HONOUR KILLING IN SHAKESPEARE

HONOUR KILLING IN SHAKESPEARE

LORAINE FLETCHER

Greenwich Exchange
London

Greenwich Exchange, London

First published in Great Britain in 2019

Printed and bound by imprintdigital.com
Cover design by December Publications
Tel: 07951511275

Greenwich Exchange Website: www.greenex.co.uk

Cataloguing in Publication Data is available
from the British Library

ISBN: 978-1-910996-26-3

for Isabella, Arthur, Cara

CONTENTS

INTRODUCTION

ATTEMPTED OR SUCCESSFUL HONOUR KILLINGS FORM the plots of a surprising number of Shakespeare's plays. Am I just giving well-known episodes a modern label without saying anything new? I don't think so. My title may seem over-dramatic, but to call his men's attacks on women by a phrase in use now clarifies what they're about: characters who judge wisely within these plays see the attacks as senseless murders too. We don't need to adjust our minds to some supposedly different culture.

The recurrent plotline appears in the Histories, Comedies and Tragedies: men put a woman on trial, formally or informally, meaning to kill or disgrace her. They see her as an Eve figure from the Eden story in Genesis, tempting and deceitful, and claim that justice demands her death. But she is, at the least, better than the men who judge her. The audience, already knowing she's innocent in terms of the moral judgments prevailing in her world, is positioned at the trial to sympathise with the woman and assess the men's mental states. We see how their indoctrination with Old Testament assumptions, the reading that's formed their education and their own personal weaknesses feed into their suspicions. We see the terrible effects of their misogyny on individuals, families and countries.

Audiences and critics of the plays often grew up with them; their plots may be over-familiar to us from our schooldays, so the innocent-woman-on-trial scenario may not strike us as quite so odd and innovative as it would have struck the first audiences. Many critics have analysed

Shakespeare's battles of the sexes, and some have discussed the prevalence of domestic and state violence towards women. But none has so far registered how often it's men's misjudgements of women, not fate or male-against-male aggression, that drive his plots towards tragedy.

Shakespeare's plays don't of course reflect what life was like in his time. They're based on prose romances, histories or legends, set in distant times and places, written in blank verse and prose that's stylised and thick with imagery. They acknowledge themselves as fictional. But their preoccupation with men's fears of women's deceit and with women's fears of men's violence was gripping for the first audiences, and has been ever since. It's a winning formula. The plays focused the audience's real-life hopes and anxieties at a time when concepts of love, marriage, women's independence and the relations between the sexes were changing fast. They still do that.

I've considered whether to put inverted commas round each use of the term 'honour killing'. That would be irritating, and I decided not to: it's a phrase that's passed into the language. By it I mean the murder of a woman who's incurred the jealousy of her husband or fiancé, or whose family consider her and themselves shamed by her rape or seduction. But though the woman's supposed transgression is usually sexual, she may simply have violated in her dress or behaviour expectations for women based on custom or religious texts. I consider plays where the aim may be to confine the woman for life rather than kill her, and plays in which she escapes her murderer.

A man's need to protect his shaky self-esteem by destroying a woman in the name of justice is central to *Much Ado About Nothing*, *Othello*, *Cymbeline* and *The Winter's Tale*. In these four honour-killing plays, the audience must assess, not the woman's guilt or innocence, since her innocence is established early on, but the pathology of men who try to destroy what they can't understand or control. Trial scenes make good theatre, and there are many trials of men in Shakespeare, notably Antonio's (in *The Merchant of Venice*) and Othello's. But overall there's more public and private arraignment of women than of men.

That impulse to judge and control is apparent though not so central throughout Shakespeare's History Plays, from *Henry VI Parts I, 2* and *3* to *All Is True; or, Henry VIII*. In his earliest Histories, Joan of Arc and Eleanor

Cobham are guilty of witchcraft as charged, but they're destroyed by English nobles more dangerous to their own country than either woman. *All Is True* shows a succession of trials. Katherine of Aragon, who's arraigned apparently for incest but really because her husband needs to get rid of her, is an interesting variant on the honour-killing pattern. Anne Boleyn, the most famous honour victim in English history, makes brief stunning appearances; everyone knows what's going to happen to her.

In 'Tales of Philomel', I discuss a narrative poem, a Tragedy and a Comedy which gain from consideration together; each has a setting in the classical world, where male power is overwhelming. In *The Rape of Lucrece*, Lucrece carries out her own honour killing, judging that best for her husband and children. In *Titus Andronicus* and *A Midsummer Night's Dream*, fathers carry out or contemplate the honour killing of their daughters. These two narratives bear striking resemblances but translate into their horrific or magical forms as polar opposites.

Honour killing can't be considered in isolation from lesser misogynies. With 'In the Suburbs', I discuss the widespread marginalisation of Shakespeare's women by his men which makes any mistreatment possible. There are comic and false allegations of female adultery in *The Comedy of Errors* and *The Merry Wives of Windsor*. *Measure for Measure* takes honour killing out of the family and relocates it in the judicial system. We might see Ophelia's madness and death as driven by her inability to satisfy conflicting male judgements. Plays as different as *Love's Labour's Lost* and *King Lear* begin with open acts of misogyny which are condemned by the development of their plots. 'Lesser' misogynies than honour killing often lead to death.

The cross-dressing Comedies acknowledge the near-impossibility of women's remaining unhurt as women; they escape violence only by disguising themselves. In 'The Truth of Girls and Boys', I trace some of the ways the usual limits of gender were broken and reconfigured when boy actors played women who survive and make happier relationships as boys: I consider how far Shakespeare sympathetically promotes homosexual or homosocial bonds as closer and more genuine than straight ones. *The Merchant of Venice* is the odd one out here in that Portia chooses disguise, it isn't forced on her, and she, rather than a man, wields the authority of the law. I propose an entirely new reading for this play.

Once we call the actual or attempted honour killings by their right name, it's easier to see how Shakespeare analyses and condemns misogyny. This perspective sheds light on the silencing and confinement of women throughout his plays. Of course, many of Shakespeare's women, including some of the most memorable, are not victims of men's mistreatment but great manipulators of men and events. I've tried not to distort characters or episodes to bolster my argument.

Honour Killing in Shakespeare is aimed at a wide readership, at students, film- and theatre-goers, actors, academics and general readers. It's for those who've seen only one or two plays and would like to read something about them, though perhaps not initially the whole book, so some explanatory passages, on Eden and the Fall of Man, for instance, or spousal marriage, appear more than once. It's also for those who know his plays well and want to read the book from start to finish. I hope they can be patient with the occasional repetition.

Unless otherwise stated, quotations are cited from *The New Oxford Shakespeare: The Complete Works*, edited by Gary Taylor, John Jowett, Terri Bourus and Gabriel Egan (OUP, 2016). I add a short bibliography of works cited, and 'To The Great Variety of Readers', the Preface to the first edition of Shakespeare's collected plays, *The First Folio*.

Loraine Fletcher, 2019

1

FOUR HONOUR-KILLING PLAYS

On *Much Ado About Nothing; Othello; Cymbeline; The Winter's Tale*

SHAKESPEARE STAGES THE UNEQUAL WAR BETWEEN men and women most fully in *Much Ado About Nothing*, *Othello*, *Cymbeline* and *The Winter's Tale*. Here the honour trials or tests are the central action and our condemnation of them is absolute; from near the start, we know the woman is wrongly accused. In each play a jealous man decides to destroy the woman he supposedly loves.

Much Ado About Nothing is set in Sicily with its long tradition of honour killing. The war between Don Pedro and his illegitimate brother Don John is over by the play's opening, and Don Pedro has won. There's been a formal reconciliation between the brothers. Don Pedro and two of his officers, Claudio and Benedick, are friends who've known each other a long time. Leonato, the Ruler of Messina, who welcomes Don Pedro's entourage to his house after the decisive battle, is notably diplomatic. The mood is celebratory; Leonato's daughter Hero, her cousin Beatrice and Hero's waiting gentlewomen Margaret and Ursula make a cheerful and companionable group. Aggression seems to linger only in the war of words between Benedick and Beatrice. They have some back-story we don't understand and score off each other with sophisticated skill.

Cracks in the smooth surface begin to appear. Don John is still smouldering, and he particularly hates Claudio, who distinguished himself in the fighting. Claudio sees Hero again for the first time after the war and decides he wants to marry her. But he's an inadequate lover from the start, consulting Don Pedro and Benedick about her character and looks instead of making his own mind up; Don Pedro vouches for her worthiness after briefly meeting her once. Claudio wants a girl who's quiet and biddable:

> Claudio: Is she not a modest young lady? I pray thee, tell me truly how thou likest her.
> Benedick: Would you buy her, that you enquire after her?
> Claudio: Can the world buy such a jewel?
> Benedick: Yea, and a case to put it into.
> Claudio: In my eye she is the sweetest lady that ever I looked on. (1.1.129-37)[1]

He's sentimental, but he doesn't forget to ask if Leonato has a son, establishing before he commits himself that she'll inherit all her father's money.

Too insecure to risk a direct refusal from Hero or Leonato, he accepts Don Pedro's offer to court her for him, then is easily persuaded his boss is courting her for himself. He's petulant, not grieved, and quick to rationalise Don Pedro's deception, as he thinks it:

> Friendship is constant in all other things
> Save in the office and affairs of love (...)
> Let every eye negotiate for itself,
> And trust no agent; for beauty is a witch
> Against whose charms faith [loyalty to a friend] melteth into blood [desire for a woman] (...)
> Farewell, therefore, Hero. (2.1.135-43)

He blames Hero for Don Pedro's apparently deceiving him, though at this point Hero owes Claudio no loyalty while Don Pedro made him a promise. But it's Hero's fault: she's broken up the men's long friendship with her dangerous witch's beauty. The business language and association of women with witchcraft suggest a commodification and fear of them which foreshadow his violent attack on her later. He reconciles himself to his loss without complaint to Don Pedro, who's Prince of Aragon.

Benedick is unconstrained by respect for his betters, and tackles Don Pedro about the supposed theft of Hero, allowing it to emerge that Don Pedro courted her only for Claudio's sake. None of the men considers how a courtship by deputy may affect Hero. Soon afterwards, Don Pedro is busily trying to bring Benedick and Beatrice together. There's an officiousness, an 'ado' about Don Pedro's relationships which permeates the play. It's shadowed in Dogberry, Chief Officer of the Watch, with his 'Be Vigitant, I beseech you!' (93.3.72) and his explosions of rage when he's called an ass.

This is a play about Noting, as Nothing was pronounced then. Everybody observes everybody else: watching, calculating, eavesdropping and misunderstanding what they think they see or hear. The audience alone is aware of what's really happening. Everybody acts a part, using wit to maintain their self-image. Benedick and Beatrice are brilliant exemplars of wit as self-defence, but all the characters hide behind ironies, humour, inflated rhetoric and absurd speculation apart from two sleepy Night Watchmen, and even they remain vigilant long enough to overhear and arrest the minor villains. The play's mainly prose style lends itself to cascades of idiomatic competition.

Once Claudio learns that Don Pedro is disinterested in courting Hero, a wedding day is set, but he declares himself ready to accompany Don Pedro on his return to Aragon the day after the marriage. There's nothing to suggest that they're gay, but Claudio is and always will be more devoted to his social superiors than to any woman.

As Hero's wedding preparations are concluding, Don John finds a means of revenge on Claudio. He stage-manages a compromising scene at Hero's bedroom window in which his servant Borachio talks about past sexual encounters to Margaret, Hero's waiting woman dressed in Hero's clothes, and he ensures that Claudio and Don Pedro overhear the conversation. Don John is a familiar character-type in plays of the 1590s, a stock Malcontent seething with resentment. He has good reason to hate Claudio, and anyone with half a brain would suspect him even if they hadn't, like the audience, watched him and Borachio planning this together. But he's not much more than a plot device. Responsibility for Hero's near-death rests with her suitor, his boss and her father, and with their culture's marriage customs, which are undermined by the presence of Benedick and Beatrice. These two may both be what Hero calls Beatrice, 'odd and from [out of] all fashions.' (3.1.72) But they are the hero and heroine of *Much Ado*, exemplars of a better fashion in courtship and marriage.

Claudio and Don Pedro believe Don John's slander very easily. There's no scene that shows them watching the false Hero and Borachio, but their reaction is a foregone conclusion given Don John's careful preparation. Claudio decides even before he sees the amorous couple at the window that instead of challenging her supposed lover on the spot he'll shame Hero publicly, though the result will be her death or confinement for life in a convent:

> Claudio: If I see anything tonight why I should not marry her, tomorrow, in the congregation where I should wed, there will I shame her. (3.2.88-90)

It's not an emotional outburst but a balanced sentence, suggesting a temperament cold and punitive beyond his years.

Here as elsewhere the quick cynical misjudgement of the woman comes out of a military culture. Returning from war, the men are obsessed with cuckoldry and joke constantly about it. The contemptuous term 'cuckold' for a husband whose wife is unfaithful seems to be derived from the cuckoo's habit of laying its eggs in another bird's nest. However, it's the female cuckoo which does that, so it's not a very logical metaphor. The men talk a lot about horns, which were fancifully imagined growing on the foreheads of husbands with unfaithful wives. The fantasy seems to date back to early chicken-farming customs in Germany and the grafting of spurs on capons' (castrated cockerels') heads, but this is uncertain. Claudio and Don Pedro, unlike Benedick, are quick to accept unconvincing evidence of female deceit, beginning to believe Don John's story as soon as he starts telling it.

In a refinement of cruelty, they go early next morning with other young men of the town to escort the bride and her attendants to the wedding. We hear them arrive outside as the women are getting ready. They want the largest possible audience for their revelation, and they'll find it in church. It's surprising that so many critical accounts of *Much Ado* play down or even fail to register the spitefulness of Claudio and Don Pedro. They're a mixture of self-assertion and weak judgement. It's been argued that Claudio needs to make her supposed liaison public to break off his engagement to her, which had a legal force little short of marriage. But he could do that by telling her father and uncle about it, rather than the whole town. Their reaction springs only from wounded egotism, and would be dishonourable at any time, even if Hero were guilty. They turn the church into a kangaroo court, waiting until the last possible moment to spring their accusation, ensuring her the greatest physical and mental shock.

As her father Leonato formally gives her in marriage to Claudio, Claudio pushes her back to him:

> There, Leonato, take her back again.
> Give not this rotten orange to your friend.
> She's but the sign and semblance of her honour (...)
> (...) Would you not swear
> All you that see her, that she were a maid
> By these exterior shows? But she is none.
> She knows the heat of a luxurious bed,
> Her blush is guiltiness, not modesty. (4.1.26-37)

After the urbanity of most of the dialogue so far, after the intimacy of the women teasing each other as they help Hero dress, the accusation in church is raw and violent. Among other things Claudio is implying that Hero is venereally diseased as well as a good faker of innocence.

Don Pedro backs him. He's as self-absorbed as Claudio. This tragedy is also about him:

> What should I speak?
> I stand dishonoured to have gone about
> To link my dear friend to a common stale [prostitute]. (4.1.58-60)

Don John rivals Iago in hypocrisy:

> Thus, pretty lady,
> I am sorry for thy much misgovernment. (4.1.93-4)

Claudio can manage only a simple binary categorisation for women. At first he thought Hero like

> Dian in her orb,
> As chaste as is the bud ere it be blown. (4.1. 52-53)

Now, he finds her

> more intemperate in [her] blood
> Than Venus, or those pampered animals
> That rage in savage sensuality. (4.1.54-56)

Hero is of course neither. She's a nice ordinary girl who's happy to obey her father and take Don Pedro if he offers, but acquiesces when it turns out she's to marry Claudio. Beside Beatrice she looks dull, as any woman would, but she's not a nonentity. Though a conventional girl and an obedient daughter, she's playful and inventive in 'gulling' Beatrice, convincing her that Benedick is madly in love with her. She's perhaps not as eager to marry Claudio as her friends think:

Beatrice: My cousin tells him in his ear that he is in her heart.
Claudio: And so she doth, cousin. (2.3.238-9)

Given the frequency of mishearing in *Much Ado*, Beatrice may be wrong in what she thinks she hears. Claudio is as fatuous as usual. Hero can be critical of Beatrice. Her description of her cousin, who she knows is listening:

Disdain and Scorn ride sparkling in her eyes
Misprising what they look on, and her wit
Values itself so highly that to her
All matter else seems weak (3.1.50-4)

is sharp enough to come from some personal resentment. She's interested in fashion and knows what suits her. She can make a punning joke about Benedick and Beatrice found between the sheets of their letters, but she's shocked or embarrassed on her wedding morning when Margaret jokes about the imminent consummation of her own marriage.

When her life is threatened she finds a new voice. Leonato can't meet the force of Claudio's first violent attack and weakly supports the continuing interrogation:

Claudio: Let me but move one question to your daughter (...)
(...) bid her answer truly.
Leonato (to Hero): I charge thee do so as thou art my child. (4.1.69-72)

Hero busts out clear and furious in response:

O God defend me, how am I beset!
What kind of catechising call you this?' (4.1.73-4)

It's a question that invokes her early childhood when she first learned her Catechism[2], and so invokes also what should be his protective role as her father, a role he's abandoning without a struggle. She's at the altar as she speaks, and her 'trial', for however brief it is one, is violent and dramatic, partly because of its location, partly because she defends herself unexpectedly well, boldly asserting her name and reputation, maintaining 'I talked with no man at that hour.' (4.4.81)

Leonato is a complex character. At the beginning we have no way of knowing whether he's sincere in his graceful welcome to Don Pedro or how he would have reacted if Don John had won the battle, but he's careful to keep on civil terms with the loser. He runs his household efficiently and arranges a wedding suitable to his family's social position. Though impatient with Dogberry and Verges when they come to report the strange conversation between Borachio and Conrad, and convinced they're wasting his time, he makes sure they have a drink before they leave. He's a man to whom decorum is almost everything, but there's a certain kindness in his dictatorial manner. He's an affectionate father to a child who obeys him.

In church all his confidence deserts him. He makes only one attempt to argue with the three powerful men confronting him. He asks if Claudio himself has had sex with Hero before the wedding, since, if so, there would be no reason to reject her as a wife, but rather the opposite. To Elizabethans, a public agreement to marry followed by intercourse constituted a marriage, even without a formal ceremony. Claudio's denial is interesting. He claims that he:

> Never tempted her with word too large,
> But as a brother to his sister showed
> Bashful sincerity and comely love. (4.1.47-9)

It's an odd, perhaps a slightly sick way to describe lovers about to marry. His determination never to court another woman when Hero apparently proves disloyal seems childish.

Leonato accepts without further hesitation Claudio's and Don Pedro's version of events, melodramatically wishing himself dead:

> Hath no man's dagger here a point for me? (4.1.104)

Hero sees the effect on her father, is overwhelmed with grief or fear, and faints. Don John, Don Pedro and Claudio leave, the last two having achieved, as they think, their aim of killing her. Don John's declared aim has been to revenge himself on his brother and Claudio, but they remain unscathed while Hero and Leonato alone are injured. At the least, she'll be shut up in a convent for life. Even the kindly Friar thinks this the best outcome unless she can clear herself.

In Kenneth Branagh's 1993 film of *Much Ado*, which is very engaging in its Benedick and Beatrice thread, Claudio is thoroughly whitewashed. Branagh produces a scene at Hero's window, absent in Shakespeare's play, which would convince most onlookers of her guilt, with a Margaret who duplicates Hero in build and hair-colour standing up and seen only from the back as she's energetically shagged by Borachio. Claudio is very young and impulsive; he's physically prevented by Don Pedro and Don John from attacking Borachio on the spot. It's a version that saves Hero and Claudio as a romantic couple truly in love despite misunderstandings, and so, I think, a misreading of the play. Though of course anything goes in productions. If we don't like one, there'll be another one along shortly.

Leonato wants his daughter dead as well as himself, as he goes on to exclaim:

> Do not live, Hero, do not ope thine eyes,
> For did I think thou would'st not quickly die,
> Thought I thy spirits stronger than thy shames,
> Myself would on the rearward [in the wake] of reproaches
> Strike at thy life. (4.1.119-123)

The images that convey his horror are intimate and domestic. She has 'fallen into a pit of ink', (4.1. 136) as though she's paper that should stay white until neatly written on. All the salt in the sea cannot season 'her foul tainted flesh' (4.1.139) and keep her good enough for consumption. These are household images, gross perhaps, but they convey an intense gut reaction too fundamental to be reasoned away.

As always when a daughter is recalcitrant or shamed, the father's violated sense of ownership breaks out into 'mine, mine, mine', and the past tense:

> (...) mine I loved, and mine I praised,
> And mine that I was proud on, mine so much

That I myself was to myself not mine,
Valuing of her. (4.1.132-5)

The possessive pronoun echoes through many of Shakespeare's father-daughter confrontations. Leonato wishes he'd adopted a child, 'took up a beggar's issue at [his] gate', (4.1.128) so her shame might not involve him. He can't love her independently of her genes, or what was then called in one sense of the word her 'blood'. But most people will still try IVF rather than choose adoption; his are feelings few parents can disown completely though obviously they take different forms now.

He's too shaken by the sudden attack to think clearly. And unlike Claudio and Don Pedro, he has some excuse for his murderous reaction. Hero's apparent loss of virginity before marriage means disgrace for himself as well, since a man who can't control his daughter will be thought ineffectual in other ways, and Leonato prides himself, fairly enough, on his ability to manage people. In the longer term it means the end of his family line. He has already mourned the children he didn't have:

Grieved I I had but one?
Chid I for that at frugal nature's frame? (4.1.123-4)

There will be no grandchildren if Hero is unmarriageable.

She's of course entirely innocent of an intrigue with Borachio. But in a sense she is 'every man's Hero' (3.2.75) as Don John calls her, willing to accept Don Pedro or Claudio as her father directs, despite Beatrice's belated effort to get her cousin to think independently. The first sign of vivacity she shows is when she dances with the masked Don Pedro, whom she thinks she's going to marry. She's unusually lively, even flirtatious here. Like Ursula and Beatrice, she can see who her masked partner is:

Don Pedro: Lady, will you walk a bout [go down one set in the dance] with your friend?
Hero: So [if] you walk softly, and look sweetly, and say nothing, I am yours for the walk, and especially when I walk away.
Don Pedro: With me in your company?
Hero: I may say so when I please.
Don Pedro: And when please you to say so?
Hero: When I like your favour, for God forbid the lute should be like the case. (2.1.62-9)

It's not the most sparkling dialogue in the play, but it shows her able to hold her own with this great man who, she thinks, has fallen in love with her. She knows better than to seem overeager to please, but she is animated. It might be argued that she's trying to put Don Pedro off, but her teasing would have the opposite effect.

She resigns herself to the truth when it emerges, but her heart is heavy on the morning of her wedding to Claudio, not, I think, because she has a premonition of what's going to happen in church, or to give Margaret a chance for an easy joke, but because she still prefers Don Pedro, who's the most important man she's met. I've never seen a production that acknowledges this.

Leonato's judgement is compromised by his sense of inferiority to Don Pedro, who is royal, and to Don John, who is also royal though illegitimate. Even Claudio outranks him. His betrayal of Hero is worse than theirs, but it's brief. When his social superiors leave the church he can think again, and he begins at last to listen to the Friar and Hero.

The Hero-Claudio thread of narrative in *Much Ado* has at least six possible sources in old stories. In some of them the lover is censured as being too easily deceived, but in each case he's represented as a lover, not just a suitor-turned-enemy, as Claudio is. Beatrice and Benedick's courtship story is original except for its sketch in *The Taming of the Shrew*, probably six years earlier. It sparkles against the hackneyed parallel of Hero and Claudio's manipulated betrothal, manipulated misunderstanding and final manipulated marriage. Beatrice and Benedick have known each other a long time. In the opening scene where she's joking about him, she's desperate to find out if he's survived while trying not to let her anxiety show. They skirmish through the first three acts and are ready to drop their pretence of dislike by Hero's wedding day.

Benedick remains with the women, the Friar and the old men when the young men leave the church. His switch of loyalties doesn't begin here: he's already decided to ask Beatrice to marry him and he quickly guesses that Don John is behind Hero's disgrace. Beatrice says little as Hero is accused. She has 'wept all this while' (4.1.253) and can't continue to act a part after the savage attack she's seen. When the rest of the wedding party leave and she's alone with Benedick, the only two lovers in the play declare themselves almost at once. But love this serious can't exist in isolation from the social group it must inhabit:

> Beatrice: I love you with so much of my heart there is none left to protest.
> Benedick: Come, bid me do anything for thee.
> Beatrice: Kill Claudio.
> Benedick: Ha! Not for the wide world.
> Beatrice: You kill me to deny it. Farewell. (4.1.278-84)

She bitterly regrets her own inability to fight and kill Claudio, the only redress she sees to Hero's situation. The helplessness of her sex strikes her as never before. It's the gratuitous spite shown by Claudio and Don Pedro quite as much as the truth or falsehood of the accusation itself that infuriates her:

> Beatrice: What, bear her in hand [behave politely to her] until they come to *take* hands, and then with public accusation, uncovered slander, unmitigated rancour – O God that I were a man. I would eat his heart in the market place. (4.1.297-8)

The last phrase has lost some of its shock value because it seems so bizarre, but that probably did happen in war. The men's violence finds its full answer in her reaction.

Benedick doesn't promise to do so much, but he does finally burn the bridge back to his friends when he agrees to Beatrice's demand that he challenge Claudio. It's a large concession, given the 'inwardness and love' (4.1.242) he still feels for them, but it's the only chance to save Hero. The code of duelling may seem nearly as shocking now as the code of honour killing. The 'wrong' man often won. But duelling or the threat of duelling was then seen as the only way to protect a woman from slander. If a reputable man was willing to risk his life to defend her, she could be assumed innocent. The audience knows what the lovers don't, that the evidence which will exonerate Hero is already with the Watch, the early form of the police, citizens who took turns to patrol a town from dusk to dawn. But while this lessens the tension, I think it frees the audience to concentrate more on the strange psychopathologies they observe among the men, and to sympathise more with Hero and with Beatrice's attempt to defend her.

After the great packed scene in church, the mutual declaration and resolve of Benedick and Beatrice once they're alone is often played as the moment of their marriage. They stand at the altar where Hero and Claudio just stood and commit themselves to each other, knowing Benedick may lose. They stay funny and endearing enough to float the vicious attack they've witnessed into comedy and the possibility of a better kind of marriage.

Beatrice's evidence in the church that for once she didn't share Hero's bed the night before is surprising. But in contrast to the prevailing ethics of Messina, she tells the truth at once without thought of the consequences. As Balthasar's song has it, men are the deceivers, of themselves and each other. Though needy women can deceive too: Margaret is desperate for male attention. Her part in her mistress's near-ruin is never explained.

The Friar advises that Hero should feign death, but he's optimistic in predicting that if she does, Claudio and Don Pedro will soon regret their actions. Even though they think Hero has died from the shock of their accusation, they remain unrepentant. Leonato and his brother Antonio quickly come to believe that Hero is slandered and challenge them to fight, but they're contemptuous about fighting two old men. Claudio tries to take the same tone to Benedick, whose challenge he's very reluctant to accept.

Before the duel can happen, the Watch reveal how Hero was impersonated at the scene in the window and slandered by Don John. Claudio expresses regret but continues to maintain that 'yet sinned [he] not/But in mistaking.' (5.1.241-2) He and Don Pedro go through the motions of repenting her death in a quasi-religious ritual:

> Pardon, Goddess of the Night [Diana, goddess of chastity]
> Those who slew thy virgin knight [Hero] (...) (5.3.12-13)

It's the dead language of the formal apology.

Next morning, when 'the wolves have preyed', (5.3.25) or prayed, Claudio in reparation agrees to marry Leonato's unknown niece, Antonio's daughter. The two young women look alike, Claudio is assured, and the niece will have Hero's dowry as well as her own, so this marriage is even better. He and Don Pedro all but make the point themselves:

> Don Pedro: Come, let us hence, and put on other weeds,
> And then to Leonato's will we go.

Claudio: And Hymen now with luckier issue speed's [us]
Than this [Hero] for whom we rendered up this woe. (5.3.30-3)

The rhyme underscores the triviality of Claudio's feelings. It's 'Farewell, therefore, Hero' again, but now as a response to her (supposed) death.

Beatrice's and Benedick's reaction to what they see in church shows that my condemnation of Claudio and Don Pedro is not a modern misinterpretation. Both the characters we care about in *Much Ado* come to think the bullies deserve death or injury for what they do to Hero. The audience, however it might consider the matter theoretically, is positioned by the unfolding action to understand that the motives of the three principal killers are spiteful, that the father is hopelessly weak and disloyal, that 'honour' is not easily assessed.

By the end, Claudio and Don Pedro have learned nothing. They lapse into the worn-out cuckoldry jokes about men whose foreheads grow horns, or who wear the yoke of marriage like driven oxen. Benedick recycles the old joke too, but to call Claudio a pathetic bastard; their friendship won't be easily resumed. Though adultery may be funny in social conversation, the suspicion of it can mean lifelong disgrace for the woman; what Benedick and Beatrice see in the church changes their lives. The existence and malignity of Don John silently attest to the destabilising consequences of male adultery, as they will with more force through Edmund in *King Lear*. Dogberry with his uneasy officiousness is a parodic version of Don Pedro, who will never feel secure, never have everything handsome about him, until his brother is dead.

Will that be tomorrow? The elephant in the room of *Much Ado* criticism is Benedick's final verdict on Don John, who is taken and brought back to Messina: 'Think not on him till tomorrow. I'll devise thee brave punishments for him. Strike up, pipers.' (Final lines) What does this mean? Do we take it seriously? It may go to the heart of our problems in understanding Shakespeare. We don't want to think Benedick, of all people, means it. 'Brave punishments' or their consequences were always on view in London and most of the audience would have had some sight of judicial sadism. Benedick's threat calls our attention back to judgements and cruelties inside and outside the play as the happy ending kicks in. Or is it just that tomorrow never comes in the theatre?

The audience of *Much Ado* sees two types of courtship and marriage contrasted: one arranged between near-strangers by family and friends, the other negotiated with difficulty but also with a lot of fun between the two people concerned, and cutting across old loyalties. Any young man or woman in the audience will be drawn to the latter model. *Much Ado* was sometimes named as their play: 'Bennedike and Betrice' was written beside the title on Charles I's copy.

Marriage is always in a state of flux and was especially so during the long change from Catholic to Protestant dispensations. When Henry VIII began his reign, about a quarter of the population was vowed to lifelong celibacy. The shift in the national sensibility required by the Dissolution of the Monasteries[3] is unimaginable now. Brexit is nothing to it. Long-established schools, hospitals, pharmacies and inns disappeared along with their parent religious houses. Peasant boys who liked Latin better than digging turnips could no longer be monks or friars. Girls disinclined to marry a stranger and die in childbirth could no longer enter a convent. Homosexuals could no longer find refuge in same-sex communities. Celibacy was no longer a holier state than marriage; on the contrary, marriage itself was now presented as the second chance at Eden. This understanding of marriage continued under Edward VI.

During Mary Tudor's reign everything went into reverse for five years. Elizabeth renewed the marriage project, putting pressure on single clergy to marry. If a Catholic were to seize the monarchy and take the English Church back to Rome, unmarried clergy could probably make their peace with the new regime and continue in their houses and livings. A married clergyman was committed to the Protestant side, as Rome wouldn't take him. The power of the Church then is almost unimaginable now, especially the power of a literate parson over his uninformed parishioners, who must listen to him every Sunday.

Simultaneously another pattern was slowly emerging, from arranged to consensual marriage. Thomas Cranmer's *The Book of Common Prayer* (1545) requires verbal and public assent from both parties, though no form of service could prevent the application of force in private. English law allowed people over twenty-one to marry without their parents' consent, and forced marriage was illegal, though almost impossible to prevent.

Aristocratic, landed and middle-class parents still tried to arrange their children's marriages, but heirs and heiresses were beginning to expect at least a negative vote. Enlightened gentry families gave their daughters some choice and avoided compulsion. Among families with little or no money or property there was much greater freedom to choose one's own partner.

Juliet Capulet's parents are exemplary, allowing her to meet and make up her mind about Paris' proposal, though they want her to marry him. She agrees to like him if she can. Capulet at first pretends he's reluctant to accept Paris' offer for her, claiming she's too young. Later, to her and his wife, he rages that he's worked night and day to bring about this marriage. The parents of a daughter couldn't look too eager to accept a proposal for her. That lowered her value and left her humiliated if for any reason the marriage didn't come off.

Capulet is a careful negotiator for Juliet, and he gives her some latitude. It's her sudden unexplained change of mind about Paris when she meets Romeo that angers him. Leonato is not acting like any father of the time when he abruptly tells Hero 'you know your answer' (2.1. 49) to Don Pedro's supposed courtship. Capulet and Leonato are both wealthy commoners who see a chance for their only daughters to marry into nobility. But compared to Capulet, who negotiates his daughter's marriage fairly until events overtake him, Leonato is autocratic.

The dramatic contrast between arranged and consensual marriage would be easier to pick up in 1598 than it is now. The social network brings Benedick and Beatrice together too, but Beatrice is not coerced like Hero. She and Benedick are deeply involved from the start. Their friends tricking each of them into overhearing reports of the other's love makes their confession in church easier, but their guard is down anyway after the brutal scene they've witnessed. And they're ready to break up the social network altogether when Benedick undertakes a more valid form of honour killing, a duel with Claudio, which if he wins it will give Hero the possibility of some continuing life in Messina.

*

Much Ado About Nothing's ending, superficially happy for Hero, smooths over the ugliness of the men's attack, but the spring of its action appears again in *Othello*, *Cymbeline* and *The Winter's Tale*. In all these, the hero's tragic flaw, to use the Aristotelian term, is unfounded jealousy. But each has a different weakness that channels his jealousy towards murder. The four plays differ so much that somebody going to one a night for four nights in a row wouldn't necessarily spot the similarity, or not at once. In three, the honour killers' intended destruction of a woman for supposed fornication or adultery is averted. *Othello* sees its killing through to the end: Acts Four and Five in a good production are hard to watch.

Much Ado is full of amateur satirists, some inspired, some mediocre, and is itself a satire of standard English upper-class marriage-by-negotiation. 'Hero' (a contrast with Christopher Marlowe's wild girl in *Hero and Leander*) and 'Leonato' (Lion) are satiric names. Though Iago is occasionally a satirist, *Othello* generally lacks that tone. *Much Ado* in its Hero-Claudio thread makes us think, *Othello* makes us feel.

Again a slanderer incites a man to destroy the woman who has apparently deceived him. Iago is much more credible than Don John, though he uses only words, not visual deception. He cleverly argues the difficulty of providing ocular proof of adultery while forcing Othello to picture Desdemona and Cassio in bed together. But he provides fake aural evidence, the equivalent of the false Hero in the window, when he brings Othello to eavesdrop on a conversation where Cassio expresses contempt for the prostitute Bianca and Othello thinks he's talking about Desdemona. In this play too, the slanderer's main target is the man not the woman. A man's reputation is not a matter of his honesty or courage only. Once he marries, it's invested in his wife's fidelity, and can be destroyed, and the man utterly humiliated, by her adultery or the appearance of it.

The best Iagos are large, bluff, decent chaps: it's crazy to pick an actor who looks sinister, though directors will do it. He has a reputation for honesty and no obvious reason for hating Othello or Desdemona, though he has several covert ones: fury that Othello promoted Cassio as lieutenant not himself, suspicion that Othello had sex with his wife Emilia, perhaps frustrated desire for Desdemona. But no one motive is sufficient, and the impulse to destroy her along with Othello seems to need no specific motive. After a momentary flinching, with his unexpected 'but let her live', (3.4.466) he moves in to orchestrate the kill.

For the contemporary audience, Venice was famous as a global commercial centre, sited where the eastern edge of Europe met the western end of the Silk Road, on the border between Christian and Muslim powers. Traders from all over the world came to buy and sell. As in London now, there was huge cultural and ethnic diversity. The city's unique beauty, luxury, grand masques and gorgeous courtesans were legendary.

It was a place where an African might credibly head a European army, the more so because the Doge or Ruler had to be born in Venice, and there would be less likelihood of a military coup. Othello is a Christian, not a recent convert but with a faith that goes deep into his language and psyche. But despite his successes as soldier and General, when he marries a white woman of high rank without her father Brabanzio's consent there's enough racism, whipped up by Iago's and her jealous suitor Rodorigo's salacious account of the elopement, to prompt his detention and trial.

The play opens in a dark street, not to the grandeur but the sleaze of Venice: to Rodorigo's whining about Iago's failure to get him access to the heiress Desdemona despite the money and jewels he's disbursed, to Iago's fury about Othello's appointment of Cassio not himself as his lieutenant, to Iago's news, withheld for a few minutes, that Desdemona has eloped that night to marry Othello, to rumours that a Turkish fleet is on its way to seize Cyprus. Even when he learns that Desdemona has made her own choice of husband, Rodorigo is fool enough, urged by Iago, to think he may still be able to buy her. All the money Rodorigo has paid out has gone no further than Iago.

He and Iago wake Brabanzio and shout the news up from the street to the Senator at his window:

> Iago: Your heart is burst, you have lost half your soul.
> Even now, now, very now, an old black ram
> Is tupping your white ewe. (1.1.85-87)

Rodorigo adds that a common gondolier has conveyed her 'to the gross clasps of a lascivious Moor.' (1/1/122) Brabanzio reacts as they expect, like an angry farmer lamenting an escaped mare: 'How got she out?' (1.1.164) All three men use the language of miscegenation, assuming inter-racial sex and breeding to be bestial and unnatural. A little later when Brabanzio is dressed and out in the streets with Rodorigo looking for Othello, he wishes this rejected suitor had after all married his daughter: 'O, would you had had her!' (1.1.171)

Rodorigo is that great rarity in Shakespeare, a character with no good qualities and no excuses for his bad ones. Prince Cloten in *Cymbeline* is similar, but at least Cloten is powerful and feared at court because his mother is Queen. Iago and many of the villains have exceptional wit, while stupid characters are often endearing. Rodorigo has nothing at all going for him, so he may be unique. Yet Brabanzio wishes Desdemona had married him rather than Othello. The issue of miscegenation is nailed at the start by Rodorigo's and Iago's self-interested stock-yard language. If we were still in doubt, Brabanzio's bad judgement should show us how not to think. Othello's first words as he meets Brabanzio and the hostile posse looking for him reassure us there is civilisation in Venice after all:

> Keep up [return to their scabbards] your bright swords, for the dew
> will rust them.
> Good signior, you shall more command with years
> Than with your weapons. (1.2.58-60)

It's the first sound of the 'Othello music', in the critic G. Wilson Knight's phrase, inspired by Giuseppe Verdi's opera, and that amused authority at his first entry cuts the ground from under the Venetians' racism. It validates Desdemona's love and his position of trust. Nevertheless, Brabanzio accuses him of using witchcraft to win her and insists on a hearing before the Senate, in effect an informal trial in the early hours of the morning. The Senate is already in emergency session and waiting for Othello and Brabanzio to join them to discuss the threat from the Turkish fleet.

In the Senate, Othello relates his courtship of Desdemona and hers of him, on his visits to her house:

> Her father loved me, oft invited me,
> Still questioned me the story of my life

From year to year – the battles, sieges, fortunes
That I have passed.
I ran it through, even from my boyish days
To the very moment that he bade me tell it:
Wherein I spoke of most disastrous chances,
Of moving accidents by flood and field ...
Of being taken by the insolent foe
And sold to slavery (...) (1.3.127-137)

His adventures are exotic but not, as some anti-Othello critics have meanly suggested, fictional. His only impossible story concerns the tribe whose faces grow beneath their shoulders, but there was a woodcut of one of them in Sir John Mandeville's *Voyage and Travels* (1568): Desdemona and the audience were entitled to believe in them. Reports about them may have come from glimpses of gorillas or chimpanzees. Cassio, Montanto and – reluctantly – Iago corroborate Othello's heroism. He goes on to tell the Senate that seeing how intently Desdemona listened between attending to the housekeeping, he

Took once a pliant hour, and found good means
To draw from her a prayer of earnest heart
That I would all my pilgrimage dilate [report in detail] (...
...) She thanked me,
And bade me if I had a friend that loved her
I should but teach him how to tell my story
And that would woo her. Upon this hint I spoke. (1.3.164-150)

This is a marriage arranged by the two principals, not their relations, coming from a strong attraction of opposites. There has probably been more critical comment on Othello's and Desdemona's sexualities and attitudes to marriage than of any other couples I consider in this chapter, which is saying a lot. Othello has been attacked for arrogance and egotism, and frequently for his – some would say unchivalrous – deposition that Desdemona virtually asked him to marry her.

But in fact he tells how carefully they chose each other. She's an heiress with many suitors, he's a stranger on army pay, albeit a General's. Partly from that, partly from their racial difference, she knows he won't speak first. But he ensures that she gives him an opportunity to tell his adventures again to her alone. Desdemona responds as he hopes. He makes it clear that she invited a declaration in such a way that he didn't have to understand her if he didn't want to. He releases himself from the dangerous charge of witchcraft without attributing any great immodesty to her.

We have to wait a long time for Desdemona. There's a huge build-up to her entrance; she's been the subject of much of the rumour and speculation so far. In the Senate, the threatened loss of Cyprus gives way to her father's loss of her and then her husband's account of their unconventional courtship. None of Shakespeare's other heroines except Perdita has quite that concentrated focus on a delayed first appearance. And the goods are delivered. She's been waiting at the Sagittary Inn for most of that night expecting Othello to join her. Instead, she's summoned to appear before a potentially hostile meeting of grandees including her angry father, and knows by now that she and Othello are on trial. She's equal to the situation. When her father addresses her with heavy irony as 'gentle mistress', asking if she knows where her duty lies, she makes the irony sound weak, replying gently and firmly:

> My noble father,
> I do perceive here a divided duty:
> To you I am bound for life and education;
> My life and education both do learn [teach] me
> How to respect you. You are the lord of duty;
> I am hitherto your daughter. But here's my husband;
> And so much duty as my mother showed
> To you, preferring you before her father,
> So much I challenge that I may profess
> Due to the Moor, my lord. Let me go with him. (1.3.179-187)

This is Desdemona's first honour trial, for disobedience to her father in pursuit of uncontrolled desire, and she acquits herself perfectly. She maintains a certain formality, remembering where she is, and doesn't fully declare her passion until the new danger from the Turkish fleet threatens to leave her in Venice while he's sent to Cyprus. The shock of immediate separation on what she thought would be her wedding night elicits complete frankness:

> That I did love the Moor to live with him,
> My downright violence and storm of fortunes
> May trumpet to the world (...)
> I saw Othello's visage in his mind,
> And to his honours and his valiant parts
> Did I my soul and fortunes consecrate.
> So that, dear lords, if I be left behind
> A moth of peace, and he go to the war,
> The rites for which I love him are bereft me,
> And I a heavy interim shall support
> By his dear [costly] absence. (1/3/245-253)

Once Othello has promised he won't neglect his duties if she goes with him, the Duke is eager to move on to more pressing business: Othello is needed in Cyprus; everything else must give way to that, as Iago has foreseen. We have to be impressed by his way of knowing what's going on and what's likely to happen next. The Duke's attempts to console Brabanzio are clumsy:

> I think this tale [of Othello's adventures] would win my daughter too.
> Good Brabanzio, take up this mangled matter at the best:
> Men do their broken weapons rather use
> Than their bare hands. (1.3.170-73)

By reference to his own daughter he tries to defuse the situation. But the attempt is tactless to Barbanzio, who couldn't care less about the Duke's daughter, and even more tactless to Othello, who can't help seeing that he's an undesirable son-in-law, a broken sword in the dynastic mating contest, in the Duke's eyes as well as Brabanzio's, and probably in the other Senators' eyes too.

Othello and Desdemona are magnificent in the trial scene. This would make a great end to a comedy, all obstacles surmounted, a daring choice ending in happiness. But we have another four acts to go, and the first act has shown that almost everybody in Venice except Desdemona and Cassio is a racist. We can't know how the Duke or the rest of the Senate would judge the marriage and the charge of witchcraft if they didn't need Othello's immediate services in Cyprus. But clearly the Duke assumes something has gone badly wrong with Brabanzio's ambitions for his daughter.

Our attention is drawn to the deep roots of European racial stereotype, since the language itself embodies good in white, bad in black, in ways the Duke struggles with:

> If virtue no delighted beauty lack
> Your son-in-law is far more fair than black. (1.3.284-85)

Soon the racial attitudes of the majority will stain Othello's own mind. He'll become a proto-Groucho Marx, easily led to think there must be something wrong with his wife if she was willing to marry him.

The source story for Othello is racist. In the Italian Giraldi Cinthio's collection of stories, *Gli Ecatommiti*, published in Venice in 1576, a Venetian lady called Disdemona marries a Moor. They live in Venice for a time, then he's sent to Cyprus with the army and she accompanies him in the same ship. The Ensign's – the Iago figure's – frustrated desire for her turns to hate, and he decides to destroy her by arousing the Moor's suspicions that she's having an affair with The Captain. The loss and finding of a handkerchief seem to prove Disdemona's guilt. The Moor and the Iago figure club her to death, then pull the ceiling down on her to make it look like an accident, but they're caught and punished. There's a moral: Disdemona has brought about her own death through her lust in marrying a black man, and she believes this herself.

Shakespeare follows the source in outline and in some details, for example the handkerchief. But he immeasurably transforms it in scope and feeling. Othello is an alien in Venice, but his character and culture make the white Venetian men look small. Brabanzio is ill-judging and choleric. It doesn't occur to him to urge his love or anxiety for Desdemona when he questions her in the Senate, only her duty of obedience. His addressing her contemptuously as 'jewel' may not have started that night. Rodorigo is a little rat. Iago though witty has a narrowness of intellectual range which Frank Kermode well terms 'metropolitan knowingness'.[4] Lodovico is a handsome man, Desdemona notices wistfully later when Othello is treating her badly, and Emilia encourages this line of thought. But when he hears Cassio being attacked in the street at night, he's too cowardly to go to his assistance. Given Desdemona's own courage and distinction, Othello is the only man she could have married as an equal.

Cassio is an interesting example of many misogynists examined in the honour killing plays. He adores Desdemona with a fervour like the poet Petrarch's for his Laura. She embodies romance and divinity:

> Tempests themselves, high seas and howling winds,
> The guttered rocks and congregated sands,
> Traitors ensteeped [lurking under water] to enclog [trap] the guiltless keel,
> As having sense of beauty, do omit
> Their mortal [deadly] natures, letting go safely by
> The divine Desdemona. (2.1.69-74)

In the tradition of Courtly Love poetry, such devotion was offered to a woman higher in rank than the lover and expected no return. Yet Cassio does hope to get something out of his known devotion when he turns to her to reconcile him with Othello. Admittedly, Iago prompts him to this, but he takes up the plan willingly.

Iago tells us that Cassio has 'a daily beauty in his life that makes [Iago] ugly.' (5.1.19-20) His behaviour towards men and within his profession bears that out. He's deeply ashamed of his drunkenness on watch and remains loyal to Othello even when cashiered. When he learns it was Othello who had him stabbed in the street and he's still in pain, he says only, and movingly, 'Dear General, I never gave you cause.' (5.2.295)

But Iago isn't the best judge of character. Cassio's treatment of Bianca, like the Venetians' racism, is a political attitude rejected by the play. He despises while using women who don't fit the pattern of the Ideal Lady. Bianca is a prostitute, a woman with her own house and apparently with some choice in her clients. Cassio is a client, and though not a regular visitor he has no wish to finish with her so long as she doesn't make a nuisance of herself. But she loves him, as she says all along. She shows it when she runs out into the street to try to protect him on hearing a fight in the dark, at the risk of being stabbed herself, and Iago accuses her of complicity in the attack. Cassio makes no effort to exonerate her.

Bianca's name may seem a satiric comment on the link in European languages of good with white, bad with black. But like Desdemona and unlike anybody else in *Othello*, she has the capacity to love unconditionally. Perhaps it's far-fetched to see the name as part of the sexual subtlety of this play, that it suggests a woman whom prostitution has failed to blacken. I think we're meant to find Cassio cruel to her, not just to take that cruelty for granted as a contemporary and indeed as a modern attitude to prostitutes. Like *Much Ado*'s Claudio, Cassio subscribes to a simple binary division into good and bad women. There's a horrible irony in the fact that each of his bouts of contemptuous laughter about a prostitute brings his adored Desdemona one step closer to death.

Once the action moves from Venice to Cyprus where Othello is the military ruler, Desdemona has no chance to defend herself in public again. Her second honour trial takes place only in her husband's mind, with Iago as prosecuting council. Othello amasses the evidence: Iago's expert opinion on Venetian women, Desdemona's warmth of advocacy for Cassio, Cassio's overheard contempt for a woman who's pursuing him, the handkerchief, which goes from talisman to divorce court evidence. It's a 'trifle light as air', (3.3.316) but apparently as substantial to his deteriorating mind as 'proofs of holy writ.' (3.3.117) He tries, judges, condemns and executes her alone, 'else she'll betray more men.' (5.2.6)

Othello is one of many contemporary plays set against the confrontation of Turk and Christian, though here that confrontation remains in the background. Othello himself is not a Turk but North African, as we see from the title, from Desdemona's comment on the effects of the sun where he was born (3.4.24) and from his Christian assumptions and language. But the term Turkish was used quite loosely by English playwrights, who sometimes played to English xenophobia in their portrayals, but sometimes made the Turks the good guys, contrasting favourably with the self-styled Christian characters. Christopher Marlowe, Thomas Kyd, Robert Greene, George Peele, Thomas Dekker and William Percy all dramatised that cultural conflict before *Othello*: this wasn't a new area for theatre-goers. The funniest and most thought-provoking of these plays is Marlowe's *The Jew of Malta*, where a Turk is the moral hero compared to the Jew and the Christian Governor of Malta.

Othello's racial otherness gives the play its edge-of-epic quality, its vast background of conflict between Turkish and Christian powers. It gives his magniloquent language and heroic conception of life. His blackness is an advantage to a soldier as it makes his enemies fear him more. Cassio,

Montanto and the garrison admire him to veneration. Out to make trouble, Iago picks a clever song for the drinking scene:

> He [King Stephen] was a wight [man] of high renown,
> And thou [Montanto] art but of low degree,
> Tis pride that pulls the country down,
> And [then] take thine old cloak about thee. (2.3.78-81)

Montanto has just lost his command in Cyprus to Othello. Cassio will soon be cashiered, but Iago continues to address him as 'lieutenant', twisting the knife in the wound. His needling has no effect on their loyalty.

But Othello's blackness becomes a torment in his marriage, as Iago's and the Senators' perceptions begin to transfer themselves to him. Iago goes very fast and far quite early on in his deception of Othello. A tentative speculation which we don't know how Othello would have continued:

> And yet, how nature erring from itself (...) (3.3.222)

is seized by Iago for the main thrust of his slander. Iago cuts in:

> Ay, there's the point (as to be bold with you)
> Not to affect [favour] many proposed matches
> Of her own clime, complexion and degree
> Whereto in all things nature tends –
> Foh! One may smell in such a will most rank,
> Foul disproportion, thoughts unnatural. (3.3.223-8)

Though Othello dismisses Iago, the seed is planted: Desdemona must be unnatural, vicious, if she loves him. His opinion of Iago as too honest to deceive him prevails over his love for Desdemona, which is going already. He begins to look for the cause in himself:

> Haply for I am black,
> And have not those soft parts of conversation
> That chamberers [ladies' men] have, or for I am declined
> Into the vale of years – yet that's not much –
> She's gone, I am abused, and my relief
> Must be to loathe her. (3.3.257-62)

Race is only one of three reasons he weighs at this early stage. His feelings about their racial difference become mixed with a sense of the world cracking up, as his moon falls into the dirt:

> Her name, that was as fresh
> As Dian's visage, is now begrimed and black
> As mine own face. (3.3.380-82)

Much modern criticism reads *Othello*, I think rightly, as a tragedy of socially constructed racism: he and Desdemona are the innocent victims of an apartheid culture. Janet Suzman's production in Johannesburg in 1987 with John Kani as Othello is a convincing interpretation. In the film of a live performance we can see some of the audience walking out when Kani touches Joanna Weinberg, who plays Desdemona. As the audience could hardly have been unaware of what they were going to see, presumably some bought tickets on purpose to walk out, endorsing Suzman's reading.

But racism is only one element, admittedly a large one, in the tragedy. Othello's racial difference, however cleverly manipulated, is not the whole explanation for his distrust of Desdemona. To start from an admittedly wide angle, Claudio, Posthumus and Leontes are not racially or culturally different from Hero, Imogen or Hermione, yet they suspect and try to destroy them, feeling themselves betrayed and their honour compromised. Iago and Emilia too share a cultural background, but they've quarrelled already about Iago's suspicions of an affair with Othello. Though Othello personally carries out the murder, something the others don't or can't attempt (until Iago kills Emilia to silence her), he's no more deluded than his European counterparts, arguably less so. He has more excuse than they do, as Iago is the best hypocrite, and he knows Desdemona less well than the other men know their women.

In the Senate he shows perfect confidence in her. To her father's spiteful Parthian shot:

> Look to her Moor, if thou hast eyes to see
> She has deceived her father, and may thee (1.3.287-8)

he replies simply: 'my life upon her faith.' When he finds her arrived safely ahead of him in Cyprus after the storm, there's complete unity in their exchange of conventional genders:

Othello: O my fair warrior!
Desdemona: My dear Othello! (2.1.173)

He's teasing, but he admires her courage. This will be the height of their happiness, as he sees though she doesn't.

As Iago turns Othello's mind to murder, he runs two strands of persuasion together. As well as using an argument of miscegenation, of inter-racial marriage as repulsive to whites, he uses the more common argument of women's faithless and promiscuous natures. He can extemporise with humour and urbanity on the subject, teasing Desdemona and Emilia in prose and verse for several minutes as the three wait on the quayside for Othello's ship, on the theme of 'you rise to play and go to bed to work.' (2.1.115) Women are lazy and lustful, he says, but it's all very lightly done and amusing. Except that Emilia isn't amused, as she knows he's attacking her, and we've already heard him plotting to convince Othello that Desdemona is having an affair with Cassio. His affectionate banter, apparently meant to take Desdemona's mind off her anxiety about Othello, is demonic.

His tone becomes frank and graphic as he talks to Rodorigo directly afterwards:

Rodorigo: (...) she's full of most blessed condition.
Iago: Blest fig's end! [slang for women's genitals]. The wine she drinks is made of grapes. (2.1.232-3)

With Othello, on the day after the wedding night, the playfulness has quite gone:

I would not have your free and noble nature,
Out of self-bounty [generosity], be abused. Look to't.
In Venice they do let God see the pranks
They dare not show their husbands. Their best conscience [morality]
Is not to leave't undone, but keep't unknown. (3.3.195-9)

Othello's image of Dian's face begrimed by a fall from sky to earth has cosmic as well as racial overtones. A little later he muses on another Fall, as he thinks about betrayal in marriage:

'Tis destiny unshunnable, like death:

Even then this forked [horned] plague is fated to us
When we do quicken [move in the womb for the first time]. (3.3.269-71)

He's not thinking of race at all at this point: being cuckolded (horned) is the common fate of husbands, black or white, a fate inherited at conception, passed on from father to son as a consequence of Original Sin. The thought of women's deceitful natures is bound up with thoughts of Original Sin and the Fall of Man. Life in Eden was perfect, but then Eve ignored God's commandment and ate the forbidden apple, the Fruit of the Tree of Knowledge, at the Serpent-Satan's prompting, bringing sin and death on Adam and all succeeding generations. Iago is temporarily off-stage when Othello says this, but it's part of the long, intense manipulation in Act 3 scene iii, where he veers from belief in Desdemona's honesty to belief in Iago's and briefly back again to the threat of what he will do if Iago is slandering her, to Iago's pretended stupefaction that Othello can't believe him. Iago's long series of innuendoes leave Othello pondering:

O curse of marriage,
That we can call these delicate creatures ours
And not their appetites. (3.3.262-4)

Desdemona has turned into an exotic and unpredictable pet. Othello reads his wife's passion for himself as undifferentiated lust. Iago has pliable material to work with. She'll soon turn into one of a pair of copulating toads.

That happens very quickly. Othello has an odd timeframe, or rather two parallel and lightly-connected timeframes. The political and background actions happen over what we might call standard time. The Senate sends Othello to Cyprus; the Turkish fleet is destroyed in a storm. Othello needs a new lieutenant to replace the unrecovering alcoholic Cassio. In due course the Senate sends a delegation consisting of Lodovico and Desdemona's uncle Gratiano with orders to transfer Othello's command to Cassio. They are entertained at a dinner on their arrival. Back in Venice, Desdemona's father falls ill and dies, reportedly from grief over her marriage. Also during this time, Cassio visits Bianca at her house, then neglects her for a week while he struggles to get his lieutenancy back. He speaks of another meeting with her on the seashore, though we don't know how far back this was.

Three to four weeks seems the least time that could pass between Othello's and Desdemona's arrival in Cyprus and their deaths.

The honour-killing story happens in compacted time. Iago seizes the day after Othello's and Desdemona's arrival in Cyprus to poison Othello's mind. Events then crowd in on each other. Some critics calculate that she's killed in the late evening of her second night in Cyprus. The speed of course displays Othello's irrationality: there would be no chance for Desdemona to commit adultery once, let alone 'a thousand times'. (5.2.208)

The problem, if it is one, seems to arise from Shakespeare's changes to his source story. He transforms the characters of Cinthio's Moor and Disdemona so completely that his own lovers' tragedy breaks loose from Cinthio's base narrative. Given Othello's high idealism, he can't go on having sex with Desdemona once he first begins to suspect her. He says as much several times. Given her intelligence, if he stops having sex with her while he carefully investigates whether or not she's guilty, she'll have time to find out what's happening before he can kill her. As it is, given her initial trust in him and in their marriage, she doesn't grasp how quickly things are deteriorating until it's too late. There can be no second night for them. Yet the brief marriage must be stretched across the longer timeframe if Othello is to be recalled to Venice and lose his two 'occupations', as soldier and as husband, both together at the end.

It's the consummation of the marriage which begins the swift decline in trust. Only after that is he vulnerable to suggestion. When the two meet on the quayside in Cyprus, with the marriage still to be consummated that night, Othello says:

> If it were now to die,
> 'Twere now to be most happy, for I fear
> My soul hath her content so absolute
> That not another comfort like to this
> Succeeds in unknown fate. (2.1.180-4)

'To die' could have the secondary slang meaning, 'to have an orgasm' in the Renaissance, and though the secondary meaning is often absent, it must be present here. He can't imagine a long, happily married life with Desdemona after he's had sex with her. He's told the Senate that desire had no part in his marrying her or wanting her to come to Cyprus with him. Not just the audience but Desdemona is surprised now:

> The heavens forbid
> But that our loves and comforts should increase
> Even as our days do grow! (2.1.184-6)

This might be called the Desdemona music. For both, 'comfort' seems to be coming from the 'help, society and comfort that one ought to have of the other, both in prosperity and in adversity', the third reason for marriage given in Thomas Cranmer's *The Book of Common Prayer.* Unlike her husband, she imagines that night will be the beginning of a long and happy married life, sanctioned by God, since we can take her 'heavens forbid' as more than just a form of words.

As Desdemona gets ready for bed and her inevitable murder, Emilia cuts in on men's inadequacy and women's adultery. Rational, graphic, feminist, she speaks up not for perfect wives but for all the angry, disappointed ones driven to have affairs by their husbands' horrible behaviour:

> But I do think it is their husbands' faults
> If wives do fall. Say that they slack their duties
> And pour our treasures into foreign laps
> Or else break out in peevish jealousies
> Throwing restraint upon us; or say they strike us,
> Or scant our former having in despite
> Why, we have galls, and though we have some grace,
> Yet have we some revenge. Let husbands know
> Their wives have sense like them; they see and smell
> And have their palates both for sweet and sour
> As husbands have. What is it that they do
> When they change us for others? Is it sport?
> I think it is. And doth affection [desire] breed it?
> I think it doth. Is't frailty that thus errs?
> It is so too. And have we not affections,
> Desires for sport, and frailty as men have?
> Then let them use us well; else let them know
> The ills we do, their ills instruct us to. (4.3.77-95)

We don't know whether she's talking about payback of her own to Iago for his repeated rudeness to her, or whether her rebellion is theoretic. But she's thought a lot about this. She thinks conceptually, seeing marriage as a whole, in its sexual, social and financial aspects. 'Pour our treasures into foreign laps' is about husbands having sex with other women. But it's also about husbands giving money and presents to these women which should go to their wives. We can't tell which of these derelictions she thinks the worst; to her, they go together. To 'scant our former having in despite' is about the husband's cutting the wife's allowance for no good reason. Wives' absolute financial dependence on the moods of their husbands and society's demand for wives' absolute fidelity create an explosive mix, in Emilia's mind.

She's been Desdemona's waiting-woman for a very short time, but she loves her already and is sickened by Othello's striking her in public and then bullying them both in the 'brothel' scene, and she speaks freely now they're alone. She's reckless when she tries to incite her mistress to rebel by talking of peevish jealousy and men who strike their wives, and emphasising the attractions of Lodovico, the sort of man Desdemona might have married, and who, Emilia obviously thinks, would make a good lover for her now. But in a few minutes she'll put justice for Desdemona, whom she'll call once by her first name as she tries to bring her back from death, above her own life.

She's not the only character in Shakespeare to attack the double standard of sexual morality, one law for men, another for women, a standard that for centuries made unfaithful wives but not unfaithful husbands subject to rejection without the right to see their children again, and made 'fallen' women, women who had sex outside marriage, into outcasts. In *Cymbeline*, Posthumus also learns to question the double standard. But Emilia does it in a sharper and more wide-ranging way. Though there were other dissentient contemporary voices in the real world, that double standard prevailed until recently and some would say, lingers on now. Emilia's attitude to sex and marriage is patently fair, if uncomfortable. Among the failing judgments we see in Venice or in Othello's mad dedication to his wife's honour killing and the murder of Cassio, Emilia is the only character to judge rationally.

Coming vividly to life and individuality as she suddenly does near the end, her quick unexpected stabbing by her husband rivals Desdemona's death in horror. This would be a classic honour killing if Iago believed Emilia unfaithful to him. He kills, rather, in rage for her revelation of his guilt, for disobeying his order to keep silent, and this is also a form of honour killing. Women were not expected to bear witness against their husbands even in a lawcourt, and Emilia is a rebel here too.

Against Emilia's rationality is set Othello's deluded belief in himself as God's instrument of justice. Justice is his aim as soon as he starts to believe his wife guilty, and her adultery is cause enough to kill her. As he looks at her sleeping and kisses her, for a moment he thinks her perfect again:

> O balmy breath, that doth almost persuade
> Justice to break her sword! One more, one more!
> Be thus when thou art dead, and I will kill thee
> And love thee after. One more, and that's the last (...)
> This sorrow's heavenly –
> It strikes where it doth love. (5.2.16-22)

He feels as powerful as God, punishing the sinner with death, then receiving her back into his grace in heaven. But there's also the terrible underlying hint of necrophilia. The only good woman is a dead one.

The marital bed is onstage in the last scene, its sheets the focus for the misfit of the couple's feelings about sex. It's possible Desdemona wants Emilia to put her wedding sheets back on the bed as a reminder that she was a virgin on the previous night. But whether or not this is so, and *Othello* is a very graphic play, for Desdemona they are sacramental, and with a premonition of approaching death she asks Emilia to use them as her winding-sheets. They are part of herself, having her blood on them, to be taken with her into eternity. For Othello the sheets are 'lust stained' (5.1.35) – though we know their stains can only be hers and his own – and the excuse for her murder. In a last attempt to make him love her again she refuses her nightdress, by which was meant something more like a dressing-gown, and keeps her lighter and more revealing smock on while she falls asleep.

When Lodovico asks what he can say for himself, Othello answers lamely

Why, anything;
An honourable murderer, if you will,
For naught I did in hate, but all in honour. (5.2.89-91)

He tries and fails to define the crazy logic of honour killing. In the last few minutes of his life when he knows he suspected her unjustly, he feels her body again, saying

Cold, cold, my girl
Even like thy chastity. (5.2.272-3)

Desdemona's chastity wasn't cold, but the chastity of faithful sex in marriage, the second reason for marriage in *The Book of Common Prayer*. He forgets the warmth of passion, the downright violence and scorn of fortune that led her to run away and go with him to Cyprus. There's no sign that he ever retrieves that understanding of her. He imagines her staring at him accusingly 'at count', at the Last Judgement, as he's hurled down into hell. He's still attributing to her feelings she doesn't have.

From her first speech to her last words she maintains their unity. Even when he's bullying her she asserts it, with 'O, heaven forgive us.' (4.2.85) Meanwhile his sustaining sense of his own nobility breaks down as he degrades rapidly through his suspicions. At the end he begins to refer to himself as 'Othello', as if he's splitting off from agency in the murder; that split is complete as he kills himself:

in Aleppo once
Where a malignant and a turbaned Turk
Beat a Venetian and traduced the state
I took by th' throat the circumcised dog
And slew him – thus. (5.2.350-4)

The Richard Twyman production of 2018 made Othello a secret Muslim, hiding his faith to assimilate successfully into a white, Christian and colonialist state: he embodies the stresses of mixed cultural identity in Venice and in our modern society. In Twyman's imaginative leap, Iago generates the fake news that feeds xenophobia and Islamophobia.

The problem here is that the fake news is mainly about Desdemona. And there's little that's Islamic about Othello. He reveals some pagan superstition in his (apparent) belief in the powers of the handkerchief, though of course Catholic practice included the veneration of talismanic objects. Even this he may exaggerate merely to frighten Desdemona into telling the truth. His superstition has no relation to Islam, which rejects material objects as aids to faith. And he's most Christian in his thinking when he can't be acting, when he soliloquises on Original Sin when first becoming suspicious of her, and when he imagines God's rejection and his fall into hell at the Last Judgement.

Certainly his identity is fractured as a black outsider but the General of a white army, undesirable as a son-in-law but revered as a soldier. He's long been an instrument of the state; he carries out against himself the state's punishment for murdering his wife; the splits in his identity implode here. He remembers a Turk he once killed, and stabs himself as the barbarian his wife's murder has made him.

Othello and Claudio are the prime movers against the life of the woman, though for Hero her father is briefly the more serious threat. They contrast in age, ethnicity, character and motivation. Othello is immeasurably the more impressive. Claudio's petty-mindedness is the polar opposite of Othello's romantic gravity in love and in his profession. But there are resemblances in touchy egotism, and they're both too naive to see that a man who's been publicly humiliated like Don John or Iago will strike back.

With its concentration on one mad sexual misjudgement, *Othello* is the richest, most tense and linear of the honour killing plays. As is entirely possible, Desdemona speaks after her crush injury. To Emilia's 'O, who hath done this deed?' she replies, 'Nobody. I myself. Farewell.' (5.2.123-4) She reasserts their unity in marriage and tries to save him from a murder charge as she dies. Some have tried to read this line as acknowledging, like Cinthio's Disdemona, her folly in marrying Othello at all. But her 'commend me to my kind lord' (5.2.124) rules that out. The greatness of the lovers individually and together gives the play its intense pain as we watch Iago destroy them. Othello, with a mind as profound though less agile than Hamlet's, is reduced to the ludicrous dupe and bully of the eavesdropping and brothel scenes. But Iago doesn't do that alone; he draws on his culture's more toxic assumptions about women and race.

*

I will keep the spelling Imogen though she was probably meant to be Innogen, the name of the wife of an early king of Britain according to Raphael Holinshed's *Chronicles of England, Scotland and Ireland* (1577), a source Shakespeare often used. A double 'n' probably became an 'm' in the printed *First Folio*. But so many women have been named Imogen, it's a pity to change now. The honour killing in *Cymbeline* is in one respect easier to define than in *Othello*: there's no racism mixed up with the slanderer's or the honour killer's misogynies.

This play is complicated in other ways. Some see it as sprawling and incoherent, with the story of Princess Imogen's secret marriage to a man of doubtful rank and his test of her fidelity only lightly connected to two other stories, one about her abducted brothers growing up in Wales and one about a Roman invasion. Links may be found by setting Imogen, the heiress to Britain when the play opens, against a map of Britain, the attempted invasion of her body by the Roman Giacomo mirrored in the Roman invasion of her country. She repulses Giacomo, while Posthumus and her two brothers later hold a vaginal narrow lane against an invading Roman army. But the comparison is forced, and if it exists it's more for the study than the stage. It would be hard to see on a first or second reading or viewing.

The story of royal blood revealing itself in princes brought up in poverty is pleasing to a court audience, though I'd argue that the real hero of *Cymbeline* is a servant. The affectionate solidarity of Cymbeline's three children may be a compliment to King James' children, Henry, Elizabeth, later Elizabeth of Bohemia, the 'Winter Queen', and Charles. If so, there's no consistent analogy, as James would hardly be flattered by identification with Cymbeline, who's weak and ill-judging. The power of slander links Imogen's alleged adultery to the back-story in the previous generation, when Cymbeline unfairly banished the famous soldier Belarius for alleged complicity with Rome against his own country, and Belarius abducted Cymbeline's baby sons in revenge.

But as with *Pericles*, we may have to forget strict notions of coherence and accept changes of location, time, narrative direction, and tone. Change of location is usual in Shakespeare's plots, but in the Last Plays characters escape death by setting off for distant countries. Citizenship is questioned, and nationality and internationality are defined in more sophisticated ways than in Shakespeare's Elizabethan plays. Bravado like the Bastard's:

> Come the three corners of the world in arms
> And we shall shock them. Naught shall make us rue,
> If England to itself do rest but [only stays] true (*King John*, 5.7.116-8)

now feels crass. The Queen and Cloten command a fierce nationalist rhetoric undermined by their own malignity. The Queen reminds Cymbeline of:

> The natural bravery [strength] of your isle, which stands
> As Neptune's park, ribbed and paled in
> With banks unscalable and roaring waters,
> With sands that will not bear your enemies' boats
> But suck them up to th' topmast. (3.1.18-22)

But Little England rhetoric is old-fashioned in the Jacobean plays. Instead, there's a tentative inclusion of Britain within Europe. Influenced by his wife and Cloten, Cymbeline refuses to pay tribute to Rome, but he respects the Roman ambassador Caius Lucius, who's more civilised than the Brits, and a compromise and peaceful settlement with the Roman Empire is reached by the end of the play. Imogen finds original images for Britain's place in the world. Discovering on the road to Milford Haven that her husband wants to kill her, unable to return to the court, she wonders:

> Hath Britain all the sun that shines? Day, night,
> Are they not [don't they exist], but [except] in Britain? I' th' world's volume
> Our Britain seems as of it but not in't,
> In a great pool, a swan's nest. Prithee think
> There's livers [people enjoying life?] out of Britain. (3.4.135-9)

She may move to Europe. Milford Haven is not 'out of Britain' though it's distant enough from London to seem foreign. As a habitual reader, she sees the world's volume not as a great space but as a book in which Britain is a loose or detachable page. A swan's nest looks haphazard, since the weight of swans flattens it, and it's a little out of the water, a little in it.

Swans are royal, they're beautiful, and for Imogen the nest carries perhaps a trace of the notion that they mate for life, so loyalty is a part of her concept too. She coins evocative images to define Britain's relationship with Europe and beyond.

The play is wide-ranging, then, but the central story of her (attempted) honour killing probably engages us more than the other semi-historical and contemporary political threads.

Cymbeline opens with a long exposition by two courtiers, one apparently well-informed, the other ignorant though curious. It's a heavy strategy when compared to racing starts like 'what country, friend, is this?' (*Twelfth Night*) or 'when shall we three meet again?' (*Macbeth*) Cymbeline has a new Queen, the archetypal wicked stepmother who establishes the folk-tale nature of the play. Imogen has secretly married in defiance of her father a poor young man brought up at court, whom she's known from childhood, Posthumus Leonatus. The Queen informs on them; Cymbeline banishes him and tries to pretend the marriage never happened. The Queen wants Imogen to marry her son Cloten so he can be King when she's murdered Cymbeline. Though not quite qualified as a witch, she's practicing on cats and dogs to find fatal herbal mixtures. In the meantime, she orders poisonous drugs from her Doctor to give to Posthumus' servant Pisanio, who's devoted to his master and Imogen, hoping he will take them.

When courtiers define a character or situation as a play opens, they're giving us a thumbnail sketch of what we need to know, but they're not necessarily always accurate in their judgements. Posthumus' birth is obscure and his father died before he was born, as his name indicates. They praise him lavishly, but he's an inadequate young man almost from the start; at best he's unformed. In saying goodbye to Imogen before going into exile he twice calls her his Queen. This is surprising, as there's already a Queen who takes precedence of her, and a reigning King; such a premature entitling could amount to treason, and would I think strike a contemporary audience. Maybe it's just a sugary compliment, and nobody except Imogen hears him, but it might prompt the question whether her position as next-in-line to the throne has any part in his adoration of her. In return for the diamond ring she gives him, he gives her a bracelet, saying:

> It is a manacle of love. I'll place it
> Upon this fairest prisoner [her arm]. (1.1.123-4)

It's a disturbing metaphor; it seems to suggest he wants complete power over her. Later, the villain steals the bracelet as evidence she's an adulteress.

Posthumus has no status, abroad and exiled, but he seeks it through his wife. In France, he gets into a quarrel by boasting about her virtues compared to other women's. In Rome, he stays with his father's old friend Philario, who introduces him to a mixed group of men at a dinner, including a Roman called Giacomo, a Frenchman, a Spaniard and a Dutchman. Posthumus doesn't name Imogen in front of this group, but he doesn't need to; they all know who his wife is.

Giacomo and the Frenchman reveal some hostility to Posthumus before he enters but the Frenchman is civil, recalling a quarrel in Orleans when he dissuaded Posthumus and another Frenchman from duelling over the chastity of their women. Posthumus then gets into an equally stupid dispute when Giacomo, in name and character a version of Iago, persuades him to bet on Imogen's faithfulness, offering to try the seduction himself. The mixed bag of foreigners suggests an element of nationalist boasting in Posthumus' praise of Imogen.

At this point he has no suspicion of her. In the four plays I consider here, this is the silliest trial of the woman, his reaction growing merely from a stranger's barbs, against the advice of his host and mentor and prompted by nothing more than boredom and the loss of position he feels in exile.

Giacomo is a libertine who fills his time with seduction, travel and sceptical debate. He's a familiar figure in the theatre, later becoming central to the Restoration Comedies of Charles II's time, and he had his counterparts in real life. He's a younger brother of the Duke of Siena and a Roman out of dark sixteenth-century Italy, glamorous, sardonic, post-Machiavellian. Shakespeare plays another game with time here, as the political action of *Cymbeline* includes the denial of tribute to Augustus Caesar and its consequence, the Roman invasion of a Britain just pre-dating the birth of Christ.

Giacomo hasn't Iago's reputation for honesty, and though he's seen Posthumus in England and envied him, Posthumus doesn't remember him.

But his high rank and sophistication now take the exile at a disadvantage. His needling, his appearance of knowing all about women, is hard to deal with. 'You may wear her in title yours,' he says to Posthumus, 'but, you know, strange fowl light upon neighbouring ponds. Your ring may be stolen too.' (1.4.69-70) Here and elsewhere, 'ring' has its subsidiary meaning 'vagina'. Posthumus replies, 'I do nothing doubt you have store of thieves [in Italy], notwithstanding I fear not [the safety of] my ring', (1.4.76-7) where he seems to want to reassert the primary meaning of 'ring' and pretends not to recognise Giacomo's innuendo. Throughout, Giacomo is insulting Imogen and Posthumus in an apparently good-humoured way which Posthumus is too awkward to deal with.

Eventually they strike a bet. If Giacomo goes to London and brings back proof of Imogen's infidelity, he'll win the ring she gave Posthumus. If he fails, he must pay ten thousand ducats as forfeit and also fight Posthumus. Philario tries repeatedly to deter them, but he's ignored. It's an egotistical wager by Posthumus on a woman who, he knows, is already surrounded by enemies. But he's too weak to disregard Giacomo's taunts.

Giacomo goes to London with Posthumus' letter of introduction, which allows him to meet Imogen alone. He tries to make her jealous, telling her that her husband has forgotten his vows and has mistresses in Rome. For a few minutes he almost fools her, but he moves too fast and clumsily in offering to console her, and she sees he's lying. Giacomo doesn't have Iago's genius. Fake moral indignation on another's behalf is Iago's *forte*. Giacomo is quite good at it, but his is cruder: it's done partly by pretending to soliloquise about her beauty and merit, but in her hearing. Soliloquy was a familiar stage device, but it does indeed look stagey by now. Unlike Iago, he has to deceive a woman not a man, and to seduce her; he fails at both. He hastily pretends he was only testing her love for his friend and decides that the pretence of her seduction will do. It will win him the ring and a reputation as irresistible.

Unsuccessful as a seducer, he's a greater threat as a rapist. He finds an excuse to leave his large travelling trunk for safekeeping in her bedroom. He's inside it, and at night he climbs out. Imogen was reading before she fell asleep, and the page is turned down on Ovid's story of King Tereus' rape of his sister-in-law Philomel, which tells how Tereus cut out her tongue to prevent her accusing him. As he looks at her, Giacomo is thinking of another rape, of Lucrece by Tarquin, the last Prince of Rome. The threat is palpable, hell is here, as he knows, but he contents himself with making a close examination of the room and her body. Her tapestries illustrate the familiar angel/devil hologram, the division of women into two categories, with scenes of the goddess Diana bathing and of Cleopatra meeting her Roman, Antony. Giacomo also notes a mole under Imogen's breast.

Armed with this information he returns to Rome and claims he's seduced her. None of the slanderers has any particular animus against the woman, but all are indifferent to the effect on her of their competition with the man. She's a pawn only. After some resistance, Posthumus is convinced by the evidence of the mole and stolen bracelet, and Giacomo wins the ring, no longer a love-token but for both now merely code for her vagina. Giacomo's and Posthumus' attempt on Imogen is a private not a public trial, but its arrangement and some of the consequences to follow her conviction or acquittal are public.

The violence of Posthumus' anger prompts an attack on human reproduction itself, including a reappraisal of his mother and repugnance about his own conception:

> Is there no way for men to be [born], but women
> Must be half-workers? We are bastards all
> And that most venerable man which I
> Did call my father was I know not where
> When I was stamped. Some coiner with his tools
> Made me a counterfeit; yet my mother seemed
> The Dian of that time: so doth my wife
> The nonpareil [unique example] of this. (2.5.1-8)

He remembers Imogen as she used to be in bed, still modest though a wife:

> Me of my lawful pleasure she restrained
> And prayed me oft forbearance; did it with
> A prudency [modesty] so rosy the sweet view on't
> Might well have warmed old Saturn, that I thought her
> As chaste as unsunned snow. (2.5.9-13)

Her ability to retain a kind of virginity within marriage is to him the sexiest of qualities. He sees her like this in retrospect, framed by the imagination of her lust with Giacomo, with the pain of knowing, as he thinks, that her modesty with him was an act:

> O all the devils!
> This yellow Giacomo in an hour – was't not?
> Or less? At first? Perchance he spoke not, but
> Like a full-acorned boar, a German one,
> Cried 'O' and mounted. (2.5.13-17)

Claudio, Othello and Posthumus all appeal to the goddess Diana or Dian as an image of chastity just when they recognise, as they think, the guilt of the woman. Diana is often invoked in Shakespeare by men struggling to explain what they see as the complexity or duplicity of women. She's the moon, beautiful, above this earth and therefore pure. But her power is tripartite and contradictory. She's also the goddess of hunting, depicted with weapons and hounds, and potentially fatal to men who offend her, as she was to Actaeon when he caught sight of her bathing. And she's the goddess not just of marine but of menstrual tides, of mysteries surrounding pregnancy and childbirth. As a concept she represents not so much female chastity alone as a complicated set of terrors about women that men can indicate but can't quite express.

Posthumus' long post-traumatic soliloquy continues with a frenzy to identify and destroy the woman's part in himself, the genes bequeathed him by his mother. He lets loose a stream of misogynist ranting: whatever evil men do, it's women or the female part in men that incite it. A woman is a compendium of vices:

> (...) be it lying, note it,
> The woman's, flattering, hers, deceiving, hers
> Lust and rank thoughts, hers, hers, revenges, hers. (3.2.22-4)

He attacks the basis of creation; his desire for parthenogenesis and the elimination of women from the earth marks a descent into a state of mind near madness. He fantasises about returning to Britain and confronting and killing her himself.

His servant Pisanio has remained in London so he can send and receive the letters between them, and by letter Posthumus orders him to kill her and send proof of her death. As Pisanio couldn't kill her in the court and escape alive, Posthumus must incite her to run away so Pisanio can kill her on the road and get back to London before he's missed. Intending to join the Roman army and return to Britain with it, Posthumus writes asking her to meet him at the proposed point of invasion. By the time she reads his letter, one part of it is true: he has arrived at Milford Haven, though he thinks Pisanio will kill her long before she gets there.

This affectionate letter sent her along with the one he writes to Pisanio ordering her death shows him more Machiavellian than Giacomo, cunning in madness. It's cleverly under-written. He doesn't ask her to meet him, thinking (apparently) she will meet him anyway:

> Your father's wrath, should he take me in his dominion, could not be so cruel to me as you [but that you] O dearest of creatures, would even revive me [could still revive me] with your eyes. Take notice that I am in Cambria [Wales], at Milford Haven. What your own love will out of this advise you, follow. So he wishes you all happiness, that remains loyal to his vow, and your increasing in love, Leonatus Posthumus. (3.2.40-5)

'O for a horse with wings,' (3.2.46) she bursts out, asking Pisanio about that 'blessed Milford' (3.2.57) and its history as she disguises herself as a squire's wife and prepares to set out. Milford Haven was the site of Henry Tudor, Duke of Richmond's landing in 1485, with mainly French support augmented by Welshmen as he made his way towards Bosworth Field and defeated Richard III, as Henry VII initiating the Tudor dynasty from which James I derived his claim to England. Shakespeare recreates it as a place for ending old miseries and finding new directions.

Though Pisanio is supposed to carry out Imogen's honour killing, like the Woodcutter in Snow White he can't do it and instead shows her the letter setting out her husband's plan for him to murder her. Knowing he won't obey orders, he's brought along a second disguise for her, a boy's clothing since she'll be travelling on alone, and gives her the Queen's Doctor's box of drugs, which Pisanio thinks are medicinal, the Queen thinks are poison, and are in fact somewhere in between, harmless narcotics.

Posthumus' soliloquy, quoted above, on women's deceit and lust, like Othello's and Lear's speeches, was sometimes taken as an expression of Shakespeare's own misogyny. But Imogen's angry rejection of Giacomo comes shortly before it; soon afterwards she learns that Posthumus ordered Pisanio to kill her, but she goes on to Milford Haven in the hope of meeting him there. The placing of Posthumus' soliloquy emphasises the insanity of his imaginings. Though she's angry and bitter, Imogen reasserts her love for her husband at the moment she learns he means to murder her. In the clothes Pisanio has brought for her, she becomes the boy Fidele (Latin for Faithful and pronounced Fidaylay).

Posthumus is not the only enemy hunting her. Encouraged by his mother, Cloten courts her mainly to become King. Enraged when she marries a man of lower birth, he follows her to Wales dressed in Posthumus' clothes, intending to catch and rape her in them across Posthumus' dead body, then kick her back to the court to marry her there. Imogen prefers Posthumus' meanest garment to Cloten, she says, an insult uttered when she's desperate to get rid of him, and the phrase obsesses him.

Cloten is deranged in various ways. He can't speak without uttering a string of *double-entendres.* He hires musicians to wake Imogen in the morning. Arriving early he says, 'I would this music would come. I am advised to give her music o' mornings, they say it will penetrate.' (2.3.10-11) When the musicians appear, he orders them, 'Come on, tune. If you can penetrate her with your fingering, so. We'll try with tongue [singing], too.' (2.3.11-13) He's like something from a *Carry On* film but grosser, and as in a *Carry On* (except in the Sid James characters) it's not clear if he understands what he's saying. The *Carry On* people have minds so saturated in sex it leaks into their every sentence, but they manage to cling to some domestic and professional decorum. Cloten is weirder and more frightening, lacking even a superficial cloak of good behaviour to cover his obsessions.

He has lapses of memory and even moments of pathos in his psychopathic muddle:

> I love and hate her, for she's fair and royal
> And that she has all courtly parts more exquisite
> Than lady, ladies, woman (...)
> but
> Disdaining me, and throwing favours on
> The low Posthumus (...) (3.5.70-75)

As with the heroes, jealousy turns 'love' to hate.

Act Four of *Cymbeline* opens into a different dimension, harsh and limited, perhaps, but the home of the only reciprocal affections we find in the play. Fidele is faint and hungry by the time she nears Milford Haven and takes refuge in a cave, the home of her two long-lost brothers, stolen away and brought up as hunters by the old soldier Belarius in revenge for his unjust banishment by Cymbeline. The brothers, Guiderius and Arveragus, are unaware of their identity, and Fidele keeps to her disguise; of course, they bond at once. Before Cloten can find her, and feeling ill, she takes the drug given her by Pisanio and apparently dies. Her elder brother meets Cloten, and objecting to his bluster kills him, cuts off his head and rolls it down a stream towards London.

Running from her family, Fidele finds another family on the road, Pisanio, her brothers and Belarius, who accepts without rancour that his adopted sons love the boy more than him. Her relationship with Pisanio at court is that of mistress and servant, but once on their way to Milford Haven in the long, emotional scene that enlightens her about her husband's intention, they talk as equals. Pisanio advises her like a brother, though it's true she suspects him later when she believes she's been poisoned.

The great, intense and poetic passages of *Cymbeline* cluster in Act Four, scene ii, when an Aeolian harp[5] sounds and Arveragus emerges from the cave with Fidele in his arms: 'the bird is dead/That we have made so much on.' (4.1.199-200) There are reminiscences of several earlier Shakespeare plays in *Cymbeline*, here an echo of Lear entering with the dead Cordelia in his arms. Arveragus promises:

> with fairest flowers
> While summer lasts and I live here, Fidele,
> I'll sweeten thy sad grave. (4.2.221-3)

The catalogue of flowers that follows echoes the catalogue of flowers in a Greek or Latin pastoral elegy: the boys brought up without formal education are naturally learned in literature and civility as well as in hunting and fighting. They're also just boys, trying to put on a bold front against the unknown, breaking down in tears when their new friend dies.

They lay her out for burial with her head to the west in the Celtic, pre-Christian way and speak (probably because the original actors couldn't sing) the elegy 'Fear No More the Heat o' the Sun'. (4.2.260-83) The first verse is about homelessness and the road, exposure to sun and storm, about hard work and fading youth. The second is about the insecurity of cities and hierarchies, about tyranny, slander and hegemonies of power: even the golden young must submit to these, and come to dust. Death is the only refuge, and mordantly beautiful. But we know she isn't dead, and her brothers' tenderness can create a different kind of family from the angry father, honour-killer husband and horror-comic stepmother and stepbrother. Though the brothers call their cave in the woods a cell of ignorance and long to get out of it, it's a place of sincerity and possibility compared to the court.

It's also the site of one of the most bizarre episodes outside *Titus Andronicus.* Belarius lays Cloten's headless body down beside Fidele to await the burial of both. She wakes, finds the corpse beside her dressed in her husband's clothes and of course mistakes it for Posthumus. The drug is wearing off, and as she feels up and down the thighs and torso of the corpse beside her, finding it identical to Posthumus' body, her terror and incomprehension settle into realisation of widowhood, with her husband's attempt on her life left unexplained. She smears blood from the neck over her face. *Cymbeline* is seldom performed, perhaps because directors flinch from this scene. Is it grotesque, Beckettian, funny? Or should it be done dead seriously?

Posthumus and Cloten show a strong resemblance from an honour-killing point of view. Posthumus intends murder; Cloten means to keep her alive so he can become King, but he intends punishment rape. Shakespeare dramatises rape as revenge or the will to power, not as uncontrollable desire. Cloten's desire turns to hate when he finds that Imogen prefers someone else, Posthumus' love turns to hate when he thinks she prefers someone else. Cloten values her mainly as heiress to the throne, Posthumus calls her his Queen and seeks higher status in exile by boasting about her to men who know she's a princess. Fidele's hazy error has a conceptual logic. From the neck down, she finds them identical. Are they pretty much identical from the neck up?

Imogen, an energetic rap and dance version of *Cymbeline*, was produced at The Globe in September-October 2016. In the programme notes, John

Pitcher proposes that Cloten, Giacomo and Pisanio are all versions of Posthumus:

> Iachimo [alternate spelling of Giacomo] can only be scary or creepy when he is, as it were, the instrument or remote agent of the dark, jealous, unconscious and unexplored part of Posthumus. This is the aspect of the play that has most baffled its critics, who have mistaken Shakespeare's clear signals that it is Posthumus, the apparently complete man and perfect husband, who is time and again the cause of what Imogen has to go through. Prurient Iachimo itemizing her in her bedroom, beastly Cloten wanting to wear Posthumus' clothes as he degrades her sexually, loyal Pisanio (Pisania here) the servant ordered to murder her – they may look like fully separate characters but they are, one by one, Posthumus' strange doubles who act out the evil desires in him while he is offstage.[6]

This is very well put, and it's true that critical comment still sometimes tries to normalise the husbands' honour-killing aims through a cod-historical 'that's how they thought in those days', without noticing that the development of the plot exposes the husbands' thoughts as very stupid, so Shakespeare at least didn't think like that. All the men are versions of masculine attitudes to women, of course, but because of the awakening scene, in which Fidele awakens us to the two men's likeness, I think we're drawn more strongly to identify Posthumus with Cloten than with the other men. Posthumus doesn't play at life and sex like a game as Giacomo does. He never shows Pisanio's selfless kindness. Posthumus and Cloten are equally the enemy; the beloved and the hated are the same. We might even see a resemblance between Cloten's rape fantasies and Posthumus' preference for a reluctant woman.

After we hear Posthumus attacking the flaw in creation which makes women necessary, after we hear his letter ordering Imogen's murder, we next see him back in Britain under cover with the Roman army, and carrying the cloth Pisanio sent him stained supposedly with her blood. The visual evidence of her death, something he never fully imagined before though he can imagine her having sex with Giacomo, is so sickening that though he still thinks her guilty of adultery, he's now suicidal with remorse for killing her when she was, he decides, less sinful than himself. He invites married men in the audience to share his fears and discoveries:

> Yea, bloody cloth, I'll keep thee, for I once wished
> Thou shoulds't be coloured thus. You married ones,
> If each of you should take this course, how many
> Must murder wives much better than themselves
> For wrying [going wrong] but a little (...
> ...) Gods, if you
> Should have ta'en vengeance on my faults, I never
> Had lived to put on this [urge her murder], so had you saved
> The noble Imogen to repent, and struck
> Me, wretch, more worth your vengeance. (5.1.1-11)

He's deserved the Gods' vengeance, we must assume, because he's had sex outside marriage too, presumably before they married but possibly afterwards in exile, a cultural norm for many of Shakespeare's contemporaries but one Posthumus now questions. It's not his urging Pisanio to murder his wife that makes him the guiltier. He refers to sins committed before that. If the Gods had punished him earlier, he says, he wouldn't have lived to incite Imogen's murder. Unlike the other killers, Posthumus expresses extreme remorse for her (supposed) honour killing while he believes her guilty, and he still considers her noble, capable of repentance and of continuing as his wife. This is, I think, quite a radical proposition from the stage, though these accommodations must sometimes have been necessary in life. Of course, English law has at all times formally condemned the murder of even adulterous or apparently adulterous women by their husbands. It's impossible to guess how often such murders were condoned.

Of all writers, Shakespeare gives the greatest encouragement to 'Presentism', the critical fallacy, so called, of belief in the unchanging human condition and thus the accessibility of historical experience. That premise is written into his Histories or quasi-Histories. Posthumus appeals from a fictional pre-Christian Britain to an audience at the moment of performance, 1613, assuming a common culture.

He decides to change his Roman clothes for a poor Briton's, and seek an unrecorded death in battle as reparation for his crime. In this disguise he meets and defeats Giacomo, also with the Roman army, also deeply ashamed of his treatment of Imogen – and at this point the mirroring certainly supports John Pitcher's reading. Just as the battle is going badly for the

British, Guiderius, Arveragus, Belarius and Posthumus hold a narrow lane against the Roman advance. The Romans are routed and Caius Lucius, Fidele and Giacomo are captured. Posthumus switches back to his Roman disguise because he's still hoping for death; he's taken prisoner too and condemned to hang.

Many of the high-ranking men in power or potentially in power in *Cymbeline*, the King himself, Giacomo, Cloten and for much of the play Posthumus, lack sympathy with, or sane judgment of, women. In that, *Cymbeline* resembles the more factually accurate English Histories, though Giacomo and Posthumus repent in the last Act. Into the gap left by a crass nobility moves the kind and intelligent Pisanio, who defies his master, successfully counterplots against Giacomo's plotting and introduces Imogen to cross-dressing and escape to Milford Haven. Imogen alone in these four plays has no loyal woman friend, but though of military age Pisanio takes this part, then joins the army to go to Milford Haven and look for her. He divides a claim to be the play's moral hero with the Roman leader Caius Lucius. When the latter finds Fidele unconscious across a dead body, he takes her as his page. Later, when both are captured in the battle, he begs for the boy's life while refusing to beg for his own.

We can't expect naturalism in Shakespeare, or any dramatist, and we certainly don't find it in *Cymbeline*. It's about, in some sense, 'ordinary' things: a marriage, a separation, jealousy and anger, but all tied into a story of legends and miracles and birthmarks proving royal blood. We may accept the magical element gladly, but even then there remain large holes in the theatrical illusion: though Posthumus thinks Imogen is unfaithful to him, he still expects his letter to lure her into setting out for Milford Haven to meet him, with all the danger and discomfort that entails. With unbelievable prudence Fidele maintains her boy act while arranging her supposed husband's burial with the Roman soldiers. She gives Caius Lucius a false name for him, Richard de Champ, the French name of Shakespeare's publisher for his poems, Richard Field, also from Stratford, who may have been more surprised than gratified to find his name given to a headless body. Field already had an alias, Ricardo Del Campo, for publication of his Protestant books in Spanish, which Shakespeare and other friends might well have found funny, even hysterical. Now Fidele gives him another one.

There's obviously an in-joke here, at a tragic and gruesome moment. Later, when the ghosts of Posthumus' dead family come down from above to implore Jupiter to allow a happy ending, the verse of this Masque is so execrable either it can't be Shakespeare's or it's Shakespeare sending up the rusty machinery of Masques and happy endings. There are other pantomimic elements besides Cloten. I think we have to admit that like Homer Shakespeare sometimes nods off – keeping up a rate of two plays a year or more for most years, it would be odd if he didn't – or at least that we just can't know how some passages should be understood or performed.

And yet the recognitions (the term for dramatic recognition is anagnorisis, plural anagnoreses, if it matters) at the end are crazily effective triumphs of plotting. Almost all the characters assemble after the battle except of course Cloten, and the Queen, whom the Doctor reports dead by suicide following a full confession. Fidele is still in her disguise, as is the condemned Posthumus, who still thinks her dead, her brothers don't know who they are, many of the other characters don't know who anyone is, though Pisanio recognises Imogen as soon as she speaks. Nobody but themselves knows who or where are the four men who won the British victory; only three of those know what happened to Cloten; two of those aren't telling. The audience knows all the answers except whether Cymbeline will pardon his Roman or pretend-Roman prisoners.

Caius Lucius recommends Fidele to Cymbeline's mercy; she reminds Cymbeline of somebody, and he takes a fancy to her, asking her what favour she would like from him. Caius Lucius expects that now she'll beg for his life, but she tells him his life must shuffle for itself, leaving him bitter at her ingratitude, though still the perfect stoic:

> He leaves me, scorns me. Briefly [quickly] die their joys
> That place them on the truth [loyalty] of girls and boys. (5.6.106-7)

Fidele ignores him; she's seen her diamond on Giacomo's finger:

> My boon is that this gentleman may render
> Of whom he had this ring. (5.6.135-6)

A tired and emotional Giacomo confesses, Posthumus sees how he was cheated, and the lined-up skittles go down one after the other. Like 'Pyramus and Thisbe' at the end of *A Midsummer Night's Dream*, it always works, however bad the performance in general. 'Pardon's the word for all,' (5.6.423) Cymbeline announces. His daughter, knowing Posthumus' contrition, is eager to forgive. But as she's still in her disguise as Fidele, Posthumus strikes the boy for interrupting his melodramatics. They've been apart for the whole play, but the violence of his irrational anger is re-enacted in this random blow at the end. Has he changed? His 'hang there like fruit, my soul, till the tree die' (5.6.263-4) when, now recognised as Imogen, she throws her arms around his neck, feels still unreconstructed, the tree so strong, the fruit so soft, when it's been very much the other way round.

Imogen links the three strands of narrative; she's multifaceted enough, boy/girl enough to do it. Her escape from her husband results in her finding her brothers; her presence after the battle ensures her father's recognition of his sons, his pardon for his prisoners and his accommodation with Caius Lucius and Rome. Imogen was the dearest of Shakespeare's heroines for the Victorians, perhaps for other times. Her cheerfulness on the way to Wales while complaining about how tedious a man's life is, her talent for cutting vegetables into alphabet soup for her brothers' supper, her willingness to forgive her husband's attempt to murder her combined to make her an ideal of enterprising femininity more attractive even than his other cross-dressing women. But that wasn't a unanimous judgement. Even before the 20th century, feminist writers have often found the women's instant forgiveness repugnant.

Of the main honour killing targets, only Imogen disguises herself as a boy to escape her pursuers. Hero pretends to die, Desdemona dies, Hermione dies for sixteen years. Imogen puts on boys' clothing and finds her way to Milford Haven, but her death is enacted in her coma and in the great elegy spoken over her body. Other Shakespearean women also disguise themselves as boys to escape the threat of rape, death or confinement, though Portia in *The Merchant of Venice* has a different motive. The resort to cross-dressing is closely related to the honour-killing threat, and I'll return to it later.

*

In *Much Ado*, *Othello* and *Cymbeline*, a slanderer urges towards murder a fiancé or husband already half-way there on the common assumption that women are liars and adulteresses. In *The Winter's Tale*, set in Sicilia, the same place as Sicily but more remote and fantastical than the site of *Much Ado*, there is no slanderer. King Leontes' suspicion springs not from external prompting but from paranoia triggered by or at the same time as his wife Hermione's pregnancy. *The Winter's Tale* is probably a little earlier than *Cymbeline* but the honour killing and its consequences absorb the whole action, so I leave it until last in this chapter.

As there's no slanderer inventing an extramarital affair for the woman, Leontes' jealousy can seem unexplained, sheer madness. Or Hermione's pregnancy alone may be a troubling daytime reminder of her sexuality. There's a more specific and obvious explanation. The couple already have a son, Mamillius, Leontes' heir. Judging from his conversation, he's about seven. He's still 'unbreeched', not yet in boys' breeches, wearing the unisex clothes of early childhood and carrying a blunted dagger, still part of the closeted world of women. They have no other child. Given the dynastic anxieties of European royalty, Leontes and Hermione have endured five or six years of disappointments. Now Hermione's ladies are delighted for her. They tease Mamillius with the prospect of a new baby:

> The Queen your mother rounds apace. We shall
> Present our services to a fine new prince
> One of these days, and then you'd wanton [play] with us
> If we would have you. (2.1.17-18)

It seems they hope for another boy, the spare to Mamillius' heir. But royal daughters were also welcome, securing useful connections to foreign courts when they married. We don't have to look far for the cause of Leontes' sudden upsurge of jealousy. Hermione's second pregnancy was expected for five or six demoralising years, but it happened only after King Polixenes' arrival at Leontes' court nine months ago.

The Victorian critic of Shakespeare A.C. Bradley has gone out of fashion. Influenced by the pleasures of the dominant 19th-century genre, the novel, he wrote about character, discussing Shakespeare's people as if they're real, and allowing himself to speculate about their lives in order to consider their motivation. Two generations on, inhabiting a less coherent world and influenced by postmodernist poetry like T.S. Eliot's *The Waste Land*, the critic L.C. Knights mocked Bradley's critical approach in an article he called parodically 'How Many Children had Lady Macbeth?' Knights found this sort of question absurd. He argued that we should embrace the fictionality of Shakespeare's plays and experience them as poetry rather than speculate like Bradley about individual characters and their pasts. I think we can do both.

I'm risking a 'How Many Children had Hermione?' parody if I speculate on the long gap between Mamillius and the baby she carries at the opening of *The Winter's Tale*. Were there children who died? Were there miscarriages? Bradley himself wouldn't ask such nosy personal questions. But I think we're encouraged to ask them, and Bradley's approach suits a specifically ethical account of Shakespeare.

As with *Cymbeline*, the play opens on two courtiers talking, this time about the visit of Polixenes, King of Bohemia, to Leontes and how devoted these childhood friends are to each other. The courtiers suggest an over-zealous entertainment of Polixenes by Leontes and a competitive edge to their friendship, and this is substantiated in the next scene. In emphasising that Prince Mamillius is adored by Leontes' subjects as Sicilia's one hope for the future, the courtiers are cautiously raising the question as to what would happen if he died. Children often did. Archidamus is attached to Polixenes' court and a visitor to Sicilia, Camillo is Leontes' favoured courtier:

> Camillo: (...) It is a gallant child (...) They that went on crutches ere he was born desire yet their life to see him as a man.
> Archidamus: Would they else be content to die?
> Camillo: Yes – if there were no other excuse why they should desire to live.
> Archidamus: If the King Leontes had no son, they would desire to live on crutches till he had one. (1.1.29-37)

These quiet opening conversations of courtiers give us a sense we're getting something off the record that can't be said openly. The possible failure of Leontes' dynasty, which might bring war to Sicilia, is obliquely canvassed by two experienced political hands, Sicilian and Bohemian, guardedly testing what the other thinks about the security of the Succession. Archidamus, at least, thinks Mamillius may die before his father.

Polixenes opens the second scene with his announcement to Leontes and Hermione that he must go home to Bohemia:

> Nine changes of the watery star have been
> The shepherd's note, since we have left our throne
> Without a burden. (1.2.1-3)

The watery star is the moon, Diana again, watery because she controls the tides. The first line suggests the fluidity and restlessness of Diana and the female principle in nature. Even in this short sentence there's a contrast between nature and feminine mutability, and the hard world of men. A shepherd can observe but not control nature. Back in Bohemia, a throne has been empty too long, inviting seizure; it must be resumed by its owner.

This is the only one of the four plays where we don't know for certain from the onset of doubt that the woman is suspected falsely, though we know soon afterwards. Leontes asks Polixenes to stay longer, but he refuses. As a test, Leontes directs Hermione to ask him to stay. She's older and more sophisticated than the three other women victims in these plays. She's inclined to question usages of language, and this is notable later at her trial, in her trenchant remark on the pointlessness of pleading Not Guilty in the absence of witnesses or evidence when, as civilised law in fact recognises, it's near-impossible to prove a negative. In this early scene with Polixenes, her husband and son present, she's apparently light-hearted, though teasing him about his pompous language:

> Polixenes: (...) I may not, verily [stay on].
> Hermione: Verily?
> You put me off with limber [facile] vows, but I,
> Though you would seek to unsphere the stars with oaths,
> Should yet say, 'Sir, no going. Verily,
> You shall not go.' A lady's 'verily' is
> As potent as a lord's. Will you go yet [still go]?
> Force me to keep you as a prisoner (...)
> How say you?
> My prisoner? Or my guest? By your dread 'verily' one of them you shall be.
> Polixenes: Your guest, then, madam. (1.2.46-56)

As her conversation with Polixenes continues while her husband covertly observes them, the coincidence of the nine months and the freedom with which she and Polixenes talk might raise doubts in an audience too. It seems to have been customary for men and women of a certain rank to hold hands as they talked; Desdemona and Cassio do this. Hermione of course is soon to give birth, but Leontes reads the handholding as evidence of guilt.

She asks what her husband and his friend did as children, which was the naughtier of the two. Polixenes' reply raises a set of assumptions about women unfamiliar now but powerful then. He describes Leontes' and his own boyhood in what he remembers as a sunny, Edenic world, sinless, before they knew the passions of adolescence and adulthood, sexual passions aroused by women:

> We were as twinned lambs that did frisk i' th' sun,
> And bleat the one at the other. What we changed [exchanged in conversation, or pastimes]
> Was innocence for innocence; we knew not
> The doctrine of ill-doing, nor dreamed
> That any did. Had we pursued that life,
> And our weak spirits ne'er been higher reared
> With stronger blood [had we not begun to feel sexual desire in adolescence], we should have answered heaven
> Boldly, 'not guilty'; the imposition [punishment] cleared [which is]
> Hereditary ours. (1.2.67-75)

The 'hereditary imposition' is Original Sin, the birth into sin and the sentence of damnation imposed by God on all human creatures as a consequence of Adam and Eve's Fall in the Garden of Eden, unless they're redeemed at the Last Judgment through faith in Christ and through repentance for their sins. Polixenes is referring to assumptions which though not universal were commonplace at the time. Though *The Winter's Tale* is set in a pre-Christian Sicilia, the characters' minds are late-Renaissance Christian.

This is true of all Shakespeare's plays, though in his Roman Histories he pays a little more attention to historical possibility. Othello too refers to Original Sin briefly when he speaks of the curse embryos inherit in the womb, though there he's talking about the inevitability of their being cuckolded if they're male and grow old enough to marry. The all-powerful church read Genesis literally and saw in women the original source of the world's misery. Eve listened to the Serpent-Satan in Eden, ate the fruit of the Tree of Knowledge contrary to God's commandment and persuaded Adam to eat too. So she brought sin and death into the world for all succeeding generations.

Polixenes claims that he and Leontes would have felt very confident about appearing before God at the Last Judgment if they hadn't met and wanted two such magnetic girls as Hermione and his own wife. He's blaming them, though jokingly, for arousing sexual desire. The church and the law saw women as temptations to sin, the weaker vessels, unable to govern their passions, by their natures destabilising influences, required to live under the control of husbands or fathers.

Male supremacy, female disempowerment are not, of course, peculiar to Christian cultures, or ones which accept the literal truth of Genesis. They're found in almost all societies, though the rationale and particular idiosyncracies differ. Religious texts offer varying excuses for them.

Throughout history enterprising women found ways of escaping their limits, escapes that some writers enjoyed and recreated in literature. In Chaucer's *The Canterbury Tales*, written in the late 1300s, the only two women Pilgrims described at any length are the Prioress and the Wife of Bath. Neither accepts the role her society tries to impose on her. The Prioress refuses a self-denying life in the convent, preferring to ride out with a mostly male party and display her prettiness and poise like a heroine of romance. The Wife of Bath is not the Church's domestic ideal for a married woman. She has no children, she knows a trick worth two of that, though she's had a lot of lovers and five husbands; she's on pilgrimage to find the sixth. These two are fictional women of course, but they connect with the reader's experience of life. But though some women found ways around the rules or got away with defying them, freedom and power in the Renaissance were still mainly the provinces of men.

Hermione enters into Polixenes' theological game-playing, embroiders it, and asks whether he and her husband have 'tripped', sinned, since their boyhood days. Polixenes replies:

O my most sacred lady
Temptations have since then been born to us; for
In those unfledg'd days was my wife a girl;
Your precious self had not then crossed the eyes
Of my young playfellow. (1.2.77-80)

He's teasing her back in return for her teasing him, flattering her in the courtly manner due to a Queen about how sexy she and his own wife are. But he's also continuing into that well-known complex of ideas, that women are Eves, temptresses, and but for them men would never be betrayed into sinful desires. Hermione thinks more deeply than he does, and knows that if you take this theological tenet to its logical conclusion, it's an ugly one, and incompatible with courtly deference to women:

Of this make no conclusion, lest you say
Your Queen and I are devils. Yet go on,
The offences we have made you do we'll answer [at the Last Judgement],
If you first sinned with us, and that with us
You did continue fault, and that you slipp'd not
With any but with us. (1.1.81-86)

Like Polixenes she accepts that sex even within marriage is a form of sin, though a minor one she prefers to call tripping or slipping, one she's happy to be accused of, not comparable with the Fall of sex outside marriage. And she lightly raises the subject of male adultery, claiming that at the Last Judgement she might not defend from damnation a husband who committed it.

Leontes' suspicions deepen when she persuades their guest to stay a few days longer. He sees all her speech now as hypocrisy, play-acting, not like Mamillius' innocent play. And there certainly is a forced gaiety in her responses both to him and Polixenes, a nerviness which we see again later when she's momentarily irritated by Mamillius and asks one of her ladies to take him, then quickly recovers herself. This is of course consistent with late pregnancy. But with Leontes, there are signs of deeper tension than that. When she persuades Polixenes to stay, Leontes tells her that she's only once spoken so well before. She asks when that was:

What? Have I twice said well? When was't before?

I prithee tell me; cram 's with praise, and make 's
As fat as tame things. One good deed dying tongueless [unrecognised]
Slaughters a thousand waiting upon that.
Our praises are our wages. You may ride us
With one soft kiss a thousand furlongs ere
With spur we heat [cover] an acre. But to the goal:
My last good deed was to entreat his stay;
What was my first? It has an elder sister,
Or I mistake you. O, would her name were Grace!
But once before I spoke to the purpose? When?
Nay, let me have it. I long. (1.2.90-100)

There's a strained, frenetic aggression here: 'Have I really spoken well twice in my life? How kind of you to say so!' She compares women with game birds fattened for the table and horses rowelled to go faster. Even when praised and treated kindly, women are still wholly dependent on men's approval, she says. She's picking up on his hostility, though not necessarily grasping the source of it, and not far short of accusing him of bullying and failing to appreciate her. She's about to learn that a lady's verily isn't after all as potent as a lord's. He replies that he's thinking of their courtship, when she at last accepted him, but

Three crabbed months had soured themselves to death,
Ere I could make thee open thy white hand
And clap thyself my love; then dids't thou utter
'I am yours for ever.' (1.2.102-105)

Given that her father was King of Russia, theirs must have been a great state marriage. But she was allowed a time of courtship, and a choice. She would have had many other suitors. Does he still resent that refusal to accept him at once? Resent the humility forced on a man who loves and courts a woman who may publicly reject him? She then, fatally, gives her hand to Polixenes again and continues talking to him. Leontes breaks out, aside:

Too hot, too hot!
To mingle friendship far is mingling bloods.
I have a *tremor cordis* [accelerated heart-beat] on me; my heart dances,
But not for joy, not joy. This entertainment [of Polixenes by Hermione]

May a free face put on, derive a liberty [justify a friendliness]
From [on the grounds of] heartiness, from bounty, fertile bosom,
And well become the agent [Hermione]. T'may, I grant.
But to be paddling palms and pinching fingers,
As now they are, and making practised smiles,
As in a looking glass; and then to sigh, as t'were
The mort o' th' deer – O, that is entertainment
My bosom likes not, nor my brows! Mamillius,
Art thou my boy? (1.2.108-120)

As his judgment fails, his language becomes increasingly broken and exclamatory, and he begins to suspect even Mamillius is not his own. The language he uses of Hermione suggests a sexual excitement from which he's altogether excluded. 'Agent' already had a sinister undertone. Her sigh is like the mort or death of the deer in hunting, a euphemism for orgasm brazenly if symbolically enacted in front of him. His jealousy becomes psychosomatic illness as his heart beats erratically and his brow seems to erupt in horns.

Medical expertise generally blamed infertility or sub-fertility on the woman. But as many women married more than once and some had children with one man but not another, the possibility of male infertility was inescapable, though seldom acknowledged. Leontes is only about thirty – twenty-three years ago he was the same age as Mamillius – but he is perhaps approaching the years of danger, or his gossiping courtiers may think so.

If we don't already guess, we learn at the end of this long scene that he's wrong to suspect her, when Polixenes coming back in from the garden passes Leontes going out, and sees the rage in his face. Polixenes declares aside, to himself, he doesn't know why his friend looks so angry with him. The dramatic convention is that a character is truthful in asides and soliloquies. But during the long scene we've witnessed previously, as we pick up on Leontes' suspicions, we're invited to look at Hermione's behaviour to Polixenes with no more knowledge than her husband has, and guess what it means. Hermione says, going outdoors with Polixenes, 'if you would seek us/We are yours in the garden.' (1.2.176-7) Leontes and a theologically savvy audience think, 'Garden! Eden! The Snake Polixenes!'

But it's just a pleasant remark. We have to recognise how wrong our clever deductions can be.

Like Posthumus, Leontes takes the problem of adultery directly to the audience, but while Posthumus urges married men in the theatre to recognise the injustice of the double standard and forgive their erring wives, Leontes wants to make them all as paranoid as himself:

> many a man there is (even at this present
> Now, while I speak this) holds his wife by th' arm
> That little thinks she has been sluiced in 's absence
> And his pond fished by his next neighbour – by
> Sir Smile, his neighbour. (1.2.191-5)

The Winter's Tale was probably for an intimate court audience, so 'neighbour' would mean the man sitting in the next seat rather than, as it might at the Globe, a neighbour back home in the same street. There might be some nervous laughter here.

As Hermione is Queen, pregnancy by an extramarital affair affects the Succession and amounts to treason. Leontes asks his closest courtier, Camillo, to poison Polixenes. If this is done, Leontes promises, he'll take no revenge on Hermione but treat her as before. Camillo, appalled at the thought of murdering a king, instead warns Polixenes of Leontes' intention and both, with the Bohemian courtiers, escape by night. Though Polixenes must surely know that his flight will make things look worse for Hermione, he puts his own safety before hers. Leontes, his suspicions confirmed, denounces her before the court – ''Tis Polixenes has made [her] swell thus', (2.1.61-2) – and sends her to jail to await trial. To demonstrate to his courtiers that he's proceeding with all due fairness, he sends messengers to Apollo's Oracle at Delphi[7] to ask for a decision on her guilt or innocence.

Hermione's principal waiting lady Paulina, her husband Antigonus and the whole court refuse to believe Hermione guilty and oppose Leontes' bringing her to trial. To Leontes' portentous

> We are to speak in public; for this business
> Will raise [rouse] us all (2.2.196-8)

Antigonus rejoins, in an undertone, 'To laughter, as I take it.' (2.2.198)

The honour-killing impulse invites comic deflation, and where the commentary is done by a woman it's outspoken. Like Beatrice and Emilia, Paulina launches a scathing feminist attack on male craziness as soon as she understands what he's thinking. Women had a certain license to speak their minds. Paulina has a lot of moral courage, but it's unlikely she'll be physically punished. Antigonus, to Leontes' way of thinking, should control her, and he'll be the one to suffer from Leontes' rage against them both.

Under the shock of her arrest, Hermione goes into labour and the baby is born in prison. Hers is the only formal trial with charges read aloud and court officials in attendance among these four honour-killing plots, and because Leontes is both King and judge, we have a sense of the whole state arrayed against one woman and her baby. No evidence is offered for the charge of adultery other than the coincidence of Polixenes' arrival nine months earlier and Leontes' claim that there was too much familiarity between his wife and his friend. He adds the charge of a conspiracy by Hermione, Polixenes and Camillo to murder him and put Polixenes on his throne. Fears about his sexual potency have widened into fears about his ability to retain power as King.

This is a very physical narrative, especially so in the first, Winter half. Leontes' own heart beats painfully and his brows harden, but the indignities visited on women and children are greater, suggesting all the fragility of a lightly-clad body thrown into the power of the state. Leontes fantasises that he'll feel at peace once he 'gives [Hermione] to the fire', (2.3.8) and the administrator's euphemism for the protracted process of burning a body alive is sickening. He also threatens to burn the baby, which is carried from the prison and passed from hand to hand on stage while its fate is disputed.

Through Hermione's eloquent speeches, the trial details become vividly circumstantial: she's proclaimed a whore on bills posted everywhere, dragged from her bed to the court through the open streets. The pain and danger of childbirth were acknowledged for women of all ranks in careful pre- and post-partum rituals, the seclusion in a warm room with women attendants, the long lying-in period afterwards. Instead of these observances, Hermione is brought to trial when she can hardly stand, her baby taken from her, 'its innocent milk still in its most innocent mouth.' (3.2.95)

The first half of *The Winter's Tale* dramatises a war between the state and the female principle, the world of pregnancy, childbirth and babies. Mamillius is still part of that world. His name means a breast or nipple, and it links him with his mother. He likes to tell stories, and he gives the play its title, with his 'A sad tale's best for winter.' (2.1.76) He might have grown up to invent more such tales. His fanciful imagination suggests a bodily frailty that makes his sudden death from the strain of his mother's trial more convincing. Leontes loves him and sees himself again in his son, wanting perhaps to recapture the innocence the three adults have lost. Though men are powerful, they must rely on 'weak' women to create these heirs and successors to their achievements, and short of locking the women up and keeping the keys, they can't, or they couldn't then, tell for certain if their children are their own. Posthumus laments that men can't reproduce parthenogenically. Leontes recognises 'no barricado for a belly' (1.2.203) and assumes there will always be suspicion.

Sickening violence to women and girlchildren erupts in Antigonus' threat to 'geld' his three young daughters if Hermione is guilty:

> Be she honour-flawed, –
> I have three daughters: the eldest is eleven,
> The second and the third, nine and some five.
> If this [the charge against Hermione] prove true, they'll pay for it. By mine honour,
> I'll geld them all; fourteen they shall not see,
> To bring false generations [illegitimate children]; they are co-heirs;
> And I had rather glib [castrate] myself than they
> Should not produce fair issue. (2.1.144-51)

'[F]ourteen they shall not see/To bring false generations' implies that if Hermione is guilty, any woman may be guilty, so he'll have his girls 'gelded' before they reach puberty rather than risk them having illegitimate children. To 'geld' usually means to castrate a young male horse, though it can be used for other kinds of castration, but it's an unfamiliar usage for anything female. Explanatory notes on this line in editions of Shakespeare, even recent ones, omit or sidestep the meaning.

A typical gloss is that he threatens to make them barren. But that would be impossible without killing them, and in any case he doesn't want to make them barren. He wants them to produce what he calls 'fair issue' –

children who are legitimate – but not to have children illegitimately before marriage or in extra-marital affairs with men he hasn't chosen as their husbands. Antigonus is talking about female genital mutilation, or excision of the clitoris. He's so appalled by the mere possibility of Hermione's guilt, he thinks fgm would be the better option for his daughters. If a woman feels no pleasure from sex, if she only relives the shock and agony of the excision, she won't engage in it voluntarily and shame her parents or husband.

It seems then that female genital mutilation was known or known of in England in the early 1600s. It was probably something travellers reported on their return from parts of the world where it was endemic rather than something practised here. Of course, Antigonus doesn't directly threaten to do it, he's speaking hypothetically. He believes Hermione innocent, and is imagining the worst sanction against female sexuality he can think of to convey his horror of Leontes' charge against her. He also says he'd rather castrate himself than risk his daughters producing illegitimate children, implying that they shouldn't complain about fgm, as their father would be willing to suffer greater mutilation to prevent illegitimate children in the family. This is illogical and irrelevant: self-castration would prevent his having children either legitimate or illegitimate, and it's something he'll never be forced to do. But he reserves a right to 'geld' his daughters.

He's just imagining possibilities, spluttering and struggling with them. If he'd never had daughters, he feels confusedly, these problems wouldn't arise. He can't quite remember the age of his youngest, the biggest disappointment because she's one more girl. The subject, for him, is involved with matters of property, death and inheritance. As he has no son, his girls are his co-heirs, something bound up with his need to control their marriages. In cultures where married women had no legal standing, a man with daughters but no son had to accept that his estate would pass on his death into the control of his sons-in-law. He could hope of course that there would be grandsons to inherit eventually, but that might be long after his death.

So the position of married women, in effect outside the law, presented problems for men as well as for women, in that a father of girls had to guess which young man amongst those available would be the son-in-law most to be trusted with the stewardship of his property. One can see in this context why Egeus, in *A Midsummer Night's Dream*, favours the pragmatic Demetrius rather than the romantic Lysander for his daughter. For Antigonus, anxieties about securing his property after his death and hatred of unregulated sex reinforce each other. He can contemplate having his daughters genitally mutilated, risking their painful deaths, to prevent their wanting to make sexual choices of their own and so incur rejection by their husbands, who would keep their dowries.

This is one of only two allusions I know of in Shakespeare to fgm. A pimp in *Measure for Measure* says that all the young people in Vienna will have to be gelded (men) or spayed (women) if their ruler wants them to remain chaste, where spaying seems to mean female genital mutilation. But the pimp is clearly presenting an impossibility. Antigonus goes well beyond Leonato and Brabantio in claiming complete power over his daughters' sexuality, even beyond Cymbeline, who ignores Imogen's secret but valid marriage to Posthumus and tries to marry her off again as if it never happened. They all think they can pick suitable marriage partners who will manage their property and sire better grandchildren than the daughter's choice could do.

In some respects Antigonus is kind, and not stupid. He admires and supports his outspoken wife, admitting he can't control her, but then most men, he says, can't control their wives. He's proud of her, and confident she won't ever shame him. He braves Leontes' rage to defend Hermione, and is appalled when Leontes tells him to burn the baby. He would, he says, do anything to prevent that. Then Leontes threatens to kill Paulina as well as Antigonus and confiscate all they have unless he takes the baby to a far-off country and abandons it. He can't hold out against that threat. He swears to do as Leontes asks, and leaves Sicilia before Hermione's trial.

Three generations of women are under attack in the Winter half of the play: Paulina, Hermione and the baby. Like Leontes, Paulina had her own last baby only about six years ago, but Leontes addresses her as if she's already very old, a crone or a male witch. A woman beyond her childbearing years is a butt, for Leontes – who's terrified that his courtiers think he's beyond siring children. She finds a role for herself as advisor, as the honest courtier who tells the truth without flattery, a role usually reserved for a man. She functions as Chorus in the first half, speaking what the audience thinks and other courtiers dare not say in terms more terse and homely than Hermione can use. But despite her physical weakness, Hermione hardly seems to need a loyal supporter; her defence at her trial is lucid and heroic, her anger tightly controlled, even when she sees her husband has already found her guilty.

Her trial speech is one of the longest in Shakespeare's work, though it's discontinuous, broken with brutal interjections from Leontes. Its tone changes as she responds to him. At the start, there's an element of entreaty in it:

> You, my lord, best know –
> Who least will seem to do so – my past life
> Hath been as continent, as chaste, as true
> As I am now unhappy (...) (3.2.29-32)

When he remains obdurate and threatens her with torture before death, her attitude hardens into a contemptuous stoicism:

> Sir, spare your threats:
> The bug that you would fright me with, I seek. (3.2.89-90)

She knows her baby has been taken away for exposure, but she tries to save Mamillius by defending herself. Finally she rejects the authority of the court, and appeals to the verdict from Apollo's Oracle.

Apollo's judgement, brought back from Delphos, declares Hermione, Polixenes and Camillo blameless and Leontes a jealous tyrant who will live without an heir 'if that which is lost be not found.' (3.2.132-3) Leontes reiterates his Guilty verdict, defying the Oracle. Mamillius has been ill since Hermione's arrest, the strain of the trial kills him, and Hermione falls down fainting and is declared dead. Paulina saves what she can from the wreck, concealing Hermione and eventually bringing her back to life again. But in human terms, outside art, magic or miracles, Hermione dies. When she comes back after sixteen years, her life on any normal computation is almost over.

There's a strong mythic and religious element: the baby is snatched away like Sicilian Proserpina by Dis (Pluto, god of the underworld) from her mother Ceres, taking flowers and the summer underground with her for six months of the year. Leontes' sins of distrust and hatred are punished and finally forgiven after long repentance, in a scene which shows us a kind of female Resurrection. *The Winter's Tale* offers hope for forgiveness of sin, hope for rebirths and second chances. But however loaded with mythic resonance, it's rooted in the nuclear family and centrally about misogyny. It shows how domestic violence grows, from men's ingrained distrust of women, from fears of women's sexuality that lost them their golden boyhoods, from doubts of their children's paternity.

Arriving by ship on the sea-coast of Bohemia, the home of the baby's supposed father, Antigonus dreams of Hermione or sees her ghost. She tells him to name the baby Perdita, the Lost Girl, and warns him that for abducting her he will never see Paulina again. Since supposedly only the dead could appear as ghosts, Antigonus deduces that Hermione must be dead, that if dead she must have been executed, and that if executed she must have been guilty. Logic is not his strong point, nor is the capacity to examine critically the world he lives in. He is however sorry for her, though he now drops her title, something he wouldn't have done earlier. He reluctantly lays Perdita with her christening robe and treasure in gold and jewels down on the ground, hoping she'll survive but knowing wild animals will probably get her. He manages to convince himself that this is what the gods want him to do.

If he were to keep his promise, he would go straight home and arrange for the genital mutilation of his daughters, since he's changed his mind and decided Hermione is guilty. But civilisation and nature combine to prevent him. Apollo's anger destroys the ship he came in along with its captain and crew, so he can't go back. And Nature is by now so enraged at the various misogynies epitomised in this latest insult, the waste of a girl baby, she sends in the bear. There's no controlling Nature in the wild. 'I am gone forever' (3.3.57) are Antigonus' last words, just before the best-known stage direction in history, 'exit, pursued by a bear.' He knows he's damned and will never see his wife again in the next world, let alone this. It's hard on him, as merely the agent of Leontes. But perhaps there's a kind of justice to it. He's the only figure in Shakespeare to contemplate female genital mutilation as the best solution to fears about women's sexuality.

The bear, it seems, was not a man in a funny bear suit but a real polar bear. David Wiles in the prefatory material to *The Winter's Tale* in *The New Oxford Shakespeare: The Complete Works* (2016), edited by Gary Taylor and others, notes that the Duke of Savoy gave two polar bears to King James in 1610, which were used in court Masques and plays around 1611, the year of *The Winter's Tale*. It's likely though not absolutely certain that this bear was one of them. The pair were used to draw the carriage of James I's heir, Prince Henry, in Ben Jonson's *Masque of Oberon*, so they must have been made entirely safe in some way.

There, in typical court Masque ideology, a young Prince controls the power of Nature. In *The Winter's Tale*, Nature strikes back at the worst practices of patriarchy: burning women, throwing away girls, fgm. Antigonus is quite an absurd character, but the use of a real polar bear means, I think, there's nothing comic about his exit, as a reader might assume. We may tend to think 'exit, pursued by a bear' is itself funny, but it isn't, it's just acquired a penumbra of funny quotations and misquotations. Brown bears for baiting and dancing were common in England; this scene may have been specially written for one of the two rare and impressive animals suddenly available as the incarnation of Winter's power, and the right snow white.

Migration is part of the plot in three of the Last Plays: in *The Tempest*, *Pericles* and *The Winter's Tale*, girls or girl babies escape death by risky Med crossings. Inevitably the major tragedy of our time will soon emerge into Shakespearean stage and film productions, like Guantanamo Orange. And it's fair enough for directors and actors to draw out the mutating relevance of his wars and power struggles. Everybody takes a free ride on his voluminous cloak. In the potentially revolutionary nineteenth and early twentieth centuries, he was used in English secondary schools to naturalise the class system and endorse colonialism, Divine Right and an entitled aristocracy and gentry.

Since then he's more often been a tool of the left than the right, and though I prefer that, there are problems with the suction of all things into that vast embrace. A *Lear* or *Hamlet* set in Mosul or Aleppo (it hasn't happened yet, but it will) may flatter us with the sense that we understand things we don't, feel things we can't. I hesitate to name female genital mutilation lest that trivialise the practice by making it into a 'Shakespeare

Yet Again Our Contemporary' riff. But it's there, and important to the play. Jan Kott's book on the modernity of Shakespeare's politics may be the best ever written on the subject, but Kott himself wouldn't think that in staging him we can find the right home for every horror and leave it there.

Structurally *The Winter's Tale* is a diptych, two companion pictures of Winter and Whitsun joined by a hinge. With Antigonus' death we're still in Winter, but moving towards comedy when the Old Shepherd enters and finds Perdita. The bear's eating Antigonus and the sailors' drowning are described by the Clown, the Old Shepherd's son, in serio-comic terms, and the Old Shepherd is jubilant to find 'fairy gold' with the baby. He promises to bring her up. The hinge itself is his observation to his son:

> Now bless thyself! Thou metst with things dying, I with things new-born. (3.3.98-9)

Time himself appears at the hinge, to jump the narrative over sixteen years and warn that though this story (based on one by Robert Greene) may seem odd and old-fashioned to the audience, he'll soon 'make stale the glistering of this present', (4.1.13-14) will dull the audience's silks and sequins along with their wearers. Like other choric figures, the Chorus in *Henry V*, for example, Time gracefully denigrates the author's talent while involving the audience deeper in the play: these strategies create intimate bonds between author and audience or author and reader, sometimes sparking a new work which can stand alone but which gains in intensity from its Shakespearean resonances.

A great example is Jeanette Winterson's *The Gap of Time*. She translates Sicilia to London after the financial crash of 2007, Bohemia to New Orleans. Her novel's action follows the action of the play fairly closely: Mimi is a French-Russian singer; the other characters too are credibly both Winterson's and Shakespeare's; Pauline is especially funny. At the end Mimi, back from the dead, appears lit up and singing on stage at The Roundhouse while her husband, her daughter, the other characters, the narrator and the reader watch her from the dark auditorium.

Then the narrator shockingly breaks through her omniscient narrative convention, as though Mimi's resurrection has resurrected her own hard memories, and she speaks at last in the first person:

> (...) [*The Winter's Tale*] has been a private text for me for more than thirty years. By that I mean part of the written wor(l)d I can't live without; without, not in the sense of lack but in the old sense of living outside something.
> It's a play about a foundling. And I am. It's a play about forgiveness and a world of possible futures – and how forgiveness and the future are tied together in both directions. Time is reversible.[8]

We would expect 'As I am', but 'And I am' is better. It subtly places Winterson, whose biography many readers will know a little of, in the same undated generation as Perdita. She's writing about redemption, though not necessarily in its traditional Christian meaning. A little later she says that there are only three story-endings, apart from the happy-ever-after that must be temporary: 'Revenge. Tragedy [which I take to mean death without closure]. Forgiveness.' There are so many of us to ask, how could Shakespeare's good women be so weak as to forgive everything? It's worth sourcing another point of view for once, from a woman reputedly not a pussycat. Her novel tells indirectly of her own growth towards forgiveness, and also what a lifesaver Shakespeare has been for so many people.

The Winter's Tale's second, comic half continues in Polixenes' country, Bohemia. Autolycus, travelling singer, stand-up and con-man, explodes onto the stage with 'When daffodils begin to peer', and we're into a season when 'the red blood reigns in the winter's pale', (4.3.1-4) into a pastoral where the sheep-farm and the countryside around it counterbalance the hidebound and paranoid Sicilian court. The Clown, Perdita's supposed brother, is unsuspicious to a fault. Perdita has grown up as the Old Shepherd's daughter, and of course she's met and fallen in love with Polixenes' son Florizel when his falcon flew over her adoptive father's land.

Critics often see the couple as pure and perfect, embodying innocent youth and happiness, the resurgent spring after the sin and death of the wintry first half. 'Innocent' is the most frequently-used adjective for Perdita, and it's hard to find a critical account without its being deployed somewhere. She's magical as she appeals to Sicilian Proserpina for flowers:

O, Proserpina!
For the flowers now that frighted thou let'st fall
From Dis's wagon! Daffodils,
That come before the swallow dares, and take
The winds of March with beauty; violets, dim,
But sweeter than the lids of Juno's eyes
Or Cytherea's breath; pale primroses,
That die unmarried ere they can behold
Bright Phoebus in his strength, a malady
Most incident to maids (...) (4.4.116-25)

She is Proserpina, though she doesn't know it. She reads herself into her landscape, which is both erotic and erudite. 'Innocent', with its implication of simplicity or even ignorance, doesn't seem the right word for her, or if so, it's only one of the right words. Inseparable from her lyricism is her engagement with her own emerging sexuality. She speaks of a bank for love to lie and play on, and knows her own skin is better than paint as an incitement to lovemaking. She doesn't like popular songs with dirty *doubles entendres*, she tells her brother, but she knows a lot about breeding in plants and people. As with Juliet and Viola, some of the greatest passages of Shakespeare's poetry are found in the uprush of sensuality gripping very young women. Florizel is determined they'll be handfasted at the sheep-shearing despite what he knows will be his father's rage. He hints to the rustic company about his own grandeur, imagining his father's death (a form of treason), when he'll be King himself.

Polixenes and Camillo, the latter still in Bohemia but homesick after sixteen years, discover that Florizel is spending a lot of time at a farm where the shepherd's daughter is very beautiful, and the two come to the sheep-shearing in disguise to see her for themselves. Perdita offers flowers to them, and while considering what kind of flowers might suit men of middle age, she says she doesn't plant certain summer flowers, carnations and pinks, because they're products partly of art, not of pure nature.

These were among the earliest plants used for grafting and hybridisation into new forms and variegated colours, and called 'nature's bastards' because a gardener or botanist intervened to create them. Instead of being the natural outcome of pollen and stigma meeting, there's a third party involved, a human 'lover' who creates the new plant as much as the vegetative 'father'.

Polixenes opposes Perdita's idea that cross-grafting is unnatural. He argues that hybridisation of plants is natural, since nature herself has given the gardener or botanist the skill to improve on nature. The language he uses implies that this is also true of human breeding:

> we marry
> A gentler scion to the wildest stock,
> And a make conceive a bark of baser kind
> By bud of nobler race. (4.4.92-5)

He seems to be supporting intermarriage between different social classes or between royalty and commoners. But though he may get his gardeners to hybridise his plants, he's the last person (except Leontes) likely to follow that practice when considering a marriage for his child. And he's disingenuous, since nobody is doing that. Everywhere parents are trying to marry their children up, not bind them to sturdy peasants. He's waiting to see what Perdita will say, whether she'll give away her shameless ambition by praising cross-breeding even between royalty and commoners. I think most commentators on this thickly-annotated passage would agree so far. Some go on to say that in continuing to reject hybrids, she undermines her own position as a shepherdess in love with a prince. Others suggest that as she's a princess, though she doesn't know it, she's genetically programmed to defend a strict observance of social equality in marriage, though at the moment it's apparently against her own interest.

I don't think she's speaking of cross-class marriage at all, in plants or people, but rejecting the notion of third-party intervention in any kind of mating. She's frightened that the King will be angry, and that Florizel's resolution to marry her may not hold out given the disparity in rank. It's a painful subject, and she avoids engaging directly with the stranger's fake democratic argument. But to her, the chance meeting between Florizel and herself is like pollen meeting stigma, winds of March meeting daffodils, natural and therefore right whoever their fathers are. It's the opposite of an outsider deliberately grafting a bud onto a different stock, with the risk of damage or failure to take.

She's rejecting, in short, the practice of arranged marriage, which Polixenes would demand of his son. Antigonus is at the extreme of

Shakespearean fathers who want to impose control on their children in the matter of mating, and he's eaten. Perdita supports the superiority of free mutual choice over arranged marriage that we find dramatised in *Much Ado* and endorsed almost everywhere in Shakespeare.

She takes the discussion a little further, somewhat randomly it seems at first:

> I'll not put
> The dibble [trowel] in earth to set one slip of them [carnations];
> No more than, were I painted, I would wish
> This youth should say, t'were well, and only therefore
> Desire to breed by me. (4.4.99-103)

Painting, applying cosmetics, mainly red and white paints, to make a woman look prettier is like hybridising carnations to make them look prettier, that is, with variegated reds, pinks and whites, not dull flesh colours. Attempting to improve her complexion and lips, the woman employs both her own art and the products of the cosmetician. It's the marital marketing Perdita seems to dislike. There's nothing inconsistent with her own situation in her views on carnations and pinks. Polixenes' argument for cross-breeding is sensible, but in its context deceitful.

There's another possible meaning for 'were I painted', which is, 'if I had my portrait painted'. In this reading, she wouldn't be happy if Florizel, shown her portrait, decided he wanted her for her looks alone, which were always improved by the painter's art and where the complexion and colouring would be perfect. Portraits were often exchanged in the preliminaries of royal marriage negotiations, and this is the way Polixenes would negotiate for Florizel, with pictures of suitable royal princesses.

One could argue that Perdita would know nothing of royal marriages or indeed of portraits, but given the reading she displays, it's not unlikely. She's thought about the marriage Polixenes will try to broker for his son. At sixteen, she's already more knowledgeable than her mother was in her twenties. The distaste expressed in her clinical 'desire to breed by me' suggests she's thinking of a Prince complying with his father's dynastic mating agenda though reserving the right to choose which princess' portrait most appeals, not thinking of any young man caught by the spurious beauty of cosmetic art. In the second case, he'd be hoping only for sex, not for breeding a baby.

There was an interesting contemporary event that might make us favour the 'portrait' rather than the 'cosmetics' reading. Prince Henry was resisting a state marriage to Caterina de'Medici. But then an Italian diplomat, painter and garden designer, Costantino de'Servi, who'd travelled to England as a spy in the pay of the Medici, showed him a portrait of her, and he changed his mind. It's uncertain when de'Servi showed Prince Henry the portrait, but it has to be some time between November 1610 and September 1611. *The Winter's Tale*'s first known performance was May 1611, so it's possible the court was gossiping about this.

If Perdita is dismissing the worth of a marriage based on a painter's idealised portrait, saying she wouldn't want to be chosen like that herself even by Florizel, it's a daring point to make, given that arranged dynastic marriages were the norm for princes and princesses. How irreverent could Shakespeare and his actors afford to be by now in court performances? Princess Elizabeth would also try to have a say in the choice of her husband. Perhaps Perdita's being herself an unacknowledged princess excuses her radical stance. And the Old Shepherd's comment to his son on their altered circumstances when Perdita is recognised as a princess, 'we must be gentle, now we are gentlemen', (5.3.120) is a more devastating comment on the practises of royalty and nobility as seen in the play.

However, there's no way at the moment of knowing whether Perdita's 'were I painted' means 'cosmetics' or 'portrait'. Davide Martino,[9] the Italian historian researching de'Servi's life and contacts, is unable to fix more precisely the date Prince Henry saw the portrait. He raises the possibility that the portrait wasn't of Caterina at all, but of a beautiful girl, real or imaginary, calculated to make Prince Henry comply with his father's wishes and so to please de'Servi's Medici paymasters. If so, and especially if the trick was detected, Perdita on stage is teasing the Prince in the audience about the pitfalls of relying on a portrait in choosing a wife. He died suddenly the next year, aged 18, before he could marry anyone, and his brother Charles succeeded James, with disastrous consequences.

There have been stunning productions of *The Winter's Tale* in my lifetime, especially of this second part's songs and dancing, the cheerful take on extramarital liaisons of the Clown and farm girls, with lovers not-too-threatened by the cruel world of courts and hierarchies. The best TV one I remember was in the 1960s, with Judi Dench as Perdita and a kaleidoscopic hippy festival of a sheep-shearing. Autolycus was particularly brilliant; when he substituted 'forget tomorrow and live for today' for the last line of 'when daffodils begin to peer', (4.3.1) it was not just forgivable, it was genius. Or so it felt at the time.

Polixenes, throwing off his disguise, reacts as violently as she could have imagined to the mismatch of his son and Perdita. His wife is dead or vanished, and he's become as much a tyrant as Leontes. The worst of his venom is turned on Perdita, not his son, and he threatens to 'have [her] beauty scratched with briars.' (4.4.403) He wants now to deploy the baser kind of nature to destroy the gentlest, and to disfigure her so badly that nobody, he thinks, will ever want her again. But he may have a point when he says that a father should be consulted about his son's marriage and present at the wedding. Perdita says twice that she's unsure Florizel really means to marry her.

His love for her is intense and controlling: he tells her what to wear, what to think, not to worry when worry is sensible, since she and her family will suffer more than he will if his betrothal to her becomes known. Whatever his protests, his reference to the gods in Ovid's *Metamorphoses* who took on disguises to meet mortal maidens is not reassuring; they weren't intending marriage. His love will have to change if they're to live as equals in the world of courts and politics. For all the resurgent energies in the great sheep-shearing scene, for all their own resurgent energies, or rather because of them, Perdita and Florizel embody in the younger generation a frank, sexy girl and a spoilt, wilful boy soon to re-enact the incomprehension, violence and grief of her parents. But as she's grown up on a farm, Perdita has more natural attitudes to love and hierarchy, so there's just a chance she and Florizel will survive.

Their love story, or at least Florizel's part in it, moves into the background as we return to Sicilia and Leontes learns that his daughter is alive. We witness the miracle of Hermione's resurrection following her death at the hands of her honour killer, a miracle linked lightly to the central narrative of Christianity. Paulina is the disciple calling her back to life, with 'our

Perdita is found.' (5.3.122) Her 'our' seems to claim Perdita as the offspring of Hermione and Paulina, who has suffered for her almost as much as her mother. When Flora Robson played Paulina in 1951, she half-recognised who Perdita was before the Old Shepherd's revelation.

As Hermione comes down from her pedestal, she embraces Leontes in a dumb-show of forgiveness, but she doesn't speak to him. What can she say, to the man who killed her son? She speaks instead to welcome her daughter home. Leontes' extreme domestic violence, the cruelty of his power over women, is broken. Or is it? Perhaps not entirely. Paulina receives the news of Antigonus' death and expresses a wish to live alone. Leontes immediately brokers her marriage to Camillo, whom she hasn't seen for sixteen years. That returns the play to homeliness and comedy after the high tension of Hermione's return to life. It also wipes out Paulina's autonomy. What can she say, to a King taking up the reins of power again?

*

These four plays differ in their genre, tone and characterisation. They are set all over Europe. The presence of Benedick and Beatrice lifts *Much Ado*'s darker materials into hopefulness. *Othello* delivers pure tragedy. *Cymbeline* is perhaps the most elegiac and beautiful in the brothers' lines of regret for Imogen/Fidele, in 'Fear No More the Heat o' the Sun' and all through the strange Welsh section where Briton meets Roman and legend meets history. *The Winter's Tale* connects domestic violence with the possibility of Time's renewals or re-runs in the children.

But they have a lot in common. *Much Ado* and *The Winter's Tale* are alike in tense public accusations and the return from death of Hero and Hermione. We don't see Hermione's father, but the other fathers especially Antigonus value their daughters mainly as possessions and breeders. All the women in some sense die as a result of their trials, though the genius of comedy rescues three of them. All, whether playful, passionate, enterprising or sophisticated, willingly accept patriarchal standards of chastity. The men's refusal to believe this drives the plots.

Of the four accusers, three are soldiers, and eminently successful as fighters. In that, they meet our usual expectation of 'hero', then make us question the term, perhaps even see a connection between military violence and violence against women. Claudio has distinguished himself in the war against Don John. Othello is the famous General of the Venetian army. Posthumus saves Britain from Roman occupation. We don't hear anything about Leontes as a military man, but few dare question his authority. One accuser, Claudio, is ostensibly sane, Othello, Posthumus and Leontes are judged or judge themselves mad. All have high reputations among men but a core of self-doubt in their relationships with women. Except for Claudio, the honour killers suffer greatly from their own misjudgements. Othello kills himself, Posthumus tries to get killed, Leontes lives on in misery and can't die as there's no heir to replace him.

Other than that, the four plays are connected by their principal action: the trial, one way or another, of a woman, her sentence, her vindication, and her forgiveness of her husband or betrothed husband, whose particular weakness varies. Claudio is arrogant and insecure, Othello thinks his race makes him unlovable, Posthumus is of lower rank than his wife and exiled from her company, Leontes is afraid of infertility, which will be construed as impotence. The specific flaw, combined with anxiety about the wife or fiancée as 'too hot', is the trigger for murder.

What the lover/husbands, the killer and the would-be killers have in common is their sense of the woman as Other, as Stranger, by her nature unpredictable and deceptive. However much they think they love her, they fall back on this meme when something unexpected happens. Her sexuality, however innocent or however fully channelled into marriage, deepens their insecurities, whatever specifically these may be. As Tony Curtis on the run in unconvincing drag notes with alarm as Marilyn Monroe walks down the platform in *Some Like It Hot*: 'Women! It's a whole different sex.'

Notes

[1]Quotations unless otherwise stated are taken from *The New Oxford Shakespeare: The Complete Works*. Eds. Gary Taylor, John Jowett, Terri Bourus and Gabriel Egan (Oxford: OUP, 2016)

[2]The Catechism was/is a method of preparing children for Confirmation by a series of formal questions and answers, a practice common to Protestant and Catholic dispensations. In its Anglican format, it begins, 'What is your name?' and goes on, 'Who gave you that name?' to which the correct answer is, 'My Godfather(s) and

Godmother(s) at my Baptism; wherein I was made a member of the Church, a child of God, and an inheritor of the Kingdom of Heaven.' It was intended to give children a basic understanding of church ceremonies and of their own places within their communion.

[3]Beginning in 1534 in a process known as the Dissolution of the Monasteries, Henry VIII broke with the Pope and the Catholic Church, closing down the religious orders of monks and nuns, and made himself supreme head of the Church in England, which slowly became a Protestant country. Henry seized lands, ecclesiastical buildings and treasures belonging to the Catholic Church. His daughter Mary restored Catholicism during her short reign.

[4]Frank Kermode, Introduction to *Othello* in *The Riverside Shakespeare,* p1,200.

[5]An Aeolian harp, named after Aeolus, Greek god of the winds, is a stringed instrument that sounds musical notes when the wind passes through it.

[6]John Pitcher, 'The Dark Side of Romance', in The Globe Theatre's program, *Imogen, William Shakespeare's* Cymbeline *Renamed and Reclaimed,* 2016. No pagination.

[7]The Oracle at Delphi was an ancient religious sanctuary sacred to Apollo and located on Mount Parnassus. The Oracle in the form of a priest or priestess gave advice and predicted the future for city-states and individual worshippers.

[8]Jeanette Winterson, *The Gap of Time,* pp284-5.

[9]Davide Martino, 'Art, Religion and Diplomacy in the Life of Costantino de'Servi (1554-1622).' Submitted as part of the Tripos Examination in the Faculty of History, Cambridge University, 2016, pp48-9. Unpublished.

2

WOMEN AND WITCHES: THE EARLY HISTORIES

On the three Henry VI plays; *Richard III*; and Shakespeare's disputed texts

THE FOUR HONOUR-KILLING PLAYS OF the previous chapter are mature works, but in Shakespeare's Early Histories there's already an interest in women accused and destroyed by men, whether the women are central or peripheral to the major events of fifteenth-century history. By 'Early Histories' is meant the group of four plays (called a tetralogy) which are known in most editions as *Henry VI, Parts 1, 2* and *3*, and *Richard III*. They're based mainly on Raphael Holinshed's *Chronicles of England, Scotland and Ireland* (1577), partly on Edward Hall's *The Union of the Two Noble and Illustre Families of Lancaster and York* (1548), and for *Richard III*, also on Thomas More's history of Richard (1557). Everyone in London who could walk, it was said, came to the Henry VI plays and *Richard III*. They were revelations for people hungry to understand their country's past but often deprived of books and information.

Richard III is still well known, but the three Henry VI Histories are among the least familiar of Shakespeare's plays now. It takes long-term planning and large resources to stage them, because there's not much point in doing one without the other two, then preferably adding in *Richard III*, so they're on less often and less likely to be filmed. Though the necessary back-story is included within them, the audience/reader needs to be very sharp to pick it up. The constant fighting between nobles rejoicing in the names of counties and railway stations may be a turn-off to anyone but a military historian. In fact these plays are gripping, not just on war and the causes of war but on political manoeuvring and the way men and women react under pressure. I've tried to sketch in enough plot to stay comprehensible to those who don't know them well.

In the first of this group, *Henry VI, Part 1*, Shakespeare dramatises England's gradual, humiliating loss of France. It's a loss with several causes: the incapacity of the young King Henry; the hostility between the English nobles, some of whom support the reigning King, who's of the House of Lancaster, some Richard Plantagenet, Duke of York; and the disastrous marriage contract arranged by the Earl of Suffolk between Henry and Margaret of Anjou, which hands over Anjou and Maine to the French. Suffolk intends to rule Henry and England through his power over Queen Margaret, and *Part 1* ends on that sinister threat.

But serious English losses are also inflicted by Joan la Pucelle (the Maid), later known as Joan of Arc. Here we first find Shakespeare's honour-killing pattern of a woman accused, judged and sentenced by men. Joan's life and death are givens of the period of history he was staging, of course, so her episodes don't necessarily show him drawn to a particular type of gender-war narrative this early. But the way he handles the Joan story is interesting in itself and also in the light of his later preoccupation with women on trial. She's captured by the English and condemned for defeating them, dishonouring them. There's no reference to the historical Joan's long and complicated trial for heresy, and she's not accused of fornication or adultery. She accuses herself of these things in a last, desperate attempt to avoid burning by pretending to be pregnant: the state execution of a pregnant woman was delayed until after she gave birth.

In Act One she arrives in Orleans when the French are in despair and offers her service to Charles the Dauphin, and the French army. There are several different Joans through the play, an argument for there being several hands in its composition. The first who enters is quick-witted and brave. Charles tests her inspiration by making Reignier of Anjou stand in his place as King, and she sees through the trick at once – by divine guidance, we may think at this point. She has huge confidence and charisma, heartening the French nobility, who are at first inclined to despise her.

The texts, chronology, and possible co-authorship of the Early Histories and some of the other early plays have long been, and will probably continue to be, disputed. So I'm in the quick-sands of Shakespearean attribution scholarship (did he write this bit? If not, who did?), a dangerous place to be. Act One of *Henry VI, Part 1* is particularly disputed, though Joan's early lines on her first arrival at the Dauphin's court certainly sound as if they were written by Shakespeare:

> Expect St Martin's summer, halcyon days [a summer prolonged into the autumn]
> Since I have entered into these wars.
> Glory is like a circle in the water,
> Which never ceaseth to enlarge itself
> Till, by broad spreading, it disperse to naught.
> With Henry [V]'s death, the English circle ends. (1.3.110-15)

Joan defines military fame as a stone thrown into a lake, a little boy's game – there's a big splash, then concentric circles rippling out to nothingness. She's right. From Henry V's funeral on through the French wars and the Wars of the Roses, the glory of soldier after soldier sinks and disperses. Her understanding of war, its theory and practice, is greater than anyone else's. She retakes Orleans and we see her fight on stage, challenging the great English champion Talbot, who's comically disconcerted by her ability:

> My mind is whirled like a potter's wheel,
> I know not where I am or what I do.
> A witch by fear not force, like Hannibal,
> Drives back our troops and conquers where she lists [pleases]. (1.7.19-22)

She cleverly coaches four French soldiers to imitate the accents of farmers so they can get through the gates of English-occupied Rouen in disguise carrying sacks of corn, kill the guards and open the gates to the French.

She begins to change markedly in Act Three when she appeals to England's ally the Duke of Burgundy to come over to the French side. She sounds patriotic and deeply moved as she describes the effects of the English occupation, begging him to

> Look on thy country, look on fertile France,
> And see the cities and the towns defaced
> By wasting ruin of the cruel foe.

As looks the mother on her lowly [lovely?] babe
When death doth close his tender-dying eye,
See, see the pining malady of France (...) (3.7.44-9))

But when Burgundy is convinced by her rhetoric and switches to support the French, her aside, 'Done like a Frenchman, turn, and turn again', (3.7.85) suggests she has no real allegiances.

In *Shakespeare's Storytellers*, Barbara Hardy calls her 'a compulsive liar, too brusque for eloquence.'[1] When Talbot is killed at Bordeaux, her reply to the English who come looking for his body on the battlefield is certainly brusque. Sir Edward Lucy rolls out a long list of Talbot's titles, prompting her graphic reply:

Here's a silly, stately style indeed (...)
Him that thou magnifi'st with all these titles
Stinking and flyblown lies here at our feet. (5.1.40-44)

But her reaction to heraldic pomposity comes out of the same shrewd peasant reductiveness as her wonderful stone-in-the-water simile.

From this scene onwards, Shakespeare – or Christopher Marlowe, Thomas Nashe or A.N. Other – shrinks her quickly into the English version of Joan, not la Pucelle but the 'Puzzle' or slut, denying her shepherd father, claiming noble parentage, broken by her capture.

Towards the end we see she's gained her successes only by sorcery. As the battle of Angiers approaches, she calls for her familiars, the evil spirits that attend on a witch, but they come only to show they'll no longer serve her:

Now, ye familiar spirits that are culled
Out of the powerful regions under earth,
Help me this once, that France may get the field. (5.4.10-12)
{*They walk and speak not*}

She offers them her blood (witches supposedly suckled their familiars with blood through extra nipples) but they leave without replying. She's quickly captured by the Duke of York after that. She's demoralised by imprisonment and her mock trial, where her claims of pregnancy only make York and Warwick laugh. But even Warwick flinches from the burning, and the play's later action and demonisation of Joan can't quite obliterate the starriness of her early scenes.

By the laws of Shakespeare's time and the time of her death, 1431, York and Warwick are right to send her to the stake, as she practises witchcraft. There's no formal trial in the play, only York and Warwick insulting her before she's taken off to execution. These Histories were Shakespeare's first plays, and he wasn't going to go broke challenging the audience's Francophobia. But the audience, however jingoistic, could see that the English nobles condemn Joan not because she's a witch but because she humiliates them in battle. This is a form of honour killing. York and Warwick might justify their cruelty because Joan dresses as a man contrary to Biblical commands and because the Dauphin may be her lover, but it's her success as a soldier they hate her for. In keeping with the pattern of honour killing found in Shakespeare's later plays, York and Warwick are guiltier in their lives and ambitions than the woman they destroy, and more dangerous to their country.

In her Introduction in the Norton edition, Jean Howard notes that Joan is sometimes portrayed in language used of Elizabeth I, for instance as the daughter of Justice, Astraea. Elizabeth might also be seen as violating woman's subordinate place in the hierarchy. Professor Howard suggests that some of Joan's characterisation reflects unease about Elizabeth's sovereignty and perhaps unease about all women who take on dominating roles. Howard adds:

> While this play insistently calls attention to the dangers of civil dissention among the English nobles, it also repeatedly stresses the danger caused to men by powerful women though it overtly displaces that threat onto the women of another country.[2]

Depending on our point of view, we might argue that the English Histories as a series equally stress the dangers caused to women, whether English or French, by powerful men. The men assume women should be subordinate and attack them when they're not. Shakespeare doesn't necessarily underwrite that, even in the early plays.

The inconsistency in Joan's portrayal may come from the misfit between the material he was reading in Hall and Holinshed with their English nationalist bias, and his own imaginative reconstruction of a woman capable of exceptional courage and directness as a soldier. It may be because several authors had a hand throughout the play – the scene quoted above where Joan solicits her familiars certainly sounds like Marlowe, especially in the stage direction – and Shakespeare wrote the early scenes but not the later ones. Or he may have had to reduce his first, impressive Joan to a witch to meet the expectations of others in the company or an English audience and is writing against the grain of the first scene's portrayal.

In *The New Oxford Shakespeare*: *The Complete Works* (2016), edited by Gary Taylor and others, and in the *Authorship Companion* to that edition, edited by Gary Taylor and Gabriel Egan, some of *Henry VI, Part 1* is ascribed to authors other than Shakespeare. These ascriptions are made mainly of the basis of lexical incidence, the frequency of usage of words and phrases, a signage some consider as reliable as a fingerprint. We're told that Thomas Nashe almost certainly wrote Act One, which contains the first Joan scene.

But even the *Authorship Companion* doesn't present conclusive evidence of that, and there's much in *Part 1*, including Act One, that's typically Shakespearean, though that's a very questionable concept now. The 'Glory is like a circle in the water' simile is stunning in itself and resembles other Shakespearean thumbnail sketches that deflate glory. In *Troilus and Cressida*, for instance, Ulysses tries with the most striking of them to persuade Achilles to go back out and fight the Trojans again:

> For Time is like a fashionable host
> That slightly shakes his parting guest by the hand,
> And with his arms outstretched, as he would fly,
> Grasps in the [new] comer. (*Troilus and Cressida*, 3.3.164-7)

Achilles may be admired now, but he'll be welcome at the celebrity party only as long as he can stay a celebrity. So he'd better stop sulking in his tent. None of the other putative authors, including Nashe, punctures glory as neatly as Shakespeare. Marlowe typically bigs it up. Not only language, always a matter of taste, but the great epic sweep of the three *Henry* plays with *Richard III* suggests a single conception. What happens in *Part 1*, for instance the Lancastrian and Yorkist choice of red or white roses in the garden of the Inns of Court, or the disastrous relocation of Margaret of Anjou to England, is developed in *Part 2* and *Part 3*. It's possible this unity may have been imposed by Shakespeare at a later date, of course, in an adaptation of originally discrete plays by himself and others. But there's no proof of that at the moment.

And he himself lays claim to Act One of *Henry VI, Part 1*. Shakespeare's second group of four History Plays, consisting of *Richard II*, the two parts of *Henry IV*, and *Henry V*, are about an earlier period of history. But they were written later than the three *Henry VI* plays and *Richard III*. At the end of *Henry V*, Shakespeare ends where he (I believe) first started in *Henry VI, Part 1* with the death of Henry V and the Accession of his baby son, Henry VI. The Chorus of *Henry V* tells us in a Sonnet-Epilogue:

> Thus far, with rough and all unable pen,
> Our bending author hath pursued the story,
> In little room confining mighty men,
> Mangling by starts [fits and starts] the full course of their glory.
> Small time; but in that small most greatly lived
> This star of England. Fortune made his sword;
> By which the world's best garden [France] he achieved,
> And of it left his son imperial lord.
> Henry the Sixth, in infant [swaddling] bands crowned King
> Of France and England did this King succeed
> Whose state so many had the managing
> That they lost France, and made our England bleed;
> Which oft our stage hath shown (...) (*Henry V*, Epilogue)

In this wonderful summary, it's clear that *Henry VI, Part 1*, which opens with the King in 'infant bands', is one of those histories 'which oft our stage hath shown', part of the Company's known repertoire, part of the author's known works, and that author is undoubtedly Shakespeare for the second tetralogy. Against this, it could be argued that The Lord Chamberlain's Men, Shakespeare's acting company, staged plays by many authors besides Shakespeare. But in 'our bending author hath pursued the story', it's implicit that he pursued the story faithfully through the eight plays, including (especially noted) the beginning, *Henry VI, Part 1* Act One, where the baby Henry VI is in swaddling bands, to the end, here, where Henry V dies and the Chorus reminds us of where we first started.

Of course, there may have been other hands in *Part 1*. The opening lines sound like Marlowe. But they also sound like a dramatist at the start of his career imitating Marlowe, an already successful one. We may dislike the scenes where Joan calls on her familiars, or disowns her father, or her final appearance, declaring herself pregnant to escape execution. There's been a lot of anger at this last scene and Shakespeare's betrayal of the historical Joan's courage. He can't, of course, show us the end, but at least he shows her walking out with recovered stoicism, with her curse on the English weather. Her last scene shows her not as a saint but entirely human, in the hands of sadistic enemies and terrified of the fire; it re-establishes sympathy for her in an audience now, and possibly in an audience then. Lexical incidence or our unease about difficult scenes don't justify dropping a play, or even an Act, from the canon.

Readers and theatre-goers new to Shakespeare may be disappointed to learn that there are such disputes, and that Shakespeare often collaborated with other playwrights. We may want to think he was unique, unmistakeable. In the *Authorship Companion* to *The Complete Works*, Gary Taylor puts the case for a collaborating Shakespeare vividly:

> Shakespeare freely collaborated with the living and the dead, with writers who were present and writers who were absent. Some of the collaborations were consensual, some were not.[3]

But he acknowledges that some current re-attribution, including some of his own, must remain tentative for the moment. Other contributors admit that to impute much-loved Shakespearean lines to another dramatist is a risky business. Though deploying immense erudition, they're willing to believe they could be wrong, something that, 'finally, is for others to determine. We submit our necks to posterity, the great executioner, with such grace as we can muster.'[4]

Professor Taylor himself acknowledges that the best guides to attribution are still John Heminge and Henry Condell, though they weren't omniscient. They were two actors from Shakespeare's company who collected his plays and produced the first Complete Works seven years after his death, *The First Folio* of 1623. Four hundred years on, their wit still rises off the page in its Dedication, 'To the Great Variety of Readers'. I've added this as an Appendix, since everyone should read it. It's funny and irreverent, and suggests better than anything else what it might have felt like to be part of that Company. But there's no evidence they joined it before 1594, so they may have known less about the early work.

Though his two long poems were printed with care, Shakespeare seems to have taken no trouble to preserve his plays by getting them into print, though this may be because they were the property of his theatre company, which wouldn't want them printed because that might discourage people from coming to see them. And he may have made more money from performances than from print. There was no author's copyright; the company who bought the manuscript owned the play.

Only about half the plays were printed before he died, and these were versions often assembled by somebody in the audience memorising what was said, writing it down afterwards and selling it to an unscrupulous printer, a 'pirate' of intellectual property. Before 1623, half had never been in print at all, and would have been altogether lost without Heminge and Condell. Only the prompter had a full manuscript version, and all these were missing by then. Actors had only their own lines and cues written out, and at best would remember only their own parts from a play of the 1590s. Many of the actors would be dead or scattered well before 1623. Heminge and Condell took on a massive task.

But they did it. It's not surprising if there were mistakes, but they seem to have been quite picky about the plays they included as mainly Shakespeare's. They didn't consider *Edward III*, *Arden of Faversham* or the *Two Noble Kinsmen*, all included by the *New Oxford* editors, to be his work. But they included *Henry VI, Part 1* as Shakespeare's. Given the qualities of mind shown in 'To the Great Variety of Readers', given that they were colleagues and friends who knew most of what he wrote and dedicated seven years to preserving it, we might do better to trust them rather than the incidence of key words and phrases. That incidence won't remain constant but will be skewed by whatever sourcebook he had open before him as he wrote.

But that's not to deny there are problems of attribution surrounding these Histories (and other plays) which will affect a critical assessment and especially an attempt like this one to establish a pattern of ideas. In considering Shakespeare, it's difficult to separate critical from scholarly questions, particularly in the earliest and last work. I think, then, quite possibly wrongly, that Joan is mostly his creation, at least in Act One, and is perhaps the most unusual of his women. She's the first to be interrogated and killed by men more powerful and self-interested than she is.

Unlike most of the English and French nobility, in her early scenes Joan is all she claims to be. Even when terrorised at the end, she's not contemptible, she's still quick-witted, and has black magic enough left to wreck the English climate before she dies:

> Then lead me hence, with whom I leave my curse.
> May never glorious sun reflex his beams
> Upon the country where you make abode,
> But darkness and the gloomy shade of death
> Environ you, till mischief and despair
> Drive you to break your necks (...) (5.6.86-91)

Shakespeare lets her have the last laugh.

An attack on a woman by a group of men is quickly repeated in *Henry VI, Part 2,* where Eleanor Cobham, Duchess of Gloucester is tried and condemned for witchcraft and treason. Again, this is a given, but unlike Joan she's a minor historical figure and Shakespeare had no need to make much of her if he didn't want to; her plot is dramatised in some detail. Eleanor is an Eve figure who tries to tempt her husband to seize supreme power from the young Henry VI. This allows other nobles to accuse her, and by implication her husband, to the King. She's naïve, even childish, and has no chance of influencing Gloucester to overthrow Henry. Gloucester is the King's uncle, devoted to the memory of his dead brother Henry V, and incorruptible. But Eleanor longs to be Queen, and like Joan she seeks help from black magic, co-opting a witch, two priests and a conjurer to find out how long King Henry will live. A spirit from hell, Asnath (Satan), who may or may not be fake, rises and gives ambiguous answers, like the witches in *Macbeth.*

Suffolk, Cardinal Beaufort, York, Buckingham and others have seen Gloucester's weakness, his love for his ambitious wife, and they set a trap for her with the séance, suborning her servants and probably supplying someone to represent Asnath. York is manoeuvring to claim the throne because Henry VI's grandfather Henry Bolingbroke killed Richard II and seized power, making himself and his descendants usurpers, and the Duke of York and his sons are next in the line of descent from Edward III. The nobles eavesdrop on Eleanor's séance, writing down the prophecies. It was treason to try to forecast the monarch's death.

She's seized and tried in the royal court with Henry as her judge while her husband stands by unable to defend her. The witch is sentenced to burn, her associates to hang, and Eleanor, who usually dresses more richly than Queen Margaret, is paraded barefoot through the London streets wearing only a sheet and a placard proclaiming her crimes. She's exiled to the Isle of Man.

It's a humorous choice of prison. Though Eleanor and Joan are opposites in every other way, both display 'unwomanly' ambition. But York's and Buckingham's motives for disgracing Eleanor are themselves treasonable, and Henry isn't sharp enough to see it. The nobles are trying to throw suspicion on her husband, the Regent, as a preliminary to seizing power for themselves, and they succeed in destroying the King's trust in his uncle.

There may be misogyny in these early plays which is authorial and can't be explained as the male characters' prejudice. In *Henry VI, Part 1*, the Countess of Auvergne is an ineffectual temptress. She sends a message inviting Talbot to visit her, saying she's heard much about his courage, and he agrees to meet her. The other English leaders assume she has sex in mind and decline to accompany him. But he's suspicious, and whispers something to one of his captains before he goes. The scene inside the Countess' castle, Act Two, scene iii, is funny but tense. The Countess means to imprison him and deprive the English of their best leader; she attempts the sort of military *coup* a General might plan, though she uses her rank and reputation for beauty to achieve it. She thinks she's succeeded in getting him into her power, and instead of flattering him, mocks his unimpressive appearance and size, refusing to acknowledge that he could be the heroic Talbot. He's courtly and urbane, waiting for her to reveal her intentions, allowing her to identify herself as a declared enemy of England. His pre-arranged signal ensures his captain will have men in readiness. As they suddenly enter, the Countess' triumph is shattered.

This is an odd episode for the Early Histories, because it's unrelated to anything else. There may be more than good-humoured banter in the

Countess' and Talbot's exchanges. He apparently forgives her for trying to trap him:

> Be not dismayed, fair lady, nor misconster [misunderstand]
> The mind of Talbot, as you did mistake
> The outward composition of his body (...) (2.3.73-5)

But his ostensibly chivalrous speech perhaps contains a threat. He speaks of the soldier's appetite for food:

> (...) nor other satisfaction do I crave
> But only, with your patience, that we may
> Taste of your wine and see what cates (sweetmeats) you have:
> For soldiers' stomachs always serve them well. (2.3.77-80)

There is perhaps a wink to the audience. The Countess is by now deferential and frightened. The scene ending is ambiguous. After testing her and proving her enmity to England, is he about to commit punishment rape? Henry V at the siege of Harfleur threatens rape if the citizens resist (he may or may not be bluffing), and of course rape is common in war. The scene may play to the contemporary audience's uglier responses. It's almost always cut in performance; probably most would cede it to another author.

Eleanor Cobham is saved from death, though not from exile, by her rank, and this is also true of the great termagant of these four plays, Margaret of Anjou. Though Margaret doesn't fight hand-to-hand like Joan, she puts on armour and makes herself a formidable presence on the battlefield. She breaks customary limits for women in more ways than Joan does, as she openly despises her husband and becomes Suffolk's lover. When Suffolk is beheaded she finds the head, keeps it and talks to it. Thomas More's daughter kept her father's head, and that wasn't considered a sign of insanity but of devotion; there have been changes in the way we respond to mortality and decay. But Margaret doesn't become a victim of honour killing. Though she's French, unpredictable and dangerous, the Lancastrians support her, first because they're loyal to her husband, then to her son. Her position as Queen and mother of a prince protects her for most of her life from the consequences of her recklessness. She's the only character who appears in all three parts of *Henry VI* and in *Richard III*; she functions as a running thread tying the epic together.

In her first scene at the end of *Part I*, she's cool and fearless when taken prisoner by Suffolk, who negotiates with her father, Reignier of Anjou, her marriage to young Henry. Reignier agrees that Suffolk can take her to England without delay:

> Since thou dost deign to woo her little worth
> To be the princely bride of such a lord,
> Upon condition I may quietly
> Enjoy mine own, the countries Maine and Anjou,
> Free from oppression or the stroke of war
> My daughter shall be Henry's, if he please. (5.5.107-12)

Margaret hears every word, as do both armies. Almost every character's mainspring of action is accounted for somewhere, and this public statement of how little her father loves her explains a lot. We see her toughening further when she arrives in her new country and marries Henry. He's not what she hoped, and she's enraged when he resigns their son's claim to the throne on condition he himself can reign in peace for his lifetime. This comes close to replaying the deal her father made with Suffolk, and it sends her from covert to open rebellion against female constraints.

In *Henry VI, Part 3*, she seizes her husband's authority, putting on armour to defend not just her son's rights but his life, since if the Yorkists win they'll kill him. She becomes demonic in her savagery, more so than the men. At the battle of Wakefield the Duke of York is at last captured by the Lancastrians. She makes him stand on a molehill and wipes the tears from his face with a handkerchief soaked in his youngest son's blood. At first he's silent. She taunts him to make him speak, laughing:

> Thou wouldst be fee'd [paid], I see, to make me sport.
> York cannot speak unless he wear a crown!
> A crown for York! And lords, bow low to him.
> Hold you his hands, whilst I do set it on. (1.4.92-95)

She pushes a paper crown down on his head. Finally, he's goaded into responding:

> O tiger's heart wrapped in a woman's hide!
> How couldst thou drain the life-blood of the child

To bid the father wipe his eyes withal
And yet be seen to wear a woman's face? (1.4.137-140)

This protracted scene of torture was famous in contemporary London. It's alluded to in a pamphlet addressed to fellow-authors, '*A Groats-worth of Witte bought with a million of repentance*' (1592), where Robert Greene refers to Shakespeare as an 'upstart Crow, beautified with our feathers, who with his "tyger's heart wrapped in a player's [actor's] hyde" supposes he is as well able to bombast out a blank verse as the best of you, and being an absolute Jo-hannes Factotum [Jack of all Trades, with an implied, Master of None] is in his own conceit [imagination; vanity], the only Shake-scene in a Countrey.'[5] Greene had already, then, some feeling for his lost intellectual property rights; Gary Taylor's grand concept of Shakespeare's free collaboration with the living and the dead might have consoled him. Greene knew his readers would pick up the quotation from *Henry VI, Part 3*; he involuntarily pays tribute to Shakespeare's success.

We follow Margaret's brutalisation as she ages during the Wars of the Roses. 'Captain Margaret' or the 'She-wolf of France' as the Yorkists call her, both inflicts and endures almost unendurable pain. In this Darwinian jungle she didn't choose, she adapts all too well to her environment. We see a woman becoming a tiger. After taunting York at the battle of Wakefield with the paper crown and the death of his son, she has him beheaded. But she's forced to stand by helpless at Tewkesbury while her only son Edward is killed. He asserts himself with crazy courage when taken prisoner, demanding homage as heir to King Henry, proving himself in his last moments everything his mother could wish him. He's stabbed by each of the three York boys. They deny Margaret the death she begs for, and she's forced to go free. Without a son, she's no further threat. She's never tried or killed for her adultery or assumption of male power. The three York boys are interested only in success, not in moral judgement; besides, they know she'll suffer more left alive.

Joan and Margaret break boundaries of gender, and as the Wars continue, the boundaries of rank are blurred too, in Jack Cade's rebellion but also in the imagination of the only humane character. In *Henry VI, Part 3,* Henry, hiding from the battle of Towton, bitterly regrets that he was born a King not a poor man, and imagines the supposed peace he would find in a shepherd's life:

> So many hours must I tend my flock ...
> So many weeks ere the poor fools [innocents] will ean [give birth],
> So many years ere I shall sheer the fleece,
> So minutes, hours, days, weeks, months, and years,
> Past over for the end they were created
> Would bring white hairs into a quiet grave. (2.5.31-41)

David Warner in Peter Hall and John Barton's adaptation, *The Wars of the Roses*, is brilliant as Henry, making of the King a choric commentator and the only sane character in the play. But Henry's view of poverty is sentimental, as we see seconds later when the Son Who Has Killed his Father and the Father Who Has Killed His Son reveal in antiphonal speeches not the peace but the dehumanisation and grief of poor men co-opted to fight in the dynastic wars. The scene allows the audience a chance to contemplate with Henry the effects on civil society of Margaret's savage defence of her son's rights against the Yorkists' equally savage ambition. One can't construct Shakespeare as a democrat, however, since Jack Cade's rebellion is not a bid for justice but a mirror image among the poor of the greed and envy of their rulers.

Joan, Eleanor and the Countess are not created as inexplicably bad or two-dimensional. Joan comes out of an innocent pastoral landscape and gives France her moment of glory. Eleanor was adored once. The Countess of Auvergne seems genuinely patriotic in her plan to take Talbot prisoner, while with few exceptions the English nobles have little concept of nationhood. Even Margaret, savage as she is, can arouse sympathy for the wretched life her father sold her into. These women may be guilty, though in the Countess' case, guilty only of being French. But the English lords and ecclesiastics are guiltier.

There are no formal or informal trials of women in the later stages of the first tetralogy. But we see more of the politics of gender that make honour killing possible. There's a mixture of women who try to overcome their disempowerment through their looks or wits and women who remain entirely disempowered. Two marriage proposals can construct their limited choices.

Elizabeth Woodville appears first in *Henry VI, Part 3*, after the dead Duke of York's eldest son has seized power and with Warwick's help made himself Edward IV. She petitions him for the return to her son of her dead Lancastrian husband's confiscated lands. Almost always, as here, the women act or define themselves in relation to men, but she's a cool adversary in the sparring that follows. Edward tests whether she'll sell herself for the land, offering it back in return for her sleeping with him. She replies that she'd rather sleep in prison. He then offers marriage, which she silently accepts. She rapidly becomes insecure and unhappy, Edward's brothers, George and Richard, use her birth (historically she was the first commoner to marry an English King) to discredit her, and she eventually loses her sons. Like Joan and Eleanor, she's seized and destroyed, though in a less dramatic way.

Historically she was reputed to be grasping, securing high positions for her numerous kin, but there's little sign of greed in Shakespeare's portrayal; George and Richard are unreasonable in despising her. Her marriage to Edward IV produced, as well as the murdered princes in the tower, a daughter, Elizabeth of York, who married Henry VII, uniting the houses of York and Lancaster. Elizabeth I was their granddaughter. Shakespeare treats Elizabeth Woodville more kindly than later historians.

In *Richard III*, Richard courts Lady Anne, Warwick the Kingmaker's daughter. He's killed her husband Prince Edward and her father-in-law, Henry VI; he waylays her as she accompanies Henry's coffin to its burial place. This scene, where Anne spits out her contempt for him, then passes from horror to horrified sexual fascination to acquiescence, shows her inability to run away. She's a rabbit in front of a snake, embracing her own oppression and death with no more than token resistance; there's provocation even in the insults she throws at him. Her father, husband and father-in-law are dead, and she can't live without a male protector.

There seems little reason for Richard to marry her. Historically, perhaps, it was for her vast lands and reserves of soldiers in the North, but there's no hint of that in *Richard III.* He courts her apparently to see whether he can win her despite 'her heart's extremest hate' (1.2.227) for him. She's a trophy. He then has her killed so he can court Princess Elizabeth of York, whose younger brothers, the princes in the tower, Richard has also murdered. Anne's death can't be defined as an honour killing, as she's never accused of infidelity or immodesty. She's merely in the way, and disappears without explanation, except that 'Anne my wife has bid this world goodnight.' (4.3.39) She and Elizabeth Woodville show some spirit initially, but it's broken by their marriages.

If they survive to be old, women can look back only on a register of murdered fathers, husbands and sons. The two old women in *Richard III,* the Duchess of Gloucester, Richard's mother, and the aged Queen Margaret, ancient enemies, join in lament with the much younger Elizabeth Woodville, by now a widow and bereaved of her sons. Shakespeare brings Margaret back on stage, ahistorically since she was ransomed and returned to France after the death of her son and was dead by now, to revisit old massacres as this first tetralogy draws to a close. The women's grief spans generations and factions:

> Margaret: I had an Edward, till a Richard killed him,
> I had a husband till a Richard killed him.
> (to Elizabeth) Thou hadst an Edward, till a Richard killed him,
> Thou hadst a Richard, till a Richard killed him
> [alluding to the princes in the tower].
> Duchess of York: (to Margaret) I had a Richard [York] too, and thou didst kill him,
> I had a Rutland too, thou holpst to kill him. (4.4.40-46)

The two old women blame each other, though they join Elizabeth Woodville in ascribing most of their bereavements and England's present ills to Richard. Margaret enjoys relating with entirely fake sympathy the misfortunes of the other two until her words are exhausted, merely 'poor breathing orators of miseries' (4.4.129), as Elizabeth calls them. Their grief doesn't unite them, despite the choric form of its expression. The violence they've suffered is beyond healing.

And yet they aren't wholly wasted. They've kept alive the national memory of the dead, and they keep the dead alive in Richard's memory too. By confronting him as the Battle of Bosworth approaches, where Henry Tudor, Earl of Richmond defeats Richard and becomes Henry VII, they prompt the ghostly visitations in his dreams the night before battle, unnerve him, and win the victory as much as Henry Tudor's soldiers do.

Shakespeare necessarily becomes even more constrained in handling his material towards the end. We may dislike the idea of his writing to comply with Tudor ideology, but he wouldn't have got a license to stage *Richard III* unless it was firmly behind Henry VII and Elizabeth of York. And he refuses to be completely 'tongue-tied by authority' (Sonnet 66), making Richard so entertainingly wicked and Henry so unbelievably saintly, any audience understands they can't resemble the real historical figures.

In another strategy too he admits the bias of his version. In Act Three, Hastings is falsely accused of treason by Richard, and executed. In a very short scene, Act Three, scene vi, often cut in performance, a Scrivener whose job is to record public events in London appears and admits in soliloquy that he's helping to falsify this one as it happens. He dares not write the truth, he tells us. The scene warns us, right in the middle of *Richard III*, not to trust histories, especially *Richard III*. Even the archival material they're based on is controlled by the winners. Shakespeare could have played the Scrivener himself, though that might make his point a bit too obvious for his own safety.

The contention begun in *Henry VI, Part 1* among the Temple Garden roses over who has the right of Succession, Henry VI or the Duke of York, gives way through the tetralogy to acceptance on stage and in the audience that none of the men who claim the throne are kingly both in birth and character. A viable King must be one strong enough to seize and hold power. As well as dramatising the long and complex Wars of the Roses or Cousins' Wars, the Early Histories dramatise the wars between men and women. Whether or not they're actually brought to trial, the suppression of women and 'witches' – in Joan and Eleanor, perhaps in Queen Margaret, the two terms merge – is motivated by the brutality and self-interest of the suppressors. The same Mafia ethics prevail, in the nobles' treatment of each other, and of the women.

Notes

[1]Barbara Hardy, *Shakespeare's Storytellers*, pp164-5.

[2]Jean Howard, Introduction to *The First Part of Henry VI*, in *The Norton Shakespeare*, pp440-1.

[3]Gary Taylor, *The Authorship Companion to The New Oxford Shakespeare: The Complete Works*, p22.

[4]John Burrows and Hugh Craig, *The Authorship Companion to The New Oxford Shakespeare: The Complete Works*, p217.

[5]Robert Greene, *A Groats-worth of witte bought with a million of repentance*. This was published as a pamphlet just after Greene's death in 1592; the authorship is now disputed. Wikipedia gives the text and an account, with identification of some of the other authors named in it.

3

SHAKESPEARE IN TUDORLAND

On *All Is True; or, Henry VIII*; *The Winter's Tale*; and Tudorland

HENRY VIII IS BRITAIN'S MOST FAMOUS honour killer, Anne Boleyn the classic victim. He dispensed with a trial for Katherine Howard, hastily bringing in a Bill of Attainder that allowed her execution without one. Catherine Parr, endangered because she held different religious opinions from his, managed to save herself by quickly renouncing them. His first wife, Katherine of Aragon, wasn't tried for her life, but the imputation that she'd lied about her relationship with his elder brother allowed him to discard her in a corrupt judicial process and probably hastened her death.

After James VI of Scotland became James I of England[1], dramatised royal histories more accurate than *Richard III* could at last begin to appear, though they still had to be tactful. The cult of Tudorland, the constant re-fictionalisation of the Tudor monarchies still going strong today, wasn't begun by Shakespeare, but it was at least quickly taken up by him. *All Is True; or, Henry VIII* is far from true: it shows Henry as an innocent bystander at most of its events.

It's a late History Play written in collaboration with John Fletcher and again based on Raphael Holinshed's *Chronicles* like Shakespeare's other English Histories. Its time-frame spans the Field of the Cloth of Gold, the Duke of Buckingham's impeachment, the first rumours of Queen Katherine's divorce, the fall of Cardinal Wolsey, the rise and Coronation of Anne Boleyn and the birth and christening of her daughter Elizabeth.

James I derived his English sovereignty from Henry VII, and a true account of Henry VIII's insanity was nowhere near possible. But though Shakespeare's Henry VIII is to some extent normalised, he has terrifying swings between jollity and ferocity. He's a more disturbing study in tyranny than Richard III because he's more believable. We can't laugh at him, or with him. His nobles try to, imitating his characteristic 'Ha! Ha! Ha!' like frightened schoolboys imitating a brutal headmaster, but they're terrified of him and spend their time trying to anticipate what he'll do next. *All Is True* is sophisticated post-truth narrative. While claiming accuracy, it acknowledges the fluidity of personality and the difficulty of making moral judgements about historical events, especially when you're likely to have royalty in the audience. It creates holograms that allow a choice about how we'll understand most of the main figures.

It starts with a dynastic struggle like the ones in the earlier History Plays, with Henry's cousin the Duke of Buckingham's impeachment for treason. He's the son of the Duke of Buckingham executed in *Richard III* and potentially a threat to Henry, who has only a daughter, Mary, to succeed him. Buckingham's fall is planned by Wolsey, who wants to remove other influences on the King, and who bribes Buckingham's former estate surveyor to give false evidence about his master's supposed plan to murder Henry and seize his throne. Queen Katherine tries to save Buckingham, incurring Wolsey's enmity, but the surveyor has been coached to act out, in front of Henry, Buckingham's imagined words and his gestures with a knife. Henry is frightened, and the Duke is executed.

For the first time in Shakespeare's Histories, the old axis of power, the nobility, here represented by Buckingham, Suffolk, Norfolk, Surrey and Abergavenny, whose strength derives from the men they can muster from the lands they own, is giving way to the powerful intellects of obscurely born men: Thomas Wolsey, Thomas Cromwell, Thomas Cranmer, the sons of a butcher, a blacksmith and an impoverished gentleman who died while his children were young. They rule the country with pens, not swords. These new men have come up through free grammar school and university places into government administration, into the Civil Service, as it would become. A sociologist or historian would spot that now with no trouble at all, it's the sort of demographic shift we look for, but it's interesting that

Shakespeare staged it as soon as he did, along with the resentment and insecurity that accompanied it.

Outraged by this embryo democracy, a country where, as Buckingham sees it, a 'keech', (1.1.55) a lump of butcher's lard like Wolsey rules, the nobility are at a disadvantage, though consanguinity and numbers help to compensate for their lack of political foresight. They form a mutually supportive group, though one apparently on its way out.

But the main dramatic struggle is not so much between opposed dynasties or classes as between a threatened Roman Catholicism and a nascent Protestantism. Catholicism is represented by Wolsey, the 'holy fox/Or wolf, or both' (1.1.158-9) and the rancorous Stephen Gardiner, Bishop of Winchester, but also by Queen Katherine, who is a pattern of wifehood and kindness to the oppressed. The incoming Protestants are Cromwell, Cranmer, and Anne, the last a 'spleeny [passionate] Lutheran' (3.2.100) according to Wolsey, though Shakespeare doesn't commit her to a religious opinion in the play. There isn't a complete division: Cromwell is deeply attached to Wolsey, for instance.

All Is True is episodic and spectacular, and it carries an extraordinary punch, anticipating the crack about all political careers ending in failure. It's structured like Fortune's turning wheel: as the play opens, we see Buckingham, Wolsey, and Katherine beginning to go down. Surrey is half-way down already though his father-in-law Buckingham will precede him to the block. Anne and Cromwell are at their zenith by the end, but we know they'll soon be down and on their way to execution too. There's a large cast to function as commentators and share the court gossip; the principal characters elude fixed identities more than in Shakespeare's earlier and single-authored plays.

Henry is unnerving: sometimes pitiless, sometimes unexpectedly kind. The old enemies Buckingham and Wolsey reveal new selves as life is torn from them, Buckingham through attempts to wrench his angry nature into forgiveness, Wolsey through repentance for his sins. Except in his opposition to Katherine, Cranmer is the one good man at court, and an interesting mixture of weakness and strength. He weeps with relief as Henry promises help against his enemies, and again when he and Gardiner are forcibly, and temporarily, reconciled by Henry. But he becomes a great prophet of Reformation and Empire at Elizabeth's christening. As he foretells a long and successful reign for the baby, the audience knows he won't live to see it. During this flux of political and religious systems, Henry changes a middle-aged wife for a new one.

In his *Chronicles*, Holinshed tells how Queen Katherine was charged with an unusual form of sexual transgression: that she had falsely claimed to be a virgin when she married her dead husband Arthur's younger brother Henry. This was, then, in modern terms, an honour trial; she'd committed a sexual crime, incest, and betrayed the innocent young Henry into committing it also, incurring God's punishment of withholding a son and heir from them. At the time of her marriage to Henry, it was accepted that her previous marriage was not consummated because of Arthur's youth and poor health, and so was not a valid marriage.

Twenty-five years later, when Henry decided to divorce her and marry again, the best or perhaps the only way to do it was to assert that her marriage to Arthur had been consummated and therefore she had never been free to marry her brother-in-law, a degree of relationship which precluded marriage then and for three hundred years afterwards (as was a widower's marrying his sister-in-law). At her public investigation in 1529 Katherine defended herself ably, walking across the floor of the court to address Henry, unexpectedly challenging him in front of a mixed crowd of spectators to say she was not a virgin when he first had her. He was unable to reply.

All is True was written over 80 years after that, probably in late 1612. The crux of the historical enquiry, whether or not she'd had sex with Arthur and therefore couldn't be Henry's legal wife, is missing, and she's not asked to explain where she lost her virginity to a court consisting of a husband determined to get rid of her and the husband's toadies, while curious Londoners look on. Shakespeare does justice to her courage and dignity but seems to have felt that Henry's full loutishness couldn't be shown on stage. The crux, however, is implicit, and would be understood by an audience as late as James I's court. Shakespeare's Katherine is magnificent, defending herself as a devoted wife and reserving most of her fire for Wolsey. For her speech Shakespeare uses some of the historical Katherine's phrasing and arguments as recorded by Holinshed. As in history, in *All Is True* she refuses to acknowledge the legality of the court, then walks out.

As well as representing Katherine's mistreatment with unexpected sympathy, given she was a Catholic, *All Is True* show-cases England's most controversial honour-killing victim. We see Anne Boleyn on her way to her Coronation in the height of her triumph, the London citizens fighting for a glimpse of her beauty, the courtiers imagining themselves in Henry's sheets. Everybody in the audience knows what's going to happen to her.

Unlike most characters in *All Is True*, Katherine's honesty is never in doubt. She's in conflict with herself as well as Henry, but she's always frank and convincing. Henry pretends religious scruples about their marriage:

> Would it not grieve an able man to leave
> So sweet a bedfellow? But conscience, conscience.
> O, tis a tender place, and I must leave her. (2.2.140-43)

But he's already begun to court Anne, meeting her by chance at a supper party given by Wolsey, who may have invited her on his own account or to please a colleague, and who wants Henry to marry the French King's sister. Anne is pert before Henry's entrance, silent afterwards. Her end is implicit from her first appearance. The audience is reminded of it by his sinister remark, as they go off to dance, 'Sweet partner/I must not yet forsake you.' (1.4.103-4) It's a meeting that helps to destroy Wolsey, as a letter he writes to the Pope attempting to delay the divorce from Katherine, and so to prevent Henry from marrying a mere knight's daughter, accidentally finds its way into Henry's hands, along with papers listing Wolsey's enormous wealth. The nobility thank Providence for this, but it's more likely one of them slipped the documents inside Henry's packet of letters: there are some splendid *House of Cards* manoeuvrings.

Henry's arrival at Wolsey's supper is announced by cannon fire. On 29 June 1613, when the play was staged at The Globe, a spark from one of the cannon caught the thatch and the building burned down in an hour, after only 13 years on Bankside.[2] Nobody died, but what was lost is incalculable: perhaps complete playscripts, cast lists, accounts. We can't know what the loss meant to Shakespeare. The contemporary reports are by people with no stake or interest in the theatre, and facetious.

Katherine puts Henry's motive bluntly to her enemies, Wolsey and Cardinal Campeius: he wants to be rid of her because she's too old to give him another child. Though she's stoical she's admirably angry with her clerical tormentors and her husband:

> Would you have me –
> If you have any justice, any pity,
> If ye be anything but churchmen's habits [clothes] –
> Put my sick cause into his hands that hates me?
> Alas, he's banished me his bed already,
> His love, too long ago. I am old, my lords (...) (3.1.113 -18)

Her arraignment was an unusual honour trial; there was no overt intention to kill her, merely to discard her. It was presented as an investigation rather than a criminal case, though it was intended to be a show trial, a scenario wrecked when Katherine had the courage to walk out of it, blaming Wolsey for the loss of Henry's affection.

The evidence given by a former courtier of Prince Arthur, who quoted the long-dead Prince as saying on the morning after his marriage to Katherine in 1501, 'Gentlemen, last night I was in Spain', was not heard until this investigation, nearly 30 years after that marriage. It was almost certainly invented to please Henry. Eventually Katherine was established at Kimbolton Castle, damp and isolated, with a court consisting of a few waiting-ladies, and forbidden to see her daughter. It was in effect a death sentence following a verdict without validity.

Katherine's fall is far the saddest in a play full of farewells to greatness. She represents stability; the song by one of her ladies celebrates Orpheus, who held still the running water and the seasons with his song. He

> made a lasting spring:
> Everything that heard him play,
> Even the billows of the sea,
> Hung their heads, and then lay by [were motionless]. (3.1.8-11)

Only art captures a moment forever. Patience and loyalty are qualities constantly undermined elsewhere by ill fortune, but Katherine grows more saintly as she suffers, admitting how she's hated Wolsey but trying to recognise his better qualities as she dies in the desolation he and Henry have made for her. The verse is appropriately elegiac throughout, with unstressed line-endings that give a dying fall to its majestic passages. These are characteristic of John Fletcher rather than Shakespeare, however, and a lot of the play may be by him. Wolsey, disgraced and facing death, remembers

I have ventured,
Like little wanton boys that swim on bladders [blown up bladders of animals]
These many summers in a sea of glory,
But far beyond my depth (...) (3.2.359-362)

Anne's portrayal is the most ambiguous. In her second scene, she protests her lack of ambition and her pity for Katherine. But her companion the Old Lady may be her older double, who lays bare Anne's hidden greed and ruthlessness. The Old Lady's conversation teems with scurrilous puns, pointing to the counts and emballings that secure honours and titles, the interchangeability of queans and Queens. From medieval times a woman young and old were often shown together in verse or painting. Stories about female doubles who can switch from young to old and back appear in the anonymous *Sir Gawain and the Green Knight* and in *The Wife of Bath's Tale* in Chaucer's *The Canterbury Tales.* The old one, known as the Loathly Lady, shows us what, without magic, the younger will become.

Shakespeare doesn't necessarily share the mindsets of medieval iconography. We may feel that Anne's innocence shines more brightly beside the Old Lady's corruption, or that the Old Lady's satirical comments spring entirely from envy. But Anne claims she wouldn't take on the burden of being Queen for all the world, while the Old Lady would do anything for Carnarvonshire. Anne is just about to become Marquess of Pembroke. The interpretation that she's Anne's double or truth-teller is there if we want it, though qualified by the fact that we know Anne won't grow old. Speaking of Katherine, she says:

Much better
She ne'er had known pomp; though't be temporal,
Yet if that quarrel [mischief-maker] fortune, do divorce
It [pomp] from the bearer, 'tis a sufferance panging
As soul and body's severing. (2.3.12-16)

This sounds more like her own beheading than Katherine's slow death. Katherine has 'known pomp' from her birth, being Ferdinand and Isabella of Spain's daughter, while Anne will rise from knight's daughter to Marquess to Queen. The Old Lady taunts her that as she's so humble, her back is too weak to bear a boy.

A bystander describes the seething crowd trying to barge its way into Anne's Coronation, mirroring the chaotic state of the nation following Katherine's divorce:

> Great-bellied women
> That had not half a week to go, like rams [battering rams]
> In the old time of war, would shake the press [crowd]
> And make 'em reel before 'em. No man living
> Could say, 'this is my wife' there, all were woven
> So strangely in one piece (...) (4.1.78-83)

Nobody knows for sure who his wife is now. Once a wife can be put away on a trumped-up charge because she's old, the fabric of society is wrenched and distorted. The premium placed on fertility rewrites the Coronation as a war of battering bellies. Anne was pregnant at the time of her marriage to Henry, Katherine's divorce was speeded up on that account, so Anne has herself barged her way into Westminster Abbey with her great belly and helped to create this chaos. A bystander relates how she sits wordlessly displaying her pregnancy to the spectators; she sounds like a cow in calf. Henry's appetite and desperation for a son degrade both wives before he kills them. Such passages are at odds with Cranmer's final prophecy for Anne's baby, Elizabeth.

Shakespeare has, I believe, included in the portrayal of Leontes in *The Winter's Tale* what he leaves out of his portrayal of Henry in *All Is True*. Leontes means lionlike. A lion was the emblem for every English King, but Henry's especially leonine qualities were praised everywhere. The two plays are close, two years apart, with *The Winter's Tale* coming first in 1611. It would be easier to argue that *All Is True* was the impetus for *The Winter's Tale*, that in the latter play he was moved to fictionalise and universalise the specifics of history shown in the former.

It's possible that both plays were in contemplation at the same time. And of course he knew Holinshed's *Chronicles* well at least from 1591.

Some scholars have argued an earlier date for *All Is True*, even that the play is Elizabethan. That seems very unlikely, given the portrayal of Katherine. If she's honest, and she clearly is, then her marriage to Henry was valid, which would make Elizabeth illegitimate, not a sensible line for a dramatist to take in the Queen's lifetime. But it's possible the date was, at least, earlier than 1613.

In *Shakespeare and the Nature of Women*, Juliet Dusinberre notes the likeness between Hermione and Katherine at their trials, which she considers mainly as dramatising the suspect eloquence of educated women when they enter a male sphere:

> Hermione and Katherine plead their own cause in courts which have prejudged the issue (...) He [Leontes] interprets her eloquence as effrontery, urging condemnation of her not for what she says, but for saying it at all (...) But Shakespeare demonstrates in this play almost more than any other, that conventions of femininity have no relevance in the tribunal of right and wrong.[3]

The Winter's Tale, *All Is True* and Holinshed's *Chronicles* show further likenesses in all three Queens' responses to arraignment. Hermione is strikingly like Shakespeare's and Holinshed's Katherines in composure, pride of birth, physical frailty (though this is only implicit in Holinshed), direct address to her husband in court and appeal as a foreigner to the onlookers' compassion. In Shakespeare's source story, Robert Greene's *Pandosto*, Queen Bellaria appears in court charged with adultery, but she has no speeches to compare in power and dignity with Hermione's.

Katherine was accused of incest in marrying two brothers, Arthur and Henry. Hermione is accused of adultery with Polixenes, who is closer than a brother to Leontes; in the second part of *The Winter's Tale*, Polixenes refers to Leontes as his brother. Also like Shakespeare's and Holinshed's Katherines, who defend the legitimacy of an only daughter, Mary, Hermione at her trial defends the legitimacy of an only daughter, Perdita.

Hermione's reference to her father, the King of Russia, and her wish that he might see his daughter's distress parallels Katherine's allusion in court to her father, King Ferdinand of Spain, in his day the most feared monarch in Europe, though dead by the time of his daughter's divorce. Hermione finally refuses to acknowledge the court, referring herself to a higher power, Apollo's Oracle, as Katherine leaves the hearing and refers her cause to the Pope. The unpredictable cruelty to a faithful wife that couldn't be fully shown in Henry VIII appears overtly in Leontes.

I think we're meant to notice that long gap between pregnancies in *The Winter's Tale.* Henry's desperation for a son in his first two marriages would be legendary to court audiences as long afterwards as the reign of James I. Katherine's forgiveness of her husband, her last sad letter to him a few days before she died attesting that her eyes longed for him, is repeated in Hermione's final forgiveness of Leontes, though this is mimed, not spoken.

Anne's trial and death (which are not represented in *All Is True*, though we know they're coming), resemble Hermione's trial and apparent death even more than Katherine's arraignment does. Katherine wasn't tried for her life, Anne was. Though Henry wasn't present or at least wasn't visible at Anne's trial, he seems to have hated his wife as much as Leontes does by the time of Hermione's trial, while in *All Is True* he retains some respect for Katherine. Anne was threatened with burning, as is Hermione; it was the standard form of execution for a female traitor (a Queen who committed adultery and women convicted of murdering their husbands counted as traitors), though that was commuted for Anne, and of course Hermione pre-empts Leontes' expected sentence, seeming to die when she hears of Mamillius' death. Burning, however, is also threatened for Queen Bellaria in *Pandosto*.

Anne was accused of incest with her brother (possibly some bright politico – Cromwell? – suggested this ploy, inspired by the charge against Katherine of a merely technical incest) and adultery with four other men, crimes impossible to disprove. As Hermione says, you can't prove a negative in the absence of evidence. Anne's guilty verdict would result in her daughter Elizabeth being proclaimed illegitimate for several years. Perdita's legitimacy is denied by Leontes and re-established only through Apollo's divine intervention.

So in *The Winter's Tale* we can retrospectively see a palimpsest created out of that overcharged time in English history. The seismic shocks continued to ripple long after Henry's death, and created a narrative of Hermione superimposed on Anne superimposed on Katherine. *The Winter's Tale* was the first of the two plays to be staged as far as is known, but it's possible that Hermione's Russian Doll effect was available for the first audiences, as it is for us. We can see in the first half of *The Winter's Tale* that this is a recurring story for women, and remember the histories of Katherine and Anne, even before the courtship of Perdita and Florizel warns that such tragedies may continue into the future.

Elizabeth's ginger hair, the Plantagenet DNA on her head, would tend to support her legitimacy, hence her mother's innocence, once she was widely seen. We're still inclined to judge Anne innocent of adultery because we're aware of the way the state can suppress or invent evidence and control appearances. She was of course ruthless, but as to adultery, perhaps she was guilty only of being too sophisticated, of playing the courtly love game a little too well, as Hermione does with Polixenes, and then tension tipped her from flirting to crude outspokenness when she said to Henry Norris, 'You look for dead men's shoes. For if aught came to the King but good [if the King died], you would look to have me.'[4] The remark got back to Henry, and Norris was arrested next day.

Every character in *All Is True* seems to live and die only to ensure Elizabeth's conception and survival into the future foretold for her by Cranmer. Buckingham, Wolsey, Katherine, the whole Catholic Church must go, to make way for her: most of the Catholic men sitting round the table ready to condemn Cranmer for heresy will die violently before him. The exception is the Chancellor, Sir Thomas Audley, a minor figure here, easing his way into the job as Sir Thomas More's replacement, soon to secure the execution of his predecessor and become a legend for toadying and brutality in a brutal and toadying age. Henry's savage mood softens into an equally scary jocularity as he asks Cranmer to baptise Elizabeth, and she has an elaborate christening with aged Duchesses in attendance: the nobility is being reduced to a decorative role. Cranmer will die a martyr in the Catholic Mary Tudor's reign, helping to secure Elizabeth's Protestant succession, initially signing a recantation of his faith, then holding the hand that signed it out to the fire first.

His closing vision of a saint-like Queen and an idyllic England is of course nonsense: there was huge poverty, savage repression of dissent and a lot of good luck in the wreck of the Armada. But there was no civil war in her lifetime, which may compensate for some of the methods she took to prevent it. Cranmer ends the play with praise of James I, the beginnings of Empire in Virginia, and James' 'branches', his children, especially his daughter Elizabeth Stuart, named for Elizabeth I. *All Is True* may first have been staged early in 1613 for her wedding.

In a generally male-dominated society, wanting a boy baby was not peculiar to royalty; boys to carry on the name and inherit and manage the family money were almost always more desired than girls, in families of all ranks. In an interview on television about his role as Cromwell in the adaptation of Hilary Mantel's biographies, Mark Rylance (I can't remember his exact words), pondered along the lines of 'if only they could have known how strong a monarch Elizabeth would be, how much misery would have been spared in that destructive quest for a boy'. If only society had valued girls more.

Shakespeare got there first. Elizabeth is not 'a girl [who] promises boys hereafter', (5.1.165-6) as the Old Lady smarmily announces to Henry. It's been suggested that the Old Lady prophesies James I's succession here, but that seems to strain the meaning of 'boys'. She means that Anne will have a son next or that this baby will grow up to have sons, and the audience knows she's wrong. We know that Elizabeth is a girl who promises power in her own right hereafter. That is of course another given of history, but several of Shakespeare's Last Plays, not just *All Is True*, celebrate the precarious potential of small girls and girl babies: Marina, Perdita, Miranda, losing everything but their beautiful conceptual names, unexpectedly fulfil their parents' last hopes of genetic survival. Increasingly, Shakespeare's plots celebrate girl babies who redeem the sins and mistakes of male power, though troubles lie ahead for them too.

Tudorland remains a popular destination. Why are we still fascinated by Henry VIII? Innumerable histories, novels, TV serials and films on every level of historical accuracy and none re-tread the old ground. In the hands of Hilary Mantel the subject takes on new life, partly from Mantel's success in rehabilitating figures that history decided not to like, partly from her genius for fear and physical pain. She can shift into sit-com at times. Jane Seymour asks the middle-aged Cromwell if he would like to marry her. He replies:

> 'I am too old for you, Jane. I could be your father.'

> 'Could you?' Jane says wonderingly. 'Well, stranger things have happened at Wolf Hall. I didn't even realise you knew my mother.'[5]

Mantel has both scholarly accuracy and empathy with all her people, and she translates vividly to TV.

A middlebrow novelist, Philippa Gregory in *The Other Boleyn Girl*, confers a modern sensibility, slightly proto-feminist, on her women, and makes the mainly women readers feel at home with it. Then there are no end of series using titillating executions to string along the titillating story. The axe rises and falls, or better still, a traitor meets a traitor's death. Any personable TV presenter can seemingly get a contract to reheat the familiar ingredients. We need to know what the wives looked like: there's no authenticated painting of young Katherine Howard, so my coffee mug rests on the coaster image of a woman apparently in early middle age, though the caption says she's twenty-one. She may be Jane Seymour's elder sister, though David Starkey disputes this on the basis of the jewellery, which is from the royal collection. Even as I write, another TV Katherine of Aragon is hurling china at the wall like Scarlett O'Hara.

Perhaps we're fixated on Henry VIII because The Tudors and the Second World War were not so long ago almost the only periods of English history taught in secondary schools, and TV audiences enjoy revisiting their schooldays. But Henry VII or Mary Tudor don't have the same pulling power. Henry VIII was our own little Hitler, his state murders of 'heretics' as crazy though of course nothing near as widespread as Hitler's racial murders. He's best known now for his treatment of his wives, not for his religious persecutions.

Our fascination with England's royal honour killer, lasting long after English culture has apparently changed beyond recognition, is a crude form of our continuing fascination with Shakespeare's honour trials, which still speak to the heart. Shakespeare gives his embattled women language, some of the most eloquent language ever spoken, when history often denied and still denies them a word before death. Could that be why he was said to be very popular with women? Honour trials and executions on stage and screen still connect with something permanent in our psyche, whether we're men or women. On average in the UK, two women a week are killed out of jealousy by would-be lovers or by their former partners or husbands.

Notes

[1]Henry VIII's sister Margaret Tudor was married to James IV of Scotland in an unsuccessful attempt to secure peace between their two countries. Both James IV and his son James V were killed in battles against the English, at Flodden and Solway Moss. James V's only surviving legitimate child Mary, known as Mary, Queen of Scots, became Queen at six days old. She was married first to the French Dauphin and lived during her childhood and teens at the French court. When he died she returned aged nineteen to try to govern Scotland, though warring factions and perhaps her own youth and education made this next to impossible. By her second marriage to Henry Stuart, Lord Darnley, she had a son, another James, who as James VI united Scotland and England in 1603, becoming James I. Thus James VI of Scotland and Elizabeth were distant cousins; there were other claimants to the Succession.

[2]On 2 July 1613, Sir Henry Wotton, poet, politician and diplomat wrote to Sir Edmund Bacon, courtier and politician: 'I will entertain you at the present with what happened at the Banks side. The King's players had a new play called *All is True*, representing some principal pieces of the reign of Henry the Eighth, which set forth many extraordinary circumstances of pomp and majesty even to the matting [carpeting] of the stage; the knights of the order with their Georges and Garter; the guards with their embroidered coats, and the like: sufficient in truth within a little while to make greatness familiar, if not ridiculous. Now King Henry making a Masque at the Cardinal Wolsey's house, and certain cannons being shot off at his entry, some of the paper or other stuff wherewith one of them was stopped [muzzled] did light on the thatch, where they thought it first but an idle smoke, and their eyes more attentive to the show, it kindled inwardly, and ran round like a train [of gunpowder], consuming within less than an hour the whole house to the ground. This was the fatal period [end] of that virtuous fabric, wherein yet did nothing perish but wood and straw, and a few forsaken cloaks; only one man had his breeches set on fire, that would perhaps have broiled him, if he had not by the benefit of a provident wit, put it out with a bottle of ale.'

It's a hostile account. Sir Henry resents public theatres like The Globe because he thinks them demeaning to royalty and nobility. The common herd may lose all respect if they're invited to watch and judge representations of their betters. Those actions once exposed to view by an observant dramatist, 'greatness' may indeed become ridiculous. In 'This was the fatal period of that virtuous fabric, wherein yet did nothing perish ... ', he mimics tragic language to show his contempt for public plays and players. This is sometimes described as an eyewitness account, though there's nothing to suggest it. On the contrary, he sounds as if he wouldn't be seen dead at a public performance. He was a talented poet and wit who addressed James I's daughter Elizabeth in some lovely Petrarchan poems, including 'You meaner beauties of the night' (all other women are like dim stars when the moon comes out). But Shakespeare's King's Men entertained the whole court, and the first performance of *All is True* complimented Princess Elizabeth at her wedding as one of the great family of Elizabeth I. Actors, and a tradesman's son who made good, attracted hostility. Other accounts of The Globe's loss are no more sympathetic.

[3]Juliet Dusinberre, *Shakespeare and the Nature of Women,* p220.

[4]This story is everywhere in Tudorland: it's told, for instance, in David Starkey's *Six Wives: The Queens of Henry VIII* (London, Vintage, 2004), p566.

[5]Hilary Mantel, *Bring Up the Bodies* (London, Fourth Estate), p49.

4

TALES OF PHILOMEL

On the Philomel myth: *The Rape of Lucrece; Titus Andronicus;* and *A Midsummer Night's Dream*

NEXT TO MURDER, RAPE IS THE most violent means of controlling women. It's understood now as a weapon of war, and was recognised as such by Shakespeare, as was the similarity between stranger and marital rape. Allusion to rape is frequent in his work. When Giacomo steps out of his travelling trunk in Imogen's room he notes she was reading the story of Philomel's rape in Ovid's *Metamorphoses* as she fell asleep, and we think he may act it out. She turns to *Metamorphoses* because she felt threatened by Giacomo and knows unconsciously the threat hasn't gone away. He fancies himself rather as a Tarquin to her Lucrece, a semi-historical Roman rape victim. But in *Cymbeline*, allusion to the two stories is brief.

Elsewhere Shakespeare wrote more extensively about both victims. The myth of Philomel, a woman raped and transformed to a bird, lies at the heart of *Titus Andronicus* (disputed date) and is invoked in two other works, his narrative poem *The Rape of Lucrece* (1593) and *A Midsummer Night's Dream* (1594-6). In *Lucrece*, a married Roman noblewoman compares Philomel's tragic story to her own and imagines them singing together. She reasserts her own and her family's reputation by a self-inflicted honour killing. The three texts, all set in the Ancient World, gain from consideration together.

In *Titus Andronicus* and *A Midsummer Night's Dream*, an honour-killing story is crucial to the weave of plots and integrated with other episodes of violence. *Titus Andronicus* is largely Shakespeare's invention, with no specific historical source, set in the decline of the Roman Empire. A woman raped and mutilated like Philomel is murdered by her father. In *A Midsummer Night's Dream*, a father tries to force his daughter to give up the man she loves and marry someone she hates, that is, to accept marital rape; she'll be killed or confined for life if she refuses. This is one strand out of four in an intricate plot, again with no single specific source. In another strand, Philomel is invoked to prevent a strange cross-species coupling, but she's unable to do so.

First, the myth: in Greek legend, King Pandion of Athens has two daughters, Procne (Shakespeare calls her Progne) and Philomel. Procne marries King Tereus of Thrace. After five years, she's longing to see her sister again, and Tereus goes to escort Philomel from Athens to Thrace. But instead of taking her to her sister, he takes her to a stone hut in the woods where he rapes her and, when she threatens to accuse him, cuts out her tongue. This isn't for the faint-hearted: Tereus has to pull out her tongue with a pair of pliers before he can cut it, and it's imagined wriggling across the floor afterwards. He rapes her again, then abandons her but leaves guards so she can't escape.

Philomel improvises a loom from a broken frame she finds in the hut and weaves the story of her rape into a tapestry which she sends by an old woman to her sister, who recognises the rapist as her husband. Procne rushes to the hut under cover of the riotous feast of the Bacchae, eludes the guards, releases her sister and takes her back secretly to the palace. Together the sisters kill Procne's son Itys, and Procne serves her son's flesh up to his father in a pie. Philomel appears at the banquet and throws Itys' head across the table at his father. Tereus tries to kill both sisters, but all three are transformed to birds, Tereus to a hoopoe, Procne to a nightingale and Philomel to a swallow.

The Roman poet Ovid,[1] writing in the time of the Emperor Augustus, the time of Christ, transcribed this and other myths of transformation into the sophisticated collection of stories, *Metamorphoses*. Philomel's story is in Book Six. He changed the type of bird each sister became, and Procne became the swallow, Philomel the nightingale, her plaintive night-song recounting her grief and pain. The tales in *Metamorphoses* are both violent and lyrical (Philomel's is among the most violent), and fascinating still because they show human and divine figures morphing into each other or into flowers, birds or beasts: there's a Darwinian overlap of species in them, breaking the boundaries between divine, human and animal which (except for the Incarnation) are fundamental in Christian thinking.

Metamorphoses was on the curriculum of English grammar schools in Shakespeare's time as a model of the best Latin verse style; boys learned to write poetry in Latin, not just to read it. It seems to have been Shakespeare's favourite book of poems, used or alluded to in his own work more often than any other text except the Bible and Holinshed. Classical literatures and philosophies taught in schools and universities were of course at odds with Christian beliefs; teachers and students had to reconcile them as best they might or accept that they were irreconcilable.

The Rape of Lucrece like his *Venus and Adonis* (1593) was written when the London theatres were closed in a long outbreak of plague, and dedicated to Henry Wriothesley, the twenty-year-old Earl of Southampton. *Venus and Adonis* is also based on *Metamorphoses*. Venus courts Adonis and tries to force him to have sex with her, but he rejects her to hunt a wild boar. He's killed and transformed into an anemone, though Shakespeare doesn't name the flower. The poem is comic in its wooing scenes and mildly pornographic in Venus' witty metaphor of her body as an inviting park. The focus is as much on animals as on the human figures; though nominally gods, Venus and Adonis are more like a randy English matron and a sulky young aristocrat. The animals are more sensitive and appealing than either, and the hunt and protracted death of the hare, Wat, comes closer to tragedy than Adonis' death. Here, especially, Shakespeare shows, like Ovid, a large overlap of human and animal behaviours, and we like the animals better.

Lucrece is based mainly on Livy's earliest Roman histories, where it's hard to distinguish history from legend. It's set in the time of Lucius Tarquinius, who killed his father-in-law and made himself King of Rome; his son is a Prince, in English terms. The focus is on the lead-up to Lucrece's rape and its immediate consequences, but we're also conscious of tyranny in the political background, which may (possibly) change because of her death.

The poem's Argument, the brief prose synopsis prefixed to many

Renaissance narrative poems and not necessarily written by the author, tells how Lucrece's husband Collatine boasts – like *Cymbeline*'s Posthumus nearly twenty years later – about his wife's beauty and virtue to a group of fellow officers besieging an enemy city, Ardea. The Argument tells us they're relaxing in the tent of the King's son, Tarquin, and are all in a 'pleasant humour', or as I think we may understand it, drunk. The others begin to boast about their own wives, which results in their all riding off to visit the wives in turn to see if they can substantiate their claims. Lucrece is the only one to be found spinning diligently and frugally at night among her maids; the others are out dancing. Tarquin sees Lucrece and immediately wants her.

The men go back to their camp outside Ardea, but Tarquin takes the first opportunity to return alone to Collatium, Collatine's country estate outside Rome, to try to seduce or rape her. There's nothing pornographic in the way this is told, though there's a long tense build-up in Tarquin's visit to her, supposedly to bring news of her husband, in the meal they take together and in his walk through the silent house in the night towards her apartments. Though written within a year of *Venus and Adonis* and for the same patron, the narrative is sombre, and naturalistic despite its elaborate language. The act itself is not described, except in the detail of Tarquin's pulling up his victim's nightdress and shoving the material into her mouth to stop her screaming, but it's represented in metaphor and half glimpsed in Lucrece's memory.

It's probable that rape was more common in England then than now, in a virtually unpoliced society where rape shamed the victim more than the perpetrator, often with the excuse that she'd invited it. She would be reluctant to complain. A lot of people thought that a woman couldn't get pregnant unless she experienced orgasm, so a pregnant woman who claimed rape was particularly likely to be disbelieved. Those few women who went to court and won their case might make themselves unmarriageable or if married risk rejection by their husbands. In a time of great legal and moral confusion about women, Shakespeare represents his rape victims as non-compliant and his rapists as deserving death.

At the beginning, the narrator blames Collatine's folly in boasting about Lucrece in front of Tarquin and the other officers:

> Perchance his [Collatine's] boast of Lucrece's sovereignty [superiority]
> Suggested [prompted] this proud issue [son] of a King [Tarquin] (...)
> Perchance that envy of so rich a thing,
> Braving compare [beyond comparison], disdainfully did sting
> His [Tarquin's] high-pitched thoughts, that meaner men should vaunt [boast]
> That golden hap [good luck] which their superiors want [lack, but also want, as now].
>
> (*Lucrece*, 36-42)[2]

Competition between soldiers, then, sets off the train of events, and in Tarquin, the feeling that something's gone wrong if a man of slightly lower rank has something he hasn't. As so often in Shakespeare, the judgement feels entirely modern: for Tarquin, she's a 'thing', if a rich one, and the adjective too constructs his narrow limits. What she is for Collatine is more uncertain.

We see her from the outside initially, as the ideal wife Collatine boasts about. She's mainly silent at supper with Tarquin, as a good Roman woman should be. In her sleep, she slowly becomes conscious of a hand on her breast, then the point of a sword. As she comes to consciousness, she can't see what's happening because the torch he holds is shining in her eyes. Then she's terrified prey in the grip of a predator. He threatens that if she resists he'll kill her, then kill one of the menservants. He'll tell everyone he found them in bed together and killed them for dishonouring her husband. She tries to stop him, urging her own physical weakness, his friendship with her husband and what he owes to his high rank.

Lucrece is not political: unlike the narrator she accepts social hierarchy and monarchy without question and sees Tarquin's violence as an anomaly, not a likely consequence of absolute power. When he leaves, she articulates emotions surging between grief, rage, shame and bitter regret that she was too frightened by the threat of slander to fight him. She thinks her way around the impossible choice now to be made. She never blames her husband for bringing Tarquin and the other men to assess her.

She blames herself for her failure to see the threat, though she doesn't attribute that to the disabling seclusion in which many patrician women lived. She blames Tarquin of course, and gradually resolves on his death, though she never achieves it. In a long exploration of time and chance, she blames Opportunity. As our current idiom has it, he did it because he could, but that's always an empty explanation. Her casting about to blame anyone or anything but Collatine has the opposite effect on the reader. It draws attention to her continuing devotion as a wife, but it also encourages us to judge Collatine partly culpable, though way after Tarquin.

Lucrece isn't just an obedient wife, she's in love with her husband. Her first action after she's dressed is to call for pen, ink and paper to summon him; it's impossible for her to keep this from him. We catch the sense of the domestic nature of her tragedy. Shakespeare creates an Elizabethan more than a Roman marriage and household, even to the weasels that startle Tarquin as he moves towards her room in the dark: weasels were used to keep down the rats and mice that infested English country houses. At the beginning, she seems very young.

The poem is dramatic, its action moving forward through the narrator's voice but also through the conversations and long interior monologues of its characters. As well as the narrator's, there are two major voices, Lucrece's and Tarquin's, and several minor ones in Lucrece's maid, Collatine, Lucrece's father Lucretius, and Roman patricians at the end including Lucius Junius Brutus. The narrator's and Lucrece's speech is erudite and highly complex; I've often had to read lines twice or more to get the word order right and register the annotation. It's a poem full of 'conceits' or contradictory ideas sparking off each other, it's indirect and philosophic, and studded with allusions to classical myth. What we may find difficult and artificial now was greatly admired for its learning.

Of all the speakers including the narrator, Lucrece is the most original. She can only hold up her hands in silent amazement when Tarquin recounts over supper her husband's daring in battle. Unsurprisingly, she can hardly speak at first when she must tell her husband and the assembled Roman patricians what has happened to her. But as Katherine Duncan-Jones says, 'Reading attentively, we can also observe the strong contrast between the amplitude of Lucrece's reflections in solitude and the bashful awkwardness of her speech in company.'[3] Shakespeare dramatises here as nowhere else the contrast between a woman's outer shell of passivity and an inner, overwhelming turmoil.

Soliloquies by women in Shakespeare's plays are rare. There are Lady Macbeth's forays into the dark, Ophelia's lament for Hamlet and herself, the two Helenas (in *A Midsummer Night's Dream* and *All's Well That Ends Well*) with their bitter experience of rejection, and Beatrice's brief speech acknowledging Benedick's and her own love with sudden wonder just before Hero's first wedding day. Generally in Shakespeare women speak socially or domestically or even, like Margaret of Anjou, on the battlefield, but they seldom talk to themselves. The closest self-examination to Lucrece's is Hamlet's series of soliloquies. He too meditates how to respond to massive injury in the absence of a functioning system of justice, whether to keep quiet, kill the criminal or commit suicide.

Hamlet remembers that God 'has fixed his canon [law] 'gainst self-slaughter.' (*Hamlet*, 1.2.131-2) Lucrece debates the wisdom of destroying her mind just because her body is, as she sees it, polluted. She strikes out an unusual metaphor for body and soul:

(...) the bark pilled [stripped] from the lofty pine,
His leaves will wither and his sap decay;
So must my soul, her bark being pilled away. (167-9)

Within that metaphor of desecration, death seems a natural consequence of rape. She slowly comes down on death's side. She's taken a lot of flak for her supposed feebleness, even for her failure to fight Tarquin. You have to wonder what some of her critics would do, woken in the middle of the night by the feel of a bladed weapon. Of course, it's her self-blame and her preoccupation with her own and her husband's 'honour' they find annoying. But these reactions were and are realities. Some women who've been raped or abused never get over it, though obviously the terminology describing how they feel is different now; some can't bear to have sex with their husband or lover again; her sense that her marriage is over is not particularly unusual.

Living in a pre-Christian era, she's not so open to the contemporary reader's disapproval as a Christian suicide would be. For the church and for many individual laypeople, suicide was the unforgiveable sin, since in its nature it couldn't be repented, inevitably dooming its perpetrator to hell. If an attempted suicide survived, the attempt was treated as a capital crime. Not everyone would necessarily concur of course, but suicide would probably lose Lucrece the sympathy of some readers if she were depicted as a Christian. But the poem's transgression goes further than that: she knows she may be pregnant by Tarquin, but this only strengthens her resolve to kill herself. She can't bear to think of Tarquin laughing with his friends about them while she and Collatine bring up a child that's not his.

Almost all her meditations lead to death, and the poem's form suits the subject. It's known as Rhyme Royal. Each stanza has seven lines of iambic pentameter. Iambic rhythm, a weak stress followed by a strong one, is the rhythm closest to everyday speech. Our casual sentences fall into iambic rhythms a lot of the time; it's a good form for plays and for poems like this with a lot of talking, though the characters are often talking to themselves. Each stanza ends in a rhyming pair of lines, a rhyming couplet, which sums up neatly or fatalistically what's been said in the main part of the stanza. Sometimes the rhyming couplet functions like a trap snapping shut, like the one last quoted, which imagines continuing life as death.

It's the same stanza form Chaucer used for *Troilus and Criseyde*, written two hundred years earlier, where the most interesting and powerful of his dramatic speakers is Criseyde, exploring shifts of emotion, enjoying her independence as a young widow in Troy, wondering if she will or won't take Troilus as a lover. There are strong resemblances in the depth and self-knowledge each writer gives to his woman speaker, and a link through the Troy setting of Chaucer's poem and the vivid painting of Troy in Lucrece's house. But until she leaves Troy, Criseyde is often happy.

Tarquin's thoughts as he approaches Lucrece's bedroom, uncertain whether or not he'll carry out the rape, are full of anxiety even in anticipation. He recognises the gravity of what he means to do, addressing the blazing torch he uses to find his way to her room:

> Fair torch, burn out thy light, and lend it not
> To darken her whose light excelleth thine. (190-91)

He thinks of her momentarily and with reverence as an individual, though in a very distancing way and as if agency can be transferred to an inanimate object. When he rapes her, the act happens in the gap between two stanzas, and the post-coital reaction of remorse and incredulity at what he's done kicks in instantly. But mostly these thoughts are about himself or his friendship with her husband. He considers that rape is a crime which will shame him if the truth emerges and may have political consequences. The bed he contemplates staining is at one remove from her body; it's emblematic of her family bonds as wife and mother. Collatine is his friend, famed for his military achievements and valuable in the army. Tarquin feels more shame at betraying another man than in using and humiliating a woman.

A traditional historical critic would argue that nobody thought like a feminist in those days. But as noted, from the start Shakespeare uses the 'rich thing' phrase to define Tarquin's feelings, or lack of them, and other aspects of the poem show that he creates Lucrece outside as well as inside the concept of a woman defined by her family. After she's written to Collatine she goes to look at a painting in a distant room that she knows well. She thinks it will help her to understand better what's happened to her. The moment of the Fall of Troy is the subject. That story is hers, the perfect crystallisation of many metaphors and similes that equate rape to the forced military entrance of a city, the 'fall' of a woman to the fall of a besieged garrison.

This series of metaphors begins in the poem's opening stanza:

From the besieged Ardea all in post [haste]
Born by the trustless wings of false desire,
Lust-breathed Tarquin leaves the Roman host [army]
And to Collatium bears the lightless fire
Which, in pale embers hid, lurks to aspire
And girdle with embracing flames the waist
Of Collatine's fair love, Lucrece the chaste. (1-7)

The lightless fire born by Tarquin is his hidden fire of lust for Lucrece, but it's also the fire that will consume Ardea. He carries it from Ardea to Collatium, with the same desire for conquest. The fires of lust may catch and inflame even chaste Lucrece's body, he hopes. The literal fires will girdle the towers of Ardea and burn them to the ground when the time comes. The Romans left few alive when a city refused to surrender: 'to spare the humble and wipe out the proud'[4] was Rome's boast. Cities that held out could expect no mercy. The opening image tends to put Tarquin, Collatine and their fellow officers all on the same side.

While Tarquin speaks of secret friendship for Lucrece, he acts as a ruthless enemy. The metaphors and similes connecting rape with warfare are too many to consider individually. They emphasis the brutality of rape and make an identification between the two kinds of violence. They also suggest that rape is as much a fitting theme for poetry as war, not to be side-lined as a 'woman's subject'. This poem begins like an epic in the middle of things and uses frequent epic similes. Looking at the picture of Troy, Lucrece wants to tear out the image of Sinon[5] the deceiver, who violated King Priam's hospitality, persuading him to take the Trojan wooden horse packed with Greeks into the city. She makes the explicit connection between Troy and her body:

> As Priam did him [Sinon] cherish,
> So did I Tarquin, so my Troy did perish. (156-7)

The poem's metaphors assert that the domestic is the epic; though she's quintessentially 'feminine', she's the hero.

When she looks for Hecuba in the Troy painting, she's looking for the remembered image of a woman whose life was ruined by lust. She's familiar with the Troy story and with her painting, but she knows she'll see them differently now she identifies with defeat. Hecuba, Queen of Troy, is destroyed not by lust of her own or by rape but by the lust of her son Paris for Helen, which costs her the lives of the men in her family and sees her daughters and daughters-in-law taken as sex slaves by the Greeks.

Lucrece doesn't look for the face of a young married woman, Andromache for instance, the Trojan champion Hector's wife, apparently a more appropriate mirror image for her. Andromache is a survivor. She becomes the slave of one of the Greeks, has a baby by him, outlives him, marries a former brother-in-law, has two more children and eventually dies of old age. Lucrece looks for the very old and broken Hecuba, who's witnessing in the painting the cruel death of her husband King Priam. Lucrece recognises that Tarquin's act has ended her marriage and made her an old woman overnight. Hecuba is a Revenger. Lucrece's wavering thoughts, revealed through the morning and up to the arrival of her husband and father with other Roman men, show a growing resolve to act on her own initiative, taking the aged, widowed Hecuba for her pattern.

Her invocation of Philomel is fanciful, almost playful by comparison with other phases of her grief. It comes as night ends and Philomel stops singing. Lucrece hates the dawn chorus with its cheerful birdsong, wishing she could keep Philomel's lamentation with her. She addresses her as nightingale rather than woman, too kind to dwell on the Thracian past. These stanzas are about music, Philomel's and her own, joining as mezzo-soprano and contralto in elegiac song:

Come, Philomel, that sings't of ravishment,
Make thy sad grove in my dishevelled hair.
As the dank earth weeps at thy languishment,
So I at each sad strain will strain a tear. (1,128-33)

There's a surreal whimsy in the metaphor of her hair as Philomel's forest grove, a subdued playfulness in the pun on 'strain.' The Philomel stanzas are particularly rich in puns and word-play. Lucrece dreams of escape into hiding, a nightingale her only companion, somewhere with a temperate climate and away from other people. In a lonely place far from society and shame:

(...) there will we unfold
To creatures stern [fierce] sad tunes to change their kinds [natures]:
Since men prove beasts, let beasts bear gentle minds. (1,146-8)

She imagines transformation to a woman Orpheus, the mythical poet, like him taming wild animals with her music and Philomel's, using their pain for good. But she knows this is impossible. It's a fantasy to put off for a little her resolve on death.

Other speakers in *Lucrece* are more predictable. Her maid loves her and shares her sorrow without understanding it. The manservant who waits while she writes to her husband and who carries her letter to Ardea is embarrassed and silent. He can't meet her look or say much, because he's in awe of her. She interprets this, wrongly, as his guessing that Tarquin has raped her: it's an immediate fit of paranoia. Her mind has changed overnight and she sees everything in terms of shame.

As Lucrece and her maid weep together, the narrator embarks on a discussion of women's weakness and men's strength that appears at first as sexist as possible. The concept of women as wax and men as the stamp that prints it is a familiar one of the period; it appears in the speeches of several characters in Shakespeare's plays, characters who take it for granted that men dominate women. But here, I think, it's used in a way specific to *Lucrece* and the subject of rape:

> For men have marble, women waxen minds,
> And therefore are they [women] formed as marble will [chooses].
> The weak [being] oppressed, th'impression of strange kinds [alien beings]
> Is formed in them by force, by fraud or skill.
> Then call them not the authors of their ill,
> No more than wax shall be accounted evil
> Wherein is stamped the semblance of a devil.
>
> Their smoothness, like a goodly champaign plain [open, fertile country],
> Lays open all the little worms that creep;
> In men, as in a rough-grown grove, remain
> Cave-keeping [hidden] evils that obscurely sleep.
> Through crystal walls [windows, glass containers] each little mote will peep [stand out].
> Though men can cover crimes with bold stern looks,
> Poor women's faces are their own faults' books
> [women give away their faults by their expressions].
>
> No man inveigh against [let no man accuse] the withered flower,
> But chide rough winter that the flower hath killed;
> Not that devoured, but that which doth devour,
> Is worthy blame. O let it not be hild [held]
> Poor women's faults that they are so fulfilled [filled full]
> With men's abuses: those proud lords, to blame,
> Make weak-made women tenants to their shame.
>
> The precedent whereof in Lucrece view (...) [look at Lucrece's example]
> (1,240-61)

At first sight this looks like a Renaissance *Men are from Mars, Women are from Venus*, a routine binary division we rather hoped Shakespeare wouldn't endorse: women so weak-made they shouldn't be blamed for anything. But the term is ambiguous; it can mean women made weak by men's abuses rather than born weak. But certainly the law assumed that women were born weak, so their fathers and husbands must be accountable for them.

Looking at the passage more closely, I think it's more unusual than first appears. In the first line, the narrator talks of 'minds' and it seems a dodgy piece of pleading to say that he's in fact talking about bodies. But as the stanzas go on, it's clear the weakness he refers to is women's physical weakness compared to men's physical strength, though the physical and mental are linked. That he says men are physically stronger may be offensive to some women now, who see no reasons other than cultural or accidental ones why it should be so. They may be right, but if they are, then no woman could be raped unless some other factor was involved like a weapon or a convincing threat of death. The mantra 'no man can rape a determined woman' persisted for a long time, could be used as a plausible defence in court, and may still linger in some minds. In fact the average man probably is stronger than the average woman, and as multiple police records show, rape is entirely possible by an unarmed man. Certainly by the time the narrator returns to Lucrece, it's clearly rape he's talking about.

In the third line, the narrator says that once weak women are oppressed, once men 'stamp' them, then 'strange kinds', are formed within them. We might see this, as suggested in most explanatory notes, simply as a man changing a woman's character, so she differs from what she was before they met. But if we read 'stamp' as rape, we could read 'strange kinds' as the alien invaders of women's bodies, the babies who result from rape. 'Strange' was a stronger word then than now, more akin to foreign or alien. Given that reading, the narrator is asking the reader not to blame women for their pregnancy, which may feel to them like a monstrous invasion, and he goes against the popular prejudice that a pregnant woman couldn't have been raped.

In the second stanza quoted, the narrator attacks the common contemporary view of women as Eves, clever deceivers. On the contrary, the narrator says, they're so unused to lying, so open and honest that when raped or seduced (by fraud or skill), they can't conceal it. Men are deceivers – a theme Shakespeare would later have set to music and sung in *Much Ado About Nothing* – and dwellers in the shady woods not in the open plains of social intercourse. The narrator again asks the reader not to blame women for what's going to be identified, at the end of this extract, as unequivocally rape. We should blame men not women if women are 'fulfilled' with men's abuses. Abuse is a noun that's retained and developed its sexual content over the centuries. Katherine Duncan-Jones reads 'fulfilled' as sexual, and I'd suggest that as 'filled full' it also carries a suggestion of pregnancy.

The landlord/tenant metaphor is particularly interesting. Men own the shame and should live in it. Instead, women inhabit the shame and must pay for it. Amongst other elements the metaphor admits the frequent social disparity between men and women in sexual abuse. Upper-class women were carefully guarded; rape was more likely to be by an upper-class man, a property-owner, against a social inferior of the tenant class who would be easily accessible and unlikely to go to court or have a male relative capable of exacting justice. This passage is far from a conventional Renaissance gender stereotype. Lucrece and Tarquin are not greatly different in rank; in this generalising couplet Shakespeare goes beyond Lucrece's story, anticipating Thomas Hardy in *Tess of the D'Urbervilles.*

Collatine, as far as Lucrece is concerned the good guy of the poem, says very little and is hard to read. He seems to love her, calls her his 'dear dear', (1,602) and comes at once when she summons him from Ardea with the other officers, arriving at the same time as her father, Lucretius, who comes from Rome. Her testimony on her wounded honour is given to an audience only of men. It's a variant on the honour trial pattern. Lucrece herself is her only witness and carries out her own killing, having resolved on this way to attain revenge on Tarquin and clear herself, her husband and children from shame.

One omission from the poem is any convincing sense of her as a mother. She never thinks of the effect on her children of her death, only of her shame, though it's possible that she's as yet childless and thinking of children she might have in the future. But as a political act, some could consider her suicide heroic, since she does what none of the men can do: her dead body incites the Senate and citizens to rebel against the Tarquins. Her rapist is exiled with his family while Rome becomes a Republic, with the implication that all power must become accountable to the Senate. But the hope implied in the Argument, that a new age of justice is at hand, is undercut in a cursory and deeply unsatisfactory ending.

The poem's passionate rhetoric is at its height as Lucrece tells the assembled noblemen how she was raped. She withholds the identity of the attacker until they promise to avenge her, names Tarquin though with such difficulty it's in reported, not in direct, speech, as if even the narrator can't quite authenticate it. Then she plunges a knife unexpectedly into her heart and falls to the ground. She lies like an island, her blood pooling around her and crying out for vengeance.

Collatine and her father Lucretius squabble over her body like two dogs over a bone, competing as to who should be said to own her when alive and who mourns her most:

> 'Woe, woe,' quoth Collatine, 'she was my wife,
> I owed [owned] her, and tis mine that she hath killed.'
> 'My daughter' and 'My wife' with clamours filled
> The dispersed air, who, holding Lucrece' life [last breath?]
> Answered their cries, 'My daughter' and 'My wife'. (1,800-06)

As usual in early modern poetry, when Echo, the 'dispersed air' is heard, she's mocking the human speakers. This exchange is part of a sequence of stanzas where husband and father fight over the best right to the possessive pronoun. Her death becomes farcical, its sacrificial idiom reduced to bathos. Her father's language conveys some genuine grief, but he's interrupted:

> By this, starts Collatine as from a dream,
> And bids Lucretius give his sorrow place [move over];
> And then in key-cold Lucrece' bleeding stream
> He falls, and bathes the pale fear in his face,
> And counterfeits to die with her a space
> Till manly shame bids him possess his breath. (1,772-77)

As Katherine Duncan-Jones notes, 'it is hard to avoid the sense that there is an element of play-acting here.'[6] The concept of manliness is questioned throughout *Lucrece*, and male embarrassment at grief for a wife's death is particularly jarring when the husband is partly to blame for it.

Among the Roman nobility listening to Lucrece is Lucius Junius Brutus.

The Tarquins have already killed his elder brother as a threat to the Succession of Tarquin, Lucrece' rapist. Brutus has been pretending idiocy to avoid the same fate. Now he drops his cover. But his response to her death, as he urges Collatine to act not grieve, is unexpected:

> Is it revenge to give thyself a blow
> For his foul act by whom thy fair wife bleeds?
> Such childish humour from weak minds proceeds.
> Thy wretched wife mistook the matter so,
> To slay herself, that should have slain her foe. (1,823-7)

We could read Lucrece's act as merely internalisation of savage patriarchal attitudes to raped women, that they're worthless; her intelligence and autonomy resist such simplification. Brutus' attack on her for failing to kill Tarquin is outrageous. Could she have strangled him with her bare hands? It's a parodic victim-blaming. Her suicide is a godsend for Brutus; it gives him the courage to drop his 'shallow habit', (1,814) his thin disguise of idiocy, and reveal his long-term plan. He sees he can save his life and rise higher than before by using her death to enlist the help of Rome's citizens and get rid of the Tarquins, his lethal relations. Her suicide doesn't cause the rapist's death, but it will exile the Tarquins, a better result for Brutus. He dismisses her as stupid and ineffectual. In the new Roman Republic, the highest power will be embodied in two consuls: Lucius Junius Brutus and Collatine. I don't know whether the contemporary reader of *Lucrece* would be likely to know that, but even if not, the bathos of the ending prevents any sense of gain from Lucrece's death. A competition for prestige among men resulted in her rape, a competition for power among men as she lies dead ends the poem.

Lucrece and *Titus Andronicus* share an engagement with the concept of Romanitas, of what it means to be Roman, that Shakespeare would return to throughout his career, though Romanitas is never again so brutal as in *Titus.* It's not clear which came first; it's possible they were written around the same time. The theatres closed for the long outbreak of plague from June 1592, opened again briefly then closed to the end of 1593, but there was no reason to suppose they wouldn't re-open. Given Shakespeare's later output, two plays a year, it's possible he was writing *Titus Andronicus*, not just his two narrative poems, while the theatres were closed. The constant reference in *Titus* to the story of Lucrece as he tells it suggests that the poem came first.

For all its raw cruelty, *Titus Andronicus* like *Lucrece* is very cerebral; its Rome lies in the twilight of a sophisticated literary culture. The characters echo among other writers Seneca, Virgil, Livy, Horace and of course Ovid. *Metamorphoses* is a book many of the characters have read. Young Lucius, Titus' grandson, carries a copy with his other school texts. The Goths seem to have much the same literary and historical education as the Romans, and they know the story of Philomel.

This is often described as Shakespeare's Senecan Revenge Tragedy, and it certainly is in the sense of being ultra-bloody. The Roman dramatist Seneca's stoic philosophy[7] held that as death is inevitable, it should be embraced or at least not greatly regretted. But in *Titus Andronicus*, life is still precious, the more so from its insecurity. In Act One, the Roman General Titus is bringing Goth prisoners back to Rome after his successful ten-year German campaign, along with the corpses of two sons dead in the fighting and the four that survive of his original 25, all soldiers and most now dead in Rome's cause. Titus' rhetoric in the committal of the latest sons to the family tomb has been read as Senecan manliness. Its woodenness is the most striking thing about it:

> In peace and honour rest you here, my sons;
> Rome's readiest champions, repose you here in rest,
> Secure from worldly chances and mishaps.
> Here lurks no treason, here no envy swells,
> Here grow no damned drugs, here are no storms,
> No noise, but silence and eternal sleep;
> In peace and honour rest you here, my sons. (1.1.153-9)

He consigns them to a limbo of negatives, an absence.

Macbeth is sometimes cited as uttering similar stoic sentiments:

> Duncan is in his grave,
> After life's fitful fever he sleeps well. (*Macbeth*, 3.2.24-5)

These lines are much more metrically delicate than any from Titus. But except by Cleopatra, the praise of death is suspect in Shakespeare: Macbeth has just murdered Duncan, so he'd like to convince himself he's done the old man a favour. When the Duke-as-Friar in *Measure for Measure* argues that life is something only fools would keep, we get a convincing rebuttal from a young man who thinks he's just about to die. Titus himself is not so keen on death when Rome turns against him; at least, he doesn't kill himself. His rigid Senecan aphorisms are levers that tip the play constantly into absurdity.

As always, Shakespeare blurs the boundaries of genre, but more disconcertingly here than usual. We laugh, flinch and feel sick simultaneously. The action is literally and generically Gothic. *Titus Andronicus* can be considered as an early Roman Play containing seeds of Shakespeare's later Roman and English tragedies, as an English Revenge Tragedy following Thomas Kyd (and Seneca), or as a popular precursor to Quentin Tarantino. It's all these things, but rape and a parent's feasting on a son's flesh are central, though instead of an impossible on-stage transformation to a bird Shakespeare substitutes the raped woman's honour killing. Almost any play of Shakespeare's could be defined as being about the abuse of power, but this one is without rival as a play about bad politics.

As it opens, the Emperor has recently died and his two sons, Saturninus and Bassianus, are quarrelling over their right to succeed him, Saturninus claiming on primogeniture, Bassianus on superior merit. Titus' brother Marcus Andronicus, a Tribune of the people who maintains that the crown is elective, claims the citizens want Titus to be Emperor because of his military successes against the Goths. The scene continues as Titus' Triumph, the grand processional entry into Rome with troops and prisoners granted by the Senate to returning victorious Generals, reaches the mausoleum of the Andronici family. The setting suits the spiralling necrosis of the action.

Titus and his eldest son Lucius are determined to sacrifice to the spirits of the dead Andronici brothers their most important prisoner, the Goth Queen Tamora's eldest son, Alarbus. Tamora begs Titus passionately for his life, pointing out that Alarbus too is a patriot, though on the losing side, and appealing on her knees for pity. Elizabeth's reign saw the beginnings of English colonial adventurism; some of its tensions are acted out here. I agree with Nicholas Moschovakis, who argues in 'Irreligious Piety and Christian History' that the play questions state-sponsored as much as 'treasonable' violence during the struggles between Catholics and Protestants from Henry VIII's reign on.

For Titus and Lucius, only human sacrifice can satisfy the Roman dead, and they're adamant that Alarbus must die. Tamora is desperate to save him, but:

> Patient yourself, madam, and pardon me (1.1.124)

says Titus, his phrasing reminiscent of Frankie Howerd in *Up Pompeii*. This is characteristic of his speech in Act One, which segues from pompous to uncomprehending to fuss-budgetty. Alarbus is dragged off and executed by Lucius and his brothers. Lucius returns to describe with relish the off-stage 'lopping' of his limbs and their committal with his entrails to the fire. It sounds as if he's still alive when they're placed on it. Lucius loves the smell of burning human entrails; they perfume the sky.

When Marcus Andronicus offers the Imperial crown to Titus, he says he's too old to rule and opts for Saturninus as Emperor instead. Saturninus promptly says he'll marry Titus' daughter Lavinia, and Titus as promptly concurs, though Lavinia is betrothed to Bassianus. Her brothers join Bassianus in abducting her bodily from her father's and Saturninus' control. One of the brothers, Mutius, bars his father from following, and Titus stabs him in fury for his disobedience, then tries to refuse him burial in the Andronici tomb.

At the start, Romans and Goths are equal but different in their violence; the Romans seem to kill out of civic and religious duty, the Goths for revenge or amusement, but they reveal themselves as more alike in their sadism as the play goes on. In Shakespearean politics, the extreme right can eventually meet up with the extreme left, as we find with Prince John and Falstaff near the end of *Henry IV, Part 2*. Though Alarbus is killed, Tamora's two remaining sons, Demetrius and Chiron, are spared. When Lavinia is abducted by Bassianus, Saturninus is free to marry Tamora, whom he wants as soon as he sees her. Her position is immediately reversed once she's Empress. With Aaron the Moor, her black lover, she plans to avenge Alarbus by wiping out the Andronici dynasty. It's better, Titus discovers too late, to take power while you can rather than expect gratitude for handing it to someone else. Sadly, for serious people who like to find moral lessons in Shakespeare, this is about the only one on offer.

For the morning after the marriages of Saturninus and Tamora, Bassianus and Lavinia, Titus organises a panther hunt in the woods outside Rome to propitiate the new Emperor and his bride. Aaron and Tamora meet Lavinia and Bassianus when they're out hunting and far from help. With stupidity worthy of Titus himself, his daughter and son-in-law begin taunting Tamora about her relationship with Aaron. Demetrius and Chiron now arrive, and with their mother's encouragement they kill Bassianus, drop him into a panther trap and with Aaron's help put the blame on two sons of Titus. Shakespeare then takes the Philomel myth to greater excess than Ovid: Demetrius and Chiron drag Lavinia off stage and both rape her, then to prevent her accusing them verbally or in writing they go further than Tereus, cutting off her hands as well as cutting out her tongue.

This was where the most people tended to faint in Lucy Bailey's production at The Globe in the summer of 2014. Lavinia re-entered as a crime scene. The sight elicits not so much sympathy as visceral revulsion; we can't adjust to the metamorphosis that's happened so fast. We learn little about her before she's permanently silenced. She says just the right thing to her returning father, seems to accept her re-betrothal to Saturninus and answers his rudeness pleasantly, says nothing when rescued or abducted by Bassianus. She's trained to be a robot.

But newly married to Bassianus, she attacks Tamora self-righteously out in the woods. Though powerless within her own family, she has too much sense of entitlement as a patrician Roman to see danger coming from a Goth. When it does, she appeals to Tamora to save her, not from death, since 'poor I was slain when Bassianus died', (2.3.171) but from rape before death. Here she does seem to claim that hers was a marriage of love, not just of acquiescence. Earlier, in reply to Saturninus' and apparently Bassianus' curiosity about whether she'd rather have stayed in bed that morning following her marriage, she says only that she was up very early. Until he dies she gives nothing away about her feelings for her husband. She represents not so much an individual as archetypal Suffering Woman: forced, silenced, and disarmed. Her attempts to engage Tamora's pity mirror Tamora's kneeling to Titus for Alarbus' life and are equally useless.

For Tamora, Lavinia's rape and mutilation are part of the revenge for Alarbus' death. But Demetrius and Chiron hardly think of their brother; it's sibling rivalry (like the struggle between Saturninus and Bassianus) that drives their attack on Lavinia. Their savagery is especially disturbing because they call it love. In the opening scene, Bassianus uses the language of Courtly Love for her

> (...) to whom my thoughts are humbled all,
> Gracious Lavinia, Rome's rich ornament. (1.1.54-5)

Demetrius and Chiron start fighting over her as soon as they see her, although she marries Bassianus a few minutes later. Chiron, the younger, tells his brother:

> I am as able and as fit as thou
> To serve, and to deserve my mistress' grace,
> And that my sword upon thee shall approve [prove],
> And plead my passions for Lavinia's love. (1.1.530-33)

It's disconcerting when the would-be seducer, soon-to-be-rapist Chiron adopts a similar courtly diction to Bassianus, the lover and husband, with semi-religious metaphors of service and grace. When Aaron intervenes and the brothers continue to quarrel, their language lapses into the idiom of libertine seduction. Anticipating Richard of Gloucester courting Lady Anne, Demetrius says:

> She is a woman, therefore may be wooed,
> She is a woman, therefore may be won;
> She is Lavinia, therefore must be loved.
> What, man, more water glideth by the mill
> Than wots [knows] the miller of, and easy is it
> Of a cut loaf to steal a shive [slice], we know. (1.1.579-85)

The tone changes, but he still implies a need for Lavinia's consent. This speech and the next one sound like Aaron rather than Demetrius, and Aaron not Demetrius is the early version of Richard of Gloucester. But it takes Aaron to urge that Lavinia is only obtainable by rape. When he intervenes, the brothers agree to share her, and then Aaron sketches the scenario:

The woods are ruthless, dreadful, deaf and dull.
There speak and strike, brave boys, and take your turns. (1.1.624-6)

The Goth boys' parallel with the brothers Saturninus and Bassianus' quarrel over her is unmistakable: women are loot or game to hunt, rich ornaments or dainty deer, in marriage or by rape. The rape and mutilation mimic earlier and later plot-situations, Lavinia's proposed forced marriage to Saturninus and her actual marriage to Bassianus following his abduction of her, during which she's already entirely silent. Then the loss of her hands is half-replicated in the ludicrous loss of Titus' hand, cut off by Aaron as ransom for Titus' two sons condemned for Bassianus' murder and sent back by Saturninus with the sons' heads. Her mutilated body, often on-stage though silent or uttering only muffled grunts, casts its still blacker shadow over the other atrocities. The Philomel myth re-enacted by Lavinia unifies and universalises the supposedly historical material.

There's nothing parodic or even particularly over-the-top in the piled-up horrors, as far as the men are concerned. None of the cruelties inflicted on the male characters is worse than what took place in public as judicial punishment for treason or lesser crimes under the Tudors. The play's grotesque intensity derives from there being no relief from them, no counterweight. These state atrocities were carried out for nonconformity in religion and justified by 'irreligious piety', in Tamora's apt phrase. They aimed first to prevent the overthrow of a Catholic state by Protestants, then of a Protestant state by Catholics, but doctrinal error was the excuse for most of them. Shakespeare's older contemporaries would remember the smell of Mary Tudor's Smithfield fires. In other Tudor reigns including Elizabeth's, the entrails of a 'traitor' were removed and burned while he was still conscious, as may be understood of Alarbus. In another generic layer, *Titus* is heavily disguised satire.

It wasn't only 'traitors' who suffered. In 1579 the Puritan printer John Stubbs had his right hand struck off in the crowded Westminster marketplace for displeasing Elizabeth. He'd produced a tactless pamphlet against her possible marriage to the French-Catholic Duke of Alencon, mentioning among other things that it had nothing to recommend it because she was too old to bear children. He raised his hat with his remaining hand and said, 'God save the Queen', as was expected, then passed out. Such spectacles were as easily available as visits to the theatre; in his case the crowd was silent and sympathetic.

Books grow out of books more than from raw life; *Titus* comes out of Seneca and Ovid, possibly Suetonius. But it may also come out of the first shock of London for Shakespeare. It's possible he was there by September 1586[8], when the Babington Plot was blown and the conspirators' executions were the talk of the city; he may have seen them. If not, there were plenty of later plots and reprisals. Despite his amputation, Stubbs continued his printing and political careers after a term in prison, serving as MP for Yarmouth in 1589. He died in 1590.

Marcus, Lavinia's uncle, is the first person to see her once Tamora's sons have left after a few vicious jokes. His struggle to find language to describe her articulates the audience's revulsion, the aversion of their eyes. But we start to watch her again her when she tries to identify her attackers and see justice done on them. *Titus Andronicus* is centrally concerned with justice: the aphorism, *terras reliquit Justitia*, Justice has left the earth, is a running motif throughout. When Titus encourages his friends to shoot arrows up into the sky to reach the gods, knowing they'll reach Saturninus on the upper stage, they're fletched with that complaint, and ask for the return of Justice.

Saturninus is controlled by Tamora and won't punish her sons. As is usual in a Revenge Play where the ruler is too corrupt to administer justice or is himself the criminal, a once-innocent hero is tainted by taking on the role of judge and executioner, since there's no alternative. Titus and his son Lucius are already brutalised, as they show in their lack of pity for Tamora and in Lucius' enjoyment of Alarbus' death. Lavinia has committed no great cruelty and has suffered infinitely beyond anything she could deserve merely from being Titus' moralistic daughter. She becomes her own Revenger.

First, she's a reader. As Lucrece reads her new identity in a picture, Lavinia finds hers in a literary text, then struggles to accuse Demetrius and Chiron. These are her first acts of agency and self-will, and we see a functioning mind in her for the first time. She's taught her nephew Young Lucius and read to him in the past. She follows him about, trying to borrow his copy of Ovid; he's suspicious, and won't let her near him. But with the help of Titus and Marcus she opens the book at the story of Philomel, indicating she's been raped, then mimes that it was by two men. She's still not independent; Marcus shows her how to write their names in the dust by holding a stick in her mouth and guiding it with her stumps. This in itself is painful, re-running the former controls and invasions of her body.

But she's beginning to overcome her disability, confronting life-changing injuries with immense determination. If we think we know what to expect from a 'heroine', she's grotesque. If we can get outside those limits and think instead of trauma hospitals and army rehab centres, we can appreciate her for what she is: the first severely disabled, central young woman on the English stage, and possibly the last until *A Day in the Death of Joe Egg* (1967)[9]. Joe Egg's father also wants his daughter dead. Lavinia, if anyone, is the Revenge hero of *Titus Andronicus*, initially guiltless if not very likeable, forced to act though degraded by the need to deliver justice herself. Given her genes and her culture, that can only be by revenge-murder. But unlike Procne and Philomel who kill their innocent son and nephew, Lavinia holds a basin steady with her stumps to catch the blood as Titus cuts her attackers' throats.

The only happy parent-child relationship comes where we least expect it. Aaron relates his varied atrocities, which include digging up dead bodies in the night and propping them up outside their loved ones' homes for a big surprise in the morning. However, he's on a gallows and Lucius is about to have him hanged, along with his and Tamora's baby son, when he makes these confessions. They aren't necessarily true. He claims crimes too bad for hanging, and secret information that will make him a useful witness against Tamora, as Lucius realises. Aaron ensures the double execution is postponed, and though his survival will be temporary, the baby's may not. The Moor is a Revenger only against Titus and his family, or in self-defence, his flaunted atrocities a clever ruse; he may be no worse than the white Revengers. His intense and endearing bond with his son, his determination to protect him in the 'wilderness of tigers' (3.1.53) claiming everyone else, is this play's love story.

As in *Othello*, there's a problem with timing. The pace is very fast. Tamora hasn't had time to have a baby by Saturninus, so Aaron's taking charge of his black baby and substituting a fair-skinned one in the Imperial bed wouldn't avert suspicion from her. This may however be a further two fingers up to the concept of hereditary monarchy: given enough cheek, perhaps a clever woman can expect to get away with any dynastic skullduggery.

There's no sisterhood in Rome, and Titus takes Procne's central part in the revenge on Tamora and her sons. Like revengers from Hieronimo to Hamlet and after, Titus shams madness. He deceives his brother, some of the other Roman nobility, and even Tamora, the cleverest politician in Rome. She wants to trick him into sending for Lucius, who's been banished and joined the Goths. To our surprise, Lucius agrees to return to Rome. The Goths are at the city gates, and with them Aaron as a prisoner and his baby. Lucius, exiled for trying to save his two remaining brothers from Tamora, is now the Goths' General. Aaron and the baby are taken and brought back to Titus' house with Lucius when he returns, knowing he may be walking into a trap but determined not to remain in exile.

The Trickster is tricked. Titus has a plan to outwit Tamora, who's taken off guard by her apparently easy success and allows him to capture her rapist sons. His relatives bind them, he cuts their throats, then uses the blood caught by Lavinia to make a pie, its raised pastry called a coffin, containing their two cooked heads for a banquet to which he invites Tamora and Saturninus. Lucius with some of his Goths and the Roman citizens also arrive at Titus' house, with other Goths in ambush nearby.

With Lavinia veiled and Titus hosting the party dressed as a chef, he serves up the pie to Tamora, who starts to eat. Almost casually, he asks Saturninus if the legendary Virginius was right to kill his daughter, as Livy relates:

> Titus: Was it well done of rash Virginius
> To slay his daughter with his own right hand,
> Because she was enforced, stained and deflowered?
> Saturninus: It was, Andronicus.
> Titus: your reason, mighty lord?
> Saturninus: Because the girl should not survive her shame
> And by her presence still renew his sorrows.
> Titus: A reason mighty, strong, effectual;
> A pattern, precedent and likely warrant

For me, most wretched, to perform the like.
Die, die, Lavinia, and thy shame with thee,
And with thy shame thy father's sorrow die. {He kills her}.
Saturninus: What hast thou done, unnatural and unkind? (5.3.36-47)

Several editor/commentators write about Lavinia's death as if it's part of the Revenge plot. But Lavinia is herself (with Alarbus and the Clown, a poor Fool who's hanged) the play's initially innocent victim. Her murder by her father is not a Revenge killing, it's a classic honour killing based on tradition and custom. She's murdered because in the opinion of her father and a higher authority she brings shame on her family by her rape and mutilation. She has no trial; Titus thinks by now it's self-evident she should die, and the exchange is so laconic and the killing so abrupt they're over before we see them coming.

She lives long enough to witness Tamora's beginning to eat her sons, but not to see her killed by Titus, who's killed by Saturninus, who's killed by Lucius; it all happens at once. Lavinia's murder is hideously unexpected, to the audience as well as to her, and wasteful. If we don't feel that, we're on the side of Saturninus, Romanitas and all the people in fiction and history who've thought a raped or disabled woman better dead. We know she's almost certainly going to die, but don't, I think, expect Titus to kill her.

In the Introduction to his erudite Arden edition, Jonathan Bate writes:

> The actress Anna Calder-Marshall played the raped Lavinia in the BBC television production in the mid-1980s, at a time when there was great concern about the ready availability of videos characterised by extreme violence, usually wrought upon the bodies of women. 'Someone said to me,' she recollected, 'it's just like a video nasty, isn't it? And it is very, very frightening. But,' she went on, 'somehow we've found – or I think we have – that the characters through their suffering get closer. Titus has committed the most appalling deeds and it isn't until he's maimed and his daughter's maimed that he learns anything about love.' To understand *Titus Andronicus* thus is at once to perceive its proximity to *King Lear* and to apprehend the difference between a slasher movie and a tragedy.[10]

It's not like a slasher movie, certainly, it's much too witty. It's more like Edward Bond's *Lear* than *King Lear*, but there are resemblances to *King Lear* in its father-daughter relationship. Titus' initial reaction on seeing

Lavinia mutilated is loving. In reply to Marcus' crass comment that she 'was' his daughter, Titus replies that she still is. From then on, as Calder-Marshall says, he becomes much closer to her. The empty shell of Act One begins to be inhabited. He kisses her bloody mouth and addresses her with tenderness; her pain becomes his; they suffer further torture and weep together. She's with him when his hand is cut off and then returned to him with her brothers' heads. And he grows in love not just for her but for his brother and son. Through the horrors of Act Three, his language changes from mindless platitude to poetry. Seeing Lavinia just after her mutilation, he says:

> he that wounded her
> Hath hurt me more than had he killed me dead.
> For now I stand as one upon a rock,
> Environed with a wilderness of sea,
> Who marks the waxing tide grow wave by wave,
> Expecting ever when some envious surge
> Will in his brinish bowels swallow him.
> This way to death my wretched sons are gone;
> Here stands my other son, a banished man,
> And here my brother, weeping at my woes.
> But that which gives my soul the greatest spurn
> Is dear Lavinia, dearer than my soul. (3.1.53)

He stops being Roman and becomes human. His wit is already macabre in Act One: the Goths have given him leave to come home, he says, meaning he's killed most of them. He gets funnier as he suffers, finding no escape but into laughter when his severed hand is returned with his sons' heads, then throughout his crazy exchanges with Tamora masquerading as Revenge, and into the comedy of his dressing up as a chef.

All this wit and new feeling disappears without warning in his murder of Lavinia. It's as if the honour-killing impulse goes so deep it over-rides any form of humanity or enlightenment.

If Titus and Lavinia believe they won't survive their revenge for more than seconds after Tamora sees what she's eating, we could argue that Titus must kill her quickly for her own sake. In the New Arden notes,[11] Jonathan Bate refers to a production where Titus held out his chef's knife and Lavinia ran onto it, embracing death and her father together in a high Roman way, the only way available since she can't hold a knife herself. In that production, her death was pre-arranged and consensual. There's a lot to be said for so relatively comforting an ending.

But it isn't said in Shakespeare's play, where nothing is done with Lavinia's consent except cooking her rapists in a pie. Titus appeals to the judgement of Saturninus, his own deadly enemy, the highest authority and arguably the most vicious character of all. He reverts to his insensate legalism in Act One, looking at custom and precedent not at his daughter; his shame is now his only thought, not her pain. His 'Die, die, Lavinia' is incompatible with an assisted suicide or a mercy killing; she's struggling while he says it. In a play with multiple plot-symmetries, he knifes her as Aaron knifes the Nurse who could testify against him – like a pig. Saturninus' startled question is clearly about an act which though he approves it in principle is wholly unexpected, not visibly preconcerted between father and daughter.

The argument that Titus kills her because they will die anyway is unsustainable. They can't be sure in advance they will die. Though Saturninus' Imperial Guard must be there, so are Marcus and Lucius with attendant Goths. Saturninus moves faster than anyone could predict of so dissolute a character. It's an act explained to Lavinia only as her father's justifiable escape from the horror of her continuing life. A focus on the play's honour killing refutes a reading of the Titus-Lavinia relationship as an early version of Lear and Cordelia.

Elsewhere there's much to define *Titus Andronicus* as a great cry of outrage at human cruelty. Titus organises a treasure-hunt for Justice among the patricians. Everywhere in nature he sees life defeated and sadism triumphant. The Clown, the only entirely innocent Roman, innocent because he's simple-minded, is murdered on a whim. All this makes perfect tragic sense, although or even because Titus has wasted his own life in the savagery of war and come back to Rome a zombie. We may relate especially to Lavinia's fightback from her injuries.

But though we can try to humanise *Titus*, look for the *King Lear* in it, Lavinia's honour killing resists that, and there remain episodes that mock moral interpretation. Though critics no longer look for consistency in each Shakespeare play, they look for lucidity and meaning even in the inconsistencies. But like Aaron, this play can dispense with lucidity and our approval. When Titus and Marcus exit carrying the heads of Titus' sons, with Lavinia carrying Titus' hand between her teeth, there may be, as some claim, a subliminal pun about her as the handmaid of Revenge, but that's just the sort of sick joke Demetrius and Chiron crack about her. In that episode and especially in her murder, any sense of growth towards love is aborted. Humanist criticism has to confess itself stumped. That's what makes *Titus* great.

After the multiple killings, only Marcus, Lucius and Young Lucius are left of the principal Roman characters. Marcus, an old career politician, is quick to look for a way ahead for the surviving Andronici. Amid the general *melee* of attendant Goths, Roman tribunes and citizens, and Goths who were in ambush, the three Andronici retreat to the upper stage, not knowing what the Roman citizens will make of Lucius' killing their Emperor. Marcus takes with them at least one Goth attendant, the one holding Aaron's baby. Lucius picks up his cue from his uncle, and both deploy good rhetorical skills. Jonathan Bate seems willing to suppose that Lucius may now make a just Emperor. But the concluding action suggests he's a more ruthless opportunist than anyone else, except his young son.

Marcus offers to gather up Rome's scattered corn, reknit her severed limbs. Lucius and Marcus explain some of the back-story for the Roman citizens and Goth soldiers below. Lucius is adept at praising himself while aping humility:

> I am the turned-forth [exile], be it known to you,
> That have preserved her [Rome's] welfare in my blood,
> And from her bosom took the enemy's point,
> Sheathing the steel in my advent'rous body.
> Alas, you know I am no vaunter, I;
> My scars are witness, dumb although they are,
> That my report is just and full of truth.
> But soft, methinks I do digress too much,
> Citing my worthless praise. O pardon me,
> For when no friends are by, men praise themselves. (5.3.108-17)

Marcus says the three Andronici will throw themselves from the balcony to the stones beneath if the Roman citizens consider they've acted unlawfully in killing Saturninus, but the citizens applaud him and declare Lucius their next Emperor.

Marcus points to the baby:

> Now is my turn to speak. Behold the child.
> Of this was Tamora delivered,
> The issue of an irreligious Moor,
> Chief architect and plotter of these woes.
> The villain is alive in Titus' house. (5.3.118-22)

What happens to the baby? He's not mentioned again after this point. There must be a stage direction or a line missing somewhere. Hard to believe that Shakespeare just forgot him. It's possible the Goth is holding up a dead baby. Or does Marcus throw him down with these words into the courtyard below? He's the most humane of the characters; he grieves for his niece and nephews, and volunteers his hand to be sent as ransom instead of his brother's. But from first to last he promotes only his own family, which is represented earlier as a tight, inward-looking ring. He's not likely to protect anyone outside it, least of all the offspring of Tamora and Aaron.

Lucius is the most likely to throw the baby down, but he promised Aaron to spare him, and he might hesitate, as somebody in the crowd below will remember that. It would be good to see the Goth attendant sidle cautiously off stage with the baby, who will return, we can hope, to take the city in twenty years' time. By the end, the Goth soldiers appear more like Romans than the Romans. Lucius' promise for the future is wonderfully unconvincing as he responds to the crowd's acclaim:

> Thanks, gentle Romans, may I govern so
> To heal Rome's harms and wipe away her woe. (5.3.146-7)

Adaptations always soften Shakespeare, however unsparing they mean to be. This play's queasiness is finely caught in Julie Taymor's 1999 film, *Titus*. It's an intense, imaginative production, rocking between bloodbath and farce. She finds ways to manage the violence without stylising it out of existence *à la* Vivien Leigh, whose hands were replaced with coloured streamers. But Taymor ends her film with Young Lucius and the possibility of an innocent child survivor, missing Shakespeare's brilliant ending. Far from being innocent, Young Lucius has already shown himself a good ham actor in the political drama when he becomes a messenger from Titus to Saturninus.

Once the citizens have proclaimed Lucius their Emperor and it's safe to do so, Marcus, Lucius and Young Lucius come down to the lower stage where the bodies are lying. Marcus and Lucius kiss Titus goodbye in a demonstration of warm family feeling. Lucius now wants to establish Young Lucius in the public mind as his heir. This doesn't necessarily prove paternal affection. A ruler with an heir, especially a capable boy heir, was safer and less likely to be assassinated. Lucius addresses his son over Titus' dead body:

> Come hither, boy, come, come, and learn of us [Marcus and Lucius]
> To melt in showers [weep]. Thy grandsire [Titus] loved thee well.
> Many a time he danced thee on his knee,
> Sung thee asleep; his loving breast thy pillow.
> Many a story hath he told to thee,
> And bid thee bear his pretty tales in mind. (5.3.159-64)

It doesn't sound very likely. Titus has been out of Rome for the past ten years, returning briefly at intervals only to inter another son's corpse in the family mausoleum, and Young Lucius is about ten or eleven, so in fact it's impossible. But Marcus sees the point and prompts the boy further:

> How many thousand times have these [Titus'] poor lips,
> When they were living, warmed themselves on thine!
> O now, sweet boy, give him their latest [last] kiss.
> Bid him farewell. Commit him to the grave.
> Do them [his lips] that kindness and take leave of them. (5.3.166-70)

The act of committal will establish Young Lucius as approaching years of responsibility. Three generations of Andronici are acting out an extempore play for their audience of Roman citizens and Goths, and for the play's audience. The onlookers are asked to approve Young Lucius' compassion and moral gravity. Following the beginnings of a popular revolt against Saturninus, Marcus and Lucius have finally grasped that the citizens would like to see something of these qualities in their rulers. The public image matters and should include strong family affections. Young Lucius does not disappoint, but quickly picks up his cue, showing himself a worthy successor to his great-uncle and father:

> O grandsire, grandsire, ev'n with all my heart
> Would I were dead, so you did live again.
> O Lord, I cannot speak to him for weeping.
> My tears will choke me if I ope my mouth. (5.3.171-4)

He overdoes it, but that's the Andronici for you. He'll make a good Emperor when he's killed his father. *Titus Andronicus* and *Lucrece* both end in a reconfigured but securer Succession.

Shakespeare uses a comparable plot situation later when Julius Caesar is killed and first Brutus, the chief assassin, then Mark Antony make manipulative speeches over the body to a ductile crowd of Romans. The Andronici are better orators than Brutus but not as good as Mark Antony. Luckily for themselves, the Andronici narrative is uncontested.

In the first scene and the last, the state's authority is asserted by extreme cruelty to an outsider. Lucius sentences Aaron to be buried outside the city in earth up to the chest and left to die of hunger and thirst. Tamora's body is to be thrown over the walls for animals to prey on. Both resume their alien status in death, with Lucius' closing speech settling most of the guilt on the Jezebel, Tamora, some on Aaron and none on himself, though he started off the chain of events with one of the worst horrors, Alarbus' hideous death. Lucius ends the play:

> Her life [Tamora's] was beastly and devoid of pity,
> And being dead, let birds on her take pity. (5.3.198-9)

The ugly non-rhyme emphasises the word, recalling the lack of pity shown at the start to Alarbus and Tamora and displayed by every character, especially Lucius. Like *Lucrece*, *Titus Andronicus* is circular.

In both, Romanitas, the Roman-ness of Rome created as an almost purely military culture of competing men, carries with it more horrors for women than we find even in the English Histories, except with Joan. Lucrece has her nightdress stuffed into her mouth to silence her, Lavinia has her tongue cut out. Later, in *Julius Caesar*, Portia (though far off-stage) swallows burning coals to kill herself when she learns that her husband is losing in the civil war. This, like stabbing herself in her thigh, is what Plutarch records,[12] but in all the Roman Plays, whether or not based on recorded history, the women are savagely abused or self-immolating. Lucrece and Lavinia are precursors of many other women silenced, if less brutally, in the later plays, including those depicting (wherever they're set) English cultures. Lavinia's fate is the most horrific, but they all live in a climate of fear.

There was a lot of interest in Greek and Roman political systems in the 1590s. The Ancient World, its histories and literatures were gradually recovered by scholars from the late fourteenth century on, in a Renaissance or re-birth of knowledges lost during the Middle Ages. Classical histories offered patterns of government very different from European hereditary monarchy: Republicanism in all its forms was fascinating. Rome in *Lucrece* has been a Republic in the past but the Emperor's role has become hereditary – dangerously, the narrative suggests. Lucrece's death may restore a better order. But though the reader is free to hope, I think the ending of *Lucrece* is sceptical. In *Titus Andronicus* too there's nobody we can believe either fit to be Emperor or content to hold power by election for a limited period.

At first Bassianus, the younger son of the dead Emperor, seems a better bet than Saturninus. His power base is potentially wider: he relies on votes from the citizens while Saturninus courts only the patricians. He's a romantic figure initially, prepared to defy his brother and Titus, and marry Lavinia. But in the woods he insults Tamora, pretending to mistake her for the chaste Diana. Shakespeare does a good line in dull ironies by wannabe wits; Bassianus draws his death on himself.

In the opening scene, Marcus Andronicus proclaims that Titus is Rome's choice. He omits to mention that Titus is his brother, or who counted the votes, but the citizens want Titus because of his foreign victories. We soon see how very bad he would be as Emperor, and he refuses because of his age, but he clearly expects like Lear to enjoy the dignity of high office without the responsibility. The Senate, tribunes and citizens are ignored in the opening scene when they're forced to accept the hereditary Succession of Saturninus. In the closing scene they're duped effectively by Lucius, Marcus and Young Lucius. A dynastic monarchy is re-established, partly because the Goths are inside the city and loyal to Lucius, partly because there's no other option while the Roman citizens are too naïve to see they're being conned.

Elizabeth was now into the last decade of her long reign. She had no direct heir, and there was a real prospect of return when she died to the dynastic wars of the 1400s, rendered if possible more savage by religious difference and foreign occupation. A political system capable of delivering a peaceful transfer of power on the death of a childless ruler, or a ruler with unsuitable children, looked very interesting, as did the model of election for a fixed term. This was something not to be discussed except in secret with trustworthy friends. On the stage, though, such possibilities might be explored if sufficiently disguised, and distanced into ancient history. That exploration could include the cruelties consequent on civil war. From the opening to the close of *Titus Andronicus*, the felt absence of any mechanism for the smooth transfer of power is the main cause of the chaos. Shakespeare would return to the subject as the decade went on.

*

In *A Midsummer Night's Dream*, four women rebel: Hippolyta, Hermia, Titania and Thisbe. We might add Hermia's friend Helena, as like Hermia she claims the right to marry for love in an Athens where arranged or forced marriage is the norm, but we don't learn anything about Helena's family beyond her father's name and that he's too old to worry about where she is at night. Of the five, Hermia is the potential honour-killing victim. Her father wants her to marry Demetrius, who was previously engaged to Helena but broke it off when he decided he preferred her best friend. Hermia wants to marry Lysander. The two young men are similar, but Lysander is more imaginative, Demetrius more blunt and pragmatic.

In the opening scene a day is set for Hermia's arraignment, which will be Theseus, Duke of Athens' and the Amazon Queen Hippolyta's wedding day. Hermia will have three choices: obeying her father and marrying Demetrius; death; or lifelong confinement as a virgin priestess of Diana. She says she'll choose confinement. Before the trial can happen, Lysander persuades her to meet him in the forest at night and run away to his aunt's house, out of Theseus' jurisdiction. After a lot of confusion and danger in the woods, she's saved, with Helena, by magic, and the girls get the husbands they wanted from the start.

Three other strands of narrative are interwoven with Hermia's and Helena's. The play opens after a battle of the sexes on an international scale, male Athenians against female Amazons, and Queen Hippolyta has lost her nation of women warriors. She's forced to marry Theseus, becoming a trophy wife. Titania, the Fairy Queen, refuses to accept that everything she has belongs to her husband, Oberon, and in revenge he tricks her into humiliating cross-species sex. In a play written and acted by Athenian Mechanicals (tradesmen) to celebrate Theseus's and Hippolyta's marriage, the heroine Thisbe kills herself when she defies her father, runs away from home to meet her lover Pyramus in the woods, and finds him dead.

Apart from the Mechanicals' play, each narrative is about rape. If Hermia obeys her father, she'll suffer marital rape by Demetrius. Hippolyta has no choice in marrying Theseus: she wouldn't have done so if she'd won. Titania's insisting on sex with Bottom is caused only by Puck's love juice, which is a powerful aphrodisiac; this strange cross-species coupling could be claimed as rape by either party. 'Pyramus and Thisbe' is the odd one out: there's no other suitor favoured by her parents whom Thisbe must escape.

For many readers, this summary will feel like taking a sledgehammer to a cobweb, reducing Shakespeare's greatest comedy to a Human Resources pamphlet about how to define gender discrimination and sexual assault on your company's day and night shifts. It's a grim precis, and at first sight a travesty of so much romantic richness. With *Macbeth*, this is Shakespeare's most poetic play, its verse thick with imagery, prompting one Victorian director to let loose live rabbits on the stage in an attempt to realise its verbal fertility.

But it's only by stripping it down to its bare bones that we can begin to see its geometrical elegance and how it works. Each of the interlocked stories reinforces the others, creating a sex war played out by ordinary young people, by figures of classical myth, in the night world of the fairies, and in fiction. In every great comedy there's a tragedy fighting to get out, and each of the three strands with a happy-marriage ending only just contains its tragedy inside its comedy. The Mechanicals' tragedy of Pyramus and Thisbe with its double suicide is much the funniest of the four.

There's not just the four-strand plait; we can divide *AMSND* in other ways. It can split down the middle into balancing characters and concepts:

Day		Night
Theseus, Hippolyta, Philostrate, court		Oberon, Titania, and fairies
Athenian palace		Warwickshire woods
Hierarchy/law		Broken hierarchy/freedom
Waking		Dreams
Reason, practicality, sense		Irrationalit/Imagination
Ego/conscious control		Id/unconscious fears and desires
Family, custom, a marriage,	Lovers, a child	Impulse, eroticism
Classical source, casting, reward	Mechanicals, a play	Creativeness,self-fulfilment,

In the world of Day, Theseus controls a defeated Queen, a respectful court and an uneasy Master of Entertainments, Philostrate, who knows his boss doesn't much care for plays but must have something to fill the space between the wedding supper and bedtime.

As *AMSND* opens, Theseus laments that four more days must elapse before his marriage to Hippolyta, while the old moon wanes. He at least is not frightened of Diana; he sees the slowly waning moon as a useless old woman who:

lingers [postpones] my desires,
Like to a stepdame or a dowager
Long withering out a young man's revenues. (1.1.4-6)

He feels like a young heir who must wait until his father's widow dies before he can get his hands on the whole of the estate, which her existence is steadily depleting. It's not a romantic simile, but it's appropriate, as money, or at least land, is the motivator for this marriage.

Hippolyta's attitude to Theseus is ambiguous. She takes up his Diana image, transforming it gracefully:

Four days will quickly steep themselves in night,

Four nights will quickly dream away the time,
And then the moon, like to a silver bow
New bent in heaven shall behold the night
Of our solemnities. (1.1.7-11)

It sounds beautiful. But Hippolyta is, or was before her defeat, a fierce archer like Diana. The Amazons were famed for archery and in some legends, though not in this play, they cut off their right breasts so as not to impede their bows. Is she still hoping for rescue from the skies or from her warriors when she imagines the moon as a drawn bow? There's an undertone of antagonism, a re-assertion of her unconquered self, in much of what she says to Theseus, as when she reminisces about hunting with Hercules and Cadmus, and praises their hounds when he wants her to admire his. But she recognises defeat. Most productions show her passing from concealed anger in the opening scene to acceptance of her lot by the end.

Egeus interrupts their conversation with an appeal to Theseus to confirm his authority over his daughter. He uses the possessive pronoun even more brutally than most of Shakespeare's fathers:

I beg the ancient privilege of Athens,
As she is mine, I may dispose of her,
Which shall be either to this gentleman [Demetrius]
Or to her death. (1.1.41-4)

Hermia undergoes an interrogation by Theseus, who seems to support dictatorship in the family as fully as in his foreign policy:

To you your father should be as a god,
One who composed your beauties, yea, and one
To whom you are but as a form in wax
By him imprinted. (1.1.47-50)

For Theseus the brief act of conception, another version of the stamp on wax, entitles a father to impose his will on a female child until she's married. Demetrius is ready to inflict marital rape on Hermia knowing she hates him; this is what she alludes to, modestly, in speaking of the 'unwished-for yoke' to which her 'soul consents not to give sovereignty'. (1.1.81-2) The woman's promise to obey in the marriage service (putting on the yoke) took the right of refusal from her. It would be another four hundred years before English law recognised the concept of marital rape, though English writers have recognised it from Chaucer on.

When she refuses to comply, arguing that Lysander is in every way as good as Demetrius, Theseus points out that Lysander lacks one thing, her father's approval, which is all that matters. He first articulates the play's central premise, that there's no objective value in things or people. Value lies in the judgement of the beholder and is changeable.

What happens to the four lovers at court and in the woods bears this out. The boys change their choices, Demetrius loving Helena before the action begins, then both wanting Hermia, then Lysander switching to Helena. For Demetrius, infidelity begins in the court before the play opens. The crazy, hormonal swings of desire can't be explained as the effect of Puck's love juice only. They're felt from the first, but the woods speed them up and allow them a freedom repressed in the court.

The love juice is produced by Cupid's arrow, once intended to pierce the heart of Queen Elizabeth. Oberon tells us:

> A certain [sure] aim he [Cupid] took
> At a fair vestal [virgin, Elizabeth] throned by the west,
> And loosed his love shaft smartly from his bow
> As [if] it should pierce a hundred thousand hearts.
> But I might [could] see young Cupid's fiery shaft
> Quenched in the chaste beams of the watery moon,
> And the imperial votaress passed on
> In maiden meditation, fancy free. (2.1.157-65)

Missing Elizabeth Tudor, the imperial votaress of Diana, goddess of chastity, the arrow-point falls on a pansy, which is ever afterwards streaked with purple dye like blood. If Bottom and Co. need to please Theseus, Shakespeare and Co. equally need to please Elizabeth. For her, Theseus qualifies his dismissal of the single life in his speech to Hermia: it's good for those extraordinary women who are pure enough to choose celibacy, he says. Elizabeth is immune to love, but the juice is strong enough to overcome any other mortal.

Romantic love is bad for the character. Helena betrays to Demetrius her friend's plan of escape merely so she can follow him to the wood when he pursues Hermia and Lysander. Demetrius threatens her with rape then runs away from her, leaving her to the night and its dangers. Lysander tries to seduce Hermia as soon as they're out of the city. She refuses tactfully, but his attempt on her virginity shocks her into a nightmare about a snake. Puck smears the love juice on his eyes as they both sleep. Waking and seeing Helena, Lysander in turn leaves a woman alone in a dark wood to follow a new love.

Perhaps his impulse to follow Helena is innate, though set free by Puck's love juice. Hermia won't have sex outside marriage. She brings with her more baggage from the day world than the other young people: in one production, Lysander staggered into the wood carrying her two large suitcases. Helena could be more amenable to seduction than Hermia. She's cast off some social restraints before she reaches the forest and can't retrieve the propriety she had before Demetrius courted then rejected her.

She's the first to suffer and so the first to learn and conceptualise:

> How happy some o'er other some can be!
> Through Athens I am thought as fair as she.
> But what of that? Demetrius thinks not so.
> He will not know what all but he do know (...)
> Things base and vile, holding no quantity [value]
> Love can transpose to form and dignity (...)
> Love looks not with the eyes but with the mind (...) (1.1.226-35)

We see not objectively but imaginatively. The two boys seem as silly as each other as they try to rationalise their behaviour:

> The will of man should be by reason swayed,
> And reason says you are the worthier maid (2.2.121-35)

Lysander solemnly tells Helena, falling back on aphorisms from school. But he and Demetrius appear very different to the girls. People half create what they see, more than half, perhaps. Lovers and poets make their images out of nothing, as Theseus will later explain, scornfully. While still in Athens, we see the lovers doing that, and also the 'poets', the Mechanicals, as Quince struggles to cast and bring to birth a play which the metropolitan Philostrate later describes as 'nothing, nothing in the world'. (5.1.78) In the wood the lovers' and play-makers' imaginations take them beyond their Athenian selves.

In the first scene, Lysander describes to Helena his plans to run away with Hermia:

> Tomorrow night, when Phoebe [Diana, the moon] doth behold
> Her silver visage in the watery glass
> Decking with liquid pearl the bladed grass –
> A time that lovers' sleights doth still conceal –
> Through Athens' gates have we devised to steal. (1.1.209-13)

His imagined landscape is very pretty, Rackhamesque,[13] a bit kitsch. When they get there, the forest is nothing like that, it's full of snails, snakes, hedgehogs, worms and strange noises. Their emotions – desire, fear, contempt, rage, above all hurt pride – are too devastating to allow time to look at the forest. Their dream of love quickly becomes a 'fierce vexation', (4.1.525) a nightmare.

Despite huge provocation, Helena and Hermia don't change their choices as the boys do. Helena remains faithful to Demetrius, Hermia to Lysander. But both the boys and the girls turn on their friends. Lysander and Demetrius try to fight a duel, which Puck prevents. The girls have been best friends from their schooldays, but Hermia has to be restrained from scratching Helena's eyes out when she discovers why Lysander left her. All four slowly make their way through the adolescent night towards adulthood.

For all four, the world of Night and freedom is as threatening as the world of Day and conformity, and especially for the girls. They're free of the power of fathers, but they find that young men can be as cruel as old ones. Hermia is threatened by her father and her lover. None of the young people finds a substitute in themself for the codes they once accepted in Athens. But blundering about in a wood and eventually pairing up with the right partner is their kind of rehearsal for a return, grown up, to the prosaic world of Day, a return to the marriages and children they must undertake.

They need elements from both Day and Night worlds to make a viable marriage. For their Day *personae* they need a formal ceremony and social endorsement. But they also need the freedom to discover their most desirable partner, and they can find that only in the night woods, outside family and social constraints. After confusion that brings the four close to death, the girls get their initial choices. Like all Shakespeare's plays, *AMSND* endorses marriages of choice for women, however crazy the choice may look to an outsider.

Hermia's and Helena's risks and trials are set against less dangerous but still more humiliating ones. In the anarchic world of Night, King Oberon has lost control of Queen Titania, his fairy court is divided between the two, though Puck is more his friend and co-conspirator than Philostrate is to Theseus. The Day court seems more orderly under Theseus, the Night court more anarchic with Titania's continuing rebellion, but the difference is less than first appears, and they end up symmetrical. The actors can double the parts in them as they're never on stage at the same time, though at the end Theseus, Hippolyta and their court would need to throw on fast their starry cloaks or whatever their fairy roles demand during Puck's brief 'now the hungry lion roars' (5.2.1) speech.

Oberon and Titania have quarrelled, not over a country but because Titania withholds the Changeling Boy from him. The Boy is human, so an object of desire to fairies, who in country tales loved to steal human children.

Unsurprisingly, the two sides have different stories about where the Boy came from. Puck, loyal to Oberon, says that Titania:

> as her attendant hath
> A lovely boy stol'n from an Indian King. (2.1.21-2)

Titania tells Oberon the Boy wasn't stolen but left her by a dear mortal friend. She remembers how they used to meet on a beach and watch the ships go by:

> When we have laughed to see the sails conceive
> And grow big-bellied with the wanton wind;
> Which she, with pretty and with swimming gait,
> Following, her womb then rich with my young squire,
> Would imitate, and sail upon the land
> To fetch me trifles, and return again
> As from a voyage, rich with merchandise.
> But she, being mortal, of that boy did die,
> And for her sake do I rear up her boy
> And for her sake I will not part with him. (2.1.128-37)

Is there a right and wrong to this dispute? The two different stories are compatible, but only just. The Indian King could be the Boy's father, so Titania is withholding him from both Kings. Oberon feels entitled to the Boy, and legally the husband owned all, including the children: there's a strong connection to the mortal world here. A wife who left her husband for whatever reason had no legal right to see her children again and no right at any time to make decisions for them except with his agreement. Even in the anarchic fairy world? Even if Titania cares more about the Boy than Oberon does? These questions are part of the play's preoccupation with male ownership and female dispossession.

Titania's account is circumstantial and passionate. The high risk faced by every woman who married surfaces briefly but painfully as she makes her claim to the Boy, all that's left of her votary. Her memory of two young women having fun on a beach is intimate, credible, and shows her right to the Changeling as more valid and deep-rooted than Oberon's, who only wants him to swell his royal train. In *Othello*, Emilia attacks the law that gives ownership of everything to the husband; there might be many women, even some men, who thought like Emilia and Titania in the contemporary audience.

For good measure, Titania and Oberon go on to accuse each other, accurately, of adultery. Titania has already described how the breach between them is damaging the natural world, causing the seasons to go awry:

> Therefore [because of our quarrel] the moon, the governess of floods
> Pale in her anger washes [soaks] all the air, [so]
> That rheumatic diseases do abound;
> And thorough this distemperature [disturbance] we see
> The seasons alter: hoary-headed frosts
> Fall in the fresh lap of the crimson rose,
> And on old Hiems' [Winter's] thin and icy crown
> An odorous chaplet [garland] of sweet summer buds
> Is, as in mockery, set. (2.1.103-11)

Are the seasons and the natural world out of kilter because the balance of dominant male/submissive female, part of the so-called 'natural order', is disturbed by Titania's rebellion? Sixty years ago in the critical history of *AMSND* this would be the accepted explanation. The critic E.M.W. Tillyard was influential then in arguing that the Elizabethans, including Shakespeare, believed in a 'natural order' or 'chain of being' supposedly instituted by God, a hierarchy stretching from God at the top down through the ranks of angels, to monarchs, the nobility, the gentry, and the gradations of the lower classes, then further down into animals, plants and stones. In this divinely created order, men were higher than women, and wives promised to obey their husbands when they married. Certainly some people believed this in Shakespeare's time, but there's little reason to suppose he did.

It's Titania who grieves over the spoilt crops, the floods, the loss to mortals of carols and their winter cheer. Oberon's response is churlish: 'Give me that Boy and I will go with thee.' (2.1.143) Is nature cracking up not because Titania is rebellious but because Oberon claims everything, as Theseus claims a right by conquest to Hippolyta's country?

In revenge for her refusal, Oberon wants her to mate with whatever horrible creature she sees on waking. Whether her eyes alight:

> on lion, bear, or wolf, or bull
> On meddling monkey or on busy ape,
> She shall pursue it with the soul of love. (2.1.180-82)

As she falls asleep, her fairies call on Philomel to join their incantation and warn away all harm from her:

> You spotted snakes with double tongue,
> Thorny hedgehogs be not seen;
> Newts and blindworms do no wrong;
> Come not near our Fairy Queen.
>
> Chorus: Philomel with melody
> Sing in our sweet lullaby (...)
> Never harm nor spell nor charm
> Come our lovely lady nigh (...) (2.2.9-18)

Philomel, morphed from girl to nightingale, laments every summer night her rape by Tereus. She makes her grief into song, and so becomes the symbol for the poet or makar. She should alert Titania to sexual dangers. But Philomel can't save anyone, any more than she could save herself when she was human. She's invoked in the song's two choruses, but Oberon's spell is stronger. He smears the aphrodisiac on Titania's eyelids, compelling her to mate with Bottom, plucked from the group of rehearsing Mechanicals by Puck and transformed to an ass. Their intercourse crosses two species, it's not just fairy with human but fairy with human metamorphosed to animal.

Sex is unnatural here at the central point of the play, but then it's also unnatural in Hippolyta's political marriage and in Hermia's threatened marriage. Titania experiences punishment rape for her rebellion, with Oberon deputing his marital right to Bottom and directing their actions via Puck. It's a kind of gang rape, a hideous betrayal of a wife by her husband. The cross-species sex at the core of the play makes on one level a grotesque parody of all mating, as does Lavinia's rape. If we see Bottom as the victim of a female rapist, this transaction too parodies by inversion the socially accepted Athenian bond of forced marriage. Titania, even more than the young lovers, is crazed by desire and equally quick to rationalise her madness:

> Thou art as wise as thou art beautiful (2.2.284)

she tells Bottom. Even he's a bit embarrassed by this; he just wants to go home. As she leads him away to her bower, she vaguely notices:

> The moon, methinks, looks with a watery eye,
> And when she weeps, weeps every little flower
> Lamenting some enforced chastity [rape].
> Tie up my love's tongue; bring him silently. (4.4.327-330)

Compared to Hermia's threatened honour killing or Hippolyta's loss of her nation in battle, Titania's manipulation into random lust may seem a harmless joke by Oberon. This is after all a bit of the play small children find funny. And Shakespeare is a lot more graceful and less graphic here than his source story, Apuleius' prose fiction *The Golden Ass*, written between 150 and 180 BC. Its hero Lucius has some bizarre adventures, including full metamorphosis into a donkey, in which guise he's solicited by many apparently virtuous ladies because he's very well-endowed.

It's Titania's own violated chastity the moon and flowers weep for, though she's too drugged to understand that. Elsewhere it's the woman who's silenced by marriage, subordination or rape; here it's Bottom whose tongue is bound up so he's rendered speechless, a grotesque Philomel. Each could claim rape. But for Bottom, though he doesn't choose it, his experience takes him outside the human condition altogether, his animality granting him unsought intercourse with the immortal.

Like the lovers, the Mechanicals need Night as well as Day. They need information about literary conventions and the practicalities of putting on a play, but they also need imagination to construct the story and write the verse. Between them, Quince and Bottom manage both. Quince's 'Tedious Brief Scene of Pyramus and Thisbe', though of course rubbish to the satirical courtiers and Philostrate, does just hold the attention of its audience on stage, and is always the funniest part of *AMSND* for the off-stage audience.

Odd as it seems now, entertainments like the Mechanicals' play were often put on for visiting royalty and nobility. Elizabeth could hardly enter a town or a subject's gates without some allegorical representation of her various perfections, or songs or poems in English or Latin according to the speaker's capacity, or as here a playlet in her honour presented by nervous amateurs hoping for a reward. Quince (or the eleven-year-old Shakespeare) could have seen Elizabeth on a Progress at Warwick, with a Loyal Address from the city's petrified Recorder, and amateur entertainments.

Quince, a carpenter, is the writer, and proud of his tragedy, which the others keep trying to mess about with. He knows that great works of English literature are drawn from classical sources, the best plays written in iambic verse. He wants uninterrupted rehearsals and does his best with the talent available. Like Bottom he's insecure about the meanings of longer words, but he loves alliteration and is rather good at it, knows about personification, and is beginning to see that you don't have to be entirely naturalistic, that some of the action can be represented symbolically.

He knows the *Metamorphoses* story of Pyramus and Thisbe well, down to the fact that the lovers killed themselves under a mulberry tree whose fruit turned purple from their blood. Of all the company, he at least has seen a play, possibly more than one, possibly *Romeo and Juliet* on tour in the provinces. For his *debut* he goes for a classical not a modern story, but chooses a plot involving young love, cruel fate and a double suicide caused by a misunderstanding.

Bottom, a weaver, is the company's star. He alone can speak the verse with the necessary resonance and is handsome enough, so he and the cast believe, to be Pyramus. An egomaniac, he tries to expand his part and take on additional roles – actors often had to double up, especially on tour – even when this is clearly impossible, as when he wants to be Thisbe as well as Pyramus.

Quince's casting and the preliminary discussions take place in Athens. Everyone must learn his part before the next meeting. That's in a dark forest glade, where they discuss the problem of Lion being potentially too frightening for the ladies, and consider how to bring in Moonlight, as Quince insists on it. Bottom is quick to take up Quince's idea of symbolic representation and suggests two ways to personify Wall.

Puck finds the hempen homespuns rehearsing and seizes his chance, but it's no coincidence that Bottom is just warming to his part when metamorphosis strikes:

> Bottom [as Pyramus]: Thisbe, the flowers of odious savours sweet –
> Quince: odours, odours –
> Bottom [as Pyramus]: – odours savours sweet.
> So hath thy breath, my dearest Thisbe dear.
> But hark, a voice. Stay thou but here a while,
> And by and by I will to thee appear. (4.4.226-230)

He gets no further. Puck chooses him, as the biggest ass available, to humiliate Titania.

He's dreamed of a different life from the one defined by his Day job. He's locked into that most of the time, identified as they all are by their trades: he's Bottom, like the spool his thread is wound on. His longing for something better appears in the magniloquence even of his everyday language, which aspires constantly to a grandeur he knows is out there but can't reach. It's a craving shown in his passionate commitment to verse he barely understands but feels is heroic; the play could earn him a pension, it could make him famous with the people who matter.

That craving is fulfilled in the most unexpected way. Without his own volition he experiences something no other mortal ever has. He has intercourse literally, and also metaphorically, with the world of Night and magic, that alternative world of pure imagination where Titania and her court live. He awakes not much changed outwardly. He's always been crazed by language, and he still is, groping for magnificent words he's heard in church, St Paul's *Epistle to the Corinthians* on the Kingdom of Heaven,[14] to try to define what he thinks was just a dream. Back in the real world, he's more eager than ever to get their play chosen and acted well. It can't go on without him.

Shakespeare left no overt autobiographical record, but a memoir's here if anywhere: the limitations of Stratford, the beginnings of a recognition in the night woods outside the town of who he was going to be. Apart from a slight difference in the degrees of their talent, Bottom and Quince together are Shakespeare.

The other Mechanicals have smaller parts, but Flute is important, as Thisbe must end the play. He doesn't want to be a woman, but he's good-natured and does it for Quince. At the casting stage there are parts for the parents, but these don't appear in the performance. Maybe Quince is too optimistic about what his minor actors can learn, or has to use them as Lion, Wall and Moonshine, or Shakespeare initially meant to show the feud between the parents, then decided that might really be tedious.

To the Mechanicals, 'The Tedious Brief Scene of Pyramus and Thisbe' is a great tragedy. The four young lovers in the audience can see in it the tragedy they narrowly escaped, if they're bright enough. From the first Lysander knows something about love, if only theoretically. In the opening scene he tells Hermia that it's:

> Brief as the lightning in the collied [coal-black] night (...)
> And ere a man hath power to say 'Behold!'
> The jaws of darkness do devour it up:
> So quick bright things come to confusion. (1.1.145-9)

But back at court again and married, the boys at least find Quince's play merely silly. They've forgotten how silly they were the previous night. Like Theseus they're ungracious in their response to it. Quince is well able to understand Theseus' rude comment: 'Marry, if he that writ it had played Pyramus, and hanged himself in Thisbe's garter, it would have been a fine tragedy.' He goes on to say, 'And so it is', (5.1.338-340) but too late to spare Quince's humiliation. With all his surface urbanity, Theseus is inadequate outside war and politics, and he doesn't like plays, though he puts up with them because he thinks these entertainments show how much his subjects revere him. The girls say nothing; perhaps they do see from the play how near to disaster they came.

Only Theseus can articulate the concept of imagination, though he despises it:

> Hippolyta: 'Tis strange, my Theseus, that these lovers speak of.
> Theseus: More strange than true. I never may believe
> These antique [old; crazy] fables, nor these fairy toys.
> Lovers and madmen have such seething brains,
> Such shaping fantasies, that apprehend [invent]
> More than cool reason ever comprehends.
> The lunatic, the lover and the poet
> Are of imagination all compact [made up].
> One sees more devils than vast hell can hold:
> That is the madman. The lover, all as frantic,
> Sees Helen [of Troy]'s beauty in a brow of Egypt [brown skin].
> The poet's eye, in fine frenzy rolling,
> Doth glance from heaven to earth, from earth to heaven,
> And as imagination bodies forth
> The forms of things unknown, the poet's pen
> Turns them to shapes, and gives to airy nothing
> A local habitation and a name. (5.1.1-17)

He doesn't believe in fairies, or the strange shifting perceptions the lovers have told him about. But we do, because we've seen them. We know that he, Hippolyta, the lovers, his palace, the play we're watching and everything in it are among those shapes a poet's pen has bodied forth. A poet has invented the title, the setting, the plot, and the characters including Theseus. We believe they have a meaning. He's arguing that he doesn't exist. A little later, during 'Pyramus and Thisbe', he'll say, 'The best in this kind are but shadows, and the worst are no worse if imagination amend them.' (5.4.205-6) By 'shadows' he means the actors and the actions they present, and one play is much like another. Puck in his final speech picks up the word, with

> If we 'shadows' have offended
> Think but this and all is mended,
> That you have but slumbered here (...) (5.2.53-5)

He plays along sardonically with Theseus' Philistinism, but his presence proves there's another truth beyond the one Theseus sees. Hippolyta knows that too:

> But all the story of the night told over,
> And all their minds transfigured so together,
> More witnesseth [gives proof of more] than fancy's images [figments of the imagination],
> And grows to something of great constancy. (5.1.23-6)

She sees the lovers' changing through the night into their final stasis in love as transfiguration. Her grand word dignifies their turmoil. Though constancy is usually glossed as consistency – they're all telling the same story – the word is more about loyalty, steadiness. Maybe they will stay faithful now. Theseus' scornful closing remark in his anti-imagination speech:

> Or in the night, imagining some fear,
> How easy is a bush supposed a bear (5.1.21-2)

deserves the response it gets from Anne Barton: it's safer to suppose a bush is a bear than to suppose a bear is a bush.[15] *AMSND* celebrates the transfiguring power of the imagination in love and play-making.

How seriously do we take the harsher elements, the violence to women? The play's rich verse and boundless imagining resist reduction to a vehicle for ideas, whether feminist or masculinist. There's something to support a masculinist side. Puck and Oberon are anarchic, but they're also kindly, some of the time, and want to help Helena get Demetrius back. Lysander makes only a tentative effort to seduce Hermia and takes it well when she refuses.

Oberon steals the Changeling Boy by a very dirty trick while Titania is distracted, but some might say that boys do need to leave the world of women and learn to be men. When Titania wakes beside Bottom she remembers almost nothing of the night before. She asks Oberon to tell her what happened, but now he has the Changeling Boy in his possession, he's not going to risk another domestic by a truthful answer. So is there any harm done?

Oberon and Theseus are not very sensitive, but perhaps they can't be if they have kingdoms to govern. They're two sides of the same coin, and

Oberon knows before Theseus does that he'll let Hermia marry Lysander. Though this may always have been Theseus' intention: after his interrogation of Hermia, he takes Egeus and Demetrius out of the way for no convincing reason, allowing her and Lysander to plan their flight. Hippolyta perhaps sees that, and she certainly sees the lovers' awaking and Theseus' indulgence to them, capricious as it is. She's happy by the time the play comes on, and not sorry when it's over. Their marriage is not romantic, it's a compromise, but it may be the better for that.

AMSND's distance from life also resists a strong political reading. We're always aware of its fictionality. We know it can't be true when figures from Greek myth appear, then English fairies. Hermia's risk of an honour killing or confinement for life is notional: Egeus is a flat and unconvincing threat; we know she and Helena will somehow get their way. The young lovers speak in rhyme, which helps to stylise and distance them.

In Act Five, there's a receding world of mirrors: an audience, perhaps originally at a wedding, watches a play in which an audience of recently star-crossed lovers at their wedding watches a play about star-crossed lovers. The main narrative strands feel enclosed in their fictionalities like graceful forms in amber. But the battle-of-the-sexes plots form a solid framework, and the class and sexual cruelties are quite painful, though funny, before they resolve themselves into an amateur play successfully performed, or at least performed, and eight reconciled lovers.

Diana the moon, symbol of the female principle, lights up *AMSND* from beginning to end. Everyone sees her differently. As noted, Theseus sees the waning moon as a superfluous old woman, Hippolyta sees the new moon perhaps as an ally, Lysander sees her as romantic beauty personified. Oberon acknowledges her power: as Chastity, she can deflect Cupid's arrow from Elizabeth Tudor. For Titania, the moon is in her darker phase as governess of floods, angry with Oberon for his greed, and drenching the world with rheumatic diseases. Later, she sees the moon weeping, perhaps for her own betrayal by her husband.

Other references to the moon are too many to list, but one appearance is outstanding. As disfigured or represented by Starveling, she has a cameo role in 'Pyramus and Thisbe'. From the start, Quince knows the moon has to be in it; that's what lovers always meet by. But he has to have a male moon because Flute, the only Mechanical who could play a woman, is already taken. Starveling's interpretation is memorable: it involves a lantern, a thorn bush and a dog, whether real or stuffed. He invites a lot of derision from the audience, which he gets thoroughly annoyed about and talks back to. Richard Wilson was a natural for this in Russell T. Davies' 2016 film.

Quince is at his finest and most alliterative when he bodies forth the moonlight. Pyramus addresses Moon:

> Sweet Moon, I thank thee for thy sunny beams
> I thank thee Moon for shining now so bright.
> For by thy gracious, golden, glittering gleams
> I trust to taste of truest Thisbe's sight. (5.1.257-60)

Quince's poetry scans, and his moon is almost as pretty as Lysander's. He doesn't flinch from deep theological questions, not even from that permanent headache, the problem of pain. Bottom as Pyramus, finding Thisbe's mauled cloak, asks:

> O, wherefore, nature, did'st thou lions frame,
> Since lion vile hath here deflowered my dear? (5.1.276-7)

There are plenty of unintentional *double-entendres* during 'Pyramus and Thisbe', but this one is more unfortunate than usual. We don't know if it's Quince's or Bottom's. Whichever, it glances back at the shocking intersection of carnal and immortal at the core of the main play.

It's beyond mortal wit to explain how Shakespeare could have made Quince's 'Pyramus and Thisbe' fold up so neatly inside *AMSND*. A moon presides over both plays, barriers separate lovers and leonine male power threatens ladies. To make a final diagram we might need, instead of two columns, a triangle with 'Pyramus and Thisbe' as a circle inside it. The miracle of *AMSND* could be explained only by its hero's intercourse with an alternative universe, which is the explanation we get. Kenneth Branagh once played Bottom as if Shakespeare were playing him, with Branagh made up to look as far as possible like the Droeshout portrait at the front of *The First Folio*. But that leaves out Quince the carpenter, who puts in place the structure that Bottom and the others fill in.

Of many striking films, Elijah Moshinsky's 1981 version for the BBC

Bardathon is romantic, and faithful to the text, though it looks very old-fashioned now. Everyone has his or her due weight. Hippolyta paces like a leopard in the opening scene and Titania is credibly angry over the loss of her Boy. The sweetness of Mendelssohn, as Puck wakes the lovers from their sleep, dissolves tragedy. The Mechanicals are among its great strengths, especially Quince, played by Geoffrey Palmer, who's gentlemanly, persuasive and respectful of his cast's talents. Even so, he's completely unnerved by his glamorous audience. His fluffing the Prologue and Theseus' unfunny dismissal of his play cause him an agony of shame. We're left on the dark side of hierarchy.

In Russell T. Davies' gay version, Theseus is absolute dictator in Athens after Hippolyta's defeat. She's about to be forced into marriage and marital rape. She enters bound, wheeled along like a suitcase and wearing a scold's bridle, a fixed leather and metal gag that from the Middle Ages and into Elizabethan times could be strapped onto argumentative women by their husbands or fathers. She hates Theseus; she and Titania have long been in love.

Titania has rejected Oberon, heterosexuality and male authority together. There's no need for a Changeling Boy here. She attributes to forces in the straight, competitive world run by men the breakdown in nature that fills the Nine Men's Morris up with mud. Maxine Peake puts a real charge into her climate change speech:

> Therefore the winds, piping to us in vain,
> As in revenge, have sucked up from the sea
> Contagious [toxic] fogs, which falling in the land
> Have every pelting [minor] river made so proud
> That they have overborne their continents. (2.1.88-92)

In Shakespeare, Titania never knows who set her up. When Davies' Titania wakes beside Bottom she understands everything, and tells Oberon, not Bottom, that she loathes his visage now.

Among the quick hormonal eddies that confuse the young lovers in the wood, Demetrius falls for Lysander, who looks as if he comes out of *Brideshead Revisited* and is fascinated if alarmed by Demetrius' advances. At the end Demetrius needs a second dose of the antidote to Cupid's love juice before he can return to full heterosexuality and marriage to Helena.

As in the Moshinsky version, in Davies' version too, Flute, who didn't want to play a woman, emerges unexpectedly as much the best actor. He's brilliant as Thisbe, mediating Quince's lines with feeling and stabbing himself realistically over Pyramus' body, redeeming the hopeless acting of the other Mechanicals, carrying the audience with him and earning wild applause.

As Thisbe enters for this last scene and Theseus is sneering at the play, he's struck down with a heart attack in full denial of art, imagination and everything else outside his own power. Staggering downstairs to the basement, too macho to call for medical help, he's confronted by the fairies he doesn't believe in, who gather round him with malicious curiosity. He sees at last the unbelievable truth, that he, the great Theseus, is dying, and they live, and will live on. Whatever we do with Shakespeare, love him, hate him, ignore him, get him, as here no doubt, completely wrong, one thing is certain: he will survive us.

Snout turns out to be an old rocker and plays – around four years before it was written – 'It Was a Lover and his Lass' for the final crazy marriage dance, in which everyone joins. The hated Athenian fascist flags are torn up and Flute, still dressed as Thisbe, comes out happily to a soldier of Theseus' guard.

Oberon is left as the spare prick at the weddings, while Hippolyta and Titania float together to the ceiling. Heterosexuality is not over, though; the four young lovers have reconnected with their original choices. But this is really a celebration of LGBTQ loves for Gay Pride Week, 2016. It's a version only slightly crazier than the original, whose premise is already that reason and love keep little company, and that night and imagination bring possibilities way outside the routine marriage option.

Davies has an interesting addition to a play with metamorphosis at its heart: he makes Cobweb a shapeshifter. She's embedded in Athens by Titania as a mortal market girl to find out what's happening to Hippolyta. Hurrying back to the dark wood with her news of the imminent forced marriage, she runs into Oberon, Puck and the male half of the fairy world. She's terrified, as any mortal would be. Magic seeds change her back to Cobweb again, when dressed and coiffed as trans, she frightens the men. Davies shows as empowering the change back from mortal to fairy, but more so is the implicit reassignment of her gender, from Shakespeare's male Cobweb to trans girl Cobweb in the film.

My favourite pairing at the end is Mistress Quince, the author of 'Pyramus and Thisbe', with Philostrate, Theseus' Head of Drama. Her star-struck expression when he asks her to dance is all we have to go on, but it seems to say she's more interested in getting another of her plays put on at court than in the erotic preoccupations of the other dancers. This is, I think, one of the great revisionings, where every unexpected change however radical feels authentic to the original.

It's a fun version, and of course a highly subjective one. *AMSND* is more malleable than almost any play of Shakespeare's, offering the greatest range of light and darkness in its staging. Directors can go mainly for the moonlight or mainly for the darkness. In imagining it as four stories of female disempowerment with Philomel brooding over three of them, I'm aware of the limitations of my reading. The cookie-cutter of criticism will always leave a lot outside its domesticated shapes, and never more so than here. The verse flees analysis. Not just in the beautiful Rackhamesque images, the 'I know a bank where the wild thyme grows' (2.1.249) passages, but in all the little throw-away lines:

> Every elf and fairy sprite
> Hop as light as bird from briar, (5.2.23-4)

Oberon orders his attendants as they flitter through the silent palace. Puck listens to the sounds outside as darkness returns:

> Now the hungry lion roars,
> And the wolf be-howls the moon. (5.2.1-2)

Male aggression against Diana, hard fought on both sides through *AMSND*, is distanced to a black canine silhouette against a silver crescent.

*

There are surprising resemblances between *Titus Andronicus* and *A Midsummer Night's Dream* apart from their reworking of, or allusion to, the myth of Philomel. Each play is a triumph of original plotting, full of visual and narrative symmetries, but *Titus* is like the dark obverse of a sunny *MSND* narrative tapestry. Each play is set in a version of the Ancient World and opens with a General bringing home a formidable enemy Queen as his prisoner; each Queen marries into the ruling family. Tamora almost achieves the establishment of a Goth matriarchy in Rome, her new husband is so easily manipulated. Hippolyta's Amazonian matriarchy is defeated before her play begins.

Each plot presents a contrast between apparent order and apparent rebellion, but the differences are less than first appear. In each, a father is ready to kill his child: Mutius and Lavinia, or Hermia. In each, a young woman out in the woods is threatened by rape or seduction, and by the hostility of another woman. There's a metamorphic sex act at the heart of both plays, hideous in the double rape of *Titus Andronicus*, though we can find the rape by the gang of three in *A Midsummer Night's Dream* an apotheosis for Bottom, a fusion with his creator.

A Demetrius rapes Lavinia in the woods; a Demetrius goes to the woods meaning to force Hermia back to the court and inflict marital rape on her. He also threatens to rape Helena. Titus carries out Lavinia's honour killing, endorsed by higher authority. Egeus intends Hermia's honour killing or lifelong confinement, which is endorsed but then overridden by higher authority. Aaron and Puck are supposedly servants, but both are loose cannon amusing themselves independently.

In each play there's a Changeling Boy whose presence undermines received law and custom. Tamara's son by Aaron and the white Changeling substituted for him threaten the concept of hereditary monarchy, and inheritance itself, since a king's or any man's apparent son may not in fact be his. Titania seems to have more claim than Oberon to her Changeling Boy, who was entrusted to her by her mortal friend, calling into question the absolute right fathers but not mothers had over the children of a marriage.

In each play a separate Ovidian fiction, a version of the Philomel story or the playlet 'Pyramus and Thisbe', is wound deftly among other threads of the plot.

Each play is substantially about acting: playing a public role or rehearsing a role for a play. In each Act Five, the audience joins with an audience on stage to watch a theatrical performance, either political acting by three generations of the Andronici family, or a tragic drama by the Mechanicals.

Both plays end in some uncertainty. Rome's future looks grimmer than ever under Lucius and his son; even the closing couplet grates. In their much happier play, Oberon and Titania bless the three marriage beds and the children to be born of them. But the educated theatre-goer, then anyone who'd been to grammar school, knows that Hippolyta's son by Theseus, Hippolytus, won't be ever-fortunate. When he's grown, his father's new wife Phaedra falls in love with him. He rejects her, and she accuses him to Theseus of raping her. Theseus calls down a curse on his son, which causes the sea-god Poseidon to overwhelm his chariot as he drives along the shore, and he's pulled out to sea and drowned. However, the theatre-goer is free to repress that incidental knowledge and just enjoy the magic ending.

*

The story of Philomel comes towards the end of Book Six of *Metamorphoses*. The story that begins Book Six is less well known. It's the story of Minerva, Goddess of (among other things) Arts and Crafts, and Arachne, a mortal woman. Both, like Bottom, are weavers. Before she's transformed to a bird and turns her pain into elegiac song, Philomel is also a weaver, creating such a realistic tapestry of her rape that her sister can recognise Tereus in it. Philomel, Minerva, Arachne, Bottom and Quince are all artists, Philomel in two media.

Arachne is vain and refuses to acknowledge a debt to Minerva in the beautiful artwork she produces. Minerva assumes the likeness of an old woman to come to earth and investigate, and they quarrel. The goddess reveals herself and challenges the mortal woman to a weaving contest. Arachne accepts.

Both produce scenes in subtly-graduated rainbow colours mixed with gold thread. Minerva weaves majestic gods and goddesses sitting on their thrones on Olympus, benign and just, with Jove presiding in the middle. She shows Neptune striking a rock with his trident, water gushing out, and she includes herself in her familiar helmet, striking the earth with her spear; an olive tree, her emblem, is growing from the spot. She puts in the corners four little designs of presumptuous mortals being punished, turned to mountains, birds or stone for offending the gods. A border of olive leaves completes the design.

Arachne ignores the warning signs. She weaves a vivid but disorderly universe where the gods are solely devoted to the rape of mortal women. Mostly her scenes are about Jove disguising himself as bull or swan or shepherd or shower of gold to get access to unsuspecting victims. But Apollo, Bacchus and Saturn are also depicted as rapists, while Minerva doesn't appear at all. Arachne's scene is surrounded with a border of flowers and ivy.

Minerva is furious. She attacks Arachne so violently with a shuttle, the humiliated mortal decides to hang herself with a rope. Minerva saves her life but transforms her to a spider, always hanging by a thread, her beauty shrunk to a fat black abdomen from which she can spin only cobwebs to remind her of the pictures she used to make. But Minerva's cruel revenge suggests that Arachne's vision of the universe may be the right one.

Shakespeare read this myth in *Metamorphoses* too. As a writer of tragedy and comedy, it would have interested him. Jonathan Bate proposes a later date than most editors for *Titus Andronicus*: 1596. If he's right, the two plays were written around the same time. Perhaps Ovid's Arachne myth suggested to Shakespeare a competition with himself: two contrasting plays woven from similar materials, an extreme and hideous tragedy, a comedy where all the quick bright things are allowed to escape confusion, for once.

Notes

[1]Publius Ovidius Naso, 43BC-17AD. Shakespeare probably read *Metamorphoses* first in William Golding's translation (1567), which was used in schools along with the original Latin poem. Because of my book's subject, I tend to refer mostly to sexual predation in Ovid, but he has plenty of other claims to our admiration, especially as an environmentalist who saw the wholeness of creation, the interdependency (though often cruel) of human, divine, animal and vegetative worlds.

[2]Quotations from *The Rape of Lucrece* (only) are taken from Katherine Duncan-Jones' and Henry Woudhuysen's *Shakespeare's Poems* (Bloomsbury, 2007). *Lucrece* is a poem many find difficult, and the Introduction and fuller notes in this edition are very helpful.

[3]Katherine Duncan-Jones, Introduction to *Shakespeare's Poems*, 2007, p33.

[4]Virgil, *The Aeneid*, Book 6, line 1,154.

[5]Though Ulysses had the idea for the wooden horse, Sinon volunteered to be the only

Greek ostensibly left behind by the Greek army as it pretended to depart so he could persuade King Priam of Troy to have the horse pulled into the city with its freight of Greeks inside it.

[6]Katherine Duncan-Jones, *Shakespeare's Poems,* note on line 1,776, p377.

[7]Lucius Annaeus Seneca, 4BC-65AD. His philosophy of Stoicism is generally understood as the quiet acceptance of personal misfortune and the control or suppression of the passions, especially grief and anger. But he also writes about the importance of pity and kindness.

[8]On 20 September 1586, seven convicted conspirators in the Babington Plot, a Catholic plot to kill Elizabeth and put Mary, Queen of Scots on the throne, were hanged, drawn and quartered, including Antony Babington. The next day seven more associated conspirators were allowed to die by hanging only, on Elizabeth's orders. There may have been some adverse reaction by Londoners to the butchery of the previous day.

[9]*A Day in the Death of Joe Egg* (1967), by Peter Nichols, is a play about the grief of having a severely disabled child.

[10]Jonathan Bate, Introduction to *Titus Andronicus,* Arden Edition, p2.

[11]Jonathan Bate, *Titus Andronicus,* Arden Edition, footnote to 5.3.46, p267.

[12]Lucius Metrius Plutarchus, 46AD-circa 119AD. Shakespeare's debt to his Roman Histories can best be traced through Geoffrey Bullough's *Narrative and Dramatic Sources of Shakespeare's Plays: The Roman Plays,* 1957.

[13]Arthur Rackham, 1867-1939, was a famous and influential book illustrator, including for *A Midsummer Night's Dream,* where the fairies and woods are richly imagined and only slightly scary.

[14]Bottom is vaguely remembering St Paul's *First Epistle to the Corinthians,* Chapter 2, verse 9: Eye hath not seen, nor ear heard, neither have entered into the heart of man, the things which God hath prepared for them that love him.

[15]Anne Barton, Introduction to *A Midsummer Night's Dream,* in *The Riverside Shakespeare,* p219.

5

'IN THE SUBURBS'

On some early and late Comedies including *The Taming of the Shrew*; the second History Cycle (*Richard II, Henry IV, Part 1* and *Part 2,* and *Henry V*); the Roman Plays; the 'Problem' Plays (*Measure For Measure, All's Well That Ends Well* and *Troilus and Cressida*); *Hamlet; Love's Labour's Lost;* and *King Lear*

WHAT KIND OF SOCIETY CONDONES HONOUR killing? It can't be considered in isolation from the social customs it's embedded in, growing as it does out of lesser misogynies. Shakespeare creates worlds where men's treatment of women falls short of murder, rape or long-term confinement, but where the marital or family dynamic typically denigrates wives and daughters. These plot situations are sometimes funny and sometimes fatal, the consequences ranging from minor annoyance through domestic grief to death or suicide and the downfall of the state. In tracing the topic through many plays, I'm very conscious of how much in the life of each must be omitted.

It would be tedious to try to nail every instance of misogyny in the *Complete Works*. We'd never stop. I'll look at some of the more interesting examples of women ignored, silenced or consigned to the suburbs of men's lives. 'In the suburbs' is a phrase used in *Julius Caesar* by Brutus' wife Portia. The suburbs of Elizabethan London, especially on the South Bank, were the sites of the brothels, because they were outside the city limits and the control of mayors and church officials.

Brutus is involved in a plot to assassinate Julius Caesar; Portia hears the conspirators coming to their house at night, and she's observed her husband's changed manner. She begs him:

> By all your vows of love, and that great vow [marriage]

Which did incorporate and make us one,
That you unfold to me, your self, your half,
Why you are heavy [worried], and what men tonight
Have had resort to you – for here have been
Some six or seven, who did hide their faces
Even from darkness.
Brutus: Kneel not, gentle Portia.
Portia: I should not need if you were gentle Brutus (...)
Am I your self
But as it were in sort or limitation [after a fashion or within limits]?
To keep with you at meals, comfort your bed,
And talk to you sometimes? Dwell I but in the suburbs
Of your good pleasure? If it be no more,
Portia is Brutus' harlot, not his wife.
Brutus: You are my true and honourable wife,
As dear to me as are the ruddy drops
That visit my sad heart. (2.1.271-89)

In response to the accusation that he's treating her like a prostitute, he promises to confide in her. But he goes out with a conspirator a few minutes later, and it's not clear if he ever talks to her about the assassination, planned for later that day, or if he leaves her for the last time without keeping his promise.

'Suburbs' suggest now not brothels but places of marginalisation, outside the exciting, metropolitan centres of government, and this too is implicit in Portia's and other women's complaints. The husband/wife or father/daughter relationships where women are left on the side-lines, played as pawns or banished altogether don't just 'reflect' the position of women in Shakespeare's time or in whatever period a play is set. They're constructed as wasteful or self-defeating by the way he develops the plot.

Time and war are traditionally the enemies of love. Almost anyone acknowledges that truism, in Shakespeare's plays or out of them. But uniquely, at least for his own time, Shakespeare creates misogyny even more than time or war as the enemy of love and often as the path to death. This is true of *Othello*, *Cymbeline* and *The Winters' Tale*. Without the Watch, who do their jobs, however absurdly, it would be true of *Much Ado*, with Claudio or Benedick dead, Hero confined for life.

By misogyny I mean an entrenched image of women as frivolous, stupid or weak, and therefore prone to infidelity. Within this mindset, seductive or 'bewitching' women must be avoided, or they'll tempt men away from an honourable course in life. Misogyny sees women as existing for the benefit of men, creatures to be carefully monitored if they're to fulfil their proper function. Such stereotypes often govern women's thinking as well as men's. These preconceptions motivate many more characters than those already discussed. Acts of blatant misogyny kick-start plays of very different kinds, for instance *Love's Labour's Lost* and *King Lear.*

In *The Merry Wives of Windsor*, Alice Ford is unhappy about her husband's irrational jealousy. In *The Comedy of Errors*, Adriana is first neglected then suspected by her husband. Both plays are farcical and can be very fast-paced; both show how successfully jealous husbands can be played for laughs. In 1968, Ian Richardson as Ford in *The Merry Wives* developed a frenzy like Leontes' while trying to police his wife. One critic attacked him for passing through the play without relation to any other character, but this felt right for the production. He became a demented whirlwind of suspicion, ripping himself out of venal, easy-going Windsor by the force of his own paranoia. Very early in the history of Shakespeare on TV, Brian Rix, playing Antipholus of Syracuse, produced *The Comedy of Errors* as a Whitehall Farce, a popular form of theatre in the 1950s and 60s. He captivated a lot of viewers who mightn't previously have thought themselves Shakespeareans. Here too a husband starts to doubt his wife, but with more excuse than Ford, when his identical twin comes to town.

Farce as much as comedy may have its repressed tragedy; both plays have some latent sadness in the wives' inability to make their husbands respect them. But each woman has a close friend and confidante. Windsor in *The Merry Wives* is full of incomers, from the court, from Wales and France, and it's full of competing dialects. Mistress Quickly's malapropisms are more outrageous than ever, and Pistol is still trying to talk like a hero out of Christopher Marlowe. But Alice Ford and Meg Page have known each other all their lives, speak alike and understand each other's problems. Falstaff writes identical love letters to them, which they compare:

> Mistress Ford: It [Falstaff's letter to her] would give eternal food to his [Ford's] jealousy.

> Mistress Page: Why, look where he [Ford] comes, and my goodman too. He's [Page is] as far from jealousy as I am from giving him cause, and that, I hope, is an immeasurable distance.
> Mistress Ford: You are the happier woman. (2.1.76-80)

They've talked about this often. Alice is right, and Ford is soon enraged:

> What a damned epicurean [sensual] rascal is this [Falstaff]! My heart is ready to crack with impatience. Who says this is improvident [baseless] jealousy? My wife hath sent to him, the hour is fixed, the match is made. Would any man have thought this? See the hell of having a false woman! (2.2.220-24)

He brings witnesses, the town's prominent citizens, to try to catch Alice in the act. Antipholus of Ephesus risks damaging his wife's reputation in his fury. As the wives are innocent, no obvious harm is done. But suppose they were guilty, or appeared guilty, what would the men do? What would they want to do? Each husband is jealous of a wife too good for him, as in the four honour-killing plays already considered. Ford is Leontes rendered harmless and ludicrous by relocation to a gossipy English town – though conversely, Antigonus recognises a farcical element in Leontes' tragic jealousy.

The Merry Wives are close enough to start Ford suspecting a lesbian relationship:

> Ford: I think if your husbands were dead you two would marry.
> Mistress Page: Be sure of that – two other husbands. (3.2.10-11)

They're cool enough to deflect the accusations thrown at them and have fun at their husbands' and Falstaff's expense. Adriana has her sister Luciana as her advisor.

The women survive through sense and (essential for farce or semi-farce characters) limitless initiative. Falstaff has lost most of his spark by *The Merry Wives*; he's no longer as funny as he was in the *Henry IV* plays. Reputedly this was a play ordered up by Elizabeth I, who wanted to see Falstaff in love, but the fat knight's aim is still primarily money rather than seduction. He hopes to 'gull' Meg and Alice, that is, to deceive them by a good story. He assumes they'll be easy to seduce because they're confident and sociable, and he pretends to fall in love with both to get at their husbands' money. It never occurs to him they'll compare notes. Together they fill the role of Hal in the *Henry IV* plays, becoming the witty centre of plotting. They punish Falstaff more cruelly than Hal does, at least before he's King, and make Ford acknowledge his injustice to Alice with such shame, apparently going down on his knees to her, that his friend Page is embarrassed for him.

Apart from Falstaff's grotesque wooing, which finds him taking refuge from Ford in a laundry basket kept for the very dirty linen that needs bleaching, then getting tipped into the Thames, the action centres on the projected marriage of the Pages' daughter Anne, whose parents have conflicting aims for her. Her father wants Slender for his gentility and expectations, her mother the pompous French physician Dr Caius for his money and influence. Sixteen-year-old Anne makes her own choice of an impoverished gentleman of the court, Fenton. Mistress Quickly claims close friendship with her and is making money fast by acting as sole go-between for all three suitors.

Fenton admits his initial motive was her dowry, but he's come to love her, and will risk Page's disinheriting her. A sensible girl, Anne is satisfied with that. But they add romance when she meets him at night in Windsor Great Park and marries him in a secret ceremony. All the characters end up at Herne's Oak[1], most of them to inflict on Falstaff his grand finale of humiliation, which the two rejected suitors must share when they're almost married to large awkward boys dressed as Anne.

A critical focus on honour killing and Mosaic law makes lines hitherto unnoticed, at least by me, leap out of the text. When Anne thinks she may have to marry Doctor Caius, she says:

> Alas, I had rather be set [buried to the waist] quick [alive] i' th' earth
> And bowled to death with turnips. (3.4.79-80)

She's not fanciful, and this isn't from a dream though it must be coming from somewhere, but a search of the internet and various editions' notes provides no clue to its provenance. In church she'll have heard of women stoned to death, but not turnipped to death. Turnips could be as deadly as stones. Was there rough-and-ready rural punishment for disobedient daughters in Renaissance England? Or is she just humorously transferring Old Testament laws to an English market town?

Fenton's final defence of Anne's elopement continues to urge a woman's or even a sixteen-year-old girl's free choice of husband as the happiest ending:

> Th' offence [marrying for love against her parents' wishes] is holy that she hath committed,
> Since therein she doth evitate [avoid] and shun
> A thousand irreligious cursed hours
> Which forced marriage would have brought upon her. (5.5.193-8)

The two middle-aged couples have their troubles, major ones in the case of the Fords. Anne and Fenton are lightly characterised. But consensual marriage as a sacrament and forced marriage as sacrilege are asserted more plainly here than anywhere in the emotionally deeper Comedies.

While *The Merry Wives* celebrates its women, *The Comedy of Errors* undermines them. Adriana is the suspected wife, though at the beginning she's the jealous partner in the marriage. Her sister advises her to ignore her husband's absences and reported affairs, but then it's all right for her, she isn't married, as Adriana sourly points out. Luciana tackles her brother-in-law squarely about his failures as a husband:

> If you did wed my sister for her wealth
> Then for her wealth's sake treat her with more kindness. (3.2.6-7)

But she merely advises him to conceal his affairs, since she doesn't think he'll end them, and she urges compliance with his wishes on Adriana. Her argument is based on an appeal to the old idea of the 'Great Chain of Being', the concept of a divine hierarchy in which everyone and everything has its place in a vertical chain leading from stones up to God. It's a belief dating from classical times, but it became Christianised through the later Middle Ages and gained in force under the Tudors. In the social order, God has set masters above servants, husbands above women and children. Men, Luciana tells Adriana:

> Lord[s] of the wide world and wild watery seas
> Indued with intellectual sense and souls,
> Of more pre-eminence than fish and fowls
> Are masters to their females, and their lords.
> Then let your [married women's] will attend on their [husbands'] accords [wishes]. (2.1.21-25)

Against this ancient understanding of the universe, Adriana opposes the new and radical ideal of Puritan marriage, one we find in Portia's equally anachronistic speech, quoted earlier. In Adriana's impassioned plea to the man she supposes her husband, Antipholus of Ephesus, she begs him to recognise their unity as equal spiritual partners. Her handling of religious and philosophical concepts is impressive. She refers to God's creation of Adam and Eve as one flesh, the basis for St Paul's mystical comparison of husband and wife to Christ's union with his church, the Bride of Christ, in Chapter Five of his *Epistle to the Ephesians*. She urges Antipholus to imagine how he would feel if she broke her marriage vows to him:

> How comes it now, my husband, O how comes it
> That thou art then estranged from thyself?
> Thy 'self' I call it, being strange to me,
> That undividable, incorporate,
> Am better than thy dear self's better part.
> Ah, do not tear thyself away from me;
> For know, my love, as easy mays't thou fall [let fall]
> A drop of water in the breaking gulf [shore where waves are breaking],
> And take unmingled thence that drop again
> Without addition or diminishing,
> As take from me thyself, and not me too.
> How dearly would it touch thee to the quick
> Should'st thou but hear I were licentious (...) ?
> Keep then fair league and truce with thy true bed,
> I live unstained, thou undishonoured. (2.2.116-43)

But during her very long speech, she's clinging round the knees of the wrong Antipholus, Antipholus of Syracuse, who's already fallen for her sister and whose comic mystification undermines her eloquent performance. The Abbess, a misogynist who will turn out to be her mother-in-law, leads Adriana on to confess more aggression towards her husband than she ever felt, then berates her for failing to be a pattern wife – though Luciana comes to her defence here. The Abbess, long single and in holy orders, supports the sharp end of St Paul's teaching on marriage, that wives must submit themselves to their husbands as to the Lord.

But her bias against Adriana is obvious, and she will herself soon have to emerge from the convent to become an obedient wife again, and mother to grown-up twins. The troubles of the marriage bed, as Luciana calls the problems that keep her single, are mostly played for laughs. Adriana will have to put up with what she's got, but Luciana and Antipholus of Syracuse may have a happier marriage, since he falls for her, not her dowry – though he falls for her as a mermaid, a Lorelei pulling him into deep waters. He's physically identical with his twin, but more likeable, more self-questioning and affectionate.

The farce's serious theme lies in its 'Who am I?' quest, its Syracusans' longing for identity, which Antipholus finds at last in his recovered family and Luciana, his servant Dromio in his new-found twin and his escape with bachelorhood intact from the clutches of the horrific Nell. She doesn't appear on stage, but she's the more alarming for that. She's described by Dromio of Syracuse to his master in jokes that come down from the comic riddles of Anglo-Saxon times and would go on through the Music Hall to post-war stand-ups like Bernard Manning[2]:

> Antipholus of Syracuse: what's her name?
> Dromio of Syracuse: Nell, sir. But her name and three quarters – that's an ell and three quarters [45 inches] – will not measure her from hip to hip.
> Antipholus of Syracuse: then she bears some breadth?
> Dromio of Syracuse: No longer from head to foot than from hip to hip. She is spherical, like a globe. I could find out countries in her.
> Antipholus of Syracuse: in what part of her body stands Ireland?
> Dromio of Syracuse: Marry [indeed], sir, in her buttocks. I found it out by the bogs. (3.2.106-15)

And so on. Both Syracusans almost miss their chance to find out who they are when they try to flee Ephesus to escape women threatening to engulf them. Nell's spherical body contains all women, Adriana's neediness, Luciana's scary sexiness, the Abbess' bossiness.

The twin Dromios are slaves, battered about the head by anyone who happens to be in a bad temper, starting with Adriana. But they find equality and family affection with each other, and they have the last words and the happiest ending. When Dromio of Syracuse politely indicates that his twin should precede him off the stage, Dromio of Ephesus replies,

> Nay, then, thus:
> We came into the world like brother and brother,
> And now let's go hand in hand, not one before another. (5.1.425-7)

This play's sympathies lie with them, if anywhere; it yields with difficulty to a feminist reading.

The Taming of the Shrew is of course controversial, even hated for its denigration of women, but sometimes explained as the work of a new dramatist out to please a misogynist audience. Petruccio ignores Kate's refusal to marry him, humiliates her in public at their wedding, denies her the new clothes she longs for, starves her and deprives her of sleep, the last two considered torture when inflicted on prisoners now. He forces her to see the world as he pretends to and describe it in his terms, a perverse variation on the female silencing in other plays. The title is deeply misogynistic: a woman is identified with a small rodent, who becomes legally the property of her husband, like his horse. Behind the quick wit of a funny play we may see the real history of thousands of years of domestic abuse, which *Shrew* ably endorses.

The counter-arguments are plain enough: Kate's unhappiness and isolation before Petruccio comes to Padua; the immediate attraction between them as the two most intelligent people in town, however eccentric; her desire from the first to marry, clear from her jealousy of her sister, Bianca. He never beats her like husbands in other 'shrew' stories or popular ballads, admittedly a small concession – in fact she does the beating, of him and her sister.

And he doesn't try to consummate the marriage until they've reached some accord (his) and she's decided she likes him. The delay is unexpected to her and the audience, which is waiting to see what happens at this crucial moment, as Kate hasn't consented to the marriage. He's thought about it from the start. A newly married couple of the status to afford a celebration spent the first night, usually longer, at the bride's family home, where the bride was put to bed in a semi-public way and the whole household knew what was going on, short of actually being there. Instead of this claustrophobic and vaguely incestuous arrangement, Petruccio forcibly removes Kate directly after the ceremony and takes her to his own house. He's breaking with traditional wedding customs, asserting marriage as an individual rather than a family matter. He describes how he'll throw the bedclothes around on their wedding night to keep her awake, then goes on:

> Ay, and amid this hurly I intend
> That all is done in reverend care of her. (4.1.172-3)

This is as far from his usual tone as her long final speech of surrender is from hers, and because it's in soliloquy, we can trust he's not acting. They're back in her father's house again when she decides she wants him, but by this time the attention is on Bianca as the bride.

It's a play about acting and deceit, beginning with the Induction, the lead-in to the main play. A beggar, Christopher Sly, who seems to come from somewhere near Stratford, is duped by an idle Lord into believing he's rich and propertied with a devoted wife, played by the Lord's page in disguise. Sly is reluctant to credit the story at first, but soon begins to speak in blank verse to mark his rise in the social scale. A troupe of passing actors agrees to put on a play for Sly, a play called *The Taming of the Shrew.*

In this play too, except for Kate (possibly) and Baptista Minola (Kate and Bianca's father), everybody is lying or pretending to be someone they're not, or both. Petruccio is frank about his motive for marriage, money, though as B.J. and Mary Sokol explain in their *Shakespeare, Law and Marriage*, he's unusually generous in the financial arrangements he makes for Kate. But he pretends at times to be even more dogmatic and irrational than he is. Kate doesn't appear to deceive him; her speech at the end, however unpalatable to most women, sounds sincere.

But has she merely learned to act as a conventional woman, like the Lord's page-boy in the Induction? Has she recognised, anticipating Simone de Beauvoir, that one is not born but one becomes a woman[3], that femininity is as much a construct of male power and the state as a boy's playing a girl is a construct of dramatic convention? If so, why not choose a popular role and play it enthusiastically? Perhaps she's decided she might as well take the part of the obedient wife, since she wants a life and a house of her own. Her real capitulation comes when she outdoes Petruccio in the crazy pretence that the sun is the moon and old Vincentio is a beautiful young girl. She parodies Petruccio's claim, in itself parodic, to mansplain the world for her. As Vincentio recognises, she's a 'merry mistress [Mrs]' (4.6.52) now, enjoying and competing with her husband's absurdities.

Bianca is the best actor; she dupes the audience as thoroughly as she dupes her suitors, including Lucentio, the one she marries. Obedient to her father, demure with other men, for whom she's the Ideal Girl, she pleases the audience too by her elopement, showing just the right amount of spirit.

But at her wedding supper, in the long scene that ends the play, she's drinking enough to keep falling asleep. Woken by the fights going on around the table, she joins in the men's 'horn' jokes, and asks in mock-indignation when Petruccio teases her:

> Am I your bird? I mean to shift my bush,
> And then pursue me as you draw your bow.
> You are welcome all. (5.2.46-8)

She compares his teasing to a hunter shooting an arrow at a bird in a bush, and says she's going to sit somewhere else. She leaves the room. Harmless enough, apparently, but it's a phallic joke, and 'bush' meant pubic hair in the 1590s, as now; it's a pun more subtle and disreputable than the men's. Her 'welcome all' is ambiguous. Welcome to my wedding (belatedly), or welcome to pursue her and her bush? When her new husband bets on her obedience, expecting her to come when he sends for her, he loses his money. She tells him, 'The more fool you, for laying [betting] on my duty.' (5.2.127) The Shrew will be Bianca, not just disobedient but unfaithful as well. The last-minute crossover confuses the issue of which personality-type a man can trust. Not necessarily the sweet, quiet one.

A last-minute reversal of audience perception is known as a reveal in film. A stunning example is angel-faced Jezzie in *Along Came A Spider*[4], though as her name can only be Jezebel, perhaps we shouldn't be too surprised. Shakespeare seldom uses the reveal strategy, his audience generally knows what's going on, but in *The Taming of the Shrew* he accomplishes a good reveal. Bianca's name gives nothing away.

Ann Thompson's New Cambridge edition has a helpful introduction to the difficult textual problems (there's another play, *The Taming of A Shrew*, of around the same date, causing a lot of confusion), the sources and the criticism. She shows how the 'Kate' plot comes from a mainly English, folkloric tradition, the 'Bianca' plot from Italian and ultimately classical sources, and how they relate to each other. Seen through the innocent eyes of Lucentio, Kate is a 'wench', Bianca a 'maid', true to their respective earthy or refined plot sources. Though Professor Thompson sees some overlap, notably that Bianca's suitors are also interested in money, she stops short of suggesting that at the end the binaries of maid/wench, good girl/bad girl collapse into each other. But these categories have proved false; they've misled all the men.

In the textual notes, Professor Thompson acknowledges Bianca's *double-entendres* but explains them as preparing us for her subsequent behaviour when she refuses to come when Lucentio calls her. She doesn't discuss Bianca's surprising reveal in her Introduction or put much emphasis on Petruccio's decision to wait until Kate signals her willingness to go to bed with him, which she does in her final speech, of course, whatever else she means by it. But we should recognise that in this important respect he's making an intelligent effort to be a good husband beyond the customs of his time.

After Bianca's come-on to her new brother-in-law, a final attempt to hurt her sister, he's disconcerted for a moment. Tranio takes the opportunity to tease him with the servants' gossip: ''Tis thought your deer [Kate] does hold you at a bay [keep you at a distance]'. (5.2.56) Petruccio admits to being galled a little by a public insinuation that would embarrass most men, but he doesn't say the decision not to consummate the marriage at once is his. He knows the others wouldn't understand it, since a man was expected to have sex on his wedding night regardless of the bride's wishes. A marriage wasn't legally valid until it was consummated, which is why Kate's father is still worried; he doesn't want her returned on his hands. These customs must have led to some wretched marriages for couples who hardly knew each other before the ceremony.

Any woman with a good word to say for Petruccio invites identification as a running dog of totalitarian patriarchy. And it's true his behaviour is often diabolical, especially to his servants. He turns the wedding ceremony into a riot and attacks the officiating clergy, but then marriage in Padua is a matter of selling off cows, the oldest and least valuable first to trade up the price of the younger, a sale the church cheerfully endorses as usual. Not enough is made, I think, of his abstention from sex with her, perhaps because he parodies it himself with his (reported) sermon on chastity to her on their wedding night. *Shrew* seems to be turning into an emotionally deeper play at its close, leaving riot behind and becoming comparable to later plots where a woman escapes arranged marriage and consequent marital rape. Kate is already in an arranged marriage, but Petruccio waives the man's marital right to rape her. Within the archaic and brutish 'shrew' vehicle, a different take on women's feelings is emerging. Petruccio's crude antics mask an unexpected decision, that marital sex should be consensual.

The battling Kate-and-Petruccio relationship was to appear in more glamorous forms throughout Shakespeare's career, in Biron and Rosaline, Kate and Hotspur, Beatrice and Benedick, Antony and Cleopatra.

There are many comedic variants on the theme of arranged/forced marriage versus marriage of choice. Simonides in *Pericles* and Prospero in *The Tempest* ostensibly try to prevent a daughter marrying her lover while all the time hoping for a marriage outcome. There's a certain claustrophobia about both these love affairs: young people who think they're rebelling are doing just what an indulgent father wants.

Some aspects of *Pericles* are more than claustrophobic. The Governor of Mytilene hears Marina advertised for sale and visits the brothel where she's forcibly held. 'Here comes the Lord Lysimachus, disguised,' (4.6.12 -13) the Bawd drily observes. Disguise was supposedly impenetrable on the stage, but Lysimachus is such a regular customer, a time-honoured dramatic convention gives up in disgust.

His 'trial' of Marina's chastity follows; she successfully rebuffs his attempts at rape and escapes the brothel, but with the establishment of her royal blood he decides to marry her, and does so with her father's and her own consent. This is a plotline at odds with all the other women's trials and sophisticated analyses of honour considered so far. *Pericles*' constructions of vice and virtue are extreme and archaic, from its trophy-heads-on-spikes opening to its patronising happy-marriage close; but these are the functions of its *faux*-medievalism. The couples in *The Tempest* and *Pericles* lack the tension between most Shakespearean lovers. Ferdinand and Miranda are Edenic, perfect, but like Pericles and Thaisa they're atoms in a great cosmic drive of time and space that brings them together for its own purposes, not theirs.

Not that either play lacks its own brand of realism. *Pericles* flaunts its artifice, but then the competitive mother who tries to murder her daughter's talented friend, the desolation of Thaisa's (apparent) death on shipboard –

> A terrible childbed hast thou had, my dear,
> No light, no fire (...) (3.1.55-6)

and the brisk business of a 1600s London brothel come crashing through the antique charm of the medieval poet John Gower's narration.

*

As noted earlier, Shakespeare wrote his two series of History Plays out of the chronological order of history. The first tetralogy, *Henry VI, Parts 1, 2* and *3*, and *Richard III*, was popular and called for a sequel, but it would have been dangerous to continue with a *Henry VII*. Elizabeth's grandfather briefly appears as the impossibly saintly winner at Bosworth at the end of *Richard III*, but Shakespeare couldn't risk dramatising his performance as King.

Instead he did the prequel, and cast back in time to the late 1390s, to Richard II's last years and his murder. He continued with two plays about Richard's cousin, the usurper Henry Bolingbroke, *Henry IV, Part 1* and *Part 2*. The last in this series, *Henry V*, tells how the usurper's son attempts to re-unite England through war with France. It ends with his victory at Agincourt, his marriage to Catherine of France, his early death and the Accession of his baby son. This brings us back to Henry V's funeral where Shakespeare first started in *Henry VI, Part 1*. In this second cycle he again follows mainly Raphael Holinshed's *Chronicles*.

Here the women are less combative, some may feel less interesting than in the Early Histories. But they have more depth if less energy, and their perceptiveness from the margins is subtly dramatised. Richard II and his Queen (unnamed in the play) have no children. In the 1390s as in the 1590s when Elizabeth was growing old, it was a dangerous situation. Richard is young but without a direct heir and unlikely to produce one. Shakespeare represents him as gay; the favourites who help him spend the country's money are feared and despised by the old guard, the royal family and nobility.

Richard II's father, Edward the Black Prince, died before his father, Edward III, leaving Richard to inherit, aged ten, on Edward III's death. *Richard II* begins over 20 years later. If Richard dies one of his uncles will succeed to the throne. John of Gaunt, Duke of Lancaster is frail, but he has a formidable son, Henry Bolingbroke. The Duke of York is also a possible successor with a grown-up, competent son, Aumerle. Another of the royal uncles, Thomas,

Duke of Gloucester, has just died in mysterious circumstances. Historically the heir was Edmund Mortimer, Earl of March, a descendant of Edward III's third son, but he doesn't appear in this play. In the opening scene two young and powerful members of the royal family, Bolingbroke and Thomas Mowbray, Duke of Norfolk, confront each other, calling each other traitors in front of the King and court. Richard orders a trial by single combat, though the specific cause of the quarrel remains unclear. We must wait for the second scene to understand it.

The newly-widowed Duchess of Gloucester complains to her brother-in-law John of Gaunt that her husband was killed by Mowbray on Richard's orders; Gaunt already knows that. The historical Richard had a lot of old scores to settle for the way he was treated by his uncles during his long minority when they governed the country and killed off many of his friends. But Shakespeare doesn't include the back-story, offering no excuse for Richard's hostility to them.

In the opening scene, then, Bolingbroke appears to be challenging Mowbray, but it's really Richard he's challenging, accusing him of ordering Mowbray to have Gloucester murdered. Bolingbroke has everything to gain from discrediting Richard, by whose impeachment he might himself become King after his father. The Duchess of Gloucester urges Gaunt to avenge her husband, to make a public accusation of Richard. Gaunt refuses: the stability of the country must come before family feeling or private justice.

The Duchess is old but her grief is passionate, though she struggles to convey it through formal images of holy relics and the family tree. At the time of her husband's death she still sees him as he was when young, flourishing still but fragile as glass under Richard's tyranny:

> Edward [III]'s seven sons, whereof thyself [Gaunt] art one,
> Were as seven vials of his sacred blood,
> Or seven fair branches springing from one root.
> Some of those seven are dead by nature's course,
> Some of those branches by the destinies cut.
> But Thomas, my dear lord, my life, my Gloucester,
> One vial full of Edward's sacred blood,
> One flourishing branch of his most royal root,
> Is cracked, and all the precious liquor spilt,

Is hacked down, and his summer leaves all faded,
By envy's hand, and murder's bloody axe. (1.2.11-21)

The Duchess appears to be ignoring the public good in her appeal to Gaunt to oppose tyranny. She speaks persuasively for putting justice above obedience to the King and goes on to add, practically, that Gaunt himself may be next on Richard's kill-list, so he should act fast to save himself. Gaunt's refusal to risk civil war by siding with his son Bolingbroke against his nephew Richard appears admirably selfless, since it means he must condone his brother's murder and see his son exiled. Gaunt believes in the concept of the King as God's Deputy on earth, someone who can't be judged by his subjects, someone whom only God can remove. The play questions this concept, and especially what can or should be done when the monarch becomes a murderer or thief.

Predictably, the murder of Gloucester isn't Richard's last crime. Before long, when Gaunt is dead, Richard seizes his lands and property, giving Bolingbroke an excuse to head a rebellion and ensuring civil war after all. Gaunt refuses to be influenced by the Duchess of Gloucester, but later developments show her demand was worth his taking seriously, even considering only the public good: if Richard had been checked firmly at this point, the civil war might never have happened.

In 'Mutant Scenes and "Minor" Conflicts in *Richard II*', Molly Smith points out that 'the play itself neither condemns nor trivialises the Duchess's request for a revenge play.'[5] She shows how later the dying Gaunt's accusation of Richard echoes the accusations of the Duchess; he has been more impressed than he showed. The Duchess ages even during her short scene. After her failed appeal, she realises there's nothing she can do to change events, forgets what she was going to say, contradicts herself and wanders off to die.

The scene is sometimes cut, leaving the audience struggling to understand what the challenges between Bolingbroke and Mowbray were about. By removing a seemingly superfluous old woman, directors ignore the way Shakespeare shows national politics invading the intimate reaches of a family, and how the women's judgments tend to operate compared to the men's. The women speak for families broken by tyranny and for human justice, rather than from devotion to an ideal nation-state.

The single combat between Bolingbroke and Mowbray is set to go ahead. But after the formal challenge and response in the lists at Coventry, Richard cancels the fight before it starts and exiles both men. He wants to get rid of Bolingbroke, who's strong, popular and too close to the throne; he looks like an ideal King, until he's King. For Richard, the consequences of a tournament win by Bolingbroke are not worth risking. For the medieval age – and *Richard II* opens in a richly medieval world – God intervened to ensure that the man telling the truth was the winner. Richard exiles Mowbray too, who knows at first hand about Richard's guilt in Gloucester's murder.

The medieval world of the opening scenes is corrupt and violent but beautiful, with its formal challenge and counter-challenge by the heralds, its roll-call of ancient Lancastrian and Norfolk titles – though Joan of Arc might have found something to say here. Then monarchy and warfare change their style, and by the end Bolingbroke's men are bringing home his enemies' heads at their saddlebows.

Bolingbroke crowns himself Henry IV, but usurpation is not as easy as he thought. As the aged Bishop of Carlisle foresees at Richard's forced Abdication, the country won't heal. Because of Bolingbroke's rebellion, English blood, he says, will manure the ground for generations:

> Disorder, horror, fear and mutiny
> Shall here inhabit and this land be called
> The field of Golgotha and dead men's skulls. (4.1.134-6)

The Bishop of Carlisle publicly challenges Bolingbroke's right to judge Richard, braving his own arrest for treason; in this, Shakespeare followed history. Carlisle's speech has additional authority because some of the audience will have already seen the horrors he prophesies in the early History Plays. He reasserts the concept of divine kingship we've doubted while watching Richard's guilt and incompetence; but he's old, like the others (apart from Richard) who believe in divine right. England now fractures, and Bolingbroke is increasingly beleaguered and desperate.

Surprising as it may seem, the contemporary audience was probably more sympathetic to Bolingbroke than to Richard. Sir Gelly Meyrick, steward and supporter of Robert Devereux, Earl of Essex, commissioned *Richard II* (c.1595) to be revived just before Essex's 1601 rebellion against Elizabeth's inner circle, in the expectation of raising support or accustoming Londoners to a monarch's overthrow, if only a staged one. The Essex rebellion failed, but an Elizabethan audience was not necessarily as convinced of the divine right of monarchs as we might expect. It was a view held most firmly by monarchs and their dependents. Elizabeth is reported as saying, 'I am Richard, know ye not that?'[6]

As Stephen Greenblatt notes[7] in *Tyrant: Shakespeare on Power*, Shakespeare's Lord Chamberlain's Men were questioned about the performance and maintained they'd done it only because they'd been paid extra as was standard for a revival, knowing nothing of the rebellion. This was almost certainly true: it would have been crazy to tell them, given the reward any one of them could get for informing – though in fact Robert Cecil already knew of it. Meyrick, who contacted and paid them, was hanged, drawn and quartered, though presumably more for taking a leading part in the rebellion than for commissioning the performance. Still, the actors, possibly Shakespeare too, may have had a bad time before their plea was accepted.

There are many responses to Bolingbroke's return to England. The Duke of York also knows that Richard ordered Mowbray to kill his and Gaunt's brother Gloucester, but he still makes a muddled, increasingly hopeless effort to hold the country for Richard, who's in Ireland when Bolingbroke returns from exile ostensibly to claim his father's confiscated lands. The Percys, that is, the Earl of Northumberland, his brother the Earl of Worcester and Northumberland's son Harry Percy, nicknamed Hotspur, quickly see loot for themselves in a rebellion. The only disinterested reaction is a gardener's.

Richard's Queen is fictional, though loosely based on the historical Richard's first wife Anne, who was his ally and best friend during his minority but died young. The Queen at the time of Bolingbroke's rising was Isabella of France, who was ten. Shakespeare had, then, no need based on truth to history to create a part for an adult Queen at all, any more than he needed to create the Duchess of Gloucester's conversation with Gaunt, and it's interesting that he does so. In the scene before the Queen first speaks, we hear that Bolingbroke is on his way back from France, in defiance of Richard's sentence of exile and before his lands are seized, though he quickly gives that seizure as the cause of his return. Northumberland is gathering support for him and planning Richard's overthrow. So far nobody at court or on Richard's side has heard of this. But the Queen senses something frightening in the air.

As her scene opens, Richard has just gone to Ireland and the Queen is left with a skeleton court, including Bushy and Bagot; Green enters later. These are Richard's favourites or gay lovers, the caterpillars of the commonwealth, as Bolingbroke calls them; we've already seen them reacting to the prospect of Gaunt's death when they're summoned to his sickbed:

> Richard: Pray God we may make haste and come too late.
> All: Amen. (1.4.63-4)

The Queen's first speeches are not logical but strained and intuitive, as she struggles with something she can't explain:

> methinks
> Some unborn sorrow, ripe in fortune's womb
> Is coming towards me, and my inward soul
> At nothing trembles. (2.2.9-12)

Something is ready to be born. But she doesn't know what, so the something is a nothing. And yet it affects her enough to make her inward soul tremble. It's the metaphor of a full-term pregnancy just about to become labour, and we could read her trembling as slight, sympathetic early contractions as her sorrow approaches.

Bushy can't make anything of this and belittles her fears with his own superior learning. He explains her sorrows as a single sorrow multiplied into many through the prism of her tears, or a triple mirror which produces multiple reflections. He then compares her perceptions to views of perspective paintings, where objects appear when seen from an angle which are invisible looking at the picture straight on.

Probably the most famous of these 'trick' pictures is Hans Holbein's 'The Ambassadors', where a skull becomes visible when the painting is viewed from the side. But Bushy himself is muddled in his explanation. He says the Queen is glimpsing a frightening portent, which isn't there if you're looking straight at the picture. But if you're looking straight at the picture, there's just a formless mass; spotting the skull from an angle is the main point of viewing the painting. It's a stunning image for a woman's point of view, seeing things more clearly from the side-lines, bringing the formless into focus, though Bushy himself doesn't see that. He's saying, look at the situation head on, like us; there's nothing to worry about.

The Queen, unsurprisingly, isn't reassured:

> Howe'er it be
> I cannot but be sad: so heavy-sad
> As thought – on thinking on no-thought I think –
> Makes me with heavy nothing faint and shrink. (2.2.29-32)

'Heavy' often meant pregnant. She knows it won't sound like thinking to the men, but she insists that though she's thinking of nothing, that is nevertheless painful thought: 'on [when] thinking on no-thought, I [still] think.' That thought makes her 'with heavy nothing' [a full-term baby which however isn't there] faint and shrink, as if this were a real childbirth.

She's giving birth to nothing, merely to apprehension. She's experiencing phantom pregnancy. Bushy says it's just her 'conceit,' her fancy, and she tries again:

> Conceit is still [always] derived
> From some forefather grief; mine is not so;
> For nothing hath begot my something grief –
> Or something hath the nothing that I grieve [somebody else has cause for the grief I feel] –
> Tis in reversion that I do possess [my grief comes before I know the cause of it],
> But what it is that is not yet known what,
> I cannot name; 'tis nameless woe, I wot [think]. (2.2.34-40)

That imagination of disaster always comes from some cause for fear, she says. She has no known cause for fear, and yet she fears and trembles, and her feelings flow into the sensations and language of pregnancy and birth. But this baby will never have a name.

Green then enters to tell her and his friends about Bolingbroke's landing in Yorkshire and his gathering support. The Queen's intuitive grief is now clear to her:

> So, Green, thou art the midwife to my woe,
> And Bolingbroke my sorrow's dismal heir.

> Now hath my soul brought forth her prodigy [monstrous birth],
> And I, a gasping, new-delivered mother
> Have woe to woe, sorrow to sorrow joined. (2.2.60-4)

The dots are joined. The metaphor is now graphically about a tragic birth, where the pain of labour is followed by the pain of seeing a dead or disabled baby. She apprehends Bolingbroke's rebellion as a real and monstrous child of her own, which in a way it is, since her childlessness has largely contributed to it. If she and Richard had a son, or even shown themselves capable by having a daughter, Bolingbroke wouldn't be able to count on the support she knows he'll get now. She has herself by her childlessness given birth to the monster, rebellion. She doesn't blame Richard, though his defects must be obvious to her. We don't need to assume she has second sight. She knows Richard, she knows the caterpillars, she's seen and heard Bolingbroke's challenge. She's highly intelligent and understands the workings of her adoptive country. She was apprehensive before Richard left; she could have dissuaded him from going to Ireland, if he listened to her.

Katharine Eisaman Maus says of this scene that the discussion encourages speculation about

> (...) the 'right' or 'centred' way of seeing and an oblique outlook from which shapes look very different. Of course, [the Queen's] presentiment of disaster turns out to be more apt than her male companions' optimism. Perhaps the women's [the Duchess of Gloucester's and the Queen's] different perspective implies that the history play's focus on traditionally male political concerns may exclude whole realms of human experience.[8]

This is well put, though I'd argue that the women's perspectives are not only included but shown to be the intelligent ones. The women struggle to find convincing expression for their ideas, but that's part of the concept: plausible political language, like action, belongs to the men, which is why the country is in a desperate state. The Duchess thinks via what has been her life: real and family trees, veneration for antiquity. More interestingly, the Queen is thinking, though not writing, from the body, a 1390s Julia Kristeva[9].

There was cultural pressure on almost all married women to have children; for a Queen that pressure was intense. Shakespeare shows it seeping into her every word and response; she suffers the anxieties of hereditary monarchy in the most intimate way possible, in her guts.

The Queen of Act 2, scene ii seems to me the weirdest instance of Shakespearean empathy in the whole *Works*. Though nothing human was alien to him, childlessness and phantom pregnancy must be as far from his personal experience as it's possible to get for a man who had a baby at 18, then twins.

A little later York enters, and a confused plan to deal with the emergency is put together. Bushy, Bagot and Green think of escape routes, Bagot being notably the keenest to leave (has he a Plan B?), and they say goodbye for what they guess will be the last time: they have their political acumen too.

The refusal by the Duchess of Gloucester's brother-in-law and the Queen's courtiers to recognise their points of view is not of course honour killing, or even ill-meant. But it's a dismissal of their perceptions and identities. An old and a young woman are brushed aside by the force of male-constructed history. This critical point is nothing new, it's the usual way of understanding the women in Shakespeare's Histories. But Molly Smith emphasises the Duchess of Gloucester's attempt at political intervention. From the Queen we get intuitive foresight of a frightening development which the men would do well to attend to, but don't.

The Queen's isolation at court is absolute, patronised as she is among the favourites. Even her kind uncle-by-marriage, York, who's aging rapidly under the stress of events, feels free to tell her, 'Come, cousin, I'll dispose of you.' (2.2.116-7) She's not an idealised Queen in a medieval tapestry: she's petulant and unjust in York's garden, wishing her own infertility on the Gardener's plantings. But as she says goodbye to her husband, we see their marriage is a real and lasting one, and for once his egotism is in abeyance. He concedes that this is her tragedy too, when she's returned to France from which she came:

> ... adorned like sweet May –
> Sent back like Hallowmas or short'st of day. (5.1.79-80)

Bolingbroke has Bushy and Green summarily beheaded at Bristol, an action scarcely legal in a King, let alone in an exile on unauthorised return to England. He takes along York, the Regent, to give himself some semblance of authority, but he's claiming absolute power through this. He accuses Bushy and Green:

> You have, in manner, with your sinful hours
> Made a divorce betwixt his Queen and him [Richard],
> Broke the possession of a royal bed,
> And stained the beauty of a fair queen's cheeks
> With tears drawn from her eyes by your foul wrongs. (3.1.11-15)

In fact he's the one who divorces them by sending her back to France. He executes Richard's favourites apparently for distressing her, for being Richard's gay lovers and for wasting the resources of the country, knowing this will be a popular move.

Some elements of chivalry still appear in him. We may sympathise with his list of grievances against Bushy and Green. They've influenced Richard against him and unjustly seized his confiscated lands, even, he says:

> felled my forest woods,
> From mine own windows torn my household coat [coat of arms],
> Razed out my impress [heraldic Lancastrian emblems] leaving me no sign
> Save men's opinions and my living blood
> To show the world I am a gentleman. (3.1.23-27)

Though he disdains rhetoric, his language can be more effective than Richard's.

We soon learn how ruthless he's rapidly become, or perhaps always was, from the ideal figure he first appeared. He captures Bagot, who saves his skin by agreeing to help him disgrace Aumerle, son of the Duke of York; this may be Bagot's Plan B. At the opening of the great dramatic scene in Parliament where Richard abdicates and Bolingbroke takes the crown, he makes a determined effort to rid himself of Aumerle, using Bagot, still under guard, to do it. Aumerle would be (apart from Edmund Mortimer, who doesn't appear until the next play in the series) next in line to the throne after his aged father, if Richard died and Bolingbroke were to be impeached for treason. Bolingbroke is desperate to close off all possible challenges to his power, and he knows that Aumerle, his own and Richard's first cousin, is the most dangerous.

Bolingbroke hears that his old enemy Mowbray, Duke of Norfolk whom he accused of murdering Gloucester, has died abroad. That leaves an unsolved murder lacking a perpetrator, and Aumerle is the best candidate for the vacancy. On Bolingbroke's signal, Bagot starts off the accusations and is quickly joined by Fitzwalter, then Harry Percy (Hotspur), then another lord, who all want to stand well with Bolingbroke. It's clear from inconsistencies that they're lying. The sudden détente between the despised prisoner Bagot and the haughty Bolingbroke is disconcerting, and only Surrey defends Aumerle. Fitzwalter says that Mowbray also claimed that Aumerle had Gloucester killed on Richard's orders, so Bolingbroke, reasonably enough, says that Mowbray must be recalled from exile to give evidence. But throughout these exchanges Bolingbroke and possibly his supporting lords are acting, knowing Mowbray is already dead.

When Bolingbroke declares that Mowbray must come home, the Bishop of Carlisle announces his death in ten lines of lucid elegiac verse. He describes Mowbray's fighting in the Crusades, ending with how he

> toiled [tired] with works of war, retired himself
> To Italy, and there at Venice gave
> His body to that pleasant country's earth,
> And his pure soul unto his captain, Christ,
> Under whose colours he had fought so long. (4.1.88-92)

Then comes the following exchange:

> Bolinbroke: Why, Bishop of Carlisle, is Norfolk [Mowbray] dead?
> Carlisle: As surely as I live, my lord.
> Bolingbroke: Sweet peace conduct his sweet soul to the bosom
> Of good old Abraham! (4.1.93-6)

Bolingbroke, who's not stupid, pretends not to grasp what Carlisle is saying, then responds with saccharine piety. His apparent ignorance of Mowbray's death, whom he accused of Gloucester's murder in Act One, is meant to make a little less obvious his attempt to fit Aumerle up for the same murder now, using Bagot and anyone else who wants to ingratiate themselves with him. The trial by combat is deferred, but it can only end one way for Aumerle with several challengers to be faced in succession.

Unsurprisingly, he decides to join the Bishop of Carlisle and the Abbot of Westminster in their plot to assassinate Bolingbroke at Oxford. This plot is defeated when York discovers his son is a 'traitor' – by this time the term is meaningless, as nobody knows to whom allegiance is owing – and betrays him to Bolingbroke, we must assume to avoid the charge of complicity, though Bolingbroke is likely to condemn his son to death. Bolingbroke's rebellion is demoralising his whole extended family. Aumerle grovels at Bolingbroke's feet, the Yorks descend into figures of fun, and Aumerle is allowed to live, as he's now harmless.

In Greg Doran's stage-to-cinema production of *Richard II*, it's Aumerle not Bolingbroke's supporter Exton who murders Richard. At Pomfret Castle, as Richard is attacked, he pulls off the assassin's balaclava and finds himself face to face with his cousin and old friend. It's a startling moment and very effective, though going right against Shakespeare's text. In several ways it makes sense: Aumerle is getting back into favour with Bolingbroke, but also hoping to eliminate Richard so as to stand next in line of Succession after his father York if Bolingbroke is killed or impeached. In the play, Aumerle is relatively innocent like his father, trying to reconcile opposing loyalties, while Bolingbroke is even more unscrupulous, I think, than he's generally acted. To have Aumerle suddenly emerge as the most ruthless of the three cousins overplays the House of Cards element, strong enough already, and takes the focus off Bolingbroke, whose trajectory must continue through two more plays. If Aumerle was that ambitious and formidable, he could have stopped Bolingbroke earlier.

All this seems a long way from honour killing and the waste of women's lives and abilities. But it's only by looking at the Machiavellian cunning of the men that we can see the pattern made by the brief intercut women's roles, and how Shakespeare is constructing perceptions of gender. In the final Andronici power-bid, in Antony's rhetoric over Caesar's body, here in Bolingbroke's Accession scene, in Prince John's cunning pretence of an amnesty in *Henry IV, Part 2*, and in Hal's elaborate public performance in *Henry V* with the Archbishop of Canterbury and the Bishop of Ely about his lineal right to claim France when the decision to invade has already been taken, it's the men who are the actors and hypocrites. The Greek-derived term 'hypocrite' meant an actor. Based on the Eve stereotype, women were generally thought to be the devious and hypocritical sex, but with some notable exceptions Shakespeare makes his women candid and loyal.

The Queen tries to persuade Northumberland to let her stay in prison in England with Richard. She's too innocent to see that Bolingbroke's men won't leave her alone with him for a minute, much less let her live with him. If she became pregnant, the whole situation would change again.

The lines in *Lucrece* quoted earlier on gender difference are fully realised in *Richard II*:

> Their [women's] smoothness like a goodly champaign plain [fair open field]
> Lays open [reveals] all the little worms that creep;
> In men, as in a rough-grown grove, remain
> Cave-keeping [hidden] evils that obscurely sleep. (1,247-50)

The Queen with her little worms of petulance and Bolingbroke with his well-hidden, murderous designs exemplify that theory.

In *Henry IV, Part 1*, the Percys, that is, Northumberland, his son Harry Percy (Hotspur) and his brother Worcester are planning a *coup* against Bolingbroke. They helped him to power and fought for him against the Scots, he promised to repay them substantially when he was King, but once King he won't even let them keep their important prisoners. The quarrel in Act One is about money, about who will get the prisoners' ransoms. Prisoners legally belonged to the Crown, but a King ideally allowed his nobility to keep their prisoners after a battle and get the ransoms, making it worth their while to support his wars. With an empty Treasury, Bolingbroke can't afford that. To the Percys, he's ungrateful, and Hotspur, who now supports a claim of his wife's brother Mortimer to the throne and has also a possible claim himself through his wife, is gathering troops against the King.

As his nickname proclaims, Hotspur is reckless. His father and uncle constantly warn him about it, but unsuccessfully. He tries not to recognise the dangers in rebellion, but he's more apprehensive than he wants to admit. His treatment of his wife Kate[10] is funny and crass at the same time. They're a bit like Petruccio and his Kate but long married and still in dispute. This is probably the best of the young or youngish marriages represented in Shakespeare's plays. They're still in love, though there's patronage in everything he says to her and annoyance in everything she says to him. He doesn't suspect her fidelity, but though spectacularly indiscreet himself he doesn't trust her discretion: women talk.

Act Two, scene iv opens with his reading and commenting on a reply he's had to a letter he sent to a friend, which described his plans for rebellion and asked for support:

> 'But for mine own part, my lord, I could be well contented to be there [with Hotspur] in respect of the love I bear your house [family].' He could be contented; why is he not, then? In respect of the love he bears our house! He shows in this he loves his own barn better than he loves our house. Let me see some more. – 'The purpose you undertake is dangerous.' Why, that's certain. 'Tis dangerous to take a cold, to sleep, to drink; but I tell you, my lord fool, out of this nettle, danger, we pluck this flower, safety. (2.4.1-8)

As he continues to read the letter aloud and make disgusted comments on his correspondent's cowardly refusal to join the rebellion, we gather that he's given away the name of every major conspirator in the plot, when and where they plan to meet, and that some of them are already on the move. He goes on:

> What a pagan rascal is this, an infidel! Ha, you shall see now, in very sincerity of fear and cold heart will he to the King, and lay open all our proceedings ... O, I could divide myself and go to buffets [beat myself up] for moving [urging] such a dish of skimmed milk with so honourable an action! Hang him! Let him tell the King we are prepared: I will set forward tonight. (2.4.21-6)

At this point Kate Percy enters. For two weeks he hasn't allowed her in his bed, but before that she's watched him in his sleep, when

> Thy spirit within thee hath been so at war,
> And thus hath so disturbed thee in thy sleep,
> That beads of sweat have stood upon thy brow
> Like bubbles in a late [just]-disturbed stream. (2.4.47-50)

He doesn't want her to learn what's planned when he cries out in nightmares. At the end of the first tetralogy, an audience has seen Richard III the night before Bosworth, when his murders come back to haunt him. Hotspur has a few things to repent too, betraying Richard II, slandering Aumerle for Bolingbroke, now betraying Bolingbroke because the Percys haven't done well enough out of the new regime. These aren't crimes on Richard III's scale, though, and Hotspur doesn't see them as crimes at all. But Kate's long description of the changes in him acknowledges the acute anxiety even reckless men suffer before battle.

His first response is to ignore her, instead calling a servant to make sure his horse is saddled. She persists:

> Lady Percy: What is it carries you away?
> Hotspur: Why, my horse,
> My love, my horse.
> Lady Percy: Out, you mad-headed ape!
> A weasel hath not such a deal of spleen [aggression, unpredictability]
> As you are tossed with.
> In faith, I'll know your business, Harry, that I will.
> I fear my brother Mortimer doth stir
> About his title [entitlement to the throne], and hath sent for you
> To line [support] his enterprise. (4.2.65-72)

She's guessed right, though she doesn't know the details. She doesn't know either that Hotspur is playing with the idea of kingship himself. Referring to his horse, he says more to himself than to Kate or the servant, 'that roan shall be my throne.' (4.2.61) He, Mortimer and the Welsh chieftain Owen Glendower, Mortimer's father-in-law, have a plan to carve the kingdom into three and each rule their own third. But Hotspur is also thinking of a claim to the whole through his wife, like her brother a direct descendant of Edward III.

She grabs hold of him and threatens to break his little finger if he won't confide in her. The intense intimacy of their marriage with its past battles and reconciliations is re-enacted in brief, but he remains adamant:

> But hark you, Kate,
> I must not have you henceforth question me
> Whither I go, or reason whereabout (...)
> (...) constant you are,
> But yet a woman, and for secrecy
> No lady closer [more discreet], for I well believe
> Thou wilt not utter what thou dost not know.
> And so far will I trust thee, gentle Kate. (4.2.90-100)

He's cheering himself up with these old jokes because he's stupidly revealed the plot in a letter that will find its way to Bolingbroke. Kate never has a chance to dissuade him from rebellion. She probably couldn't, but at least she would advise him not to trust an untried friend.

Hotspur is right about the friend's next move. In the following scene, Bolingbroke's son and heir Prince Hal is waiting for his friends Falstaff, Bardolph, Peto and Gadshill to come back to the Eastcheap inn where they meet. The previous night he and Poins, in disguise, robbed them and frightened them into running away, just after they'd robbed a group of wealthy travellers of money going to the King's Exchequer. Hal plans to get Falstaff to boast about his courage, then expose him as a braggart.

The Eastcheap scenes are the greatest moments of the Histories. We're in a different world from anything we've seen before, in the underbelly of East London with its crimes, aspirations and angry friendships. It's like the court but funny, which the court seldom is. The comic subplot of robbers robbing robbers echoes the main plot of the Percys and their allies who try to rob the robber Bolingbroke of the crown. It defines the great battles for crowns and countries, led by noblemen and dignified by the name of dynastic wars, as no better than highway robberies, though costlier in human life. In Eastcheap there's plenty of aggression too, and Hal never forgets his own place in the hierarchy, but though he's using his friends, and they him, this doesn't preclude bonds like the ones we see among the nobility.

Just when Hal has exposed Falstaff's lies and cowardice in front of the clientele, and the two agree to act out extempore a play about Hal in trouble with his father, the landlady Mistress Quickly reports a nobleman at the door sent from the King with a message to Hal. When Falstaff investigates, he comes back with news of Hotspur's rising and the names of the chief rebels. Hal must talk to his father, recruit troops and prepare for a battle. There's so much going on and Eastcheap feels so far from the court, we may not take in at first where the news is coming from. Hotspur's friend has ratted, as Hotspur belatedly saw he would. Hal remains apparently unperturbed and stays on to act out the roles of son and father with Falstaff before he leaves, though he knows when he hears the message that he and Hotspur can't both survive the coming rebellion.

Though Hotspur ignores or patronises Kate, he can't do without her, and offers to take her on the campaign, at least as far as Wales: 'Will this content you?' Kate bitterly understands the helplessness of her sex: 'It must, of force.' (2.4.105) Of force: necessarily, and also literally by force. The same rule that applies in war applies between husbands and wives. She must give up her own better judgment to Hotspur's greater power.

In Wales, they're in a country of legend where Kate's brother Mortimer is enthralled by his new enchantress wife, Glendower's daughter, and Glendower claims magical powers. Hotspur remains the blunt Northerner, making fun of the old faker, teasing Kate by saying in the hearing of the father and husband that he'd like to share the Welsh lady's bed, the classic error for soldiers abroad. He tries Kate's patience to the limit, and she stays loyal.

He makes several mistakes which affect the outcome of the Battle of Shrewsbury. He quibbles about the land allotted to him, offends Glendower and possibly Mortimer, and relies on his father's troops arriving in time though his father's support for the rising was always tepid; it's the brainchild of Worcester. But the mistake he makes by confiding in a man, not Kate, is the crucial one. His refusal to say what's frightening him is nothing like the jealous rage that drives honour killing. It's just dismissive, the old joke that women talk too much, stemming from his need to pretend he has the better judgement. He trusts a frightened man instead, somebody he's fool enough to take for a friend. His mistake forces him to move against Bolingbroke too soon, Glendower and Mortimer don't turn up, and Hal kills him at Shrewsbury before his father's reinforcements can arrive.

We can understand Mortimer's failure to join Hotspur at Shrewsbury in two ways. Is his singing, clinging wife a Welsh siren who lures him away from honour on the battlefield and a possible crown? A castrating woman like the literally castrating wild Welshwomen alluded to earlier in the play? Or is Wales an enviable haven from military politicking for Mortimer, who sensibly decides to save his own life rather than continue in the relentless dynastic wars? Falstaff's mid-battle interrogation of Honour and how little it does for its devotees, along with Hotspur's early death, might support the second reading. But it's only because Mortimer 'doth stir about his title', has agreed to be the figurehead for the rising, that the battle happens at all, and he leaves his supporters to die there.

Mistress Quickly appears briefly in *Part 1*, vividly enjoying the 'royal' play Hal and Falstaff act out, which is better than anything by the 'harlotry players' (2.4.325) she's seen. The two other women appear together in the

Welsh scene. One is, I think on balance, an Eve figure. The other is as clever as a Comedy heroine, a Rosalind or a Beatrice, but as a woman she's ignored on military and political matters, so her intelligence is useless. In *Part 2*, she's embittered by her father-in-law's failure to join her husband and will never forgive him. She and Hotspur are the saddest examples in the English or Roman Histories of the waste caused by consigning women to the suburbs. With his death, her life is also over.

The last play in this tetralogy has Hal, now Henry V, the legitimate victor or the thief of France according to our point of view, reconciling opposites, soldier with Machiavellian ruler, military courage with charm enough to persuade the French Princess Catherine to marry him willingly, though she knows men's tongues are full of deceits. As in the Petruccio-Kate story, even the macho male must gain the woman's consent. *Henry V*, I think, is Shakespeare's only play where militarism finds any endorsement at all. Though Henry is clearly wrong, legally and morally, to invade France and does it only to unite England behind a usurper's son, the male bonding and language of great last-ditch heroism make the day their own. A student once described *Henry V* as an anti-war play often subverted by a sense of the glory of war, and that's probably as good as it gets. As with the Battle of Bosworth, a peace brokered by marriage offers the obligatory happy ending which we don't have to believe in, and even if we do, the Chorus tells us it won't last long.

*

Shakespeare's Roman women have an even worse time than his English ones. Julius Caesar is desperate for a son to back his ambition for lifelong monarchy, insisting his wife Calpurnia must stand in the way of the ceremonial runner, Mark Antony, to be touched by him on the Feast of the Lupercal, the feast of fertility. That assumes the childlessness is her deficiency not Caesar's; the Roman ritual is a painful public ordeal for childless women. Historically, Julius Caesar adopted his great-nephew Octavius, later the Emperor Augustus, as his son. Though Shakespeare follows Plutarch here, he also continues to treat the political preoccupation of the English 1590s, the lack of an heir.

Caesar and Calpurnia aren't funny and charming like Hotspur and Kate, but his life ends through a similar masculine misjudgement. The night before the Ides of March when he's due to go to the Senate, she has a nightmare, crying out in her sleep that he's being murdered, and next morning she tries to dissuade him from going. Though she doesn't consciously know the conspirators' intentions, the nightmare comes out of her greater sensitivity to their facial expressions or body language. Though he scoffs at the fear of death, initially he agrees to stay at home. But when the conspirators arrive to escort him to the Senate with a promise he'll be offered imperial power that day, ambition overcomes caution, and he changes his mind. As we know he's going to die, we recognise as she speaks how prescient Calpurnia is.

The subjection of Roman women is extreme. They're silenced, if not as savagely as Lavinia, almost as effectively. Octavius uses his sister Octavia as a pawn in the imperial game; she knows what he's doing but has no choice. Her marriage to Antony is broached at a meeting between the main players in Rome by Octavius' friend Agrippa, clearly by prior agreement. Antony could evade it, but he doesn't. When in Rome he's Roman, and himself feels the advantage of a family connection with the autocrat who's rapidly becoming his enemy.

Enobarbus knows that Antony will soon tire of Octavia's 'holy, cold and still' (2.6.120) personality and will return to his pleasures in the East. This gives Octavius an excuse for his hostility, as he foresaw when he planned the marriage. According to Plutarch, Octavia was forceful and adventurous, going on campaigns with Antony and eventually taking charge of his children by Cleopatra along with her own. Shakespeare drains the life out of her to contrast with her vivid, verbal opponent.

There are many variants of the woman played as pawn. In *King John*, for instance, English Blanche is traded as a wife to the French King's son to secure her uncle King John's right to the English throne against competing claims by France and by the real King, the boy Arthur. The marriage is just celebrated when a message from the Pope changes the political landscape again, and Blanche is forced to leave everyone she knows and go with her inane new husband, who's once more an enemy of England. The futility of marital bargaining, the misery inflicted on the woman, is played out at greater length in *King John*. But in *Julius Caesar*, the later play, Octavia's cold disposal is the more effective for its economy.

For the first four Acts of *Antony and Cleopatra*, the East/West divide between Egyptian sensuality and Roman austerity is never morally absolute either way. Octavia is affectionate if dull, Cleopatra cruel and childish, disturbingly surrounded by eunuchs she laughs at. Though a Queen, she's serially dependent on powerful men, and causes Antony's disastrous flight at Actium. Only in Act 5 with Antony dead can she re-cast their tacky, compelling story as a triumph over mundanity and military power. She's a poet-imaginist like Quince or Bottom, and like Bottom a great comedian.

Coriolanus' wife Virgilia is a nonentity; actors stuck with the part have a hard time. She's overwhelmed by her husband's and nightmare mother-in-law Volumnia's psychotic devotion to military violence. Coriolanus addresses his wife approvingly as 'my gracious silence'. (2.1.142) In *Titus Andronicus*, Bassianus calls Lavinia 'gracious', and the compliment seems to praise female acquiescence conveyed by body-language rather than words, the ideal (for many of Shakespeare's powerful men) of female manners.

Volumnia's first speech reveals her identification with Roman military glory and her strong conviction that she'd make her son a better wife than his wife does:

> I pray you, daughter [in-law], sing, or express yourself in a more comfortable sort [cheerful way]. If my son were my husband, I should freelier rejoice in that absence wherein he won honour than in the embracements of his bed where he would show most love. (1.3.1-4)

Women exist to serve the military machine. Volumnia goes on to describe how she brought Coriolanus up, encouraging him to seek danger and injury very young. Virgilia expresses her first and last reservation about the wisdom of the cult of war:

> Virgilia: But had he died in the business, madam, how then?
> Volumnia: Then his good report should have been my son. (1.3.14-15)

Titus Andronicus and *Coriolanus* create a Roman state more indifferent to life than *Julius Caesar* or *Antony and Cleopatra*. They book-end the Roman Histories, *Titus* first performed probably in the first half of the 1590s, *Coriolanus* in 1613. But they cross over chronologically: *Titus* is set in the decline of empire, *Coriolanus* in its fifth-century BC beginnings, when the Romans are intent on subduing their near neighbours, the Volscians, and the great imperial adventure is still in the future. There's a resemblance in the plots: in each a banished Roman patrician makes peace with Rome's enemy and returns with a hostile army to attack the city.

Though women can't participate in war, they can share the glory. Even more than Titus Andronicus, Volumnia is Rome incarnate. Both send their sons to war and revel in the destruction of everything non-Roman. The cult of war flowers into homoerotic passion between men who go into battle together in the ultimate sensual bonding. Meeting his general, Cominius, on the battlefield after being nearly cut to pieces inside Corioli, Coriolanus embraces him as eagerly, he says, as he embraced his wife on their wedding night. Aufidius, the Volscian general, makes the same erotic comparison when Coriolanus, his old enemy, comes disguised to his house in Corioli, seeking death or revenge on the Romans who've banished him. They fall in love. Battle is sexier than sex. The homoeroticism is played out in fighting and wrestling that deify the male body, in bleeding wounds and scars that write the patrician male as superhero, though lacking any quality that fits him for government or family life.

Much of the interest comes from debate on how the Roman body politic should work to distribute health and goods to all its members. The plebeians are starving, but Coriolanus is indifferent to their suffering; he despises their cowardice; they're fragments, not Romans. The wily old patrician Menenius produces a specious political fable for them about a head, a belly and limbs that comes nowhere near their economic reality. The debate remains unresolved. When Coriolanus, who would certainly define himself as among the 'head' citizens, not the lower 'belly' or 'limb' groups, cuts himself off from Volumnia and Rome, his death is inevitable. He can't find his 'world elsewhere' (3.3.135) outside the city that spawned him; his enemy/lover becomes his killer, and stamps on his head.

This has been called Shakespeare's most anti-war play, and there's much to identify war with culturally-induced insanity. But as with any short general statement about any of the plays, there's much diametrically to oppose that label. There's no other emotional centre or value system on offer, in Virgilia or the plebeians, so we're swept along with Romanitas Triumphant, with risk and blood as the only game in town. Coriolanus has been much admired. In his *History of English Patriotism*, Esme Wingfield-Stratford called him:

> (...) every inch a gentleman. He possesses in overflowing measure all the virtues peculiar to aristocracies. Brave, courtly, generous, modest, he is of a type which, with increasing difficulty, we try to turn out from Eton and Oxford.[11]

This is particularly poignant given the date, 1913.

To return to Portia's appeal to Brutus: like Hotspur he hasn't confided in a wife whose advice would be for caution, or if he does confide in her, it's too late to affect plans already made. But all the examples of marital imbalance are different and they don't universally support the woman's superiority of mind. Portia's objection to being left in the suburbs is followed by some doubtful claims to participation in his affairs:

> I grant I am a woman, but withal
> One that Lord Brutus took to wife.
> I grant I am a woman, but withal
> A woman well-reputed, Cato's daughter.
> Think you I am no stronger than my sex,
> Being so fathered and so husbanded?
> Tell me your counsels, I will not disclose 'em.
> I have made strong proof of my constancy,
> Giving myself a voluntary wound
> Here in the thigh. Can I bear that with patience
> And not my husband's secrets? (2.1.290-300)

She assumes that women absorb strength from their husbands and fathers rather than find it in themselves; a lot of Shakespeare's women find it in themselves. With 'here', does she/the boy actor display the scar? In her *Letter to Shakespeare* on the internet, Harriet Walter chooses this passage to explain her unease with women's parts in Shakespeare: his women define themselves only in relation to men, and all their conversation is about men. Because Shakespeare's words, she says,

> are still the highest form of expression of our human condition, we [women] still swallow your plots and social attitudes even if they don't fit us anymore.[12]

I agree that from the mid twentieth century on an increasing distance has opened between modern and Shakespearean women.

But Portia's disdain for her own sex, her identification with her suicidal father and her manipulative self-harm don't have to be understood as admirable or even sane. Stabbing herself in the thigh disturbingly imitates rape. More fundamentally, self-harm with a knife or sword mimics the men's devotion to the cult of war. Displaying or indicating her scar, she also displays her inability to direct that energy outside herself; literally, she internalises their drive to kill. As so often, rape and killing in war are closely connected.

Shakespeare stays close to Plutarch's account, which at least to an English reader suggests she was mad. The speeches he writes for her first appearance must accommodate that possibility, though in the speech quoted earlier her devotion to Brutus is uppermost. But a little later that day she panics in the street and despite her promise to him gives away to the boy Lucius and the Soothsayer that some frightening event is imminent. Later still, before the Battle of Philippi, news comes that she's died by swallowing burning coals, as Plutarch records. Historically, other means of suicide were taken away, but her captors overlooked the fire.

Shakespeare's extreme Roman women are more distorted by their masculinist culture than his English ones: in no situation is Kate Percy likely to start stabbing herself in the thigh. Portia's identification with men and Romanitas doesn't appeal to us now, and I'd suggest it wasn't necessarily appealing then. In *Julius Caesar* as in *Richard II*, there's a delicate balance between the claims of stable tyranny and of disruptive justice; if we favour the latter, Brutus may be right to keep her in ignorance. Kate Percy and Calpurnia show no such contempt for their own sex, and though they do live through their men, their men don't govern their judgements. Hotspur's rising would be better abandoned, as Kate sees. At best it would divide the country in three.

Only *The Merry Wives of Windsor* is overtly set in contemporary England, but in fact all the plays are. Whenever and wherever a play is set, it's also about the condition of Shakespeare's England, as the first performances acknowledged. A picture of an early production of *Titus Andronicus*[13] shows the cast in part-Roman, part-Elizabethan dress. Already at this first staging there's a combination of two historical cultures, togas and doublets mixed, signalling that this is not just about Rome but about England, about Then, certainly, but also about Now, that explosive Now of the late 1500s and early 1600s. The distancing in time and space cuts out inessentials; the plays escaped their historical moments, both the one they represent and the one they were written in. They went on into a future that has seen them embrace Darwin, Marx and Freud among others.

*

By the Problem Plays are usually meant *Measure for Measure*, *All's Well That Ends Well* and *Troilus and Cressida*. If they've been thought especially problematic by critics, it's because their women resist relegation to suburbia more fiercely than most. They make more troubling choices than in other plays and initiate more of the action. In *MM* and *AWTEW*, major problems of attraction and repulsion are solved by a bed-trick, the substitution of one woman for another. In the dark, a man has sex with a woman he's already contemptuously refused, believing her to be the woman he wants. In each play there's a precontract or formal marriage ceremony in place, so he's legalising a marriage he thinks he's escaped. The all-cats-are-grey-in-the-dark trick humiliates both parties, but it's an interesting variant on comedy's happy-ever-after bromide. The Problem Plays disturb theatrical expectation.

In 1585 Edwin Sandys, Bishop of London and later Archbishop of York, addressed Parliament on the need to introduce Mosaic law for adultery and other sex offences, which he described none-too-originally as a river overflowing its banks. In the late 1590s a group of Puritans following Sandys, also proponents of Old Testament law and morality, again tried to drive through Parliament a bill that would make sex outside marriage a capital crime for both men and women, whether it was adultery, where one or both sexual partners are married to other people, or fornication, where neither is married. There was little enthusiasm among MPs for the project, and it was abandoned. But the attempt shows a formidable tranche of Puritan morality underlying Elizabethan and Jacobean life and aiming to control the morals of both sexes. Fifty years later adultery, though not fornication, became a capital crime during the ten years of Cromwell's Republic. In practice, even under the Republic, jurors were reluctant to bring in a Guilty verdict and there's no record of an execution for adultery.

The Puritans' projected law is the point of departure for *Measure For*

Measure (1604). The Duke of Vienna hands over his authority to a puritanical Deputy, Angelo, pretending he's going away, but he stays on in Vienna disguised as a Friar to see how Angelo stands the test of absolute power. In a variation on the honour-killing theme, Angelo reinstates an old law that prescribes the death penalty for men or women who commit adultery or fornication. This time the play takes honour killing out of the family and embeds it in civil law.

Two luckless young upper-class people, Claudio and Juliet, are arrested. Though they're precontracted (engaged), their marriage has been delayed because her family hasn't handed over her dowry, and she's pregnant. They're condemned to death under the new law, though as was standard for a pregnant woman in England, her execution will be delayed until after she gives birth, which is imminent. Claudio will be executed in under twenty-four hours.

His sister, Isabella, is on the point of entering a convent to escape the sleaze of Vienna. She's eager to make the strict rules of the order of St Clare even stricter. This narrative doesn't show young women as marginalised but as targets for state retribution equally with men, self-consigning to a convent or working in the sex trade.

It's a great high-stakes opening and the tension continues to ratchet up to the end. How will the lovers escape the new law? What argument or cunning can get them off? We're pretty sure they'll survive, but we can't be certain it won't turn into a tragedy. It's a play full of trials and interrogations. I think we know from the start that the real villain will turn out to be Angelo, but we don't know how he can be beaten before the axe falls on Claudio.

The Viennese setting is uncannily apt because the play explores the Freudian concepts of sexual repression and its sublimation, in this case into cruelty and self-righteousness. Angelo is the chief Puritan. Isabella is due to take her vows the following day; the city is Catholic, and she takes for granted that celibacy is a higher state than marriage. The Duke too has 'ever loved the life removed [monastic]' (1.3.8) and dismisses any thought of love or marriage. These three Puritans are in dramatic opposition to Pompey the Pimp and Mistress Overdone the Bawd, workers in the sex trade that preys on 'fallen' women, takes over their babies and spreads syphilis through Vienna. The third enemy of Puritanism is Claudio's friend, the stud Lucio.

There's a whole range of erotic sensibilities on display. Angelo is excited by Isabella because she's a virgin and soon to be a nun. His morality cracks and he offers to exchange Claudio's life for her virginity. When she threatens to reveal his hypocrisy, his 'Who will believe thee, Isabel?' (2.2.154) and her despairing 'To whom should I complain?' (2.2.171) as he leaves her to decide, are frequently asked questions few women find an answer to. Of course, he reneges on his promise once he's (as he thinks) had her. Isabella can't make this sacrifice for her brother, and whether she should or shouldn't remains open to debate. We might assume that the Christian response should be to save her brother's life. We might equally defend her right to refuse compliance with a corrupt regime. But she refuses Angelo in disturbing Freudian terms. Rather than agree to his demand, she says:

> The impression of keen whips I'd wear as rubies,
> And strip myself to death as to a bed
> That longings have been sick for
> E're I'd yield my body up to shame. (2.4.99-104)

Her sensibility falls somewhere between religious martyr and Sadeian complicit victim.

But however we judge her, her mind soars above the range of most Shakespearean men. Suppose we were asked to guess who said:

> But man, proud man,
> Dressed in a little brief authority,
> Most ignorant of what he's most assured –
> His glassy essence [his intellect or spirit] – like an angry ape
> Plays such fantastic tricks before high heaven
> As make the angels weep, (...) (2.2.121-6)

who would we give the speech to? The lines might be Hamlet's. There's hardly anyone else in the canon who could speak them. Among powerful minds, Lear isn't detached enough, though his trenchant 'a dog's obeyed in office' (4.6.144) comes close to the sentiment. Hal is too political, Prospero too focused on himself and his Masterplan. If we didn't know, I doubt we'd guess it's a woman, Isabella. There are moments when women move intellectually well outside the limits of love and family.

On the other end of the spectrum, Pompey's response to reproof is whingeing self-justification: 'Truly sir, I am a poor fellow that would live.' (2.1.188) Lucio's celebration of free love is intensely sexist. He tells Isabella:

> Your brother and his lover have embraced.
> As those that feed grow full, as blossoming time
> That from the seedness [sowing] the bare fallow brings
> To teeming foison [harvest], even so her plenteous womb
> Expresseth his full tilth and husbandry. (1.4.39-43)

It's a witty extended metaphor that compares sex to farming, with the husband and the husbandman (farmer) neatly linked in the last word. In the 1960s it was sometimes read as Shakespeare's personal feeling about sex. Now, I think, we can recognise it as merely libertine rhetoric. Lucio's appeal to nature ignores context and consequence in the human, social world. His male is the actor/hero, his female just the passive earth waiting to be tilled, her risk in bearing and her work in nurturing a child unrecognised. Lucio's attitude to Isabella is aggressive from the start. When he addresses her as 'a thing enskied and sainted', (1.4.33) he's speaking satirically, as she knows. She answers, arrogantly, 'You do abuse the good in mocking me.' (1.4.37)

Juliet stands between the extremes of repression and promiscuity, the angel that Angelo isn't, an angel who acknowledges her own sexuality when it might be more sensible to claim rape, if this isn't her last confession:

> Duke-as-Friar: Repent you, fair one, of the sin you carry?
> Juliet: I do, and take the shame most patiently. (...)
> Duke-as-Friar: Love you the man who wronged you?
> Juliet: Yes, as I love the woman who wronged him.
> Duke-as-Friar: So then it seems your most offenceful act
> Was mutually committed?
> Juliet: Mutually.
> Duke-as-Friar: Then is your sin of heavier kind than his.
> Juliet: I do confess it and repent it, father. (2.3.20-31)

His calling her baby a sin deserves a different answer. But in silently enduring his crass judgement, she makes a dignified attempt to win clemency for Claudio as well as herself and prompts the audience to take her side. The Duke-as-Friar's questioning feels intrusive and prurient and would probably seem so to many in the audience, with the confessional now obsolete in England. His little joke about her sin being of 'heavier' kind than Claudio's would be cruel at any time, let alone made to a woman who'll be hanged as soon as she's lighter. His character and motives are ambiguous throughout. In making Angelo his Deputy he sets him up for failure, as he knows, and gets rid of a dangerous rival.

Claudio, facing death, can't meet it as an audience might expect of a young nobleman. He's momentarily convinced by the Duke-as-Friar's advice to see life as something only fools would keep, but his stoicism can't last. He can imagine physical dissolution too vividly:

> Ay, but to die, and go we know not where,
> To lie in cold obstruction, and to rot,
> This sensible [sensitive, emotional] warm motion [movement, moving body] to become
> A kneaded clod (...) (3.1.117-20)

He breaks down and begs his sister to agree to Angelo's demand. She reacts with contempt, with doubts of his paternity and their mother's fidelity. His weakness is endearing, perhaps, but his insistence on waiting for Juliet's dowry before marriage though he won't wait for sex has been disastrous. Isabella, Angelo and the Duke reach a stalemate when Isabella refuses to have sex with Angelo. Coincidentally or not, the play turns from mainly verse to mainly prose at this point, and ceases to sound much like Shakespeare while Isabella and the Duke substitute Angelo's cast-off betrothed Mariana for Isabella in a bed trick. Then it recovers, and Shakespearean verse returns for the great last Act. It's likely that Thomas Middleton is the author or part-author of the Fourth Act.

Shakespeare isn't of course the first to attack honour killing or Mosaic law. Christ advises the men who catch a woman in adultery and want to stone her to leave the stoning to those who've never sinned themselves. They evaporate. The play's title comes from the Sermon on the Mount:

> Judge not, that ye be not judged. For with what judgement ye judge, ye shall be judged, and with what measure ye mete it shall be measured to you again.[14]

Commentators on the play including the great Shakespearean editor and critic Samuel Johnson have regretted that Angelo gets off scot-free after intended rape and intended murder covered by so much hypocrisy. At the end, Isabella, her certainties shattered by all she's witnessed, reluctantly kneels down beside Mariana to beg the Duke for Angelo's life, still believing he's had her brother murdered. The above recommendation in the Sermon on the Mount has never been put into any country's legal practice, as far as I know. To see it implemented even on the stage is a shock.

Measure for Measure and *All's Well That Ends Well* end in more than usually troubling marriages. One of many problems in *Measure for Measure* is that under English law Claudio and Juliet have been married all along, since a precontract or spousal marriage, which could be just a verbal promise between two people, not necessarily a written document, amounted to a legal marriage when followed by consummation. The marriage was supposed to be made public, however. I think we have to assume that with the new regime in Vienna, along with Angelo's death penalty for sex, has come the abolition of spousal marriage, something which was being canvassed in England at the time. Yet both the Duke and Isabella are happy to promote another spousal marriage as a way out of their *impasse*. Angelo and Mariana were once betrothed, but he broke it off when she lost her dowry, pretending she'd lost her reputation. So one act of intercourse, the Duke alleges, even though Angelo doesn't know who the woman is, is not a sin but will turn their relationship into a valid and indissoluble marriage. The inconsistencies suggest the near-impossibility of the state's regulating love relationships.

Two other marriages are hastily thrown together by the Duke: Lucio with the discarded mother of his child, in a ducal Child Support Act; the Duke himself with Isabella, though we can't be sure of her response to his sudden proposal. Three out of the four marriages, then, feel more parodic than romantic.

Marriage is the comfortable Anglican middle way between celibacy and promiscuity, and yet two pairings are devised as punishments for the men, who won't make their wives happy. The play proclaims its cynicism about happy-marriage endings unlike, say, *As You Like It*, where some of the final pairings are cobbled together but an air of celebration prevails and Hymen turns up in person to take the four weddings.

For *All's Well*, Shakespeare creates an enterprising, reckless heroine, unusually from the professional class, a doctor's daughter now orphaned,

Helena. She's in love with a nobleman, the lying young toad Bertram, who despises her for her low birth. His particular brand of misogyny consists in evaluating a woman not by her character or even her looks, but by her rank – which always went hand-in-hand with money and influence. Marriage is a means to an end, the individual woman irrelevant.

Helena's love is the only silly thing about her, but it's been her life since childhood:

> T'were all one
> That I should love a bright particular star
> And think to wed it, he is so above me. (1.1.73-5)

She's clever enough to understand the massive gamble of marriage when everything hung on one throw of the dice: whether to take an immediate offer or hope that a (possibly) better one will come good. Paroles, a womanising liar like Lucio in *MM*, advises her to use her virginity to make a marriage as soon as possible while she's young, since an old virgin is no use to anyone. Helena sees as well as he does how easy it is for a woman to miss her matrimonial market by hankering after the unattainable, but she refuses to be frightened by the pressure of time:

> I will stand for't [defend my virginity] yet a little, though I therefore die a virgin. (1.1.17)

Unusually, Helena initiates almost all the action, not just at the beginning like Desdemona, but all through her play, and she has by far the most lines to speak. She adopts her father's profession and uses his expertise to cure the French King's illness. The King offers any reward she wants, and she chooses Bertram. Shakespeare anticipates novelists of the eighteenth and nineteenth centuries in analysing female romance as a construct of class, a woman's dream of 'rising' not consciously linked to money but supported by everything in the culture. Unlike many of the novelists, he withholds the endorsement of a credibly happy ending.

Expected gender roles are reversed. Bertram has to obey the King and go through a formal wedding ceremony. But unlike a woman, he can refuse to consummate the marriage, and without this it won't be valid. He runs away, leaving a letter to tell Helena he will be her husband when she can get the ring from his hand and a baby fathered by him. He sets her the conditions of a chivalric quest, though of a bizarre type, reversing the pattern of a knight's adventure usually to be rewarded with a lady. Helena pursues him across France to the war in Italy, and with the help of a hastily-assembled girl gang fulfils his conditions through the bed trick.

She's had some distinguished fans, especially among the Romantics, and she has some of the most plangent lines of verse anywhere. Until recently readers and audiences have often found her boldness unlikeable, but she's finally come into her own. Bertram continues lying and slandering to the last; when he finally accepts her, forced by the King and his mother, it's impossible to believe he's changed.

In the Globe production of 2018, Paroles was played by a woman. Given that he's a stud and also treacherous and cowardly, this seemed an unfortunate decision, unrelated to anything in the play. Cross-casting has to be done with an idea behind it, and it was hard to see the rationale for this. In the *Julia Caesar* of 2012 where Frances Barber played Caesar and Harriet Walter Brutus, one could believe the women's release from the frame prison setting took them straight (back) into political action.

All's Well That Ends Well is a sad, resigned title. This is more tragedy than comedy: 'the web of our life is of a mingled yarn, good and ill together'(4.3.54), a choric onlooker remarks, but in the ending ill seems to predominate. We're left with a sense of the waste of so much courage and devotion in Helena, loyal to the last but pointlessly so, still duped by the dream there's no chance Bertram will fulfil.

The love story of Troilus and Cressida doesn't appear in *The Iliad.*[15] Shakespeare based his (pre-1603) play mainly on Chaucer's *Troilus and Criseyde*, which drew on several medieval Troy narratives. After long resistance, Cressida confesses her love to Troilus, a son of Priam, King of Troy. When they swear fidelity, Troilus says that faithful men henceforth will be called 'as true as Troilus', (3.2.162) Cressida says that unfaithful women will be called 'as false as Cressid'. (3.2.176) They anticipate the judgements of history, though the play's satiric angle tells us that history gets it wrong: the Trojan War wasn't heroic, and history got Troilus and Cressida wrong too.

When the lovers have spent one night together, the Trojans send her as an exchange for a captured Trojan lord, Antenor, to the Greek camp to join her traitor father Calchas, a priest who's foreseen the fall of Troy and defected to the Greeks: she's the classic pawn in a wargame that's even more futile than usual. Once she's with the Greeks she quickly takes Diomede as her lover. So it's easy to see her as an Eve, a deceiver, which is how she's usually played. But there's a counter-narrative.

She's one more proof, if we need it, of Shakespeare's ability to be ever-new; hers is a story with no date except today's. She's young, a virgin not a widow like Chaucer's Criseyde, with a lot of urban wit. Her uncle Pandarus is willing to trade her not so much for money as to ingratiate himself with the Trojan Royals. The Social Services aren't there for her either. She wants Troilus with a desperation too intense to control, though she knows he'll probably lose interest once he's had her. Why does she betray him for Diomede? She must necessarily take a Greek lover if Shakespeare is to tell her story, and infidelity is right for this wonderfully cynical play. But we need to look also at Troilus' failures as a lover.

When the Trojan War Council debates whether Helen should be returned to her husband, Menelaus, Troilus is for keeping her. His reasons are interesting. He hypothesises that he himself takes a wife:

> I take today a wife, and my election [choice]
> Is led on in the conduct of my will [that choice resulting from my desire for her].
> (...)
> How may I avoid [get rid of],
> Although my will distaste what it elected [when I don't want her any more],
> The wife I chose? (...)
> We turn not back the silks upon the merchant
> When we have soiled them, nor the remainder viands [leftover meat]
> We do not throw in unrespective sink [the garbage]
> Because we now are full. (2.2.60-71)

His contribution to the debate is irrelevant, since Helen is the wife of Menelaus, not Paris. But it's revealing on his attitude to women. Once you've had one, you'll get bored with her. If you marry one, you're stuck with her, though she's damaged goods now you've had her.

His anticipation as he waits for Cressida in Pandarus' orchard is epicurean, a matter of the 'watery [watering] palate'. (3.2.18) Then the metaphor turns, as so often, to battle:

I do fear besides
That I shall lose distinction in my joys,
As doth a battle when they charge on heaps,
The enemy flying. (3.2.23-6)

He fears it'll be all over before it starts, in short. He's focused wholly on the degree of pleasure he'll get. And she's the enemy, an especially sinister term here against the war background. His habit elsewhere of referring to himself as 'we', though he's only one of fifty sons of Priam, not the King, might be a warning to a woman less isolated and desperate than Cressida.

After he's spent the night with her, they meet Pandarus in the hall as he's leaving, and Troilus joins in the old man's laugh at her expense. When Aeneas arrives to tell them she's to be exchanged for Antenor, Troilus' response is, 'we met by chance; you did not find me here.' (4.2.72) We may suppose it's her reputation he's thinking about. But Paris and Aeneas already know Troilus expected to spend the night with her, Paris from Pandarus, so that Paris could make excuses for Troilus' absence from supper to their father; Aeneas from Troilus. It's not her reputation Troilus is thinking about, it's his own, and his father's anger if he finds his son is having an affair with a traitor's daughter.

The couple's vows in front of Pandarus followed by intercourse may amount to a marriage, and this is supported by the Sokols' examination in *Shakespeare, Law and Marriage*[16] of what constituted spousals, legal marriages made without clergy or a formal ceremony, though as usual Anne Barton got there first. The Sokols don't discuss *Troilus and Cressida*, but their analysis of spousal marriage puts the whole play in a new light. Though there's no priest, ceremony or ring, the vows the couple swear before they go to bed probably are enough to make a valid and permanent marriage. It's true that Troilus never mentions marriage before they become lovers (except to imply in the War Council he's not going to marry anyone) or afterwards when he hears she must go to the Greeks. His anxiety about keeping their meeting secret from his father and elder brother Hector shows he has no intention of marrying her.

But intention, being so nebulous, was less important in spousals than the handfasting (joining hands), and the vows made. Cressida's fears of losing Troilus once he's had sex with her show she's not sure this is a marriage, though she may hope it is. Only Pandarus acts as if it's a marriage, disclosing it to Paris, encouraging handfasting with himself as witness, calling on them both to say 'Amen' when they exchange vows of fidelity. He makes a parodic parson. His oiling up to the royals is embarrassing, and he'll be one of that family if Troilus marries Cressida. That's his erotic fantasy.

Does Troilus let her think beforehand that this is a marriage, as it could be in Elizabethan law? His behaviour next morning wonderfully demonstrates why serious people were trying to ban the practice of spousals in the 1590s. We may even be grateful for our present bank-busting, cast-of-thousands white weddings; at least neither party can wake up next day and pretend it didn't happen. If he acknowledged her as his wife, that bond would supersede her bond with her father. It would buy time to find another exchange for Antenor. But like her father, he abandons her. He concurs in her transfer to the Greeks and repeatedly questions whether she'll be faithful to him, as if it's inevitable she won't. His sparring with Diomede, who comes to escort her to the Greeks, is boastful, not protective of her; he makes it obvious that they're lovers, which won't do her any good in the enemy camp. After a few miserable questions, she's silent for the last part of the scene. How should this be played? Is she too shocked to speak? Embarrassed by so many men turning up? Looking Diomede over?

As she comes into the enemy camp with Diomede, she's surrounded by the Greek 'heroes' as Achilles' Myrmidons will later surround Hector. They pass her around and start to kiss her one by one. Initially she's silent. When it's Menelaus' turn, though, Patroclus and Achilles push in before him, and she joins in the men's horn jokes about the cuckold who's the butt of both armies. She gets the other men laughing with her, and evades Ulysses' grasp altogether, which angers him. Has she changed in a few hours from the girl in love of last night, who can imagine a time 'when waterdrops have worn the stones of Troy' (3.6.165) but when she and Troilus will still be remembered as lovers? Is she already the hardened prostitute Ulysses calls her? Or is she terrified, and trying to defuse a situation which might easily end in gang rape by treating the men as mates and turning the laugh against someone else?

In Act Five, scene ii, Troilus and Ulysses, spied on by Thersites, eavesdrop on Cressida and Diomede talking at night outside her father's tent. The scene opens with a brutal revelation of the way the Greeks treat Calchas when they're not in a public meeting:

> Diomedes: What, are you up here? Ho! Speak!
> Calchas [at the door]: Who calls?
> Diomedes: Diomede. Calchas, I think. Where's your daughter?
> Calchas: She comes to you. (5.2.1-4)

Cressida comes out of the tent and tries to keep Diomede's protection without promising to have sex with him. Dropping his pretence of chivalry, he repeatedly threatens to walk away if she won't promise, and eventually, reluctantly, she does. If another Greek hero turns up the next night, or a pack of them, her craven father will send her out again. But Troilus and Ulysses hear the betrayal they expect, though it's Troilus' betrayal that delivered her to Diomede. The last time the audience hears of her, she's written to Troilus. Unusually for a letter delivered on stage, he doesn't read it aloud, he just skims it and tears it up, so we don't know what she wrote. 'History' tells the man's story; the woman's version is silenced. She passes into legend as another deceitful Eve like Helen, and the play demonstrates how that happens.

The women in the Problem Plays, or whatever we choose to call them, still disturb our expectations: Juliet's stoicism facing death, Isabella's conceptual intellect and retreat into celibacy and Helena's alternate delicacy and boldness are more than usually surprising. Cressida's spiky vulnerability and dead-end choices have been re-enacted in cities across the UK over the last twenty years, and nobody except Sara Rowbotham and Maggie Oliver[17] did much about it.

*

A husband accuses his wife of lust for his brother. We're not sure if the incestuous couple began an affair in her husband's lifetime, but two months after the husband's death the widow marries her brother-in-law – and the death turns out to be murder. Being dead, the husband can't investigate his wife's degree of guilt or punish his brother, but he can depute these tasks to his son. The son's interrogation of his mother forms the ghost of an honour trial behind the more overtly political events of *Hamlet*.

King Hamlet is bitterly eloquent about the murder and remarriage. Much of our understanding of Claudius and especially of Gertrude is refracted through his and Hamlet's minds. Though Hamlet may be the most intelligent person ever represented in literature, he's surely one of the least objective. Unsurprisingly so: a Renaissance Oedipus, he inhabits a fallen world where the Serpent-Satan that took his father's life now wears a crown and rules jointly with his mother. He can make no sense of that.

Gertrude is affectionate, physically protective of those she loves but crass about their mental states, stupid, taking aphorisms for original ideas, so sexualised she'll remember the coarser name for the wildflower dead men's fingers as she describes Ophelia drowning. The Adam and Eve story is conflated here with the story of their sons, the murderous Cain and his brother Abel. Gertrude is perhaps half the reason Claudius took his brother's life and turned Denmark from Eden to un-weeded garden. The other half is his understandable confidence in his own fitness to rule; he makes an efficient administrator for a complex state. King Hamlet, gambling Danish territory against Norwegian in single combat with King Fortinbras, belonged already to another world.

Even before Hamlet meets the Ghost and learns of the murder, he's sickened by his mother's hasty marriage and her passion for his bloated, heavy-drinking uncle. Claudius has displaced him, both in her affections and in his hopes of Kingship. Monarchy is not hereditary in Denmark, we infer, but there's been no Election either, and Gertrude, Polonius and others in the Danish court have connived at Claudius' Succession.

Unlike Shakespeare's many guiltless heroines, Gertrude and Ophelia are arguably tainted by the society they live in. Past criticism tended to accept that Hamlet has something to be misogynistic about, but that's changed over the last hundred years. We'll be more sceptical also about the Ghost's memories of himself as a radiant angel with a celestial bed, from which his ungrateful wife turned to prey on garbage, that is, Claudius. In 'Gertrude Talks Back', Margaret Atwood's Gertrude calls her husband a bore, mocks her self-righteous son and admits that she, not Claudius, committed the murder.

Others may baulk at young Hamlet's disgust with his mother's middle-aged sexuality when he's just run a rapier through an old man trapped behind a tapestry and will soon commission the deaths of two of his schoolfriends, all without remorse. This is not a modern problem of interpretation: revenge and 'casual slaughter' (collateral damage, casual meaning 'accidental' rather than 'indifferent') were never considered compatible with Christianity. *Hamlet* is both a Revenge play in which Hamlet has little choice but to take the part assigned him by his father and a Christian play in the professed faith of most of its main characters. The clash between the two belief systems can't be reconciled.

When 'The Mousetrap' confirms Claudius' guilt, Hamlet is wildly excited, confronting his mother in her room, forcing her to sit down again when she tries to leave. As she cries out in fear for her life, Polonius calls for help, giving himself away: for all his toadying, he's loyal. Hamlet kills him, mistaking the shape behind the arras for his uncle. As he begins to see what revenge will bring him to, he exaggerates her possible complicity:

> Gertrude: O, what a rash and bloody deed is this!
> Hamlet: A bloody deed! Almost as bad, good mother
> As kill a King, and marry with his brother. (3.4.25-7)

He's not far from 'look what you made me do'. She repeats, stunned, 'as kill a King?' It satisfies Hamlet and us she knew nothing of the murder. It's not a false note like Lady Macbeth's giveaway, 'what, in our house?' (*Macbeth*, 2.3.82) when trying to look surprised by Duncan's death.

And though Hamlet acts as a violent prosecutor, she's never in danger of an honour killing; the Ghost expressly forbids that. Claudius in effect kills her, or fails to save her life, since knocking the poisoned cup away as she lifts it to her mouth would reveal his intent to murder Hamlet. Her choice of her new lover-husband brings about her death, as Eve's choice of the Serpent-Satan ensured hers. Each death in *Hamlet* is particularly neatly tailored to its owner.

We can consider the play as *The Tragedy of Ophelia*, not an unusual critical approach. Hamlet loved Ophelia, and recently, but his disillusion with his mother poisons his understanding of all women. In his first soliloquy, misogyny is shown in the process of its creation. Already, with 'Frailty thy name is woman', (1.2.146) he's jumped without logic from the individual to the general, his private sense of betrayal by his mother finding its home in a commonplace.

Ophelia starts out sane and humorous. When her brother Laertes misinterprets the early stages of a love affair as Hamlet's attempt to seduce her and thinks it's his duty to warn her to be careful, as a Prince is not free to choose his own wife, she flips the warning deftly back to him:

> I shall the effect of this good lesson keep
> As watchman to my heart. But good my brother,
> Do not, as some ungracious pastors do:
> Show me the steep and thorny way to heaven
> Whiles, a puffed and reckless libertine
> Himself the primrose path of dalliance treads
> And recks [heeds] not his own reed [advice]. (1.3.44-50)

She has independent judgement and rejects the double standard of morality that Laertes and Polonius take for granted. Then Polonius goes well beyond Laertes' advice, warning her to suspect everything Hamlet says, to imagine the disgrace if she gets pregnant, to avoid speaking to him again. Though she can tease and temporise with her brother, she's not strong enough to disobey her father.

Everyone is under surveillance at Elsinore. 'Who's there?' (1.1.1.) a sentry calls out as the play opens. He's nervous about a ghost, but in fact there's somebody there a lot of the time as in every European court, especially England's. Polonius is at the centre of the network, getting reports on his daughter, sending a spy to hang around at his son's university, encouraging Claudius to eavesdrop on Hamlet and Ophelia, volunteering to hide in Gertrude's room. He too dies in a horribly appropriate way, a rat behind the arras. Claudius and Gertrude also recruit Hamlet's old friends Rosencrantz and Guildenstern; Claudius needs to know what Hamlet intends.

Ophelia is constrained by her duty to her father and to the King. She complies with their directions to talk to Hamlet where they can listen. Her father gives her a prayer book to explain her being alone, and Hamlet notices this prop at once:

> Nymph, in thy orisons
> Be all my sins remembered. (3.1.90-1)

But he knows Elsinore and recognises as he says it that she's a plant. For a moment, despite this, there's a chance they'll talk openly. She meets his brutal rejection with dignity, neither pretending indifference nor asking for sympathy. He knows who's listening, and becomes increasingly aggressive, finally asking, 'Where is your father?' She lies: 'At home, my lord.' (3.1.127-8) Could she answer honestly? He's just said he never loved her, so it would be expecting a lot of her to anger her father and the King by giving them away. By her one, uncalculated lie she stamps herself as the thickly-painted, deceitful harlot of popular male myth. His repeated, 'get thee to a nunnery' (3.1.120) in one sense recommends celibacy and childlessness as best for this fallen world. But a nunnery was also slang for a brothel. Unlike Brutus, Hamlet consigns her to the suburbs deliberately.

Later, as they wait for 'The Mousetrap' to start, we watch a classic example of sexual harassment and its motivation by contempt, not desire. His 'Lady, shall I lie in your lap?' and 'That's a fair thought, to lie between maids' legs', (3.2.97-101) harp on 'lie' to remind her she betrayed him by lying about her father. He continues in this strain as 'The Mousetrap' goes on. His 'It would cost you a groaning to take off my edge' (3.2.223) is a threat about the defloration of a virgin, frightening her with sexual experience she doesn't have, and she struggles to keep up a veneer of composure. His innuendoes are insulting to an unmarried woman; he's treating her like a prostitute again, knowing his rank means he can get away with it. Her brother is in France and her father no threat to anyone. In short, he's a bit of a shit.

When she sings 'Tomorrow is Saint Valentine's Day' in Act Four, scene ii, she plays out the seduced and abandoned young girl of her brother's and father's imaginings, and enacts Hamlet's insinuations and rejection. Her family first silence her, then Hamlet's hysterical misjudgement about the spy behind the arras maddens her. As she's on everyone's margins, completely in the suburbs, she never learns about his suspicions of Claudius, so she can't make any sense of his killing her father by mistake. At her funeral, Gertrude reveals that she wanted Ophelia to marry Hamlet; the social barrier assumed by Polonius and Laertes was their own invention. Her own hold on life is slight. As with the speaker of Sonnet 111, her nature is coloured like a dyer's hand by the element she lives in. A twig she's holding breaks, plunging her into water; her clothes are enough to take her down.

*

I'll end with two very different plays where initial acts of misogyny drive the rest of the plot.

Love's Labour's Lost starts off with a Misogynists' Manifesto. Four young men sign a document promising to devote themselves to a life of undistracted academic scholarship. Women, except for servants, are banished from within a mile of the King of Navarre's court on pain of losing their tongues, though as the men belatedly recognise that the penalty is at odds with the civility they aspire to, they assure themselves it's only there as a deterrent.

Well into the twentieth century, the older English universities retained traces of this ideology. Not that academics were still forbidden to marry then, but women weren't welcome in college except on rare social occasions. Wives had their evening meal alone at home while their husbands dined at High Table to discuss important scholarly subjects undisturbed by women's chatter – and to eat and drink very well.

The King of Navarre and three of his courtiers, Biron, Dumaine and Longueville, propose to study and stay celibate for three years. The King calls his friends:

> brave conquerors – for so you are
> That war against your own affections [passions]
> And the large army of the world's desires (...)
> Our court shall be a little academe. (1.1.8-13)

They see learning as the way to acquire lasting fame. We know their passions and the large army of the world's desires are going to win, of course. Biron, the wittiest of them, starts backsliding in the opening scene:

> Small have continual plodders ever won
> Save base authority [elementary knowledge] from others' books. (1.1.86-7)

Gary Taylor recalls seeing the play as a student and empathising strongly with its subject. The 'play's battle between hormones and homework was one we had all been fighting, and often losing, for years.'[18] His recollection, surprisingly, is that critics were then mostly on the side of the homework.

Navarre and his courtiers must revise their promise when the French Princess and three of her ladies, Rosaline, Catherine and Maria, arrive on an embassy from her father. Given the one-mile-limit clause, they can't be admitted to Navarre's palace, so they're forced to lodge in tents in his park, though the tents would be beautiful pavilions. But the young men have to meet the ambassadresses, who immediately become objects of intense desire. It's possible the Princess rather than a male ambassador represents her father to get a better outcome in his financial dispute with Navarre. Her three ladies have met Navarre's three friends before, and liked them, with some reservations about their unremitting irony; they may have accompanied the Princess from France to meet and assess them again.

Love's Labour's Lost is the most difficult of all Shakespeare's plays. The cross-fire of allusion and *double-entendre* is too much for most of us, and that certainly includes me, to pick up the first time around, or the second. This one needs study before watching as a straight performance, though Kenneth Branagh's musical film would help.

There's almost no plot, but an elaborate dance of personalities and courtship rituals expressed in fashionable verse forms and far-fetched figures of speech. For the men, love and courtship are matters of the written word, occasionally in prose letters but more often in a range of Courtly Love, Petrarchan, anti-Petrarchan and erotic poetry. Some of this was lifted from its context in *LLL* and went into contemporary verse anthologies. But they're also good at badinage. The verbal tennis is stunning, with the women as quick as the men – and amongst themselves quite competitive about their weight.

'Courtly Love' poetry is poetry in a European tradition that began among the minstrels or troubadours of Southern France; it goes back as far as the 11th Century and was originally written to be sung. The poem's male speaker/singer adores a lady higher in the social scale than himself. The poet expresses his despair that he can never possess her because of the social distance or because she's married, or both. The language used was the language of religious devotion, of 'service' to a superior being, of seeking 'mercy' or 'grace', comparable to God's mercy and grace, from the lady, in other words, acceptance as her lover. Not surprisingly, the church wasn't happy about any of it.

The classic text is *The Romance of the Rose (Le Roman de la Rose).* It's an allegory of love and of the arts the lover needs in courtship, the lady imagined as a rose growing in a garden surrounded by thorns representing the obstacles to winning her. It was written by at least two hands, Guillaume de Lorris and Jean de Meung, between 1230 and 1280, and was immensely popular throughout Europe, not just in France. And not just in courts and among the upper classes. As its imitators grew, its language became common currency, as Chaucer shows in *The Miller's Tale*, where Nicholas solicits the Miller's wife Alison for sex, but she succumbs only when he brings in the 'have mercy or I die' line.

As the *genre* grew in sophistication over the centuries, the poet described the beauty of the lady's face and sometimes her body in a tribute known as a 'blazon', seen as the equivalent of a man's heraldic shield, and as powerful. Her eyes dazzle like suns, her lips are like cherries, her hair like jeweller's golden wire. She's itemised into an ideal as impossible for most women to achieve as photographic models are now. The male poet was probably as much interested in his own literary success as in the adored object.

Less cynically, we can assume this tradition expressed the pain of being young in a religious and military European culture that channelled desire into the consolidation of a stable, hieratic state. Many young men and women among the aristocracy and wealthier classes were contracted as children and married off young. Though there must have been instances of mutual love leading to marriages of choice, they were probably rare, so the culture favoured poetry lamenting or celebrating relationships that were unconsummated or adulterous. The immensely influential *Rime* of Francesco Petrarch (1304-74) fed into the courtly love tradition. Petrarch's sonnet sequence defines earthly love for an unattainable woman, Laura, as an impulse that leads, though with many doubts and hesitations, to her Creator, to God.

In England, Richard II's court allowed peace enough for Geoffrey Chaucer to flourish. Some of *The Canterbury Tales*, notably *The Knight's Tale*, are stories of courtly love. His epic *Troilus and Criseyde* brilliantly exemplifies the narrative of a secret, transgressive courtship and passion. There was little place for court poetry in the following century in a country ripped apart by civil war. But under Henry VIII, England began to catch up, with Thomas Wyatt and the Earl of Surrey appearing as talented Petrarchan sonneteers. Edmund Spenser domesticated the *genre* with a sequence that tells the story of his own courtship and marriage and ends with an Epithalamion (marriage song) for his bride.

By Shakespeare's time, English versions of courtly love tended towards the debunking, libertine or aggressive. Shakespeare's own 'My mistress' eyes are nothing like the sun'[19] is a funny example of the first type. John Donne retains traces of the devotional aspect while incorporating an explicit sexiness: in *Love's Labour's Lost*, Dumaine's verses to Catherine, 'On a day – (alack the day!)' are of this sort. Michael Drayton's sonnet speaker in *Idea's Mirrour* seems driven as much by hatred as desire. If the lady won't come across, he hopes he'll live to see the day when she's so old her teeth fall out and her nose drops down to meet her chin.[20] This sentiment is close to the possessive rage that drives honour killing.

The four young men in *Love's Labour's Lost*, Navarre the King, Biron, Dumaine and Longueville, are as well-read in these poetic cultures as in the classics. Biron is the first to fall, for Rosaline, whom he calls:

> (...) a whitely wanton with a velvet brow,
> With two pitch balls stuck in her head for eyes
> Ay, and, by heaven, one that will do the deed
> Though Argus[21] were her eunuch and her guard. (3.1.173)

Women don't just tempt men away from the intellectual study that brings fame. They're strange and fearful creatures in themselves. Biron speaks the classic misogynist stereotype of his time: women are deceitful and oversexed, hellish in their darkness – and Rosaline is very dark. They can't be trusted for a second even when they're locked up. Biron assumes she's wanton, a slut, because she's beautiful. He invokes courtly luxuries like velvet to describe her brows, but he also compares her eyes with pitch, that defiles. His allusion to the monster Argus, who even with a hundred eyes can't ensure a woman's chastity, attests to a classical but limited boy culture that's cut all four young men off from educated (early) modern women. But the girls are irresistible, and each of the men writes verses in praise of his beloved, which he reads aloud when he thinks he's alone.

Serial eavesdropping is followed by serial exposure. Biron is the last to admit breaking the promise, but insists he did so on rational grounds, since:

> love, first learned in a lady's eyes
> Lives not alone [only] immured in the brain,
> But with the motion [mobility] of all elements [living things]
> Courses as swift as thought in every power [mental and physical function] (...)
> (4.3.297-300)

Yet he and his friends remain stuck in their boy gang, still seeing women as the enemy, as foreign creatures to be conquered; they remain half-abject, half-hostile in their courtship. When they can no longer conceal their promise-breaking from each other, Navarre urges them on to visit the women and engage in the battle of the sexes:

> Navarre: Saint Cupid! then, and, soldiers, to the field!
> Biron: Advance your standards [flags, flagpoles, erections], and upon them, lords,
> Pell-mell, down with them, but be first advised
> In conflict that you get the sun of them. (4.3.336-39)

Get the sun in their eyes in battle, get them pregnant with a boy; they know they have to marry some time for dynastic reasons. Again, courtship, sex and warfare blend into each other, here in mock-heroic style. The courtiers can't find a language that's free of hostile overtones. They try to sound threatening because they're scared. If an aristocratic woman's family gave her a choice in marriage, courtship was the one time she enjoyed real power, if only the power to reject. These men aren't used to rejection.

The 'mocking wenches' (5.2.258) enjoy innuendo and puns as much as the men, but Rosaline's companions, including the camp Boyet who's trying to look after them, seem to consider her particularly 'light' or wanton. She says nothing to contradict them, as if it's irrelevant or as if she expects a potential husband to take a risk on her chastity. It's part of her refusal to inhabit either stereotype, chaste maiden or whitely wanton. In her last exchanges with Navarre, even the sophisticated Princess, by then a Queen, carefully asserts her own virginity. Rosaline's carelessness about her reputation makes *LLL* feel particularly modern.

All the women tease their lovers by ignoring them, by disguises, by reversing the usual gender stereotype and blaming the men for promise-breaking. When they impersonate each other by wearing masques and each other's jewellery, the gifts of the men, they seem to make the point that the men can't tell them apart as people except by extraneous signs. However, disguise usually was impenetrable on the stage.

The linguistic excesses of Navarre's court are imitated by the visiting Spaniard, Adriano de Armado, whose grand circumlocutions are sent up relentlessly by his page, Mote. Armado too promises to study for three years, imitating the young aristocrats, and he also reluctantly falls in love with 'a child of our grandmother Eve, a female', (1.1.241) Jacquenetta the dairy maid. He too sees women as temptations to avoid but can't avoid them:

> Love is a familiar [a witch's companion-spirit, often an animal]; love is a devil. There is no evil angel but love. Yet was Samson so tempted, and he had an excellent strength. Yet was Solomon so seduced, and he had a very good wit. (1.2.137-9)

He's absorbed the image of women as seductresses or witches from the Old Testament, where most of the named women are bad news for somebody, and even Susanna is bad news for the Elders. 'Who can find a virtuous woman, for her price is far above rubies?' the *Book of Proverbs* rhetorically asks.[22] Though a long profile of such a woman is posted, nobody, sadly, ever reports finding her. Armado's courtship of Jacquenetta is also a matter of writing, his love confessed in a highfalutin letter it's unlikely she can read. His fear of deceitful women comes from his religious education, as the courtiers' fears come from their literary one. Jacquenetta, though she has a small part, is as much fun as Rosaline, an Essex Girl unimpressed by Armado's and the nobility's pretentions.

The courtiers dress up as Muscovites, hoping to put on a Masque and dance with the women, who instead retreat to their tents. So the men are particularly aggressive when Armado with a little group of aspiring middle-class eggheads puts on a Pageant of the Nine Worthies for all the court characters. This was a favourite subject for scholastic entertainments. It's under-cast, and they have to make four actors go round nine Worthies. Costard, the only one emphatically not an egghead, is a workman on Navarre's estate. He's formally uneducated and has the usual problems with long words but, like Armado's Mote, is as sardonic as the courtiers most of the time:

> Mote [of his betters]: they have been at a great feast of languages and stolen the scraps.
> Costard: O, they have lived long on the alms-basket of words. (5.1.31-2)

But the classics aren't Costard's thing, and he mangles Pompey the Great. Holofernes, the earnest schoolteacher, doesn't get far as Judas Maccabeus. Navarre and his friends, smarting from their rejection by the Princess and her ladies, are much ruder than the audience of 'Pyramus and Thisbe'. The Princess is unfailingly good-mannered, but Holofernes is forced off the stage by the men's fusillade of crass jokes and catcalls, though not before he's made a judgement the audience endorses:

> This is not generous, not gentle, not humble. (5.2.611)

In all their dealings with the women, the courtiers are trapped inside language that's either Petrarchan-idealist or schoolboy-bawdy; both dialects are inadequate for the purposes of normal communication. Towards the end Biron promises he's going to be straightforward and sincere with Rosaline:

> Taffeta phrases, silken terms precise,
> Three-piled hyperboles [piled-up exaggerated praises], spruce [dressed up] affectation,
> Figures pedantical [learned figures of speech] – these summer flies
> Have blown me full of maggot ostentation
> [inflated me so I'm like a flyblown corpse].
> I do forswear them, and I do protest,
> By this white glove, how white the hand, God knows!
> Henceforth my wooing mind shall be expressed
> In russet [brown or grey wool] yeas and honest kersey [thick warm wool] noes.
> And to begin, 'wench, so God help me, law [rustic for 'Lord' or 'Lord have mercy'],
> My love to thee is sound, sans [without] crack or flaw.'
> Rosaline: Sans sans, I pray you. (5.2.408-18)

Even as he's rejecting courtly poetic language he lapses into the tired old 'hand whiter than your glove' chat-up line and the unnecessary French word. His attempt to switch to simple Mummerset doesn't work, and he can't keep a straight face while he's doing it. For all their formidable education and verbal skills, or because of them, the men can't talk to intelligent women.

By Act Five, their obsessive sexual puns are growing tedious, their pyrotechnics repetitive rather than illuminating. There's a growing seriousness as the realities of death and birth creep into Arcadia. Speaking to Catherine of Cupid, God of Love, Rosaline says:

> You'll ne'er be friends with him, a [he] killed your sister.
> Catherine: He made her melancholy, sad and heavy.
> And so she died. (5.2.13-15)

As the Pageant of the Nine Worthies collapses, Costard re-enters to report that Jacquenetta is pregnant, 'two months on her way'. (5.2.649) He fixes responsibility on Armado, though from earlier scenes we can guess that he himself is probably the biological father. Courtship and sex have consequences in the messy real world they don't have when confined to writing. Of all the men, uneducated Costard seems to be the only one who scores in the mating game. Luckily Armado is pleased to believe his story. The courtiers get an alarming visual lesson on the ease with which a man can be cuckolded.

Then the messenger Mercade arrives from France, and the Princess, now a Queen, guesses his errand from his clothes before he plainly tells her that her father is dead. All the women must go into mourning.

Navarre begs the Queen, his courtiers beg her three ladies, to promise marriage at once, though they know they've probably lost their chance:

> Navarre: Now, at the latest minute of the hour
> Grant us your loves.
> Queen: A time, methinks, too short
> To make a world-without-end bargain in. (5.2.753-5)

All the women are unconvinced of the promise-breakers' sincerity, and all want to split up the boy gang. Catherine and Maria ask Dumaine and Longueville, politely, to spend a year growing up. The Queen wants Navarre to live for a year as a hermit. Rosaline's demand is the best: Biron must leave his life of privilege and spend the year in a hospital trying to make the sick and dying smile. He must learn about pain and death, and adapt his wit to that knowledge.

The songs of Spring and Winter, Ver and Hiems, that end the play look out from the court towards nature, though not towards simplicity. Spring has flowers and maidens bleaching their summer smocks, but it also has the cuckoo to remind married men of potentially cheating wives, and cuckoos in their nests. Winter has aches, coughs and frozen milk, but it also has mulled ale and the merry owl of a wiser old age. This diptych is among Shakespeare's greatest dramatic songs, directing the dilettantism of the academic courtiers out towards the painful, beautiful, mutable world, as the women hope to do.

Even such a bare outline of *Love's Labour's Lost*'s coruscation is enough to show misogyny controlling the action, from the men's first idiotic attempt to eliminate women to the anti-comedic ending, when the women decide their suitors are still too emotionally immature for marriage. All four courtly romantic relationships are antagonistic, though Biron's and Rosaline's is much the most cutting and sexy. They have that in common with almost all Shakespeare's clever couples. Romeo and Juliet are exceptions; even they spar a little when they first meet, but they're too young to foresee any problems beyond the feud.

This time Jack doesn't have Jill; the men must wait another year while the Queen mourns her father, her ladies with her. Men as much as women may miss their matrimonial market if they spend too long reading or showing off or worrying about being cuckolded. Four such sparky girls are seldom found together. Despite their mourning and conditional promises, perhaps Rosaline, the Queen, perhaps all four will meet somebody new before these men see them again.

Misogyny drives both the main and the subplot in the most powerful of all the tragedies, though 'main' and 'sub' are inadequate categories for a narrative that closely knits Lear's and Gloucester's children, and where the subplot of Edmund's rise is usually more gripping than Lear's fall.

Lear commands his three daughters to speak in front of his court, expecting them to say what he wants to hear, displaying them like circus ponies. Approaching dementia, he needs professions of love and gratitude when he decides to abdicate and divide his kingdom between them. Goneril and Regan act fairly well; Cordelia refuses to act at all.

The Love Trial is a variant on the honour trial of a wife's fidelity. Lear's demand to hear who loves him best issues from quasi-sexual jealousy, and Goneril and Regan know what they're doing when they claim to love him better than anyone or anything else. Cordelia's

> Why have my sisters husbands if they say
> They love you all? (1.1.83-4)

points to the incestuous nature of his love and the elder sisters' ability to exploit it. We know before he does that he's going to repudiate her and reward the two tigers. His judgement of her, 'Better not to have been born than not to have pleased me better', is a definition of herself she must reject if she's not to fade out like Ophelia.

King Lear has a source in Holinshed's *Chronicles*, like the English Histories. Another and more intriguing source was closer to home in the family life of a once-prominent London citizen, Sir Brian Annesley, a well-to-do old gentleman with three daughters. By 1603, he was ageing badly enough for the eldest (and possibly the middle) sister to try having him declared insane, so they and their husbands could enjoy his money and estates. But their plans were wrecked by the youngest sister, who counterclaimed that her father was not mad, that greed alone was behind this. There was a widely-discussed lawsuit, and the youngest sister won. Sir Brian died a year later, not on the best terms with his elder daughters. The name of the youngest was Cordell, an uncommon name at any time.

What does this mean? It's anyone's guess. But it might help to account for what a lot of people have thought about *King Lear*: that though it may be based on the *Chronicles*, though Lear's Kingship and the government of Britain is the ostensible subject, the play's impact comes from the sight of two wrecked families. Only if we can believe in Lear and Gloucester as fathers ageing badly can we understand the hate that Goneril and Regan feel for Lear and that Edmund, perhaps Edgar too, feel for Gloucester. Simon Russell Beale caught the comedy and unpredictability of Lear's dementia in a Mendes production where for once the Lear story was more exciting than the Edmund one.

Lear and Gloucester are both misogynists. The play opens with Kent in conversation with Gloucester, whose illegitimate son Edmund is listening in apparently respectful silence:

> Kent: Is not this your son, my lord?
> Gloucester: His breeding, sir, hath been at my charge. I have so often blushed to acknowledge him that now I am brazed to it.
> Kent: I cannot conceive you.

Gloucester: Sir, this young fellow's mother could, whereupon she grew round-wombed, and had indeed sir a son for her cradle ere she had a husband for her bed. Do you smell a fault?
Kent: I cannot wish the fault undone, the issue of it being so proper [handsome]. (1.1.6-14)

Gloucester's reply to Kent's question is clearly 'yes'. With 'I cannot conceive you', Kent is amiably playing the straight man for Gloucester's well-known party turn. He's fatuously proud of his handsome son and enjoys lip-smacking reminiscences of the 'good sport' at his conception, not an event most sons want to visualise at the best of times. Though affectionately, he goes on to call Edmund a whore's son.

For Gloucester as for Lear, women exist for men's pleasure and prestige. Gloucester's former 'whore' (where is she now?) and Lear's daughters are in their different ways something to boast about in public. Both old men make their wills at the beginning. Gloucester won't lessen the disparity between legitimate Edgar and illegitimate Edmund. The latter, his father says, has been out nine years, and must soon be away again. To be 'out' was to be abroad on military service with the army, in which Edmund is an officer. Though patronisingly fond of him, Gloucester has no great concern for his safety, while Edgar will remain at home and inherit everything. Edmund maintains his self-control during the conversation at court, but his fury breaks out the next time we see him. Lear and Gloucester sign their own death-warrants in the opening scene.

Tragedy starts in the domestic failures; the public failures grow out of these. The division of a kingdom is first the division of a father's goods among children who've never been loved equally. Legacies highly regarded by the father mean love to the children. In the productions as in the criticism of the last 30 years, there's been a tendency to un-demonise Goneril and Regan, to bring out their bitterness over their father's preference for Cordelia that forms the basis for their later actions. It seems Lear chose Goneril and Regan's husbands for them, judging from both sisters' immediate desperation for Edmund, while Cordelia has a choice, if only of two. Goneril and Regan transfer their struggle for their father's love to a more savage struggle for Edmund's, who like Lear seeks to rule through them, playing them off against each other like their father in the first act.

Lear's misogyny runs deep, it's not confined to his insistence on a Love Trial, the staged display of his daughters' devotion. It emerges violently when he curses Goneril:

> Hark, nature, hear:
> Dear goddess, suspend thy purpose if
> Thou did'st intend to make this creature fruitful.
> Into her womb convey sterility.
> Dry up in her the organs of increase,
> And from her derogate [flawed] body never spring
> A babe to honour her. (1.4.242-8)

Cursing her reproductive organs, he wishes away any grandchildren he might have by her, in a curiously self-harming surge of anger. On the heath, he imagines putting Regan on trial, and the thought of his daughters' cruelty opens into an attack on all women's deceit and lust:

> Behold yon simpering dame
> Whose [innocent] face between her forks [legs] presages [foretells] snow [chastity],
> That minces [mimics] virtue, and does shake the head
> To hear of pleasure's name:
> The fitchew [polecat] nor the soiled horse [fed on fresh green fodder; randy] goes to it
> With a more riotous appetite. (4.6.110-115)

When Goneril and Regan are asked to act specifically as women, daughters at the Love Trial, they comply as well as they can. In their later refusal of Lear's rights, they're not behaving specifically as women, they're more like rebellious sons, and Lear knows nothing of their passion for Edmund. Yet it's in their sexuality, as women, that their father attacks them.

We return to Gloucester's original sin at the end. After their final fight Edgar taunts Edmund, whom he's fatally wounded:

> That dark and vicious place where thee he got [conceived]
> Cost him his eyes. (5.3.168-9)

He's referring to Gloucester's impregnation of Edmund's mother. It sounds like the culmination of a life's anger with his father as well as his brother. There's a latent sense of her womb as diseased, causing blindness, as if she'd been an infectious prostitute. Edmund ends as he began the play, listening to contemptuous comments about his mother that he can't respond to. Gloucester has taken the usual path of nobility whose wives have babies to nurse, and found an exciting girl. Choosing a daughter's husband and finding a mistress were common among the nobility, but they prompt uncommon reactions here.

Lear, Kent, the Fool, Gloucester and Albany understand virtue as the acceptance of divine hierarchy and fatherhood. But that order is threatened by a new world and new men, by Edmund, who has the wit to seize his opportunities, and whose looks, brains and good manners make any marriage or political position possible. On his side of the divide is his mini version, Oswald, much lower in the social scale than an Earl's acknowledged son, but ready to rise through women. Here too Cornwall belongs, turned savage by the danger posed to his new power by Cordelia's return to Britain. Edmund almost makes it from illegitimate son of an Earl to King. He doesn't try to originate a different social system, he just wants to improve his place in the established one. But Edgar emerges as the toughest in the Darwinian jungle.

Two characters opt out of the competition. Cornwall's heroic, unnamed servant throws off a lifetime's social conditioning when he intervenes to try to stop Gloucester's blinding, and kills Cornwall. Though he's killed at once by Regan and can't save Gloucester's other eye, he strikes the first blow for Lear's side. Cordelia won't join in the power struggle at the Love Trial, refusing to upstage her sisters in the bid for their father's largest legacy she knows she can easily win. She rebels, though briefly, then quickly slips back into the hierarchy as the King of France's wife.

She's seemed to some critics, A.C. Bradley particularly, sufficiently genderless to function as a Christ figure who claims 'O, father, it is thy business that I go about', (4.4.23-4)[23] when she returns to Britain at the head of an army, loses the battle and is hanged, Christ-like, on Edmund's orders. Modern criticism mostly rejects that interpretation. The play's bleak ending is no argument against it: nobody ever claimed that Christianity offers a happy ending on earth. But even if she's a redeemer, Lear can hardly be called redeemed, except in the sense that he recognises her, in one of those lucid intermissions dementia sometimes affords, and dies sane though still wrong about her, still expecting her to speak comfortingly to him. Lear's treatment of her and her sisters, Gloucester's attitude to Edmund's mother (indulged even by the good guys like Kent), and thus to Edmund's place in his family, together cause civil war and their own deaths.

Unlike most women in the Histories and Roman Plays, whose identities are stifled under a military regime, Cordelia both becomes a soldier and retains her selfhood to the end. But though they die trying, she and Cornwall's servant can't save anyone. *King Lear*'s world is incompatible with a benevolent God. It's like the rack, Kent mordantly remarks, destroying its victims as it elongates their bodies:

> He hates him [Lear]
> That would upon the rack of this tough world
> Stretch him out longer. (5.3.309-11)

If anyone's in charge, it's the psychopaths who run the Tower.

Women are silenced in different ways. Cordelia is encouraged to speak, but only if she says what her father wants to hear. When she tells the truth she's banished, which sets in motion the country's downfall. Life in the suburbs or in exile is forced on women by the limiting judgements of the men; their truths are wasted. In some Comedies, the worst consequences are averted, and Beatrice's mouth is stopped only by a kiss; the women of *Love's Labour's Lost* retain their independence as their play closes. Usually, repression can be avoided only by the woman's escape into a world of pure imagination where she can choose metamorphosis, and be male.

Notes

[1]Herne's Oak is a good place for an assignation because it's haunted at night by the ghost of a ferocious old Keeper, so the spot will be deserted. It's never been clear which of the oaks in Windsor Great Park was meant by Herne's Oak. Whichever, it has long gone.

[2]Bernard Manning, comedian, 1930-2007. His misogyny and ethnic stereotypes were popular in the 1950s, becoming less so as the 20th century went on.

[3]In *The Second Sex* (*Le Deuxieme Sexe*), 1949, Simone de Beauvoir argues that masculinity and femininity are not innate but constructions of society and of the choices we make.

[4]*Along Came a Spider*, film, 2001, starring Morgan Freeman and Monica Potter.

[5]Molly Smith, 'Mutant Scenes and "Minor" Conflicts in *Richard II*', in *A Feminist Companion to Shakespeare*, p267.

[6]'I am Richard, know ye not that?' The question is discussed in Jason Scott-Warren's 'Was Elizabeth I Richard II? The Authenticity of Lambarde's "Conversation"', in *The Review of English Studies* 64 (2012), pp208-30. It's possible Elizabeth was referring to John Hayward's *The First Part of the History and Raigne of King Henrie IIII*, a prose history dedicated to Essex and published in 1599, before the Essex Rebellion, for which the writer was imprisoned but escaped execution. Or she may have been referring to Richard II as represented in both Shakespeare's play and Hayward's history. The deposition scene wasn't printed in her lifetime, though it may have been staged.

[7]Stephen Greenblatt, *Tyrant: Shakespeare on Power*, pp17-23.

[8]Katharine Eisaman Maus, Introduction to *Richard II* in *The Norton Shakespeare*, p950.

[9]Julia Kristeva, (1941-) is a French-Bulgarian writer, influential in her work on the female body and female difference in spoken and written English.

[10]Henry Percy's (Hotspur's) wife's name was in fact Elizabeth, but either Shakespeare didn't know that or he decided to re-christen her Kate. She and her brother Sir Edmund Mortimer were grandchildren of Lionel, Duke of Clarence, a younger son of Edward III, and direct descent from Edward III was a trump card in the struggle for the Succession brought on by Bolingbroke's usurpation of Richard II. Kate/Elizabeth's brother Sir Edmund Mortimer married Owen Glendower's daughter. But Raphael Holinshed, the historian Shakespeare mainly followed, got it wrong in one respect, so Shakespeare did too: it was Sir Edmund's and Kate/Elizabeth's nephew, also called Edmund Mortimer, the son of their brother Roger Mortimer, who was the focus for the rising alluded to in this scene.

[11]Quoted in prefatory material to *Coriolanus*, in *The New Oxford Shakespeare: The Complete Works*, p2,724.

[12]Harriet Walter, 'An open letter to Shakespeare on behalf of women'. Internet.

[13]This is by Henry Peacham, a younger contemporary of Shakespeare. His drawing of *Titus Andronicus* in performance and Jonathan Bate's discussion of it can be found in the Introduction to *Titus Andronicus*, the Arden Edition, pp38-44.

[14]*St Matthew*, Chapter 7, v. 1-3: 'Judge not, that ye be not judged, for with what judgement ye judge, ye shall be judged, and with what measure ye meet [whatever penalty you dole out to others] it shall be measured [doled out] to you again. And why beholdest thou the mote [speck] that is in thy brother's eye, but considerest not the beam [plank of wood] that is in thine own eye?'

This is part of a long run of Christ's teaching known as The Sermon on the Mount, which often contradicts Mosaic Law.

[15]*Troilus and Cressida* was written for an audience educated in the classics. For modern readers and theatre-goers it may be helpful to have a quick outline of events leading up to the point where Shakespeare's play opens.

Eight years earlier, Paris, one of many sons of Priam, King of Troy and his wife Queen Hecuba, goes to visit Menelaus, King of the Greek city-state of Sparta, to ask for the return of his aunt Hesione, who's been abducted by the Greeks. Paris falls in love with Menelaus' wife Helen, the most beautiful woman in the world, and persuades her to run away with him back to Troy. Menelaus raises a Greek army to go after them, to punish the Trojans and demand the return of Helen. The army is commanded by Agamemnon, Menelaus' elder brother.

Other Greeks who join the expedition against Troy are: Ulysses, the brains of the party; Achilles, the military champion with his reputedly gay friend Patroclus and his subjects the Myrmidons, half human and half ant; the elderly Nestor; Ajax, who's all brawn and no brains; the cynic Diomedes; and Thersites, the 'clown' of the play, who comments scathingly and accurately on both Greeks and Trojans. With their troops they besiege Troy, with occasional truces and parleys but getting nowhere until the point where Shakespeare begins.

In Troy, King Priam's command is as shaky as Agamemnon's. On the Trojan side are Priam's sons: Hector, the military champion; Troilus; Deiphobus; Helenus; the illegitimate Margareton; and of course Paris. Aeneas and Antenor are also important Trojans. The priest Calchas foresees that Troy will fall to the Greeks and he defects to the Greek camp. The story of Troilus and Cressida does not appear in Homer's *Iliad*, but in Shakespeare's play Calchas' daughter Cressida is left in the inadequate care of her uncle Pandarus, who likes to ingratiate himself with the Royals. Cassandra, Priam's second-sighted daughter, also knows that Troy will fall if Helen is not returned. The play opens with Councils of War on both sides, Greek then Trojan.

The audience knows from the start there's no hope for Troy, and the Greeks will get in via a wooden horse, a bright idea from Ulysses. Aeneas however will escape to found Rome, as told in Virgil's *Aeneid*, and Menelaus will spare Helen. Most of the other Trojan men will die; the Trojan women including Hector's wife Andromache and his sister Cassandra will be taken as slaves.

[16]*Shakespeare, Law and Marriage* (2003), by B.J. and Mary Sokol, suggests new ways of understanding some of Shakespeare's lovers. There are several spousal marriages: Othello and Desdemona's, Posthumus and Imogen's, the handfasting almost achieved by Florizel and Perdita but broken off by Polixenes and, as noted, possibly the 'true contract' of Claudio and Juliet. The Sokols don't discuss the Orchard Scene in *Troilus and Cressida*, but their book as a whole suggests that the declarations of love by the couple, accompanied by vows and handfasting in front of a witness and followed by their going to bed combine to make them husband and wife in English law (and of course it's English culture not Trojan we're in). The Sokols' research exposes Troilus' failure to make clear his marital intentions (or lack of them) to Cressida, to acknowledge her as his wife or to oppose as her husband her transfer to the Greek camp.

[17]Sara Rowbotham was a Sexual Health Worker and Maggie Oliver a police officer who worked for eight years to expose the sexual abuse of young girls in Rochdale while the Social Services and police refused to recognise the problem. Sara Rowbotham was sacked for her intervention.

[18]Gary Taylor, prefatory material to *Love's Labour's Lost*, in *The New Oxford Shakespeare: The Complete Works*, p773.

[19]Shakespeare, sonnet 130:

My mistress' eyes are nothing like the sun.

Coral is far more red than her lips' red.

If snow be white, then are her breasts but dun,

If hairs be wires, black wires grow on her head (...)

[20]In Michael Drayton's *Idea's Mirrour*, Sonnet 8, the speaker looks forward to a time when:

Thy pearly teeth [are] out of thy head so clean [completely]

That, when thou feedest, thy nose shall touch thy chin.

[21]Argus, in Greek myth, is a monster with a hundred eyes: a strict guard.

[22]*Proverbs*, Chapter 31, v. 10-28: 'Who can find a virtuous woman, for her price is far above rubies? The heart of her husband doth safely trust in her, so that he shall have no need of spoil [no need to beg or borrow]. She will do him good and not evil all the days of her life ... She riseth also while it is yet night, and giveth meat to her household ... She layeth her hands to the spindle, and her hands hold the distaff ... She stretcheth out her hand to the poor; yea, she reacheth forth her hands to the needy. She is not afraid of the snow for her household: for all her household are clothed with scarlet ... She openeth her mouth with wisdom, and in her tongue is the law of kindness. She looketh well to the ways of her household, and eateth not the bread of idleness. Her children arise up and call her blessed; her husband also, and he praiseth her ... '

[23]*St Luke*, Chapter 2, verse 49: 'And he [Jesus] said unto them [Mary and Joseph], how is it that ye sought me? Wist [know] ye not that I must be about my father's business?'

6

'THE TRUTH OF GIRLS AND BOYS'

On the cross-dressing Comedies: *The Two Gentlemen of Verona; As You Like It; Twelfth Night; Cymbeline;* and the odd one out, *The Merchant of Venice*

LIKE MANY OF HIS CONTEMPORARY DRAMATISTS, Shakespeare sometimes adopted plots where women disguise themselves as boys. His cross-dressing plays are based on early versions of novels, old Italian or French stories possibly read in translation, or for *As You Like It*, on Thomas Lodge's prose romance, *Rosalynde.* Even the earliest European storytellers noticed that being a woman is dangerous and life could be better as a boy. On the Elizabethan stage the female characters were played by boys and men; audiences seem to have accepted the cross-dressing convention without question, knowing no other way of doing it.

Actors played women, but they also played everything else they weren't: Fools, Kings, usurpers, politicians and peasants. Plays where actors representing women cross-dress and act as boys or where, for example, an actor representing an Earl's son disguises himself as a beggar, particularly emphasise the theatrical nature of all gender and class roles taught by society following the accident of birth. Provisional, uncomfortable or popular roles may be assigned to actors on the stage, as they've been assigned to actors in the audience. 'All the world's a stage,' (2.7.138-9) as Jaques says in *As You Like It*, 'and all the men and women merely players.' His speech comes in the middle of the play most apt to destabilise concepts of fixed gender.

In a novel, we're told what happens; we don't see the characters or hear their words spoken aloud. On the stage, we see and hear what happens. On the Elizabethan stage, the audience saw the adaptability of the boy actor's body, voice and emotional range as he acted girl then boy then (sometimes) girl again.

Cross-dressing is Shakespeare's narrative answer to attempts to kill or repress women. He allows women who might not survive as women to reinvent themselves as males. Jessica (*The Merchant of Venice*), Rosalind (*As You Like It*), Viola (*Twelfth Night*) and Imogen (*Cymbeline*) adopt boys' clothes to escape confinement, rape or death. Julia (*The Two Gentlemen of Verona*), cross-dresses to pursue her lover from Verona to Milan unmolested by rapists on the road. Portia (*The Merchant of Venice*) is different, secure as a woman but cross-dressing to exercise power in a profession exclusive to men.

I've been considering Shakespeare's plays as much-heightened images of his society and ours, but we enter another dimension with the cross-dressing comedies. Disguise is not a possible way out in any version of a real world – though some might dispute that. To find happy endings secured only by the heroine's disguise as a boy we must enter La La Land.[1] Which we do, in entering Arden and Illyria, imaginary green or golden worlds as critics have called them, lands of endless possibility where girls can disguise as boys and get to know and be known by potential lovers and husbands outside the fabrications of Petrarchan idealism or the reductiveness of sexy innuendo.

The transgender story is found only in his Comedies, infiltrating the dream of love and marriage, not in the Tragedies or Histories. Joan of Arc and Queen Margaret put on armour, but this is for a practical military purpose; they don't disguise themselves. Comedy with its love of changing relationships is the space for cross-dressing and role-playing, for testing the fluidity of boy and girl while staging same-sex and opposite-sex attraction.

The cross-dressing Comedies as they're performed now, with women actors playing women, invite the audience to enjoy the jokes and mix-ups caused by a woman's pretending to be a boy. They will show how well or badly a woman can pass as male, and so raise questions about the differences between men and women. Perhaps they're only physical, concealable under clothing, or a matter of socialisation, learning a role. These speculations predominate for us. But on Shakespeare's stage, because boy actors played the women, the cross-dressing Comedies offered a wider, more fluid spectrum of genders, undermining the categories of male and female altogether.

Back in the 1950s when genteel society and Shakespearean criticism openly acknowledged only two sexes, it used to be said that Shakespeare wrote stunning roles where boys playing girls become boys again because the boy actors felt easier and more convincing back in boys' clothing. That would be the tail wagging the dog. It's more likely these were boys who could pass for girls or women on or off the stage, and that the best of them would identify as transgender or transvestite now.

Although all-boy acting companies (ie without grown men) were becoming popular by the end of the 1590s, those boys were not acting in plays of Shakespeare's psychological intensity. Even if puberty was later then, it seems unlikely that a straight boy under fifteen or sixteen could play Desdemona or Lady Macbeth successfully. But this must remain speculation. Hamlet's welcome of the players to Elsinore includes a pre-pubertal boy, but the play in the visiting company's repertoire, 'The Mousetrap', is formal and declamatory, not requiring the qualities needed for Gertrude or Ophelia. For them, an actor closer to current understandings of transgender might be better.

If we admit the possibility of trans or bisexual actors, then on stage the boys escaped a mainstream culture that threatened unconventional young men, unless they were protected by their rank, more than it threatened nonconforming heterosexual women. At last they could be rewarded for who they were, boy actors who could be girls who could be boys who could be girls again, then take the girl-clothes off and leave the building as boys, then come back and do it all again next day. In the 1590s they could offer a dream theatre where desire is free of demarcation into masculine and feminine. And because dreams usually try to become possibilities, cross-dressing could give an actor or a member of the audience confidence in a homosexual, transsexual or transvestite identity to take away from the performance.

Boy actors played women's parts through the reigns of Elizabeth, James I and Charles I. Theatre attracted the interesting people then as always, young men escaping dull families and futures for a chance of metropolitan excitement, boys perhaps troubled by a sexuality they didn't necessarily understand but which felt easier when they were girls. Sadly, though something is known of the stars who played Shakespeare's heroes and his Fools, his boy actors' careers were brief and have left little individual trace. Only after the ten years of Oliver Cromwell's Republic when all the theatres were closed did women start to play women, after the Restoration of Charles II.

Now that heterosexual women generally play the women who cross-dress as boys, often as unconvincingly as possible, a layer of complexity is stripped away. Which is perhaps more enjoyable for the majority. But in performances after the mid-1660s, gay or trans people in the audience can't retrieve the sense of liberation they may have felt when they saw males as both 'heroes' and 'heroines'.

There can be no proof, but it seems probable that the percentage of people who are gay, bisexual, transsexual or transvestite remains stable over centuries. Different times and cultures may persecute, tolerate or enable difference, but it's unlikely these varying cultures will alter incidence, though of course they will alter behaviour. Looking back, an individual will stand out, a Chevalier d'Eon[2] or a Dr James Barry,[3] and we assume they were singular in their times. But in the Middle Ages, travelling bands of women knights fought in tournaments. Recently, photographs have emerged of Casa Susanna,[4] a large community of transvestites that flourished on weekends in the Catskills in New York State in the 1950s, mainly composed of married men with professional jobs in New York during the week. In my youth, gender reassignment was rare and shocking. Now most of us know or know of someone who's at least considered it. In the past, as many might have chosen it had that been possible.

Until the middle years of Henry VIII's reign, homosexual men and women could retreat to same-sex communities, to monasteries or convents. Whether they found erotic or companionate love or both or neither might depend on the individual heads of the orders. Until recently the church officially opposed homosexuality, but it's always found a home there. With the Reformation, religious communities were abolished, and that refuge closed. Some gay or trans people, we may guess, would have found their way into the theatres, the boys of Shakespeare's great cross-dressing roles among them.

They had to be exceptionally skilled to create and maintain their illusion. After Antony's death, Cleopatra wonders what it would be like to walk through Rome as a captive in Octavius' Triumph, as Tamora must at Titus'. She imagines the jeers, the parodic side-shows along the route staging her life with Antony, perhaps all too accurately. The boy playing her would have to feel very confident in a female role to say:

> The quick [lively; quick-witted] comedians
> Extemporally [unrehearsed] will stage us, and present
> Our Alexandrian revels. Antony
> Shall be brought drunken forth, and I shall see
> Some squeaking Cleopatra boy my greatness
> I' th' posture of a whore. (5.2.212-17)

How would the audience experience this? S/he's breaking the illusion s/he's sustained over four acts but daring the audience to go on believing. They know s/he's a boy, though probably not a squeaking one. S/he's also, next to Helen of Troy, the most famously magnetic woman in legend or history. Is there a meltdown in gender recognition at this point, or can the audience put the knowledge of her masculinity to one side during the performance? Not here, certainly, because they're sharply reminded of it.

In *Shakespeare & Women*, Phyllis Rackin is brilliant on the duplicity and dazzle created by the chameleon boy actors. Of the above passage, she says:

> When Cleopatra contracts for a moment to the 'squeaking boy' who acted her part on Shakespeare's stage and reminds the audience that everything they have seen so far is part of a show, she prepares the way for a new show [the rest of Act Five] that displays her virtuosity as a performer and that of the boy actor who played her part – the spectacular suicide scene that will validate both her own worth and the worth of theatrical performance.[5]

Professor Rackin links the boy-playing-girl roles to the plays' theatricality, to our constant awareness of them as performance. In doing so, she illuminates whole plays, not just individual scenes, and particularly our sense of Cleopatra's triumph over Octavius' attempt to exhibit her in his own crude Triumph to be staged in Rome. Cleopatra's romantic fictions as she looks back on herself and Antony in life, and her well-acted death, together extinguish Octavius' historical successes. But though she reminisces about changing clothes with Antony, there's no cross-dressing represented on stage. Where a boy actor starts female, becomes male and then goes back to female again, the audience's experience can be still more shifting and complicated.

The Two Gentlemen of Verona may have been Shakespeare's first play, and it's seldom anyone's favourite. Anne Barton identifies both disappointments and stunning passages of verse, as where Shakespeare writes the metamorphic re-creations of Orpheus' lute, which Proteus imagines as:

> strung with poets' sinews,
> Whose golden touch could soften steel and stones,
> Make tigers tame, and huge leviathans [whales]
> Forsake unsounded deeps to dance on sands. (3.2.77-80)

Barton's readings of the Comedies have never been equalled, I think, especially in her Introductions to the Riverside Edition (1974). With uncharacteristic severity she describes *Two Gentlemen* as a 'limping forerunner', with 'the unenviable distinction of being the least loved and least regarded among Shakespeare's comedies.'[6] But there are some vivid and beautiful things in it, and it's possible to read it as an experiment that doesn't quite come off, with explorations of courtship and gender that would clarify in *As You Like It* and *Twelfth Night*.

Ostensibly it's about male friendship, a bond highly regarded by early modern essayists and philosophers looking back to Greek and Roman models and around them to the substantial advantages of male solidarity in their own times. There are dramatic precedents which treat the subject seriously: Richard Edwards' *Damon and Pythias* (1565), John Lyly's *Endymion* (1588), George Peele's *The Old Wives' Tale* (1590). From its title and opening, *The Two Gentlemen of Verona* seems to fit the pattern. But this male friendship is fake.

Valentine and Proteus (in classical myth, a Shape-Changer from the sea) are cousins and apparently best friends from childhood, but there's a competitive edge to their relationship. Valentine leaves Verona to attach himself to the imperial court of Milan and complete his education. He falls in love with the Duke's daughter Sylvia, and she with him, but they must conceal their love as the Duke has already picked a wealthy husband for her, Thurio. Proteus is in love with Julia, and doesn't seem to want to leave Verona, but his father insists he go to Milan too. He promises to be faithful, Julia promises to marry him when he returns, and they exchange rings. Once in Milan, he immediately falls in love with Sylvia.

Valentine confides in Proteus his romantic plan to rescue Sylvia from her tower by a rope ladder, so they can run away; Proteus betrays his friend to the Duke. Valentine has to leave Milan in a hurry, while Proteus courts Sylvia. Meanwhile Julia disguises herself as a boy, Sebastian, and arrives in Milan just in time to hear 'Who is Sylvia, what is she?' sung by Proteus' arrangement under Sylvia's window. But she becomes his page and confidante.

Sylvia refuses Thurio and Proteus. She escapes from Milan to the forest surrounding the city, followed by Proteus and his page. When she contemptuously rejects him, Proteus threatens to rape her. But Valentine is now the leader of a band of outlaws in the woods; he comes forward from hiding and rescues her, and she reveals his friend's treachery. When Proteus expresses some contrition, Valentine not only forgives him but offers him Sylvia in marriage:

> And, that my love may appear plain and free,
> All that is mine in Sylvia I give thee. (5.4.83-4)

Julia/Sebastian faints at this, then reveals, circuitously, who she is by showing the ring Proteus gave her.

The two young men's friendship doesn't pass the first test. Valentine is crass and self-pitying; his servant Speed understands Sylvia better than he does. Proteus, after some deep thought about the obligations of friendship, decides:

> I to myself am dearer than a friend. (2.6.23)

There's a touch of Blackadder there. He doesn't just try to steal his friend's girlfriend, he seems to enjoy his own hypocrisy. He betrays Valentine to possible death in woods infested by outlaws, and he's capable of rape. Both young men adopt mechanically the worn-out language and posturings of the courtly lover. True love in *Two Gentlemen* is the servant Launce's love for his dog, Crab. When Crab pees under the table, Launce pretends it was him, and takes the beating for him. Crab must have been a hit in the early productions. Launce urges his dog to behave and copy him when they're in Sylvia's elegant society, but Crab fails to do so. Launce reproves him:

> When did you ever see *me* heave up my leg and make water against a gentlewoman's farthingale [hooped skirt]? (4.4.27-28)

Sylvia, and Julia in disguise as Sebastian, get to know and sympathise with each other when Proteus sends his page to collect Sylvia's portrait. Already in this early comedy, the verse and prose is easy, intimate and colloquial, especially between the two women and the two servants, Launce and Speed. Julia studies Sylvia's picture and is generous not catty about it; she doesn't blame her for Proteus' treachery. As Barton says, Shakespeare's 'tendency to hand over the initiative and just judgment to the women in his cast of characters was already well-marked.'[7] In contrast to the men, the women have a gift for friendship.

In the final scene Proteus, recognising Julia by his ring while she's still in her boy's clothing, asks himself:

> What is in Sylvia's face but I may spy
> More fresh in Julia's, with a constant eye? (5.4.112-13)

Julia is as beautiful as Sylvia and possibly younger, so he might as well stick with her. Julia complies, but Sylvia says nothing after Valentine's offer to pass her on to his friend, though she's strong and articulate up to this point. The play ends in conversation between the young men and the Duke and his entourage who've followed them to the forest. The reader/audience is left to draw whatever conclusions they can.

In *Upstart Crow*, David Mitchell as Shakespeare is commissioned to write a comedy and doesn't know where to start. But he observes sweet feminist Kate fall madly in love with Kit (inevitably: get your kit off) Marlowe, here represented as rabidly heterosexual. She gives him her precious ring, then follows him, disguised as a boy, to Verona, only to see him fall in love with Sylvia and offer the ring to her. Kate knocks him down, and when he tries to get up, knocks him down again. 'Shakespeare' adopts her story, but he's determined to finish it with a standard happy-marriage ending. Kate agrees with Anne Barton: this isn't going to be one of his best.

Unlike plays discussed earlier, *Two Gentlemen* has no development of plot or comment from a reliable character that would direct attention to Valentine's and Proteus' inadequacies. But Launce's treatment of his dog is a lot better, we may reflect, than the two gentlemen's treatment of the women who love them. The original pairings are re-established without a murmur from either woman, and Valentine's last bright idea is that the two married couples will live together.

The happy-marriage ending, then, is fake too. The play undermines conventional notions of 'romantic' love as of male friendship, though it validates a bond of sympathy between women. Each couple initially comes to some understanding through writing. Julia is embarrassed to read a love-letter from Proteus in front of her maid Lucetta and tears it up. But for her, love isn't only about writing. When she pieces the letter together again, she comments on their names touching between the sheets, the joke Hero makes about Benedick and Beatrice in *Much Ado*. When unexpectedly (to Proteus) Julia writes back, they become engaged, but when she offers to kiss him, he gives her his hand to shake instead. He goes to Milan instead of announcing their contract of marriage, with the excuse that his father might disapprove, though there's no reason why he should. He's much less keen to marry than he thinks he is. Something is struggling to be born that isn't yet clear enough to be effective.

Julia's boy name, Sebastian, is interesting: St Sebastian, shot to death with arrows, was a favourite subject for Renaissance painters, including Mantegna, Botticelli, Titian and Reni. He was often depicted as epicene, with phallic arrows; the name had already taken on undertones of gay martyrdom. Julia's cross-dressing is more graphic than the other Shakespearean women's. For her disguise to be convincing, Lucetta decides she must wear a fashionable cod-piece[7] with decorations on it:

> A round hose [britches, tights], madam, now's not worth a pin [worth nothing],
> Unless you have a cod-piece to stick pins [small brooches, as now] on. (2.7.55-6)

So after Act One, Julia's boy/girl range of behaviours is emphasised in the most blatant way. The Julia/Sebastian image becomes a composite.

While wearing her boy's clothes and cod-piece she remains very feminine by traditional standards like Viola later, not a he or a she but a s/he or a 'they'. The road she takes from Verona to Milan might be understood as the transition from she to they, the 'journey' that's become the accepted metaphor of rebirth in our time. In *Trans Like Me: A Journey for All of Us*, C.N. Lester chooses 'they' as the best third-person singular and plural pronoun for transgender and transsexual people, and these choices are becoming better understood.

Julia is still dressed as a boy when Proteus falls instantly back in love with her. The shadow story of Proteus' attraction to the boy Sebastian lies beneath his half-hearted and socially-acceptable love for Julia: his protean, shape-changing tendencies embrace more than just switching from Julia to Sylvia and back; he's gay, but not out. Valentine tries to give Sylvia away as soon as he's sure of her. Read like this, *Two Gentlemen* is about male friendship after all. But the effects of Julia's cross-dressing are blurred and tentative. The potentialities of same-sex love are developed with far greater depth of feeling in *As You Like It* and *Twelfth Night.*

In *As You Like It*, violence in two families separately threatens a young man and a young woman. Orlando's elder brother Oliver has inherited their father's whole estate as was usual for an eldest son. But he won't fund Orlando's education or settlement in life as expected. There are the beginnings of a political agenda here, in that it seems unjust for the eldest to inherit everything. Primogeniture, the absolute right of the firstborn boy, creates a lot of ill-feeling, as we find in other plays. Oliver tries to trick the professional wrestler Charles into killing his younger brother in a wrestling match at court. There Orlando and Duke Frederick's niece Rosalind meet and fall in love at first sight, but trapped inside constraints of rank and gender, Orlando can hardly speak to her.

When Orlando unexpectedly wins the match, Oliver plans to kill him in a fire. Orlando runs away to the Forest of Arden accompanied by the ancient family retainer Adam, who offers his life's savings as their escape fund. In that respect Orlando plays a role more often written as female, escaping with a faithful servant from a ruthless male relative as Rosalind, Celia and Touchstone escape, though winning the wrestling match stops him looking too girly.

Duke Frederick has power of life and death over his niece Rosalind and his daughter Celia. In this thread too, primogeniture means trouble. He's usurped the throne of his elder brother, Rosalind's father Duke Senior. She's more popular, or so he thinks, than Celia, and as the rightful heir too dangerous to live, so he banishes her. She must leave the court alone and at once, to survive as best she can outside. Even in Shakespeare's England, let alone in the uncertain time the play is set, she wouldn't last long.

Duke Frederick, then, plans a kind of honour killing to protect his new status, though it's motivated by Rosalind's potential rather than her actual disobedience. Unexpectedly to Frederick, who has no notion that women can be friends, Celia decides to run away with her cousin, and the court jester Touchstone goes too. They mean to join her exiled father in the Forest of Arden. 'Beauty provoketh thieves sooner than gold,' (1.3.99) Rosalind observes, and to avoid rape on the journey they adopt disguises, Rosalind as a boy, Celia as his sister, a woman of middling rank who might respectably travel with only a brother. Celia calls herself Aliena, alienated from her father and previous life.

Rosalind moves sideways not just into another gender but another *genre*, leaving her girlhood at Frederick's frightened court and stepping confidently into pastoral as a boy. Pastoral was a style deriving from Greek and Latin literature, and popular: as they liked it. Set in a rustic world inhabited by shepherds and shepherdesses, the form tended to political and philosophic debate. Perhaps the best way to explain pastoral now is by comparison with the Western. We'll usually find good cowboys, Indians or bad cowboys, and a young woman at risk in the Wild West, but these ingredients animate very different politics.

In *The Searchers* (1956), Ethan is strong, silent and brave. He's also phobic about inter-racial sex, convinced that death is best for a young white woman who's lived among Indians; he hates people of mixed race. This film examines the South's hostile response to the 1950s Civil Rights movement, though the issues are fudged at the end. In *Soldier Blue* (1970), attitudes to race are changing, and the Indians are now the goodies. The massacre of Vietnamese civilians at My Lai[8] divided America, and radical American anger at their army's violence in Vietnam rewrites the cowboy's old enemy. *Soldier Blue* stages the most brutal film slaughter ever attempted, and it's by American military. The heroine is now the hero.

Similarly, pastoral in Shakespeare's time offered not just love in the country, but ideas. Edmund Spenser's *The Faerie Queene*, which has elements of pastoral, is a good example. It's a story of knights, ladies and dragons as a complex allegory of Protestant resistance to a resurgent Catholicism. In a pastoral drama too, the audience would expect difficult sub-textual concepts.

Rosalind, Celia and Touchstone are already inside a fiction at Frederick's court, but they enter a deeper layer of fiction when they get to the forest, though given the way drama works, they become freer there. In one Stratford production, the clock in the foyer of the Royal Shakespeare Theatre was replicated in a clock that appeared over the Arden setting. The audience went in to watch a potentially tragic play, then into a play inside that, a pastoral comedy.

As You Like It is very radical about gender. Though it ends with four heterosexual weddings, they're non-traditional ones, and on the way to them there's a lot of diversion into same-sex attraction. Rosalind is perhaps the most likeable of Shakespeare's women, and the one who enters into masculinity the most wholeheartedly. For most of her short life she's been heir to a Dukedom, brought up to function like a man some day, and it shows. She calls herself Ganymede, in classical myth Jove's cupbearer and boy lover. S/he doesn't drop her male disguise, though there's no reason to retain it once s/he reaches the safety of the forest and buys a cottage. S/he's in no hurry to join her father and go back to being girl.

Celia plans their escape and is initially the more confident, but Rosalind becomes the stronger once they're in Arden. It's hard to separate her pleasure in her boy identity from her resurgent sense of her own rank: once out of Frederick's usurping court and into some version of nature, she's the next-in-line again. She dominates Arden as Hal dominates Eastcheap. *AYLI* is conservative socially, though radical sexually.

In Arden, she finds Orlando's terrible Petrarchan love poems to herself hanging on the trees:

From the East to Western Ind
No jewel is like Rosalind. (3.2.71-2)

Touchstone parodies the verses, cutting the idealism down to what is, for him, just sex:

> If the cat would after kind [mate]
> Let him seek out Rosalind. (3.2.84-5)

But Rosalind/Ganymede plays Rosalind to coach Orlando in a middle way of love, which is intelligent, funny and down to earth: if your love is unrequited, don't imagine you'll die. If you marry her, don't expect too much, she'll change for the worse, and so will you. Marriage is a big risk, with cheating on both sides a possibility.

Still playing Rosalind, she 'marries' Orlando in a wedding rehearsal conducted unwillingly by Celia/Aliena, whose own jealous devotion to Rosalind isn't displaced by heterosexual love for a penitent Oliver until the end. Any performance tends to stand or fall by its Rosalind and Celia. They go back a long way. Celia gives up a Dukedom and risks her life for her cousin, and that homosocial bond stays as strong as any formed later. Her remaining single and un-courted through most of the action emphasises this. Their love is not a stage on the way to heterosexual love, as it is with Helena and Hermia in *A Midsummer Night's Dream*, but co-exists alongside it. These bonds are emphasised now women play women. In an RSC production, Juliet Stevenson as Rosalind, and Fiona Shaw as Celia, paired off in the final marriage dance which symbolised universal harmony in Elizabethan comedy; they were drawing same-sex love into the cosmic scheme of things.

Rosalind/Ganymede, Celia/Aliena and Orlando all vaguely remember the wedding service:

> Rosalind: Come, sister, you shall be the priest, and marry us. Give me your hand, Orlando. What do you say, sister?
> Orlando: Pray thee, marry us.
> Celia: I cannot say the words.
> Rosalind: You must begin, 'Will you, Orlando – '
> Celia: Go to [shut up]. Will you, Orlando, have to wife this Rosalind?
> Orlando: I will.
> Rosalind: Ay, but when?
> Orlando: Why now, as fast as she can marry us.
> Rosalind: Then you must say, 'I take thee, Rosalind, for wife.'

> Orlando: I take thee, Rosalind, for wife.
> Rosalind: I might ask you for my commission [a fee for providing a service, ie, as Ganymede, procuring Rosalind]; but I do take thee, Orlando, for my husband.
>
> (4.1.95-107)

The absurd business term 'commission' suggests the comic viability of Rosalind/Ganymede's double nature; they're two people inside one body, but both can benefit from that, Ganymede financially, Rosalind emotionally. And since penniless Orlando will become joint-ruler of a Dukedom by marrying Rosalind, Ganymede earns his commission. When the rehearsal breaks off, Celia falls asleep in the daytime, as if deeply depressed.

Most people got married in church and according to *The Book of Common Prayer.* But marriage was less regulated in Tudor times than now. As mentioned in the discussion of *Measure for Measure* and *Troilus and Cressida*, it could consist in a promise to live together and the exchange of a ring followed by intercourse, a bond known as spousal marriage. Even the ring was not essential to the legality of the marriage, though it was customary. That would be valid even without witnesses or a clergyman, though the couple were supposed to be open with their family or community about the contract. Such a casual system led to abuse, with husbands sometimes disappearing a year or two on.

It seems sexist to say husbands, when there must have been plenty of wives wanting to escape early entanglements. But it was easier for a man to move on and start another life than for a woman, who would be regarded with suspicion if she turned up in a new town or village, assumed to be a prostitute or to need financial support, especially if she had children with her. By the 1590s, in an attempt to stop men leaving their wives and children as a charge on the parish, church authorities were beginning to insist that only weddings in church conducted by the parson according to *The Book of Common Prayer* and recorded in the parish register should be considered valid.

Touchstone isn't ready for that commitment. He arranges his wedding to Audrey the Goatherd with Sir Oliver Martext, a 'hedge priest', one without a church. With no register to record the ceremony, it should be easy to deny it later. Jaques, always other people's finest moralist, thinks he can use his superior rank to talk Touchstone out of this; he sends Martext away and recommends a church marriage. Like some contemporary clergy and magistrates, he disapproves of the ease with which people could enter and leave spousal marriages. But his attempt to settle Touchstone and Audrey into long-term respectability isn't going to work. When we next see them, they listen to the greatest of all seize-the-day lyrics, 'It was a Lover and his Lass', celebrating springtime, impulse and an absence of civic regulation. Here as elsewhere Jaques is ineffectual.

The Arden passages flow easily from scenelet to scenelet as characters meet and score off each other in argument. Rosalind/Ganymede wins her wit contest with Jaques, mocking his ironic detachment: if it's good to be silent and say nothing, it's good to be a post. His Seven Ages of Man speech traces the cycle of life from helpless infancy to helpless senility. Everything's a zero: the nurse's encircling arms, the satchel, morning face, snail, bubble, cannon's mouth, spectacle lenses, pouch, the cross-section of youthful hose and shrinking thigh, sounds coming up from a piping throat. It all says O.

But this is Shakespeare's most optimistic play. Into the stunned silence as Jaques ends with 'sans everything', Orlando carries Adam. The old man knows better than Jaques what senility is like – 'unregarded age in corners thrown' (2.3.42)[9], Shakespeare's bitterest single line – but he's given his life savings to Orlando while expecting nothing from Oliver. His entrance refutes Jaques' miserable determinism without a word spoken. The nihilism of 'All the world's a stage/And all the men and women merely players', (2.7.138-9) all mere stereotypes acting out their stereotypical lives, is not the last word on life or plays. In *As You Like It*, Rosalind and Celia create different roles from the ones they were assigned.

Rosalind/Ganymede seldom scores off Touchstone. Her patronising 'Thou speak'st wiselier than thou art ware of' (2.4.48) gets an acid put-down. He declares himself more willing to bear with Celia than to bear her, a tempting option still when asked to bear with our respondent on a phone. Touchstone, Feste (in *Twelfth Night*) and Lear's Fool confirm that wit is the only indicator of wisdom. They aren't detached spectators as Jaques tries to be, but deeply involved in similar passions to their employers and acquaintances, so for Touchstone too, 'wedlock would be nibbling',

(3.3.60-1) but the Fools' commentaries on people and events are the more acerbic for that.

The little scenelet between Touchstone, Audrey and 'William' is mysterious. 'William', who believes he has a pretty wit of his own, was once courting Audrey, but he's warned off by Touchstone. It's an odd, inconsequential scene. In so sophisticated a literary play, we might see the death or banishment of an Author. 'William' admits to 25, while Shakespeare would be closer to 40 now – though that may be part of the joke, of course.

Phoebe and Sylvius are straight out of pastoral poetry, playing the game of courtly love, Sylvius begging, Phoebe refusing. Both are literary, especially Phoebe, who quotes Marlowe and knows she deserves something better than life as a shepherdess. It leaves her with rough brown hands like old gloves, as Rosalind/Ganymede doesn't fail to point out. This is a class not a racial signifier, as I think are many Renaissance images of the dark and the brown: they identify women who worked on the land and couldn't afford to buy masks or gloves to protect against sun and wind.

Phoebe's long rejection of marriage and immediate attraction to Rosalind might suggest a homosexual element in both, now and when they were played by boys; her sudden passion responds to the cavalier superiority of rank Rosalind displays with everyone. 'Let me tell you plainly in your ear,' s/he says, 'sell when you can, you are not for all markets.' (3.5.59-60) S/he says she likes the looks of Sylvius better. But immediate antagonism is the mark of sexual attraction in all Shakespeare's fighting pairs of lovers. S/he drinks in Phoebe's beauty while pretending to disparage it and doesn't forget to say where s/he lives. Whether we see her as most Rosalind or most Ganymede, whether she and Phoebe are played by boys or women, s/he's same-sex attracted as well as same-sex desired.

The church marriage Jaques recommends to Touchstone, like the form of service at the wedding rehearsal, are Christian, specifically Anglican ceremonies. But in the end, Christian marriage doesn't happen for anyone. The Greek and Roman classical worlds were more accepting of homosexuality than official Christianity ever allowed itself to be. So Hymen, the Roman God of Marriage, turns up in person to solemnise the four weddings. His ceremony marks a social bond of board and bed, without reference to marriage as an image of Christ and the Church or to any transcendental element. Rosalind is not given away in silence by her father to Orlando, as in an Anglican ceremony. Rather, she gives herself freely to them both. Nobody has to promise to obey anybody else.

Hymen's 'You and you no cross shall part' (5.4.113) is his one allusion to Christianity. For Rosalind and Orlando, it may prophesy Christian lives containing some pain but redeemed by their faithful love. The words can bear another meaning: the cross, symbolising the Christian church, shall never part you, never enforce its intolerant laws against you. Shakespeare's verbal ambiguities peak when the subject is ambiguous gender. Amid the 'howling of Irish wolves against the moon', (5.2.89-90) when Phoebe, Silvius and Orlando are proclaiming what they're made of, sighs, tears and other boring things, Ganymede/Rosalind's repeated 'And so am I for no woman', (5.2.83) works whether we see her as Rosalind, Ganymede or the boy actor underneath both. In Shakespeare's sonnet, 'Let me not to the marriage of true minds', the final line is ambiguous, the 'no man' can be either the subject or the object of the verb 'loved':

> If this be error and upon me proved,
> I never wrote, nor no man ever loved (Sonnet 116).

Hymen's form of service removes the regulation from marriage, allowing it to be more as gays might like it. Call it coincidence, but the only unequivocally heterosexual couple, Touchstone and Audrey, Jaques proclaims, will be the soonest to part, within two months. Maybe she'll be pregnant, and Touchstone will be off. Or maybe Jaques is just wrong again.

In 1599, Celia's conducting the wedding of Rosalind/Ganymede to Orlando could represent a real wedding, when an exchange of vows alone was still legal. A wedding, though on stage, incomplete and fictional, between a couple in male clothing, one of whom was not a woman dressed as a boy, as now, but really was a boy, must have been an interesting sight when homosexuality was theoretically, and sometimes in fact, a capital crime. It might even constitute a real wedding, if actors as well as audience could confuse real-world with sim.

Not only the wedding rehearsal but Hymen's marriage of the four couples at the end may have found Rosalind in boy's clothing. Usually our texts read:

> Hymen: Good Duke, receive thy daughter
> Hymen from heaven brought her,
> Yea, brought her hither,
>
> That thou [the Duke] mightest join **her** hand with his [Orlando's]
> Whose heart within his bosom is. (5.4.93-7)

In this reading, we have Rosalind back in women's clothing, a wedding dress of some sort, and recognised as Rosalind by everyone. But as Laurie E. McGuire points out[10], the reading of these last two lines in *The First Folio* of 1623 is:

> That thou [the Duke] mightest join **his** (Rosalind/Ganymede)'s hand with his [Orlando's]
> Whose heart within his bosom is.

An easy printer's error, when dealing with two other 'his'. The emendation of the first 'his' to 'her' doesn't come until forty-one years later in the third edition of the First Folio (1664). Later still, in 1709, when Nicholas Rowe edited the plays, came the additional stage direction that Rosalind is back in women's clothes. And even if we take my first-quoted version above, the emended one, as the right version, it's a mess anyway, as it leaves Orlando's heart within his own bosom when it should be in Rosalind's. To make it work, we'd have to change the third 'his' to 'her' as well.

The *New Oxford Shakespeare: The Complete Works* (2016) solves that problem by saying firmly that 'Whose' refers back to Rosalind. That is not what the words say. If Rosalind is still in boy's clothes as the play ends, Orlando's and Phoebe's reactions to her only make sense if they can at last see the woman inside the boy's clothes and acting. Hymen's 'Good Duke, receive thy daughter' might make them look rather carefully, but that's stretching probability a bit. Directors usually go for the big heterosexual wedding with Rosalind and Celia in white dresses. However Rosalind is dressed, the Epilogue remains as dazing and confusing as before, as Rosalind/Ganymede speaks of herself as 'the lady', then says 'if I were a woman' (meaning 'but I'm not'), then promises to curtsy, not bow.

If we do accept the *First Folio* reading rather than later emendations, we have two young men, both dressed as young men, as the principals both at the first wedding by Celia and at Hymen's marriage. It's taken over 400 years to get to this point off stage. The Cheek By Jowl, all-male productions of the 1990s restored a boy's form to Rosalind/Ganymede as public opinion warmed towards same-sex marriage. The ending may have been staged differently for different occasions.

Rosalind/Ganymede inhabits not a double but a triple pleat of genders: a boy actor plays Rosalind who disguises as Ganymede who acts like Rosalind, then as Ganymede leaves the stage to come back (probably) in a wedding dress as Rosalind, then as one or the other or both comes forward in the Epilogue to draw attention again to their shifting nature but also, cheekily, to encourage men and women in the audience to kiss, as s/he sends them back to the simpler heterosexually-oriented world outside. S/he's the embodiment of wit, beauty and authority, and genderless.

Twelfth Night advances the gambit that boy-girl twins can be identical. The fantasy allows a seaside holiday from the constraints of binary gender when Viola changes clothes and becomes Cesario, visually indistinguishable from her twin, Sebastian. Their shipwreck, which washes them up on different beaches, demands that for safety from sexual attack Viola must dress as a boy and find employment as a page in the household of Duke Orsino. This is not her first choice. She'd rather join the Countess Olivia. But Olivia is in mourning and seeing no visitors. If Viola is to join a bachelor's household without risk at any level above a menial, she'll have to be a page. As the action continues, we see that she's not like Sebastian in character, and in this respect also boy/girl twins can be no more alike than ordinary brother and sister, as Shakespeare obviously knew, having boy/girl twins himself. The relationships forged between same-sex or apparently same-sex pairs are closer and more authentic than the final heterosexual pairings.

Viola has much less fun playing a man than Rosalind; she falls for Orsino at once, but he's courting Olivia. His Petrarchan adoration of the standard unattainable lady, who doesn't know him by sight, is perhaps useful in deferring marriage to anyone. He doesn't consciously fall in love with his new page, but their relationship quickly becomes intense and confidential.

He begins to feel curious about his acquisition, asking if he's been in love, asking about his family. This intimacy switches to violence when he thinks Viola/Cesario has betrayed him and deliberately stolen Olivia's love, but it's also where he begins to see that he loves his page too.

Sebastian is saved from drowning by a sailor, Antonio, who falls in love with him and tries to buy his love with gifts and services. This relationship is sometimes played as if Sebastian is gay: his name is code for that, chosen by Julia of Verona. But until the end, everything suggests he's trying with a mixture of compunction and awkwardness to get away from Antonio. He's embarrassed to take the purse Antonio presses on him, though he agrees to be the purse-bearer, to look after it but not to spend the money. Then, among the final recognitions, Antonio claims that the two have never parted day or night for three months. And yet it's a dream come true for Sebastian when Olivia marries him out of hand, thinking he's his twin. Antonio, like Antonio in *The Merchant of Venice*, is left solitary when the heterosexual marriages are accomplished, here more by accident than design, at the end.

Viola stays more conventionally feminine than the other cross-dressers, always about to give herself away, hoping that time will untangle her problems for her, witty but often lost in dreamy devotion. When Olivia asks what she would do if she were Orsino, she answers, thinking of Orsino:

> Make me a willow cabin at your gate,
> And call upon my soul within the house,
> Write loyal cantons [stanzas] of contemned [despised] love,
> And sing them loud even in the dead of night,
> Holla your name to the reverberate hills,
> And make the babbling gossip of the air
> Cry out 'Olivia' (...) (1.5.221-27)

One can't imagine Rosalind saying anything quite that crazy. But it's what makes Olivia fall for her. Words construct love, are love. Women recognise and respond to the right language, and Orsino doesn't have it:

> If music be the food of love, play on
> Give me excess of it, that surfeiting
> The appetite may sicken and so die (1.1.1-3)

doesn't cut it. He's a would-be consumer of music and women, but images of anti-peristalsis aren't attractive. The epicure is foremost too in his lines on choosing very young women, since women are:

> as roses, whose fair flower
> Being once displayed, doth fall that very hour. (2.4.36-7)

He's too sickening and surfeiting, too remote and conceptual. Orsino, Orlando and Biron all need re-education in finding better language in a culture where the language used to and about women – heavens on earth, roses, jewels, whitely wantons – has become ossified.

Viola's language wins Olivia more than her looks, though her looks help: she's small, in everything 'semblative a woman's part', (1.4.33) unthreatening. Muscles needn't apply. Felicity Kendal was fun as Viola/ Cesario in the BBC Bardathon production, though like most woman actors hardly even attempting masculinity in the boy role. Viola's downright rejection is much more attractive to Olivia than Orsino's literary courtship. None of Shakespeare's clever women wants to be on the receiving end of the Petrarchan scam; Olivia itemises her own features, parodically. Mourning was one good inarguable excuse for postponing marriage; Olivia claims seven years to mourn her brother, then falls in love at first meeting with Viola. She insists on their instant marriage, but by accident she marries Sebastian.

So there are four strong same-sex attractions, Antonio for Sebastian, Olivia for Viola/Cesario, Orsino and Viola/Cesario for each other. As he's saved Sebastian's life, Antonio is enraged when he thinks Sebastian is leaving him to execution. As Olivia's desire is awakened only by language, we have to hope Sebastian can equal the language of his twin. Viola doesn't change back into woman's clothing at the end of *Twelfth Night*, though she's just about to. We never see Orsino's reaction to her as a woman, but they've established an intimacy he never had with Olivia.

As You Like It is mostly about love, while in *Twelfth Night* the lovers' stories are intercut with Sir Toby Belch's plot to marry Sir Andrew Aguecheek to Olivia and get his hands on Olivia's house and money, with Maria's two plots, to marry Sir Toby Belch and to punish Malvolio, and with Malvolio's consequent plot to marry Olivia. These are in their way love stories too, of course, but love in its commercial rather than romantic aspects. They give *Twelfth Night* a different tone from *As You Like It*, more cruel in its wit and action, more grating. Its song, 'O Mistress Mine', is elegiac not carefree, though the voice can register high and low. Time is running out for them all. Feste is more melancholy than Touchstone, painfully hard-up but resentful of Malvolio's attempts to rise, touchy about his own status.

Imogen makes much happier relationships out of her woman's clothes. Pisanio becomes less a servant and more a brother. For him, the erotic is definitely feminine, 'woman it[s] pretty self', (3.4.156) as he calls it. But he knows being a woman is dangerous and helps her become Fidele. Her father, her husband, her rejected suitor and her Italian visitor all treat her brutally while she's a princess. Released into boyhood, she meets her unknown brothers, and of course bonds with them as we'd expect. But s/he also gains another lover, the Roman General Caius Lucius, whose devotion is understated and protective.

He finds her/him in that hard-to-credit moment, discussed earlier, when s/he comes round from fainting across (apparently) Posthumus' body, though in fact it's Cloten's. Surrounded by Roman soldiers, Fidele invents the fiction that the body is Richard du Champ, the name of Shakespeare's printer, Richard Field, a man she calls her master. Caius Lucius is curious about Fidele, reads his character accurately and takes her/him on into Wales as his own servant, first ordering his soldiers to bury the body reverently for the boy's sake.

As the battle starts to go against him, he sends Fidele to safety, and when the Romans end up as Cymbeline's prisoners he won't ask for his own life but asks for Fidele's. Either as Imogen or Fidele, s/he might do better with him than with the crass and murderous Posthumus. Then Cymbeline gives the boy the right to ask for another life, but Fidele ignores Caius Lucius to retrace all that's happened in the past. His life must shuffle for itself, s/he says. Caius Lucius has good reason to accuse her/him of ingratitude:

> The boy disdains me,
> He leaves me, scorns me.
> Briefly [quickly] die their joys
> That place them on the truth [fidelity] of girls and boys. (5.6.105-08)

The lines are metrically jerky, but that's the only way he shows his bittterness and anger, his self-control a marked contrast to Posthumus' rages. It's romantic comedy's classic case of bad timing; in that moment she's seen the ring she gave Posthumus on Giacomo's finger, and the secrets begin to unravel. Posthumus is stricken with greater guilt when he hears of Imogen's innocence, and reprises his mistreatment by striking her, a mere page, for interrupting his lamentations. S/he of course instantly forgives this, along with his other gross misjudgements. Her chance of a better friend/lover surfaces at the end; Caius Lucius remains stoical as it sinks again.

Cross-dressing typically questions a 'natural' division into masculine and feminine. Though Julia becomes Sebastian, Rosalind Ganymede, Viola Cesario, and Imogen Fidele to avoid death, rape or confinement, in disguise they attract and explore homosexual or homosocial sensibilities and are tested, Imogen especially, in painful circumstances. We find they're as capable as their male counterparts, or more so. But though they become male successfully most of the time, they lack physical toughness. Julia faints, Imogen is tired by the long journey to Wales, even Rosalind faints at the sight of Orlando's blood. Viola is terrified by the prospect of fighting Sir Andrew Aguecheek, not a formidable adversary for her brother. Sir Andrew is terrified too, so physical courage is not an innate male characteristic. But Sir Andrew is an unsuccessful man, while Rosalind and Viola are very successful women. In this respect Shakespeare strengthens gender stereotypes. Except for Viola, who doesn't put on boy's clothes until she's in Illyria and who acts the least convincingly, all the cross-dressers must make a journey while they transition from girl to boy.

Portia and Nerissa make that journey in *The Merchant of Venice*, crossing from Belmont to Venice. We find the familiar honour stories of young women escaping their fathers' control and false reports about their faithfulness, but the balance of sympathy changes here. This play is as far from my central topic as I can go and a bit further, since Portia cross-dresses by choice, not to escape death, rape or confinement. It contains Shakespeare's most famous trial scene and, uniquely, a woman controls the fate of its eventual victim. In re-reading the play, its trial and sentencing after many years away from it, I've come to a startling conclusion, so I'm allowing myself a digression.

Critics are usually divided: either Shylock is a hateful threat and the Christians are generous and warm-hearted, or Shylock is cruelly victimised and the Christians are callous hypocrites. Shakespeare is generally ambiguous, of course, but in *The Merchant* particularly directors have struggled to produce a play that's anywhere between these extremes. They do it mainly by extensive cutting.

It's generated a lot of anger and aversion over the centuries, and still does, compounded by too much quotation of Shylock's 'Hath not a Jew eyes?' (3.1.44) speech, as if Jews should be grateful if Shakespeare attributes consciousness to them. I hope to mitigate the aversion a little, if I can, by a new reading.

But first I'll review some current critical ground, which I agree with: that Shakespeare creates Shylock and the Venetian Christians as pretty equally greedy. The group who flock around Antonio, the Merchant, toady to him as the one with the money. He's in unrequited love with Bassanio, who's already borrowed heavily from him, wasted the money on luxuries, and now sees a way to make himself money enough to last a lifetime. Antonio is sad at the play's opening because Bassanio has just told him he's decided to marry, if he can make the wealthy match he wants.

Bassanio clears his journey to Belmont with Antonio first because he means to borrow more money to look prosperous when he gets there. He doesn't need to look prosperous, he only needs to turn up and guess a riddle set by her father for suitors of the heiress, Portia, but he wants to have Portia on his side. Shylock makes money breed by charging interest, Bassanio makes it breed by enhancing his appearance, engaging more servants and buying presents. Wealth is a necessity to the Christians as to Shylock, though they spend it and he saves it. Bassanio is uneasy as he meets Antonio and the rest of the group:

> When shall we laugh, say when? (1.1.66)

he asks with fake jollity. The others know what's up and helpfully remove themselves. But Bassanio is very eloquent and engaging when parting somebody from their money and makes the pitch well. He represents it as a beautiful, competitive financial venture:

> Nor is the wide world ignorant of her [Portia's] worth,

For the four winds blow in from every coast
Renowned suitors, and her sunny locks
Hang on her temples like a golden fleece,
Which makes her seat [great estate] of Belmont, Colchos' strand,
And many Jasons come in quest of her.
O, my Antonio, had I but the means
To hold a rival place with one of them,
I have a mind presages me such thrift [care]
That I should questionless be fortunate. (1.1.166-175)

There's nothing questionless about it: he could lose this money too. His allusion to the myth of Jason and the Argonauts, who sailed to distant lands to find the priceless Golden Fleece at Colchos, gives a coating of romance to his purpose, but it also emphasises that the expedition is solely financial, another form of mercantile enterprise. Her 'worth' is her monetary worth. He'll win the golden girl, whose hair signifies not so much beauty as the coin he needs to fund his spending. The Order of the Golden Fleece, instituted in 1430 by Philip, Duke of Burgundy, was a high honour. But the mythic and honorific associations of the noun 'fleece' are undermined by the verb's common metaphorical meaning, skinning someone of everything they have, a meaning extant already in, for instance, Shakespeare's familiar Holinshed. These two poles of association could be taken to exemplify the wide difference of interpretation this play has attracted.

Antonio can't refuse him. He's often played as the oldest in the Venetian group, keying into the stereotype of the wealthy middle-aged man in love with a handsome young one, but he's younger than Bassanio and the rest. Later he says, facing death:

I am a tainted wether [castrated ram] of the flock
Meetest [fittest] for death; the weakest kind of fruit
Drops earliest to the ground; and so let me.

He will die young, he thinks, before the others. The wealthy middle-aged man is a largely Victorian construct. Antonio hasn't made his money from years of hard work but from lucky chances. But his courage, along with his mordant understanding of himself as withered fruit, without an heir to his fortune and wounded in his sexuality, makes him with Shylock one of the more sympathetic characters in *The Merchant of Venice*. He's not altogether outside the Christian flock like Shylock, but he's a tainted member of it, meetest for death, uncertain of salvation. The main enemies both see themselves as outsiders.

Shylock has a similar grim self-understanding:

> you take my life
> When you do take the means whereby I live. (4.1.69-70)

And Shylock has a drier wit than the Christians:

> You [Antonio] that did void your rheum [spit] upon my beard,
> And foot [kick] me as you foot a stranger cur
> Over your threshold. Moneys is your suit.
> What should I say to you? Should I not say,
> 'Hath a dog money? Is it possible
> A cur can lend three thousand ducats?' (1.3.110-15)

Bassanio's priorities for a wife are clear; Portia is richly left, the only legatee of a dead father, fair and virtuous. It's the right order. In every speech the language of courtship and marriage is saturated in the language of finance. The loss of Antonio's ships is solely a loss of money; nobody gives a passing thought to the loss of life. As Bassanio leaves for Belmont, Antonio cautions:

> Slubber not [don't skimp] business for my sake, Bassanio,
> But stay the very riping of the time. (2.8.39-40)

You'll stand a better chance if you hedge until she's desperate for you. This is part of a conversation reported by Salerio to Salanio. Antonio's interchangeable hangers-on understand that money is Bassanio's goal, not love. Bassanio doesn't contradict the definition of courtship as business: that's what it is. One could argue that Bassanio does truly fall in love with Portia when he sees her. But he's seen her before, and he didn't fall in love with her before; he wasn't so broke then. He registered that she was in love with him:

> Sometimes from her eyes
> I did recieve fair speechless messages (1.1.162-3)

he boasts; she's a sure thing.

Once at Belmont, Bassanio compares his anxiety about choosing the right one out of three caskets, and so winning or losing Portia, to being on the rack. Portia takes up the metaphor:

> Bassanio: (...) as I am [before I choose], I live upon the rack.
> Portia: Upon the rack, Bassanio? Then confess
> What treason is there mingled with your love. (3.2.25-7)

As he continues to protest his devotion, she repeats:

> Ay, but I fear you speak upon the rack
> Where men enforced do speak anything. (3.2.32-3)

She may be expressing real doubt about his sincerity, or she may be flirting. Whichever, she makes the one point worth making about England's judicial system under the Tudors. Torture, the back-up for state interrogation of all citizens other than the nobility, invalidated every criminal trial. This was true even when the rack or other instruments weren't used or threatened; everyone knew they were there. Portia is legally acute while still in Belmont. But she and Bassanio in their privilege are callous about torture; it's just a metaphor to glamorise desire.

She evades the provisions of her father's will to marry the man she wants, giving away the clue to the correct casket out of three: gold, silver and lead. The song sung while he's making his choice has line-endings rhyming with lead, then introduces the funeral bell with its lead clapper and the implication of a lead coffin. If we weren't meant to notice these clues, we'd hear a different song. In one of the source stories, the maid arranges for the song, but Portia is in control at Belmont, not Nerissa. After Morocco's and Aragon's wrong choices, she knows the right one, as do the audience, for whom there's no suspense in this creaking pantomime. As Portia's father and Bassanio have a shared culture, it's likely Bassanio would guess right anyway, it's not that difficult and most of us would choose lead, but she's taking no chances.

She escapes her father's power, but unlike Shakespeare's other heroines, she risks nothing. The song is interesting in itself. Portia uses it cunningly, but its plain message escapes her. Fancy, attraction engendered in the eyes, sparked by handsome looks and plausible manners like Bassanio's, is quickly over. The future looks dark, as suggested too by the classical love stories Lorenzo and Jessica speak of in the last Act, all with tragic endings.

Jessica escapes in disguise from her father, Shylock, taking his money and jewels with her, to marry a Christian, Lorenzo, one of the Antonio group; she cross-dresses reluctantly at his suggestion. Shakespeare may have known about the Ghetto in Venice; she doesn't need disguise to get out of Shylock's house, but she needs it to escape a Jewish neighbourhood. Like his friend Bassanio, it's the money and jewels Lorenzo is after. Jessica supplies him, calling down from the balcony:

> Here, catch this casket. It is worth the pains. (2.6.33)

'This casket' links the sub-plot to the main plot of Bassanio and Portia with its three caskets. Both young women steal from their fathers, Jessica straightforwardly, Portia by giving the clues to his riddle. Shylock's money and jewels fund Jessica and Lorenzo as they spend and gamble their way around the Med. Portia's father, Shylock and Old Gobbo are all blind, cheated by their children. Is this to read the play too earnestly? After all, we like daughters who elude heavy-handed fathers. But Jessica's theft of her father's betrothal ring, Lancelot's callous fun at the expense of his literally blind father, tip the balance into sympathy with the older generation this time.

We've heard Portia's casual xenophobia in her dismissal of Morocco and jokes about other suitors. When she attends the court in Venice dressed as a lawyer, Balthasar, to represent Antonio in the suit brought against his life by Shylock, she proves herself the most formidable of the Jew's enemies. The public hearing is about Antonio's debt, and as he freely admits it, there's no need of a trial for that. But she cleverly turns the hearing into an indictment of the Jew. At this unique trial the 'male' accuser speaking with the authority of the law is a woman, the one on moral trial a Jew who's dishonoured the Christians by outsmarting them and who's more an outsider than any Christian woman could be. He's about to act out the old blood libel: he's avid for the flesh and blood of a young male Christian.

Shylock hears how the legal system is biased against him before the trial starts. The courtroom scene opens with the entrance of the Duke, who will preside, his Magnificoes, Antonio and his Venetian friends. The Duke addresses Antonio:

> I am sorry for thee: thou art come to answer
> A stony adversary, an inhuman wretch,
> Uncapable of pity, void and empty
> From any dram of mercy. (...)
> Go one, and call the Jew into the court.
> Salerio: He is ready at the door, he comes, my lord. (4.1.3-14)

Shylock has of course heard the Duke's opinion of him. Without embarrassment, and in front of the same group, the Duke switches to flattery, saying he knows Shylock means to change his mind, that he's too merciful to pursue the death penalty. The Duke assumes that Shylock is a fool, and that it doesn't matter if you lie to a Jew. Unsurprisingly Shylock grows ever more determined to exact his pound of flesh in retaliation for the racist contempt he encounters from Antonio, his friends and every aspect of Christian culture. He points out that the 'Christian' Venetian state is systemically hypocritical, since it owns slaves and treats them like animals.

Portia as Balthasar pretends fairness, giving him the chance to change his mind about his fatal cutting of Antonio. But she isn't fair: pretending impartiality, she's committing identity-fraud and half-way-married to the defendant's friend. Her plea to Shylock to be merciful used to be the stuff of mind-numbing School Prize Day recitations, and is sometimes taken seriously still:

> The quality of mercy is not [con]strained,
> It droppeth as the gentle rain from heaven
> Upon the earth beneath; it is twice blest:
> It blesseth him who gives and him who takes,
> 'Tis mightiest in the mighty, it belongs
> The throned monarch better than his crown (...) (4.1.178-83)

These are tired Renaissance clichés about mercy. But as she hits her stride in this unfamiliar profession, her language grows more intimate and compelling – to Christians:

> Therefore, Jew,

> Though justice be thy plea, consider this,
> That in the course of justice, none of us
> Should see salvation: we do pray for mercy,
> And that same prayer doth teach us all to render
> The deeds of mercy. (4.1.191-6)

In the distancing 'Jew', in the reference to the doctrine of Salvation[11] and to the Lord's Prayer, familiar and emotional to Christians but meaningless to him, she places him once and for all not as 'one of us' but as 'none of us'. Whether she intends it or not, it's the best way to make him refuse reconciliation.

Bassanio attacks Shylock verbally but appears to see no alternative to his friend's death. He could save Antonio by killing Shylock in the court and accepting the death penalty for it, but he's not going to. Portia stuns them all with the point of law that gets Antonio off, then produces the forgotten law that makes Shylock's life forfeit as a foreigner seeking the death of a Venetian. The state has it both ways. Jews are treated as citizens because their trade connections are important, which is why Antonio's bond with Shylock must be taken seriously. But they can suddenly become aliens again when the state sees a way to confiscate their money. Shylock's ingrained hatred puts him far enough in the wrong to allow the Duke to seize his property and force him to become a Christian. As the trial ends, Portia and the Duke repeatedly use 'Jew, Jew' as a term of contempt. Portia adopts her boy disguise to save Antonio's life; but it also gives her the power to secure what is in effect a death sentence for Shylock.

She gratifies Bassanio, Lorenzo and Gratiano by giving her fortune to Bassanio, securing Shylock's for Lorenzo and giving Gratiano a place at her court as Nerissa's husband. The Christian men marry for financial security; Shylock married for love a woman who loved him. But whatever the Christians are like, we can't sentimentalise him. He's capable of killing with a knife in cold blood, crueller than the Christians because he's abused and they're eternally privileged. He's also harsh to his daughter, isolated, and spiteful. But his is a massive presence, this is his tragedy and he draws all eyes.

Nobody seems to know who first played him, though it may have been Richard Burbage, who usually played heroes. Edmund Kean played him with romantic passion in the early nineteenth century (Jane Austen took her nieces to see him), as did Al Pacino in the 1990s, in a film of great beauty that manages to generate sympathy for almost everyone, though it can only do so by cutting and revisioning, by showing Jessica slandered in Tubal's account of her. At the end, she's still wearing the turquoise ring her mother gave her father as she gazes back across the sea towards Venice, where Shylock is barred out of his synagogue.

There's a focused intensity to his characterisation. So it may seem perverse to suggest that *The Merchant* contains undertones of a then more dangerous, more immediate religious conflict. But ...

*Religious bigotry, with Christians identifiable as such only by hatred of a different religion.
*That hatred is mostly about material possessions, not doctrine.
*A rotten judicial system.
*A nominally Christian society pursuing and wasting money, with trade increasingly based on slaving and foreign adventurism (looting).
*The state confiscating religious outsiders' wealth.
*Forcible conversion.
*A rich, much-courted lady, independent except in a weakness for handsome chancers ...

Nobody needed to look to the stage for that; it was all around them. I believe the great violence of Shakespeare's England, the violence between Catholics and Protestants, seeps into *The Merchant*. To argue this, I must mention briefly Christopher Marlowe's work and some of the forms Christianity had taken by the second half of the sixteenth century. There's no original research here, the facts I cite are well known, but I use them to support (I believe) an original argument.

Marlowe's *The Jew of Malta* played through the first half of 1592. The theatres then closed for over a year because of the plague, but the play was revived in 1594 and continued popular through the nineties. It prefigures much that's in Shakespeare's *The Merchant*, though it's funnier and farcical. Marlowe satirises institutionalised Christianity under cover of satirising Jews. There's a grotesquely wicked Jewish villain, Barabas, who poisons a convent full of nuns, but Marlowe's Christian Governor of Malta is as greedy and more hypocritical. The friars and nuns are parodically lecherous. A slave with his price on his back is bought in the market for his looks by a respectable Christian matron.

There's a sub-plot about Barabas' daughter Abigail who wants to marry a Christian. Barabas' servant Ithamore betrays him because he wants money to buy the expensive prostitute Bellamira, to whom he proposes, 'I'll be thy Jason, thou my golden fleece.' (4.2.85) Barabas ends up boiled alive on stage in a cauldron he's prepared for the Governor.

With the exception of Abigail, her Christian suitor and the Turkish leader, the characters are equally wicked whatever their religion. The Governor ends the play with smug thanks to Providence for the Christians' triumph. Marlowe obviously had a lot of fun with the writing, and it was very popular, suggesting that the audience enjoyed not just its wicked Jew's downfall but its satire of Catholic clergy and government, and might appreciate satire of other forms of authority.

Marlowe was probably an atheist, but this play could equally have been written by a witty Christian angered by the travesty of Christianity apparent in both Catholic and Protestant dispensations. Each side was committed to destroying the other in bouts of 'irreligious piety', as Tamora calls it. Mary Tudor punished usually by burning but sometimes by hanging, drawing and quartering anyone who confessed to Protestant beliefs. Elizabeth Tudor didn't kill Catholics merely for their beliefs, but if they tried to convert Protestants or supported a Catholic Succession, they were imprisoned or hanged, drawn and quartered. Catholics had to pay fines for not attending an Anglican church, so their families were reduced to destitution if they persisted, a clever form of forcible conversion. Catholic priests were banned from England; anybody caught hiding one was executed, as was the priest. After the Pope excommunicated Elizabeth, Catholics could consider it meritorious not sinful to kill her.

There certainly were devout Protestants like Thomas Cranmer and devout Catholics like Robert Southwell, willing to accept death for their beliefs, in Cranmer's case after recantations which make his fortitude as he was burned in 1556 a still more extraordinary act of will. Southwell like many Catholic priests had longed from boyhood to go down into the sun-scorched arena of martyrdom, and he got his wish when he was hanged at Tyburn in 1595 before a sympathetic crowd, some of whom pulled on his legs to ensure that the hanging killed him before the other penalties could be carried out. This was not long before the probable date of *The Merchant of Venice*.

But mostly, Protestants under Elizabeth were defending their lives and property, which they'd lose if a Catholic government came in. Just as, under Mary Tudor in the previous reign, Catholics were defending their lives and property against a Protestant rising and the overturn of the social hierarchy that seemed likely to come with it. Elizabeth's Succession in 1558 was in fact peaceful. Her Protestantism was still undefined and the chances were she'd marry, so her own beliefs would hardly matter. But in 1569 the unsuccessful Rising in the North against her in favour of Mary, Queen of Scots marked the beginning of greater anti-Catholic severity. Each of the Tudor monarchs and their families, governments, aristocracies, landed gentry and higher ecclesiastics stood to lose their property and probably their lives in a violent regime change. Since Elizabeth refused to name a successor even when approaching 70, there was growing alarm about the future. If a Catholic monarchy returned to England, leading Protestants would be killed or forced into exile, and the Inquisition would deal with the rest.

As in present-day Saudi Arabia or Pakistan, then, Protestant England in the 1590s was a repressive state and heresy, whether outspoken Catholicism or atheism, potentially a capital crime. Atheism was often understood as a cover for Catholicism or an intention to stay neutral until the next Succession. There was no freedom of speech or writing. Most people, including judges, didn't distinguish dissent from treason or criticism of the church's long-accreted malpractices from an attack on the truth of the Incarnation. Bishops and Archbishops might agree in theory that after the Fall all individuals and institutions must be subject to error; in practice, it was safer not to carp. Marlowe and (later) John Webster got away with satire of the English church by making their corrupt clergy Catholic, and therefore legitimate targets, but they took risks.

While still at Cambridge Marlowe was working in England and the Netherlands as a spy for Francis Walsingham. He was hard up as a student in the 1580s, and government agents were well paid, though only by results; if a plot didn't exist, it was necessary to invent one. It sometimes looks as if half the population was working for Francis Walsingham or William Cecil, Lord Burghley and later his son Robert Cecil before and after the Babington plot and the failed Armada invasion. Charles Nicholl in *The Reckoning*, his gripping detective work on Marlowe's death, finds that a disproportionately large number of dramatists and poets were recruited as secret agents: they were clever plotters, persuasive in speech and writing, usually poor. Walsingham died in 1590, but other ambitious courtiers, including Robert Devereux, Earl of Essex, then began to set up their own information networks, recruiting from his and the Cecils'.

In April and May 1593, there was a government crackdown on anonymous anti-immigrant incitements to violence, which were widely posted. There were many Protestant refugees seeking asylum from Catholic persecution in London, as well as a community of Jews, all seen as undercutting London tradesmen and professionals. The authorities were also looking for treasonable and heretical writings. On 11th May, Thomas Kyd, a dramatist who'd collaborated with both Marlowe and Shakespeare, was arrested and questioned about heretical papers found in his rooms, which he'd once shared with Marlowe. The papers expressed doubt about Christ's divinity and virgin birth, and suggested he was St John's homosexual lover. Nicholl thinks they were a plant. Kyd was racked, and eventually named Marlowe as their owner; Marlowe was arrested, charged and released on bail.

On 30 May 1593, before he could come to trial, he was stabbed through the eye by Ingram Frizer, a property dealer and loan shark, in a fight at a house in Deptford, a house that happened to belong to a relative of the Cecils. It was an expert killing blow practised by duellists and professional hitmen. The two other men present, Robert Poley and Nicholas Skeres, were witnesses for Frizer at the inquest. With their support he claimed self-defence and was acquitted of murder. Poley and Skeres were government spies who seven years earlier had acted as *agents provocateurs* to trap the Babington conspirators, which in turn secured Mary, Queen of Scots' execution. Antony Babington's last letter before arrest to his 'sweet Robyn' [Poley] is painful to read: 'Thine, how far thou knowest,' it ends.

Apparently Poley took his work seriously. By 1593, Skeres was working for Essex, Poley for Robert Cecil.

The reasons for Marlowe's death may never be known, but it's improbable he was killed in a fight over the 'reckoning' or bill for food and drink bought in, as was recorded at the inquest, the 'great reckoning in a little room,' (3.3.11) as Touchstone calls it in *As You Like It* six years later. From the timing, it seems likely that Marlowe's murder was connected to Kyd's enforced evidence, though that can't be known for certain. Kyd was released, but never recovered from the racking; he died a year later, aged 35.

Marlowe's new high profile and unpredictability may have made him a danger to his principals, or he may have wanted out himself, repelled by the cruelty of a government that thought it better for an innocent Protestant to die than a Catholic conspirator to escape. His *Massacre at Paris* (c. 1592), based on Catholic butchery of Huguenots (Protestants) in Paris in 1572, is of course anti-Catholic, but in Protestant London the jackboot was on the other foot. And he had a great career as a playwright going now. In any case, he would have to be silenced. Possibly his handlers didn't want him to stand public trial for fear of what he might say. The ministers investigating seditious writings were different from the ministers employing him as a spy, and one department kept its secrets from another.

He and Shakespeare had collaborated as dramatists and competed with their narrative poems *Hero and Leander* (unfinished at Marlowe's death) and *Venus and Adonis*. They came from similar trade backgrounds and were the same age, 29, when Marlowe died. Whether they were mainly friends or mainly rivals is irrelevant: the bond of collaboration on a script is probably more intellectually involving than most friendships. Shakespeare had also collaborated with Kyd, the slightly older and longer-established writer. Kyd's *King Leir* would later became the main source for Shakespeare's *King Lear*, and in *Hamlet* Shakespeare drew on his *The Spanish Tragedy* for the play within the play and for Hamlet's pretended madness. Shakespeare would have to be sub- or super-human not to feel intense shock at two state murders of fellow dramatists. It's likely he would have known more about both men's arrests and deaths than has been recovered in the centuries since.

While Kyd was dying of his joint dislocations, rumours of King Philip of Spain's continuing plots against Elizabeth persisted. A spy employed by Essex found in a coded letter what seemed to be evidence that Elizabeth's doctor, a converted Jew called Rodrigo Lopez who left Portugal as a young man to escape the Inquisition, was in league with Spain and willing to poison her in return for King Philip's favour and a large sum of money.

Essex had already quarrelled with Dr Lopez, who was also his own doctor, and who hadn't observed confidentiality about Essex's (embarrassing?) medical problems. Essex was in disgrace with the Queen and wanted to propitiate her by appearing solicitous for her safety; he had Lopez arrested. A minor suspect caught in possession of ambiguous letters was merely shown the rack; he implicated Lopez as central to a plot to poison her. Elizabeth didn't believe it. Nor did the Cecils, who knew the spy networks and were genuinely protective of the Queen. Essex was reprimanded for starting false rumours about her doctor.

Despite Lopez' adult lifetime as a practising Christian, public anger grew with rumours of his supposed treachery. He was held in the Tower while Essex tried again and this time found (or manufactured) stronger evidence of his guilt; threatened with the rack, he signed a confession. Given the way life imitates art, it's possible Essex got the idea for implicating Lopez in a poison plot from *The Jew of Malta*. But to some of the population, poisoning was simply what Jews did. Other supposed conspirators were racked and accused Lopez. Elizabeth withdrew her protection from him. He was tried by a hostile court and convicted, then hanged, drawn and quartered at Tyburn in June 1594. On the scaffold he said that he loved the Queen as much as he loved Jesus Christ. The crowd decided to take this as meaning he loved neither, and jeered him to the end.

It's likely he was innocent. If a successful *coup* put Philip of Spain or another Catholic monarch on the English throne, the Inquisition would return to England; Lopez knew its clergy often ignored Jewish (Marrano) pleas of conversion to Christianity. The ingratitude of Kings was proverbial. He was 70, rich, respected, at the height of his profession before the poison plot was 'discovered', and an intelligent man. If a Catholic regime came in through his poisoning Elizabeth, it would think him a lot safer dead, as he couldn't fail to foresee. Would he take risks to re-establish Catholicism in

England, for any money? That question would be asked at the time, though not aloud. In 1601, Essex raised an unsuccessful rebellion against Elizabeth's inner circle. He was captured and beheaded, luckier than Lopez because he was a nobleman.

Short of a miracle, we'll never know what Shakespeare made of *The Jew of Malta*, Marlowe's and Kyd's deaths or Lopez' execution. Gratiano, *The Merchant*'s crudest character, attacks Shylock in the court scene, with:

> Thy currish spirit
> Govern'd a wolf, who, hanged for human slaughter,
> Even from the gallows did his fell [cruel] soul fleet,
> And whilst thou lay'st in thine unhallowed dam [mother]
> Infused itself in thee. (4.1.132-6)

'Lopez' means wolf in Spanish. But Gratiano isn't necessarily saying that Lopez' spirit inhabits Shylock. Animals were hanged for 'crimes', and a wolf that killed people might be hanged in country districts. Lopez was executed about eighteen months earlier, not back when his soul could transmigrate into an embryo Shylock still in the womb. And Lopez wasn't, of course, hanged for human slaughter, only for supposedly plotting it, as Shylock plots Antonio's. But there may be identification of both Lopez and Shylock as Satan-wolves, joint-enemies of the Good Shepherd and his flock, in Gratiano's lurid rhetoric.

The best guess for the date of *The Merchant* seems to be 1595. Maybe Shakespeare wanted to cash in on the rich vein of anti-semitism uncovered by Lopez' arrest and conviction. But if he was cynically exploiting Lopez' fate, one would expect him in these dangerous times to avoid anything like Marlowe's satire of Christian government and clergy in *The Jew of Malta* and play it safe, make his Christians models of virtue to contrast with the Jew's total wickedness. Instead he creates Christians whose attitudes to money are as predatory as Shylock's, and a Shylock who has moments of humanity. He's subtler than Marlowe. His Christians are extravagant, adventurous. He allows room for a censor or superficial member of the audience to see them as glamorous, not greedy.

If *The Merchant* is about Protestant-Catholic bigotry, it won't show in any obvious way. The play wouldn't have been licensed if it was openly critical of the current Protestant ascendancy. It had to work, if I'm right, by stealth and inference, in a technique of subject-displacement from the dirty present to a magic past of quests and caskets, golden girls and wicked villains. The reading may seem far-fetched, but displacement is everywhere in Shakespeare: in *Richard II*, as noted earlier, Richard's lack of an heir and the consequent instability of the country were recognised as a comment on the present. Ubiquitous spies in Elizabeth's court relocate to Elsinore.

The plays are always about more times than one, about Now as well as Then. We could argue that *The Merchant* is indeed about Now, the 1590s, without looking beyond its obvious subject, because it was staged at a time of prejudice against immigrants and Jews. But that prejudice existed from medieval times and was fairly constant, not distinctive of the Now. It's always seemed strange to me that Shakespeare stole Marlowe's bad Jew/ bad Christians idea so soon after its original staging. If he wanted to put a deeper subtext into *The Merchant*, that's less surprising, and Protestant triumphalism and Catholic menace haunt the play.

Displacement is common in all types of historical fiction. It offers a three-dimensional rather than a flat narrative, engaging us because it makes us think harder about ourselves: 'that's true of our time too,' we realise. We wonder if other people get the point; we want to talk about it. Though the two Westerns I mentioned above are set in the nineteenth century, I claimed that they're also about, in *The Searchers*, the white South's resistance to Civil Rights in the 1950s, and in *Soldier Blue*, liberal America's changing view of race and its own imperial role in the 1970s. How do I know that? I don't. There's nothing in the films specifically to say so, and I haven't consulted the writers' or directors' intentions. But for anybody knowing the major national anxieties at the moments of the films' production, knowing what writers and directors do for a living, a current political meaning floats up into sight, and few would disagree with my readings of these films, at least.

Especially in a contemporary production, the tension would be unbearable as Shylock approaches Antonio with his knife. He means to act out the Jewish blood libel, certainly. But nine years later the Gunpowder Plotters would try to cut the heart out of James I's government; they believed there were enough covert Catholics to take over in the chaos that would follow. They failed, of course, but only by a fluke. Everyone in the 1590s felt under threat from an imminent Protestant-Catholic showdown.

Shakespeare lived and wrote where words could be fatal, at the intersection of the theatres, the court, and the underworld of night's black agents and their prey. Touchstone's full allusion to Marlowe's death is:

> When a man's verses cannot be understood, nor a man's good wit seconded with [supported by] the forward [precocious, clever] child Understanding, it strikes a man more dead than a great reckoning in a little room. (3.3.9-11)

Touchstone notes that a man's writing may be read by powerful people too stupid to understand it, and then he may die. He's remembering a line from *The Jew of Malta* where Barabas gloats over his treasures, his 'infinite riches in a little room.' (1.1.37) But he's also remembering the very small size of the room in Deptford, which was Poley's and Skeres' ridiculous excuse at the inquest for their claimed inability to separate Frizer and Marlowe as they were fighting, when they were probably holding on to Marlowe's arms. In the coalescence of the two rooms, Touchstone seems to be paying tribute to all that was lost that day. Marlowe was back in the news again in the year of *As You Like It*; his translations of Ovid's poems were burned in June 1599 along with other supposedly heretical or obscene works.

Touchstone goes on to say that 'the truest poetry is the most feigning.' (3.3.15) He's talking to Audrey about artificial, Petrarchan love poems, but he knows Audrey can't understand a word he's saying, so he is in effect talking only to the audience. The phrase is loaded with implication. It may mean that the best poetry is the most mannered and artificial, like the pastoral frame Touchstone is standing in, or the richest in imagery. Maybe it's a simpler paradox: the truest poetry is the kind that must disguise its meanings.[12]

The audience, and not just the intellectuals, were used to decoding metaphors because they went to church every Sunday. Realism was still centuries into the future; parable and symbol were the norm in both religious and secular poetry and prose, as in visual images. Elizabethans were more inclined than we are to look below the types and shadows of a surface for an underlying world of meaning. The great epic of the 1590s,

The Faerie Queene, is an extended allegory of the struggle between the Protestant and Catholic Churches for the Soul of England represented by the Red Cross Knight. Una is the pure Protestant Church, Duessa the deceitful Catholic one, Gloriana, the Faerie Queene, is Elizabeth, Archimago the Pope. Of course it's more complicated than that sounds, but we're in no doubt how to understand it: Spenser promotes the ideology of the current Protestant government, demonising Catholics.

Shakespeare couldn't afford to be easily understood if he wanted to write even-handedly for an elite part of the audience about 1590s Christian, inter-sectarian violence and live to write another play. He needed a convincing narrative vehicle. He took the model for a cunning Jew ready to hand in Marlowe's successful *Jew of Malta*, along with the Christians who travesty Christianity. He's more cautious than Marlowe. The slower sections of a contemporary audience could take his play as a romantic love story, though even they might notice that the Christians' only sign of Christianity consists in their hating Jews. The middle range might see it as critical of both Jewish and Christian cultures. The most sophisticated might see a deeply coded attack on Christian inter-denominational hate.

Shakespeare took risks in *The Merchant*, I think, as he did in *Richard III* when he wrote in the Scrivener. He wasn't trying to put anti-semitic bums on seats, but letting an audience consider religious bigotry *per se*, between Protestants and Catholics as well as between Christians and Jews. I've suggested there's satire of contemporary religious barbarity in Alarbus' death, and other readers have seen that too. *Titus Andronicus* is not primarily about a clash of religions or cultures, but it shows an impulse to attack the butchery carried out in the name of religion and patriotism.

Using Marlowe's successful anti-semitic formula was a blind to get the play past the Master of the Revels, the pleasant job-title for a censor in the equivalent of the Home Office, racist then as ever, and to avoid charges of heresy once in performance. It was an unfortunate choice, because of course he did it too well. Shylock walked out into history, time-travelling proof that Shakespeare was anti-semitic, so anti-semitism must be part of true Englishness, while the play's real satiric targets are, I suggest, the two broken and bloody forms of Christianity attacking each other in his lifetime.

The plot and characterisation are gripping. Embodying every

stereotypical Jewish libel imaginable, Shylock seems such a huge and convincing Jewish figure (though what does that say about us?) we can't see round him. James Shapiro's *Shakespeare and the Jews* traces his origins and afterlife. But Professor Shapiro doesn't engage with the subject of Christian cruelty, theft or sexual exploitation, either in *The Jew of Malta* or *The Merchant of Venice*. He doesn't apparently see either play as satire of the depths to which Christianity had sunk but seems to assume that Marlowe and Shakespeare shared the most ignorant bigotry of their time. He says that:

> ... some of the darker currents of early modern English attitudes towards the Jews informed Shakespeare's *The Merchant of Venice*: Jews were aliens, they were a separate nation, racially set apart, and, most ominously, they secretly desired to take the knife to Christians in order to circumcise or even castrate them.[13]

He concedes it's the flesh nearest to Antonio's heart (though that's itself an ambiguous phrase) that the bond specifies, but this only emerges when Portia reads its wording in court, after she's said that the cutting must go ahead. Up to that point, and especially in Antonio's self-identification as a 'wether [castrated ram]', the audience might harbour a still more grisly expectation.

Shapiro traces medieval and early modern Christian anxieties about ritual castration by Jews, which he sees re-activated by Antonio's bond and by the court scene. If he's right to see that, and I think he is, his reading supports mine. Public, ritual castration happened only as part of the legal process of quasi-hanging, drawing and quartering, devised by Christians mainly for Christians. Taking the pound or so of flesh came between the hanging and the disembowelling stages; such cutting couldn't be far from any late 16th-century man's consciousness, whether or not he'd actually seen it. Wouldn't the more intelligent tranche of an audience make the connection?

In *Tyrant: Shakespeare on Power*, Stephen Greenblatt doesn't discuss *The Merchant of Venice* but he refers generally to strategies that citizens and dramatists use to avoid accusations of treason. In his opening chapter, 'Oblique Angles', he says:

> As with modern totalitarian regimes, people developed techniques for speaking in code, addressing at one or more removes what most mattered to them. But it was not only caution that motivated Shakespeare's penchant for displacement. He seems to have grasped that he thought more clearly about the issues that preoccupied his world when he confronted them not directly but from an oblique angle. His plays suggest that he could best acknowledge truth – to possess it fully and not perish of it – through the artifice of fiction or through historical distance.[14]

I think *The Merchant*'s anti-semitic Venice lies at just such an oblique angle to Shakespeare's anti-Catholic London. He used Marlowe's *Jew of Malta* concept as an extended metaphor for the Christian sectarian hostilities that killed Marlowe and so many others.

Even if Shakespeare is dramatising mainly Protestant-Catholic bigotry in *The Merchant*, there's still casual anti-semitism in the *Works*, for instance, in Benedick's 'If I do not love her [Beatrice], I am a Jew.' (2.3.207) But Benedick makes several crass remarks. It's Shylock who's placed Shakespeare among the full-blown anti-semites. My alternative reading is of course open to the charge of distortion to fit my own times, and that goes with the whole territory of Shakespearean criticism. He reveals new possibilities in every age, and every reader will see something new in him. We're not necessarily all wrong. We may be re-connecting with lost meanings.

In Act Five, Bassanio's quest for the Golden Fleece seems accomplished, Gratiano claims his share in that achievement, and the Venetians are coming back to a moonlit Belmont of magical serenity. Shylock, if not quite forgotten, is remembered only for the money Portia has extracted from him. But false reports about two women's faithfulness make a little ripple in the happy ending. Portia and Nerissa punish their husbands for giving away their wedding rings, especially Bassanio for putting his loyalty to Antonio before his wife.

It's Antonio who persuades Bassanio to give Portia's ring to 'Balthasar', and that male bond prevailed over the marriage bond, as Portia has seen. Far from forming a closer relationship with her husband-to-be through disguise as a boy like Rosalind and Viola, she's learned that she comes a bad second. Both new husbands denigrated their wives in court, so the women pretend they've had sex with Balthasar and his clerk. It's meant as a lesson not to take them for granted.

Bassanio and Gratiano threaten the absent (supposed) lovers but seem not to know what else to do. There's nothing they can do. They aren't legally married yet, as the marriages haven't yet been consummated; they won't be if the men become violent, and then the great Fleecing can't happen either. As ever in this play, money governs all responses except Shylock's and Antonio's. As they want the money, the new husbands are going to have to put up with the infidelity. Their paralysis is momentary, then the light breaks in on who the lawyer and his clerk were.

Gratiano is the most racist of the Christians. Lorenzo is late turning up when he's due to elope with Jessica, and Gratiano implies that he's already had her, so he doesn't need to be attentive. Gratiano will continue to disparage her, and she'll never be one of them. Fittingly, he has the last words:

> Well, whilst I live, I'll fear no other thing
> So sore as keeping safe Nerissa's ring. (Last lines)

In the incongruous vagina joke (apart from *Troilus and Cressida* this is the only play that ends on a sex joke) lies a threat. It reminds us of all the rings including Shylock's turquoise, and what they've signified or failed to deliver. Tomorrow, Bassanio and Gratiano will be married and controlling their wives entirely, like other unreconstructed husbands in Shakespeare. As a boy, Portia is cleverer and more analytical than the men. As a married woman, those qualities won't help her. She and Nerissa hear in disguise how little their husbands value them, something the audience already knows. Then they, and Jessica, walk back into danger voluntarily, dressed again as women.

The homosexual undertones of cross-dressing are missing here. But in Bassanio's gallant speeches we hear how well the language of heterosexual love can be faked by an educated man on his uppers, and in Portia's agony of suspense as she awaits his choice of caskets (he may miss the clues), how completely a clever woman can fall for it. The only lover in *The Merchant* is Antonio, who gives and hazards all he has and ends up alone.

This play is the odd one out in a more fundamental way than in its trial and cross-dressing. It's died. It's too deeply imbricated in the 1590s to live. Only a child, and an ignorant child at that, could now enjoy a magic-courtship and hiss-the-villain version. In recent productions of *The Merchant*, the Christians are sometimes played as worse than Shylock. I don't think they're worse. Shylock means to be extremely cruel when he thinks he has the chance, as a Catholic government restored to power would be. A cut text wrenching Shylock into the flawed-but-loveable hero is so hopelessly well-meaning it's an embarrassment, though the Al Pacino film is an exception. We'd need to be back in the day, watching the callous winners, the murderous loser, seeing how vicious both are and how fast their positions could change to feel what dynamite it once was.

Shakespeare explores the homosexual implications of cross-dressing in only four plays: *The Two Gentlemen of Verona*, *As You Like It*, *Twelfth Night* and *Cymbeline*. Here he removes the props and fixed boundaries of heterosexual identity to dramatise other affinities. When boys played the women who disguise as boys, erotic bonds were sketched in between men. Now women play the women, erotic bonds are sketched in between men in all four plays and also between women in *As You Like It* and *Twelfth Night*. In *The Two Gentlemen of Verona*, the meeting between Sylvia and Julia-in-disguise is a plot-situation very like that between Olivia and Viola-in-disguise, but there's no element of attraction or flirtation between the women in the *Two Gentlemen* scene. In *Cymbeline*, there's no other young woman to fall for Fidele.

The cross-dressing comedies and the *Sonnets* cheered LGBTQ people in the centuries when difference was isolating. Oscar Wilde's *The Portrait of Mr W.H.* is a great example of a Victorian response.[15] In *The Guardian* of 1 July 2017, fifty years to the day after the decriminalisation of homosexuality, eighteen gay writers were invited to nominate the book that first spoke to them about their own lives. One choice was Virginia Woolf's *Orlando*, a revisioning of *As You Like It*. Rabih Alameddine (*An Unnecessary Woman*; *The Hakawati*) sent the most heartfelt response:

> A number of queer books that I'd read in my twenties changed my life, from Gide and Genet to Maupin and White (Ed and Patrick), as did the poems of Abu Nuwas and other Arab poets. If I were forced to choose, I'd go back to my teenage years when I was more impressionable. A teacher mentioned in passing

> that many of Shakespeare's sonnets were written for another man and in that instant, my life, my soul, unfurled like a corolla. Yes, yes, please, compare me to a summer's day. You're right, I am more lovely and more temperate. Go on, please. (Have I mentioned that I was impressionable?) I devoured the sonnets. I began to feel that I could be loved by a man, maybe even a man as great as Shakespeare. I, master-mistress of his passion, was worthy. The sonnets quenched a thirst I did not know I had. So long as men can breathe, and eyes can see, so long lives this, and yes, this gave life to me.

It's a pity Shakespeare can't read that.

He constructs sexual difference with urbanity, not with the raw pain of the present. In Arundhati Roy's *The Ministry of Utmost Happiness*, the story of a girl caught inside a boy body, the girl's grief and terror as she becomes suddenly very male in adolescence are as grim as anything in *Metamorphoses*.

There's no generalisation to be made on the authenticity of girls and boys or their changing shapes. Whether boys or women play the girls who play boys then girls again, their roles differ greatly according to their play, Julia setting out on uncharted paths in his first comedy, Rosalind suggesting the possibility of a permanent bisexuality, Viola taking a brief gender holiday, creating havoc, then returning with relief to (almost) her previous identity. Imogen's play is closest to tragedy; she wins a greater love as Fidele, but it comes to nothing.

Women characters disguising as boys let us fantasise that women can escape the category of wife or daughter along with the entrapment attached to those roles, can find new identities and ways of forging closer relationships. But the dressing-up and the acting remind us we're in a theatre, and we'll soon be returning to the wind and the rain outside. In a way, the plays are closed circuits. Yet, as Feste says, 'we'll strive to please you every day', (last line) and there'll be another one or a rerun tomorrow. 'William' must leave Arden, but Touchstone and Audrey remain.

As You Like It and *Twelfth Night* are the most exhilarating and truest, just because they're the most obviously feigning. The cross-dressing Comedies have slowly helped (with much else) to create a climate of liberal opinion in the US and UK where people feel freer to live as they like. And both heterosexuals and homosexuals in audiences who don't know or care that boys once played women can still enjoy their premise: if men and women are willing to move outside the clichés of masculinity and femininity, they can negotiate their turf wars into an amnesty.

Notes

[1]La La Land: the land of dreams, once known as Cloud Cuckoo Land. The name refers to Hollywood, Los Angeles, and the film industry's fantasies, which the film of 2016 mocks and celebrates.

[2]Le Chevalier d'Eon (1728-1810) was a talented French scholar, soldier and diplomat. In his lifetime, gossip had it that he was a woman. He was born hermaphrodite but brought up as a boy by his father probably because he could inherit from his mother's family only if he was male. He kept his secret all his life, but there was an inquest, where it was decided he had characteristics of both sexes.

[3]Dr James Barry (1795-1865) was born female, but a strong sense of vocation and family poverty led her with the help of enlightened friends to change her name and gender. He trained as a surgeon, something he couldn't have done as a woman, and joined the medical corps of the British Army, rising to a rank equivalent to Brigadier-General. He performed the first (known) successful Caesarean in Africa, mother and child surviving.

[4]Casa Susanna: in 2006, a cache of photographs was discovered in a New York street market, showing two transvestite communities, one called Chevalier d'Eon, the other Casa Susanna, that flourished in the Catskill mountains in the 1950s and 60s, weekend retreats for male-to-female cross-dressers. The photographs formed part of an exhibition, 'Another Kind of Life: Photography on the Margins', at the London Barbican, Feb-May 2018.

[5]Phyllis Rackin, *Shakespeare & Women*, p90

[6]Anne Barton, Introduction to *The Two Gentlemen of Verona* in *The Riverside Shakespeare*, p143.

[7]Anne Barton, Introduction to *The Two Gentlemen of Verona* in *The Riverside Shakespeare*, p145.

[8]My Lai: in March 1968, about 500 women, children and old men were massacred by US troops in the village of My Lai, Vietnam. The resulting publicity helped to change mainstream US attitudes to the war.

[9]Unregarded: *The New Oxford Shakespeare: The Complete Works* has 'unrewarded.' The Riverside and Norton editions have 'unregarded', which I prefer as starker and more imaginative, about the invisibility not just the poverty of old age.

[10]Laurie E. McGuire, 'Feminist Editing and the Body of the Text', in *A Feminist Companion to Shakespeare*, ed. Dympna Callaghan, p62.

[11]Salvation: Portia urges on Shylock the Christian doctrine that everyone is sinful and deserves eternal damnation. At the Last Judgement, the dead can achieve Salvation, eternal life in heaven, only through God's mercy and their faith in Christ. Nobody

can be saved through good works or their own merits. We should all show mercy, she says, because we will all need mercy at the Last Judgement.

[12]Charles Nicholl in *The Reckoning* puts a different construction on Touchstone's words. He claims that Touchstone is refuting a rumour that Marlowe died in a fight over a boy. See pp85-90.

[13]James Shapiro, *Shakespeare and the Jews,* p199.

[14]Stephen Greenblatt, *Tyrant: Shakespeare on Power,* p3.

[15]Shakespeare dedicated his Sonnets to a 'Mr W.H.', wishing him 'all happiness'. There has been much speculation about Mr W.H., none of it conclusive. Oscar Wilde's *The Portrait of Mr W.H.,* published in 1889, fantasises that Mr W.H. was a boy called Willie Hughes who acted female parts in the plays. This is a love story, and fictional, but some of its fans think that Wilde makes a case for the theory. *The Portrait* was published in fuller form in 1958, edited by Wilde's son, Vyvyan Holland.

7

RE-WRITING EVE

On contextual criticism; some Shakespearean Eves including Lady Macbeth, Goneril, Regan and Cleopatra; two Susannas; a re-cap; *Arden of Faversham*; and *The Duchess of Malfi*; a conclusion

THOUGH EVERY AGE IS AN AGE of change, in the mid-1500s vast tectonic plates were moving. Knowledge of Greek and Roman cultures was sifting down from clerical scholars into the educated laity, creating scepticism and alternative belief-systems. Ideas about the social contract, marriage and women's rationality were in the air, though as yet inseparable from religious assumptions and language; there was little other than religious language for any form of politics. But by the end of the 1580s, the theatre was evolving a wittier, more secular response to the human condition. Each of Shakespeare's women is unique, but her humanity is at home in a tradition of prose and poetry that was shaping the intellectual life of his time. Representations of the ideal woman were multiple and evolving: the greater the writer, the greater the number and depth of tributary streams feeding into the work.

The new Protestant religion challenged old authorities and instated new ones. It allowed clergy to marry and compared marriage to the union of Christ and the Church. Protestantism stressed the individual man or woman's personal connection to God without mediation by a priest, on the premise that both sexes have an independent conscience and a capacity for self-examination. The Puritans especially opposed the old 'wicked Eve' view of women and set out to idealise companionate marriage, which should be a matter of mental affinity and mutual support, not based on romantic or carnal attraction.

But with the new print culture, readers could buy books of their own now, including stories and poetry celebrating the romantic and carnal attraction the moralists despised. Even if they'd never learned to read, Londoners could go to the theatre; people in country towns could catch the repertoire of acting companies on tour. 'Ordinary' intelligent people were beginning to have access as never before to sophisticated political ideas and engaging romantic fantasies. Then as now there was a huge range of possible responses to the plays they saw.

It's always been recognised that misogyny is everywhere in Shakespeare's work. For many, the critical assumption tended to be that this was the inevitable mark of his time. Sometimes one can sense a certain nostalgia for that time on the part of the critic. But even before the Women's Movement of the 1970s and the academic feminist criticism that's followed, plenty of masculinist critics too saw that he doesn't endorse the misogyny his characters display.

From the 1970s, feminist criticism of Shakespeare was and continues to be largely historical and archive-based, interested in other early modern writers, in women's lives and their prescriptive texts and how each fits or doesn't fit his representations of women on stage. Juliet Dusinberre is a great pioneering example. In *Shakespeare and the Nature of Women* (1975), she writes of the cultural background:

> The drama from 1590 to 1625 is feminist in sympathy. Shakespeare's modernity in his treatment of women has always attracted attention, but it is not nearly so well known that his attitudes to women are part of a common stock to be found in the plays of almost all of his contemporaries – in Marston, Middleton, Dekker, Webster, Heywood, Jonson, Massinger, and to some extent even in Beaumont and Fletcher. These dramatists ask the same questions about women as Shakespeare, about their natures, about the stereotypes society imposes on them; in many cases they find the same answers, and these are essentially the Puritan answers: that the old Pauline [St Paul's] orthodoxies about women and about marriage must give way to a treatment of women as individuals. Like the Puritans, the dramatists reject or ridicule the old pieties, and struggle to realise, and then to test, the new. Shakespeare's women are not an isolated phenomenon in their emancipation, their self-sufficiency and their evasion of stereotypes. The women in Marston's plays share many of their characteristics. Shakespeare's are different only in the degree of his artistry.[1]

Dusinberre is erudite on the intellectual context of that explosive thirty-five years after the public theatres opened. If 'Puritan' means to us a hypocrite like Angelo or Malvolio, or a sober-suited citizen of Cromwell's Republic, we'll be surprised by her claim that Puritan ideas influenced Shakespeare. But she makes her case, citing Martin Luther and John Calvin among the Puritans as sources of ideas. Thomas Cranmer was also a huge and continuing influence. People listened to his magnificent prose in church every Sunday, felt his humane take on marriage and death along their veins as often as they went to weddings and funerals. We can hear these writers' echoes in Shakespeare's texts.

She questions a previous understanding of 16th-century women as victims. There was a Queen on the throne, widows and older single women might have a lot of power, women worked outside as well as inside the house, they often negotiated their own and their relatives' marriages, and they went to the theatre, where the dramatists sought their approval as much as men's. But her more optimistic view of women's roles can't eradicate the downside, the hanging or burning of 'witches', the absence of married women's property rights or legal sanctions against domestic violence, the sexual double standard, the ownership of children by the father.

In her Introduction to *Broken Nuptials in Shakespeare's Plays* (1985), Carol Thomas Neely offers a lucid cultural background with an overview of previous feminist criticism of plays where betrothals are interrupted by violence. After that, her book becomes a wonderfully compelling inside account of these plays. I disagree with a lot of her readings, but she's a descendant of A.C. Bradley in her focus on character as a play's principal hold on us. She's unrivalled in her response to *Measure For Measure* and *All's Well that Ends Well.* Discussing *MM*, she quotes Angelo's bed-trick partner Mariana in her final confrontation with him in front of the Duke, when she throws back her veil and demolishes his pretences, revealing her rejected face, hand and

> the body
> That took away the match from Isabel
> And did supply thee at thy garden house
> In her imagined person. (4.4.23)

Acknowledging that felicitous 'imagined person', for all objects of impersonal lust are imagined persons, Neely goes on:

> Mariana testifies with still more painful frankness than Helen [in *All's Well*] does to the dark delusion and mechanical workings of lust and the consequent fragmentation of identity (...) Her bold reconciliation of love, desire and marriage makes possible the denouement of the plot. Her example might induce the other characters to achieve intimacy, accept desire, and move towards regeneration, as she has.[2]

Neely traces that fragmentation and partial reconciliation through many plays. Though she acknowledges some hope in Mariana, she sees *Measure For Measure* mainly as the equation of sex and death, no longer in the jokey way of the early Comedies, but for real. Even so, she's more optimistic about the ending of both plays than I can be.

In *Shakespeare and the Loss of Eden: The Construction of Family Values in Early Modern Culture* (1999), Catherine Belsey documents many different forms of the Adam and Eve narrative in Shakespeare's time. Influenced by New Historicist thinking, she concentrates on specific objects and ideas rather than on creating a generalised historical context. She shows how people lived among a multiplicity of Eve artefacts and texts. The Loss-of-Eden story was carved into marital bedheads, onto wooden dishes and wedding chests, analysed in sermons and treatises on marriage and pictured in stained glass windows. Belsey finds it difficult to correlate the plays she discusses, *Love's Labour's Lost*, *As You Like It*, *Cymbeline* and *The Winter's Tale*, with the artisanal and clerical understanding of marriage elsewhere in Shakespeare's culture, the understanding that women are the weaker vessels, frail and needing control if they're not to destroy their men and themselves.

In some passages, she attributes the lack of trust between Shakespeare's couples, the loss of a marital Eden, to men's jealousy rather than to women's deceit. But she appears to conclude that Shakespeare's audience would sympathise with that jealousy more than we can. She ignores, it seems, the fact that for audiences of his own and every later generation he depicts his jealous men as just plain wrong. She notes that:

> to counter the dangers intrinsic to the marriage state, some of the clerical treatises

> and the domestic conduct books of the period recommend unceasing vigilance [by men over women], as if a contradiction could be overcome by an act of will.[3]

It's precisely that unceasing vigilance, that failure to trust women, which Shakespeare identifies as the problem, not the solution. This is clear in the four honour-killing plays discussed earlier and in the systemic misogyny shown in many others. The warning artefacts and domestic conduct books cited by Belsey were preaching to men already quick to suspect women.

In her work on the boy actors who disguise as women, Phyllis Rackin vividly defines Shakespeare's theatricality, his ability to dazzle our perception of what's real and what's fiction. But in 'Misogyny is Everywhere' (2000), she tries grounding literary discussion in general historical context. She considers various contemporary and recent critical constructions of sixteenth-century women: their supposed unruliness, their alarming bodies, their varying degrees of power and autonomy, their occasional right to vote, the jealousy they aroused in men, the cheering proportion of female heads of households in Southwark [though many of these would have been madams]. Only near the conclusion to her article does she acknowledge that Othello and Leontes cause great harm, Ford looks very foolish, and all three are completely mistaken. Maybe this shouldn't be a conclusion but a starting-point, as it's the starting-point of the plays. Rackin's article is highly sophisticated, however, written to try to nail down the slippery issue of historical context, the 'what they thought/did in those days' fallacy, once and for all.

But it keeps coming back up again. Cristina León Alfar's *Women and Shakespeare's Cuckoldry Plays: Shifting Narratives of Marital Betrayal* (2017) examines contemporary marital conflicts, from Anne Boleyn's (fictional) 'last letter' to Henry VIII to the trouble and strife of less famous marriages, and compares them with Shakespeare's warring couples. She compares real-life slander cases to the effects of slander on Shakespeare's women and their husbands. She writes on Beatrice, Emilia and Paulina as brave, articulate defenders of their own sex, relating them to real-life networks of woman friends and to the 'gossip' networks of god-siblings, set up by parents' choices of godparents for their babies. The latter ideally lasted down several generations, as valuable as blood ties. She considers among other educationalists the Humanist Juan Luis Vives' writing on women's conduct.

Vives was a learned and conflicted man, born in Spain into a Jewish family, forced converts to Christianity. His father practised Judaism in secret and was burned at the stake for it; his mother's body was exhumed and burned twenty years after her death, also for privately practising her faith. Vives escaped to the Netherlands, visited England, and because of his erudition acted as occasional advisor to Katherine of Aragon in educating her daughter Mary. He was rigid in his attitudes to female propriety (especially we may suppose when mentoring Henry VIII's Queen and heiress), and his *Advice to a Christen Woman* is scary: behave, or you may be locked in a stable by your male relatives and eaten alive by hungry horses. But he was one of the few who stayed loyal to Katherine when Boleyn came along. He died in 1540.

Professor Alfar notes Vives' and other moralists' prohibitions on women's speaking in public. She says:

> Like [real] women in the period, therefore, whose lives both corresponded to and contradicted their culture's assumptions and laws, the women in Shakespeare's cuckoldry plays (...) are and are not virtuous, for while they maintain a bodily continence, their revolt against male tyranny exceeds the bounds set by early modern moralists on silence and obedience as evidence of bodily virtue.[4]

She's trying to relate separate and unrelatable value-systems. Shakespeare consistently refutes a belief in silence and obedience as evidence of any kind of virtue, in men or women.

Some grounding in historical background, then, seems indispensable to most critics of early modern literature. But women's lives and the judgements made on them were and are unimaginably various, each one differing from year to year if not hour to hour. Women's lives in history will always owe a lot to the individual writer reconstructing them. Shakespeare's texts, even after radical editors have done their grim cull of our favourite lines, are relatively stable compared to the best social histories, which are constantly upended by new research and changing cultural priorities. Historical detail is fascinating, but does it help us understand what's happening on stage? The He said, She said conflicts, the deadly effects of slander and women's passionate loyalties to each other are made incarnate within the plays themselves. How far do we need to look outside?

To take, perhaps, a simplistic parallel: somebody gives me a copy of James Joyce's *Ulysses* and I can't make anything of it. I've read *The Odyssey* in translation years ago, but maybe I should re-read it, or learn Greek. I think Joyce must have been a Catholic, given his date and place of birth, so I try to find out what the contemporary Catholic Archbishop of Dublin thought about marriage, adultery and novels. His voluminous published sermons aren't a problem, but his private letters are hard to locate. I decide to supplement my research by choosing three typical Dublin citizens and establishing exactly what each did on 16 June 1904. I spend many years in archives and libraries, and uncover some interesting facts. I doubt if I understand *Ulysses* any better at the end of it.

A stiffening of historical and archival research is reassuring for teachers. It arms us with new factual information, so we're not just sitting there with some students and a book, no backup save their opinions and our living blood to show we're actually doing some work. It professionalises a beleaguered subject, makes it compete with the sciences, wins funding. I don't underrate the patience and eye for detail needed for archival research, but it's not the only lens for reading Shakespeare. The strong conceptualising mindset it requires tends to pull his diversity into the slipstream of a thesis. At its worst, it reduces a Shakespeare play to one more contemporary document.

But then, inconsistently, I too use selective background material, stressing the proximity of rack and scaffold to the theatrical performance, in attempting a new interpretation of *The Merchant of Venice.* And research like the Sokols' gives us confidence that a reading sympathetic to Cressida is not a modern misunderstanding but inherent in the play for the contemporary audience too.

I admire criticism that lives mainly inside the play and expresses itself with clarity, like Anne Barton's and Carol Thomas Neely's. But there should be room for all sorts in this inexhaustible playground. Even if, like mine, it waffles a lot, goes off down an alley, risks a wild speculation, cuts the monumental critical reading though that may mean missing or duplicating something. An earnest critic of Shakespeare would end up like Tristram

Shandy, never getting to start, buried under an avalanche of ancient and oncoming interpretation.What matters most is to speak what we feel, as Albany advises, not what we ought to say, and if we're teachers, encourage students to do the same.

A major regret for me is the divergence of academic and non-academic but educated language. They've parted company. What can the brightest non-specialist reader, young or old, make of a prose style that seems designed to mystify? Some of it reads like wading through lexical cotton wool. Incomprehensible (to the amateur) books on Shakespeare costing over £120 and available in only the richer university libraries are part of other developing class and fiscal divisions across American and British society. In print culture, the privileged are hi-jacking him, like so much else, though the great new blessing of stage-to-cinema or stage-to-TV production pulls in the other direction. And my grumbles were ever the infirmities of age.

Simply or simplistically, then, I've argued throughout that the main way Shakespeare engages us on the side of women is by his killing/suppression narratives in all their forms. The patterns in his plots have received less attention than other aspects of his work. He makes us spectators at a judgement, formal or informal, positioning us with the inside knowledge that makes us want to see a woman vindicated. This is true of the honour-killing plays but also of the many scenes where clever women are quickly relegated to the edges of men's lives or forced to flee in disguise.

For the audience, what's on trial is not so much the woman, whom we know is innocent, or at least more innocent than her judges, as misogyny itself. From the start of the play we see the men's fixed theological concepts, the formative reading, often Petrarchan or debased Senecan, the individual weaknesses that feed into it. We're shaken by the harm it inflicts on individuals, families and countries.

Despite the Puritans' attempts to whitewash women, Eves were still everywhere in Renaissance culture, attesting to a lot of anxiety. For most of Shakespeare's contemporaries, the Bible was literally true, each story put there by God for a purpose. Though Eve was Adam's ideal mate, made from his rib as his help and comfort, her disobedience to God's law lost Eden for everyone, bringing sin and death into the world instead. That takes a lot of whitewashing. A happy marriage may for a while re-create a little domestic Paradise, but the original seeds of deceit remain in Eve's daughters, ready to spring up again.

Sometimes Shakespeare too endorses the story of woman as the root of quite a lot of evil. Not all his women are blameless victims of men's misunderstandings, nor are they all pushed to one side while men rule the world. Some are as unscrupulous, power-crazy or murderous as their equivalent men. He has plenty of Eve figures, at least as interesting as his kind and threatened ones. Among the most ruthless are Lady Macbeth, Tamora, Goneril and Regan, but other, very different women approximate to the Eve pattern: Cleopatra, Helen of Troy, Bianca Minola, Gertrude, Eleanor Cobham, Glendower's daughter, the Daughter of Antiochus. Some of these, though, are Eve-like only by circumstance.

Lady Macbeth is the most disturbing Eve. She's a practising witch, though passing as a noblewoman, then a Queen. She calls on her familiars, the spirits that tend on mortal (murderous) thoughts, as the Weird Sisters call on Paddock and Greymalkin, or as Joan of Arc calls on her familiars. When Lady Macbeth prophesies like the witches, she's as accurate, or inaccurate, as they: Duncan's entrance under her battlements is indeed fatal, though for herself and her husband as well as for him.

Her calling on her familiars to unsex her is crucial; she wants to be free from the constraints of her gender, to make herself a man. She's so completely internalised the military culture she's grown up in she thinks herself, mistakenly, more ready to kill than her husband. Her standard of manliness is simple: to be a man is to show physical courage and ambition. Her husband is aware of competing concepts: gratitude, loyalty, shared dangers past, the connections that as much as courage form a sustaining male network on a battlefield. His consciousness is profoundly moral: damnation, a great battleground of good and evil forces, the hope of salvation are visual and tangible realities to him. But none of this deters him. Only the chance of the deed being blown in every eye, of getting caught, frightens him. He'd destroy heaven and earth, kill his friend and his friend's son, just to eat his meals and sleep in peace. His goals are as material as his wife's, whose conscience only nightmares can access.

Unlike Adam, Macbeth is not even initially innocent. He's raised the enterprise of Duncan's murder with her before the play begins. At her first appearance, she's reading a letter from him which tells her of the witches' prophesy. It's cautiously worded but alerts her to be ready for Duncan's arrival. When he returns, he tells her:

> Macbeth: My dearest love,
> Duncan comes here tonight.
> Lady Macbeth: And when goes hence?
> Macbeth: Tomorrow, as he purposes.
> Lady Macbeth: O, never
> Shall sun that morrow see. (1.5.54-7)

The intercut iambics show them at one; his 'as he purposes' seems innocuous but signals his own purpose. Knowing it, the Weird Sisters have appeared to him already. In later, whispered conversations with his wife, she seems much the more determined of the two. But he knows how she'll respond to his hesitation, and he deceives himself, clutching onto some remaining humanity and renouncing the murder plan, then appearing to yield only to her persuasion. When it comes to the point, she can't kill either Duncan or the grooms. He can do both and could do both without her; he doesn't need an Eve to tempt him.

Whatever we think about her degree of guilt, this is mostly a woman-hating plot. The witches prophesy that no man born of woman can defeat Macbeth. His nemesis, Macduff, reveals himself as a man 'untimely ripped' (5.9.17) from his mother's womb, born out of her death. Only a hero who bypasses vaginal birth can restore justice. Vaginas contaminate. The 'finger of birth-strangled babe/Ditch-delivered by a drab' (4.1.30-31) is *Macbeth*'s imagination of natural birth – though the querulous Lady Macduff's first thought is for her husband and her son's safety when the killers come in.

In *Exodus* 22, verse 18, the Bible says, 'Thou shalt not suffer a witch to live.' Nothing in the Bible could be wrong, so witches existed and must be caught and killed. Witchcraft and treason were often linked in contemporary political thinking; together they might overthrow divinely-sanctioned male authority; *Macbeth* dramatises that possibility. The concept of woman easily elided into the concept of witch: Shakespeare takes from Holinshed's *Chronicles* the element of witchcraft for his scenes of Joan of Arc and

Eleanor Cobham. The *Chronicles* describe Scottish women as savage, ruthless, and again Shakespeare seized the dramatic charge offered by 'history'.

Macbeth was written and staged soon after the Accession of James I, who was an expert on witches. His parents died violently, his father when he was eight months old, murdered probably by James Hepburn, Earl of Bothwell, who just afterwards married his mother, Mary Queen of Scots. Except as a baby, James never saw her. After 19 years of captivity in England she was beheaded. There were attempts on his own life too. While still in his teens he was kidnapped in the so-called Gowrie Conspiracy, and held for a year by Scottish nobles hostile to Catholic influence on him; he believed witches assisted his captors. He published extensively on witches in *Daemonologie*[5] and elsewhere. In 1605 came the Gunpowder Plot, which might aggravate anyone's paranoia about dark forces at work. *Macbeth* followed in 1606.

We think of witch belief as flourishing among the uneducated, but it was defined and judged by the educated. Trials were long and complex, not run by the locals but by learned judges. James I's writing on witches was intended to make him a credible player among European intellectuals working in theology, then known as the 'Queen of Sciences'. The subject carried immense prestige in universities, though it flourished among the peasantry too.

It's impossible to guess how many women died terrible deaths when something went wrong in their neighbourhoods: a failed harvest, or cattle disease. Or they grew facial hair or warts, or roused suspicion by being a bit odd or just too old. The numbers run into hundreds of thousands, perhaps millions across Europe. It's a subject that went missing from history books for centuries, like the slave trade. Few critics mention it, much less blame Shakespeare for endorsing the belief.

Macbeth is unsurpassed in its richness of verse, creating a Scotland of blood and terror. In the long Northern twilight:

> Light thickens, and the crow
> Makes wing to the rooky wood;
> Good things of day begin to droop and drowse
> Whiles night's black agents to their preys do rouse. (3.3.51-4)

Lady Macbeth and the witches make up much of that darkness.

Ostensibly the play goes back into history to validate the divine right of James' Accession to the monarchies of Scotland and England. But for Alan Sinfield and others, a messenger's report about Macbeth and Macduff killing the rebels against King Duncan and making a new Calvary by their slaughter casts doubt on legal as well as illegal violence. Duncan is old enough and wise enough to let his Thanes do his killing for him now, but we don't know how he came to power. The 'traitor' Thane of Cawdor faces his execution with studied grace: 'Nothing in his life became him like the leaving it.' (1.4.7-8) He would have made a good king in other circumstances. The politics of *Macbeth* are more ambiguous than they seem. On women and witches, however, there's little room for doubt: they melt into each other.

The play endorses witch-belief, then, for whatever reason. Because they come with the Scottish territory, with the Holinshed source, and witches make great drama? As a compliment to James appropriate in this first tragedy performed for the new court by Shakespeare's company, now the King's Men? Shakespeare's plays have affected the way people think and feel. *Macbeth* sits uncomfortably at the heart of any debate on the rival claims of art and ethics.

Tamora almost succeeds in replacing Roman patriarchy with her own imperial matriarchy. Like Edmund in *Lear*, she uses her outsider's glamour to rise to Olympian heights. A tiger-mother in a wilderness of tigers, her ambition seems almost incidental, a side-effect of her passion to avenge her eldest son. Until she relaxes her guard and lets herself be tricked by Titus, she's the cleverest of the political players. She has elements of Cleopatra, but she makes Cleopatra look Home Counties English. We pity her first agony as Alarbus is dragged off, but by the time she realises she's eaten her younger sons' flesh, the audience is, I think, beyond pity. Like Eve, she becomes a scapegoat in a Last Judgement, but for the audience her violence is almost condoned by the Roman savagery that produced and will succeed it.

Stemming from their relationship with their father, Goneril and Regan are alternately manipulators and victims in their relationships with men. They're not identical; Goneril is sharper, wittier, Regan more crude and direct. But for once Regan grovels, almost stammers as she questions Edmund about her envied older sister:

> Now, sweet lord,
> You know the goodness I intend upon you:
> Tell me, but truly, but then speak the truth,
> Do you not love my sister?

There's graphic detail in the sisters' marriages and their competition for him. Regan feels lucky in losing her husband, as it frees her to marry again. In the BBC Bardathon series, Diana Rigg as Regan turned contemptuously away from Cornwall's silent plea for comfort as he died. Goneril and Albany's incompatible marriage has never been negotiated into an amnesty. When Regan openly claims Edmund as her future husband, while Albany has just learned that Edmund and Goneril are planning to marry once his wife has murdered him, he rises to unexpected decisiveness and wit:

> Edmund, I arrest thee
> On capital treason; and, in thine attaint [arrest],
> This gilded serpent [Goneril, his wife]. For your claim [to Edmund], fair sister [Regan],
> I bar it in the interest of [on behalf of] my wife.
> Tis she is subcontracted to this lord [Edmund],
> And I her husband contradict the banns [Regan's notice that she'll marry Edmund].
> If you will marry, make your loves to me. My lady is bespoke [spoken for].
> Goneril: An interlude! [comic turn]. (5.3.81-8)

He sees Goneril not just as Eve but the Serpent-Satan. He's been earnest and ineffectual up to now. 'Your sister,' Oswald smirks to Regan, 'is the better soldier.' (4.5.3) But with his recent information about his wife's loathing of him, Gloucester's blinding and the country in turmoil, the funny side suddenly hits him. *Lear* is one of the wittiest of all Shakespeare's plays. With his deft summary of the family chaos, Albany manages to stay sane and (just) in control.

Like Lady Macbeth, Cleopatra can be played as an Eve who tempts a man to his disgrace and death, but unlike Lady Macbeth she's human, funny and deeply engaging. The historical Antony ordered the decimation of his soldiers when a battle went badly, Cleopatra tested poisons on her slaves to find the easiest way to die, so Shakespeare cleaned them both up a lot. But it's easier to see *Antony and Cleopatra* as the story of the world well lost for love if you haven't read it for a while and forget how childish the lovers can be, how contemptibly they bully their servants. The critical history of each play changes as British cultural history changes, and *Antony and Cleopatra*'s reception has been a barometer of England's imperial role. This may be urban legend, but one Victorian lady is said to have exclaimed as she left the theatre, 'How unlike the home life of our own dear Queen!' Though it may have been not so unlike as the lady thought.

Whatever we think of the balance between seamy love and sterile duty in the first four Acts, in the fifth Cleopatra re-invents herself and Antony, now dead, to show love eternal. She edits out the rows and treacheries, making their defeat into triumph. The friendships of women with women and men with men cluster on the Egyptian side. Cleopatra's women stay loyal and follow her willingly into death. Antony's friend and fellow-officer Enobarbus voices the shifting sympathies and antipathies of the audience, holding the balance between Egyptian and Roman claims. He abandons Antony in anger for his cowardly flight at Actium, then when Antony generously sends his chests of treasure after him, dies of shame at his own disloyalty, vindicating the Egyptian Antony after all.

Cleopatra's deception of Antony, sending Mardian to report her own death, leads directly to his botched suicide, though she can't foresee this. Again the source, Plutarch, dictates much of the action. How far is she playing only for herself and Egypt throughout? For her, there's no distinction between self and country.

In Act Five, the tone changes. Here the action starts to move into an honour-killing pattern, its magnificent, archetypal Woman threatened with a shameful death by Octavius, the coldest Roman of them all. Despite his denial, she sees he means to take her back to Rome for public humiliation in his Triumph, which was followed by the death or enslavement of the prisoners. His need to inflict this on her for the sake of his pride is the punitive anger that drives honour killing. She's challenged the might of Rome, his own authority. It wasn't a fate reserved for women heads of state: Vercingetorix, King of the Averni, had to walk in Julius Caesar's

Triumph before execution, and foreign prisoners were desirable spoils for exhibition. But Cleopatra adds to her political rebellion the reputation of a whore, and this will figure in the side-shows and catcalls as she's paraded through the streets. She'll be humiliated before she's killed.

All through Act Five she's both celebrating Antony's life and planning how to die. We know she's fictionalising as she praises Antony:

> Realms and islands were
> As plates dropped from his pocket (...)
> Think you there was, or might be, such a man? (5.2.90-92)

Dolabella replies, 'Gentle madam, no.' But her fictions are truer than Octavius' victory. Rome is the death of Eros and imagining in all the Roman plays, here especially, and we're glad when she finds a loyal subject with a snake to take her out painlessly. The last Act shows the greatest of all the escapes from honour killing, scripted and choreographed by Cleopatra herself. For once in the unequal battle between Woman and Romanitas, a woman wins.

In *Troilus and Cressida* there are two great female legends for infidelity, Helen and Cressida, but Helen is bored and boring, and the play shows how Cressida's legend is falsely created by the men around her. This generically indeterminate play may have been written for a clever Inns of Court audience. It's cynical about the two great themes of epic, military heroism and love. Of all Shakespeare's women, Helen of Troy best fits a downmarket Eve stereotype: seductive, trivial, she causes the Fall of Troy as brainlessly as Eve causes the Fall of Man. In this respect, Homer and the Old Testament speak as one: uncontrolled women are very dangerous.

The heroes' legendary status is equally undermined. The Trojan Prince Hector sends a challenge like a medieval knight, boasting he has a lady fairer, wiser, truer than any known to the Greeks. Trash, Achilles calls it, and he's right. In private, Hector's manner to his wife Andromache is barely civil. The ideals of chivalry are repeatedly undercut. On the battlefield he sees a suit of gold armour on a corpse and decides to loot and wear it, taking off his own. Here Achilles finds him, and gloats over his unarmed prey:

> Look, Hector, how the sun begins to set,

How ugly night comes breathing at his heels;
Even with the vail and darkening of the sun
To close the day up, Hector's life is done. (5.10.5-8)

Hector responds, lamely, 'I am unarmed, forbear advantage, Greek.' (5.10.9) Earlier, Hector allowed Achilles time to recover when the two were fighting and Achilles was winded, but Achilles won't reciprocate. Hector is surrounded and killed by the Myrmidons, though Achilles claims the glory: 'Achilles has the mighty Hector slain.' (5.10.14) The Myrmidons were robotic, antlike creatures, and at this moment of horror the play turns into science fiction. There's no such thing as glory, and with the death of Hector, 'the dragon wing of night o'erspreads the earth.' (5.10.17) Shakespeare's constructions of war, here as in most of the History Plays, are a long way from the heroics of *Henry V*, and even in *Henry V* what we see of Agincourt, as opposed to what we hear of it, is only an English bully frightening a timid Frenchman.

There's a desperate gaiety to Paris and Helen, trying to be funny but unequipped with wit. Helen urges Pandarus to sing to them, and as ever the song is dramatically appropriate, both idiotic and orgasmic:

These lovers cry, O! O! they die,
Yet that which seems the wound to kill,
Doth turn O! O! to ha! ha! ha! (3.1.102-5)

Thersites' judgment, fools on both sides, is accurate. Cressida and Aeneas are the only sympathetic figures in the play.

Bianca Minola's sweet duplicity is very Eve-like, misleading everyone including the audience until the end. Eleanor Cobham, Duchess of Gloucester longs for the golden apple of a Coronation, but so do the nobility, who are more ruthless and efficient than she is. Glendower's daughter with her siren song is an ambiguous figure, dishonouring or saving her husband according to whether or not we admire his commitment to his military cause. Gertrude is one strong incentive for the murder of King Hamlet; her compliance in marrying the serpent Claudius supports his Succession and turns Denmark into an un-weeded, fallen garden. However, she's not aware she's being used. The incestuous Daughter of Antiochus in *Pericles* enjoys a game where she lures suitors to their deaths if they can't guess a riddle about her. They have their heads cut off and stuck on spikes around the battlements of her father's palace (or the railings of the Upper Stage). So she's more like Salome, joint-killer of St John the Baptist, than Eve or Jezebel. Interestingly, given that she's the deadliest woman in the *Works*, the *Authorship Companion* to *The New Oxford Shakespeare* (2016) claims these early scenes are not by Shakespeare but by a collaborator, George Wilkins.

There are a rich variety of Eves in Shakespeare, then, but the greatest of them are treated with some authorial sympathy, their failings partially accounted for. And deceitful women and broken promises are rarer than frank, generous women and difficult but close love relationships. There's no chronological development or generic fashioning in this: throughout his career and in all types of play we find cruel and lying women, as we find candid, affectionate and forgiving ones.

Where do his good women come from? A Humanist tradition of writing on women's rational natures underpins them, but that alone couldn't spark them into life. Good women in the Old Testament are conspicuous by their rarity, but there are a few. In the story of Susanna and the Elders[6], two clerical judges spy on a married woman, Susanna, as she bathes, try to blackmail her into having sex with them and when she refuses accuse her of adultery with a third man. She's tried and condemned to death in what would be a classic honour killing. But the boy Judge, Daniel, establishes that the Elders told inconsistent stories, so she's reprieved and they're condemned instead. Shakespeare or his wife or both chose her name for their first baby.

What people call their children can be revealing. Perhaps the story of Susanna fed early into his perception of the way jealous or thwarted men take out their aggression on women. Was the name chosen only for its pleasant susurration, or was there already some attachment to a plotline that he'd heard, perhaps both he and Anne had heard in church from the Geneva Bible still in use then, and that he later rewrote in many versions? Susanna was an unusual name in 1583. Did Anne herself meet some hostility from her elders when she got pregnant by a nameless boy of eighteen, or did their hasty marriage avert that? Whichever, this Old Testament trial, condemnation and vindication of a sexually desirable woman, all blame fixed on lecherous clergy, was unique, and dramatic enough to invite updating. Unsurprisingly, it was soon relegated to the *Apochrypha*.

None of Shakespeare's plays exactly replicates the Susanna story. But in the four which are centrally about honour killing, *Much Ado*, *Othello*, *Cymbeline* and *The Winter's Tale*, a man of flawed self-esteem tries and condemns an innocent woman he thinks has committed adultery, or fornication in Hero's case. His suspicions are reinforced by other men he trusts, by his competitive military culture, by his conviction that women are daughters of Eve and naturally deceitful. The woman suffers a form of death and the man's misjudgement spreads misery far beyond the couple alone. All the women are vindicated and the men proved wrong. In *The Winter's Tale*, Leontes' rage kills Hermione. But the devotion of Paulina and the return of Perdita eventually restore her. Shakespeare comes close to rewriting the Crucifixion, Resurrection and evangelical role of St Paul the Apostle as a miracle with a female hero brought back to life by her friend and daughter. In his Tale, misogyny not woman's disobedience is the primal, death-dealing sin.

When he stages English History, he can't stray far from the historical records of Holinshed and Hall. But except for Margaret of Anjou, his women are created with unexpected sympathy, and even Margaret's cruelty may be a response to her treatment by her father. Joan is a unique and luminous figure on her first appearance. The Eleanor episode is an early example of a woman trapped by predators; they use her without pity to discredit her husband, a political rival. Her story is told in some detail, though we're never sure if Asnath is Satan or a talented retainer of Suffolk. Other women use their brains to read and try to guide events, though they're generally ignored. Unlike Henry VIII's other victims, Katherine of Aragon is kind and blameless, her longing to hold back time caught lyrically in the Orpheus song.

Rape in war aims at the suppression of a nation or an ethnicity, rape in peacetime at the contemptuous obliteration of the woman's identity. Whoever first told Philomel's story knew what s/he was doing when s/he took out Philomel's tongue. Shakespeare went a stage further and took out Lavinia's hands. From at least his early teens he absorbed Ovid's *Metamorphoses*, its pages crawling with sexual predators and their frantic prey. In his formative years he would imitate its Latin verse in school, and the book became part of his understanding of his own world. Lavinia's double rape and mutilation only just off stage and audible is in a league of its own, but elsewhere he shows marital rape as comparable with stranger rape and forced or even arranged marriage as cruelty. All his courtship stories assume that women should have a least a negative vote in the choice of a husband, and most are ready to fight for this freedom. Kate Minola's negative vote is ignored, but Petruccio risks his reputation among the boys to give her time to get used to him, even get to like him, emerging (in this respect only) as one of our leading proto-feminists.

Misogyny pervades every area of experience, the early and late Comedies, the English and Roman Histories and the Tragedies. Women are kept in the suburbs, silenced or side-lined. There's infinite variety in their responses, from Portia (*Julius Caesar*) who self-harms, to Isabella who violently refuses to meet men's expectations, to Ophelia who wants to please all her men and melts away into water, her natural element. The cards are stacked against them, but far from this being represented neutrally, as just the way things are, men who reject women's intelligence and autonomy undermine themselves, wreck their whole family or bring about the overthrow of the state.

Shakespeare's finest women break through their claustrophobic family and social circumstances by disguising as boys or by finding some freer way to live, not just in the cross-dressing Comedies but in every genre except the Histories: Beatrice, Rosalind, Desdemona assert their own judgement, with happy results for the first two, though Desdemona's courage leads her to what feels like the most tragic of all Shakespeare's deaths. Many of his women are complex to a degree that leaves modern psychiatry behind; Rosalind and Ganymede share a body for much of their play. His courtship, marital and familial relationships are full of tension and misunderstanding.

Before the Fall, the Church taught, life in Eden was simple. In the Anglican Marriage Service, Thomas Cranmer, who lost his Cambridge Fellowship by his first marriage then took a huge risk as a widower and re-married secretly when in Catholic orders, constructed the best conventional relationship for his time: the husband is protective, the wife compliant. He promises to love her, comfort her, honour and keep her. She promises to obey him and serve him, love, honour and keep him. Sadly, his promise to endow her with all his worldly goods was the one the law didn't support. A husband was expected to keep his wife at whatever standard of living he could afford for himself, but she owned no money, everything legally belonged to him, and so she had no choice about how money was spent unless she could exact that freedom for herself. She lived his life. It was a difficult, perhaps an impossible model for many women.

The large difference, then, between Shakespeare's lovers and the lovers and married couples in the pre-Fall Eden images, the Marriage Service and the early modern how-to books is that with Shakespeare the closest relationships aren't serene and paradisal but wary or hostile, conducted between two people of formidable and equal intelligence whose interests diverge. Even Romeo and Juliet, the least contentious of his lovers, weigh each other up and compete in 'sonnets', rhyming quatrains, checking each other out for literary accomplishment as they might now for musical taste. Romeo begins:

> If I profane with my unworthiest hand
> This holy shrine [her hand, as he takes it] (...) (1.5.89-90)

He moves straight into the language of courtly love, where erotic feeling is mediated through religious imagery. Juliet takes up his metaphor of a pilgrim at the shrine of a saint and turns it to the Petrarchan Lady's expected repulse of her suitor:

> Romeo: Have not saints lips, and holy palmers [pilgrims] too?
> Juliet: Ay, pilgrim, lips that they must use in prayer. (1.5.99-100)

They both know how to play these literary games; you kiss by the book, she says, laughing at how good he is at it. Later, on the balcony, she drops the Petrarchan Lady pose because she's given away her secret before she knows he's listening, but she sets out her condition firmly with

> If that thy bent of love be honourable,
> Thy purpose marriage (...) (2.1.185-6)

Almost all his women from innocent Juliet to sophisticated Beatrice know they must negotiate if they're to stand a chance of survival. The other Juliet, in *Measure for Measure*, fails to see this in time, and she confronts her failure stoically. Cressida is too desperate for love to sustain a negotiation.

To return at last to *Much Ado About Nothing*, then, Claudio's division of women into two types, Diana or animal, angel or devil, probably sounded simplistic already to many in the audience. He says to Hero:

> You seemed to me as Dian in her orb,
> As chaste as is the bud ere it be blown;
> But you are more intemperate in your blood
> Than Venus, or those pampered animals
> That rage in savage sensuality. (4.1.52-6)

For Claudio, as for many of Shakespeare's ill-judging men, there's nothing in between.

Hero is interesting precisely because she is so in-between, an average young woman who may or may not want to marry the man who satisfies her father but who knows she must take what's going and make the best of it. She walks a tightrope, like most young women before the 1960s; she has to be immaculate in her conduct, though she's allowed, indeed expected, to know about sex. Her father asks Claudio to repeat her joke about Benedick and Beatrice between the sheets, and Claudio is reluctant to do so; it doesn't quite go with the 'Dian in her orb' that he thinks her. Leonato is used to a household full of lively young women and knows something about them.

On Imogen's bedroom wall, the virginal and the wicked woman are contrasted in tapestries of Diana and Cleopatra. There's no familiar image who can represent a good wife. Diana can't represent Imogen because Diana is a virgin, and like the Virgin Mary, who is both maiden and mother, an impossible model for wives. In his memory, Posthumus approximates Imogen to Diana as far as he can, as he does also with the memory of his mother. But then his mother's image is desecrated by his sudden recognition that she too was a sexual being who bore a child, himself. So she must have been promiscuous. Claudio, Othello, Posthumus and Leontes all find women's sexuality confusing.

If Shakespeare's narratives of love come from anywhere, they come not so much from religious cultures as from poetry about love, from Chaucer and his many successors down to the 1590s. In *The General Prologue to the Canterbury Tales*, and in many of the Tales themselves, Chaucer creates women who don't do what men or society expect of them. In Thomas Wyatt's 'They flee from me that sometime did me seek'[7] a woman comes to his bed but won't be tamed. In Michael Drayton's violent sonnets and in the long contention in Philip Sidney's sonnet sequence *Astrophil and Stella*, love is a struggle. In Spenser's sonnets too there are quarrels, and time and circumstance are also divisive, though the erotic *Epithalamion* resolves all troubles. These stories are more dramatic than the pre-Fall Genesis or Marriage Service harmonies, which assume that the man is the boss and the woman accepts that – until she doesn't.

There are many tributary streams, then, too many to trace here. But no cultural background or literary history can explain Shakespeare. In a nuanced book, Catherine Belsey examines the cultural/contextual approach and finds it wanting. But she doesn't completely cut the link between dramatist and context. And she's right, as he doesn't so much go against the grain of his time as combine its multiple grains, ending up with a richness like none of them. His women are honest and intelligent, the Humanist or Puritan prescriptions for good women, but they break Puritan prescriptions in their sensuality and in their reliance on their own judgement. These last two qualities threaten the power of Mosaic law as it remained embedded in English culture.

There were many contemporary versions of the self-sufficient and emancipated woman, as Dusinberre argues. In an ancestor of the novel, Philip Sidney's *The Countess of Pembroke's Arcadia*, Pamela has brains and distinction comparable with Shakespeare's women. She's probably based on Lady Jane Grey, who was Sidney's aunt by marriage, and executed just before he was born. Sidney creates in Pamela a woman of heroic strength and patience. But though Jane Grey was married, Pamela is neither believably a wife nor a marriageable girl. She's all but asexual, and she goes to a martyr's death. This is not a study of love relationships as Shakespeare's plays are. The Pamela thread of the narrative is hagiographic, the story of a saint.

Devils are more popular than angels; the anonymous *Arden of Faversham* has a good example. It's dated at around 1591 when Shakespeare's career was beginning and it's sometimes ascribed to him, at least in part, because it's a brilliant play and not obviously the work of anyone else. Some of its images foreshadow Shakespeare's. For instance, Alice Arden longs for a horse with wings to carry her husband away and buck him off into the sea. But this is rather different from Imogen's fervent 'O, for a horse with wings' (*Cymbeline*, 3.2.46), and Pegasus drops by in many Renaissance works.

This one is a docudrama based on a notorious Kent murder of forty years earlier. Alice has a rough-trade lover, Mosby, and wants to be rid of her husband to remarry. Her husband knows about Mosby but he's badly advised by his best friend, and condones her adultery. In the historical account, Holinshed's *Chronicles*, this is because he doesn't want to offend her relatives, with whom he has business dealings. There's no hint of that in the play, where his failure to control her comes from excessive fondness. As a landowner he's unrelenting, which emphasises his feebleness, by common contemporary standards, as a husband who should rule his wife.

Alice hires a succession of men to kill him, most enjoyably a cross-talking, accident-prone duo called Black Will and Shakebag. Sadly, these are the nicknames of the historical hitmen, not the anonymous author's catty allusions to Shakespeare. There are some funny near-misses, one where a falling window-frame pens the killer's arms while the prey walks off. In the subplot, the Ardens' manservant Michael is desperate to marry Mosby's sister Susan, and Mosby will give his consent only if Michael agrees to help kill Arden, which he does. Desire corrupts, whether or not marriage is intended. Finally, many of the *dramatis personae* help Alice with the on-stage stabbing of her husband on the family dining-table.

His body is hidden in a field. Providentially, enough snow falls for the murderers to leave footprints from the Arden home to the corpse, but not enough to cover them, so it's quickly discovered. The body bleeds as Alice is forced towards it, an infallible sign of her guilt, and she confesses. The men involved in the murder are hanged along with Mosby's sister, who learned of it only after its commission, and Alice is sentenced to be burned at Canterbury, as she was in fact. Legally, she'd committed a form of treason in killing her husband, violating the social order where a husband is 'above' his wife, so her sentence was worse than hanging.

It's a subtle play psychologically, with a convincing ebb and flow of nerve in Alice and Mosby. Alice has been compared to Richard III in hypocrisy and engagement with the audience, but she's not as clever as she thinks. Mosby becomes alarmed by her short way with husbands and means to kill her for his own safety, something she doesn't anticipate, as soon as he's married her and secured her money. But events overtake him. It's clear, I think, that it's Arden's weak fondness for her which makes her despise him. She loved him once, but she's attracted to Mosby precisely because he's dangerous and treats her badly. Arden's failure to govern his wife leads to her adultery and their deaths, and to the corruption and death of most of the other characters. The play is the perfect updated Eve story.

It was popular, one of many contemporary portrayals of women as Eves or Jezebels, as Shakespeare's career began. If he did write *Arden of Faversham*, he quickly revised its Eve ideology: he makes his later small-town Alice, lovely Alice Ford of Windsor, into Alice Arden's polar opposite.

Dusinberre argues that Shakespeare's women differ from those of his contemporary dramatists only in the degree of his artistry, but they differ too in their placing within an innocent-woman-on-trial plot, so with Shakespeare the play's focus is on their vindication and the emergence of a truth that the men, or at least the audience, have to acknowledge.

John Webster's career began as Shakespeare's was ending, and he's deeply indebted to Shakespeare for *The Duchess of Malfi*, the one great feminist play of the early modern period. We can call Shakespeare a feminist in the sense that his women are often intellectually and morally superior to his men. But though his good women claim the freedom to choose their own husbands or remain single, a freedom in fact underwritten by the Church and the law however difficult that could be to access, they aren't otherwise rebellious against male systems. They have much the same expectations of themselves as men have of them, and they define themselves mostly in relation to men. Even Beatrice doesn't fundamentally reject her society's standards for women, though she sees how open they are to abuse.

Shakespeare's men are initially brave and intelligent. Their friends admire them and their wives and daughters love them, though they turn out to be capable of every form of misogyny from casual contempt to murder. That plot is in some ways more disturbing than Webster's Gothic horror story, where the killer males are psychopaths from the start.

Webster's sexual politics are extreme. The Duchess, a young widow, falls in love with, takes the initiative in courting and secretly marries her Master of Horse, Antonio, a man of lower rank than her brothers think suitable. Neither wants her to remarry at all. One, a Duke, is insane and sexually fixated on his sister; the other, a Cardinal, is a murderous hypocrite. Of course, nobody in the contemporary London theatre audience would think she deserves punishment for her choice, let alone death.

Her brothers discover the marriage through their catspaw Bosola, who's spying for them in the Duchess' household. His mordant wit is almost a medical condition in itself, one which keeps human feeling at bay. Though she escapes them all for a while, Bosola overtakes her on the road and takes her back to her palace, where on her brothers' orders he has her strangled on stage in a protracted honour killing. Her 'trial' makes no pretence to reason, it's an imaginatively-scripted Theatre of Terror accompanied by singing and dancing. The Duchess couldn't live in the world Webster creates; no happy ending is remotely possible. Like Samuel Richardson's Clarissa Harlowe, she has nowhere to go but a coffin, which Bosola thoughtfully brings along to her murder.

Webster couldn't have written *The Duchess* without Shakespeare's defiant models and their honour trials. But in the protracted preliminaries to her strangling, Antonio is all but forgotten by the Duchess. With the garotte around her neck, she asserts herself alone:

> I am Duchess of Malfi still. (4.2.139)

She doesn't consider herself defined by a man, though a purist might argue she's still defined by her first husband. However, she does identify to the end, passionately, as a mother. The Mad Men here are impossible to circumvent or enlighten, whereas in Shakespeare they learn to regret their actions.

Over the next four hundred years, dramatists and novelists found in Shakespeare patterns for their own intelligent, determined women. By the second half of the 18th century, a knowledge of Shakespeare and an ability to quote him were replacing a knowledge of Latin as the definition of an educated person, a definition women could at last share. Female authors, often with restricted access to books, Frances Burney, Charlotte Smith, Jane Austen, the Brontes among many others, found in their fathers' libraries what they needed for a writer's education, a *Complete Works*. Austen especially drew on Shakespeare, re-writing in *Persuasion* the winter bleakness and spring renewal of *The Winter's Tale*, and a heroine who is her mother's self with a second chance. The re-writing continues, by Jeanette Winterson and many others.

The present theatre-going, Shakespeare-reading, Shakespeare-producing constituency in the West may have lost some sympathetic connection to his women. The heroines kept their full hold into Victorian and early twentieth-century times. Then in the mid twentieth century came women's new power to control their own fertility, and that changed a lot, including the fictions they need. We're more likely now to see integrity in a woman as loyalty to a worthwhile occupation than as long-term commitment to a love relationship. But long-term commitment retains its appeal; people keep on moving in together, getting married, often spousally.

*

Shakespeare's men accuse women of deception because they're humiliated or irrationally jealous, and because that's what their culture has conditioned them to do. In a surprising reversal of the Eve story, tragedy strikes repeatedly in Shakespeare not because men trust their women too much but because they don't trust them enough. He rejects the narrative of female weakness and deceit. Instead he focuses his audience's sympathy firmly onto his embattled women, making the audience confront the madness that drives the men to suppress or destroy them.

Even Lady Macbeth and Cleopatra are sexually faithful. None of his women goes off with a snake except Margaret of Anjou, Helen of Troy, Goneril and Regan, whose husbands have apparently been picked by Lear, and Cressida, who has the excuse that it's wartime, she needs a protector, and Troilus has made no effort to keep her. In *Much Ado*, *Othello* and *Cymbeline*, it's the men who listen to snakes and bring death to their worlds, while in most of the other plays too, men are deceivers ever, if only of themselves and each other, and distrust of the woman is unfounded. Where men disregard women's perceptions and intelligence, they're almost always wrong to do so.

I don't believe Shakespeare wrote for anyone's moral edification. He wrote, I assume, to entertain, and debateable new concepts of love and marital relationships are entertaining for both sexes. Because his plays are not reflections but indictments of misogyny, edification followed, and a slow shift towards enlightenment. He replaced the Eve story with the Susanna story in the national consciousness.

Notes

[1]Juliet Dusinberre, *Shakespeare and the Nature of Women*, p5.

[2]Carol Thomas Neely, *Broken Nuptials in Shakespeare's Plays*, p97.

[3]Catherine Belsey, *Shakespeare and the Loss of Eden: The Construction of Family Values in Early Modern Culture*, p81.

[4]Cristina León Alfar, *Women and Shakespeare's Cuckoldry Plays: Shifting Narratives of Marital Betrayal*, p4.

[5]*Daemonologie, In Forme of a Dialogue, Divided into three Books*: by the High and Mighty Prince, James, etc, 1597. Partly in the form of FAQs, James discusses demons, werewolves and vampires, and the urgency of identifying and killing witches. He begins: 'The fearful abounding at this time in this country [Scotland] of these detestable slaves of the devil, the Witches or enchanters, hath moved me (beloved reader) to dispatch in post [hastily] this following treatise of mine, (...) to resolve the doubting (...) both that such assaults of Satan are most certainly practised, and that the instrument thereof merits most severely to be punished.'

Not all the accused were women, but most were.

[6]Susanna and the Elders: the story is told in *Daniel* 13, which was in the Geneva Bible in use in Shakespeare's and Hathaway's youth. Though the story was retained in the *Vulgate*, the Catholic Bible, which was in Latin, under Protestantism it was soon relegated to the *Apocrypha* (hidden or secret works), texts considered too valuable to discard but of doubtful origin or authenticity.

[7]Thomas Wyatt:

They flee from me that sometime did me seek.

With naked foot, stalking in my chamber.

I have seen them gentle, tame and meek,

That now are wild and do not remember

That sometime they put themselves in danger

To take bread at my hand; and now they range

Busily seeking with a continual change.

The domesticated deer that walk upstairs into the bedrooms of a great house seeking food are images of the apparently loving woman who vanishes when a better suitor appears. This and Wyatt's 'Whoso list to hunt' may be about Anne Boleyn.

ACKNOWLEDGEMENTS

Davide Martino has generously allowed me to use unpublished material from his thesis, 'Art, Religion and Diplomacy in the Life of Costantino de'Servi (1554-1622)', part of his submission for the Tripos Examination in the Faculty of History, Cambridge University. Martino discusses the response of Prince Henry Stuart to a portrait of Caterina de'Medici shown him by de'Servi, a diplomat in the pay of the Medici while a visitor to King James I's court. This thesis opens a new reading for the much-annotated conversation between Perdita and Polixenes.

I'd like to thank Tom Woodman for information about the Old Testament story of Susanna and the Elders, included in the Geneva Bible in Shakespeare's youth, then transferred to the Apocrypha.

Many thanks to Kevin Sprague (www.kevinsprague.com) for supplying the cover picture, a poster image of Hermione prepared for a 2010 production of *The Winter's Tale* by Shakespeare & Company, Lenox, MA. Jake Campbell of December Publications has been skilful and patient in adapting it to my cover. Quotation from *The Gap of Time* by Jeanette Winterson, published by Hogarth, is reproduced by permission of The Random House Group Ltd © 2015. Thanks also to Fourth Estate (HarperCollins) for permission to quote from Hilary Mantel's *Bring Up the Bodies.*

I'm very grateful to John Lucas for putting me in touch with his own publisher, Greenwich Exchange: I've been lucky to find with James Hodgson an academic press willing to make a quick decision and go straight to paperback at an affordable price, something I'd almost given up hope of. Patrick Ramsey and Janet Davidson have been scrupulous readers and constantly helpful at the layout and editing stages, while Peter Randall oversees promotion and distribution. The team at Greenwich Exchange has been a pleasure to work with.

I'm very grateful also to Katherine Duncan-Jones for the encouragement she gave by her sympathetic discussion of my 'animal rites' reading of *Venus and Adonis* in the Arden Edition of Shakespeare's Poems (2007).

Honour Killing comes from a lifetime's reading, seeing and teaching Shakespeare. A brief outline of Chapter One and a sketch of the argument, 'Misogyny on Trial: Shakespeare and Honour Killing', appeared in *Form and Feeling in Modern Literature: Essays in Honour of Barbara Hardy*

(2013): pp 122-31, edited by William Baker with Isobel Armstrong and published by Legenda, permission kindly granted by Taylor and Francis. Barbara was my Ph.D supervisor, greatly missed by me and all her graduates.

I remember fondly the generations of Reading University students, day and evening, whose interest and enthusiasm took the Shakespeare seminars way into overtime.

Error and wild speculation I acknowledge mine.

TO THE GREAT VARIETY OF READERS
[Preface to Shakespeare's First Folio, 1623]

From the most able, to him that can but spell: There you are numbered. We had rather you were weighd [to see how full of money your pockets are]. Especially, when the fate of all Books depends upon your capacities: and not of your heads alone, but of your purses. Well! it is now publique, & you will stand for your privileges we know: to read, and censure [criticise]. Do so, but buy it first. That doth best commend a Book, the Stationer [Bookseller] saies. Then, how odd [different] soever your brains be, or your wisedoms, make your licence [spending] the same, and spare not. Judge your sixe-pen'orth, your shillingsworth, your five shillingsworth at a time, or higher, so you rise to the just rates, and welcome. [Plays were priced and sold individually as well as collected in the one-volume First Folio, thought to be priced at around £1]. But, whatever you do, Buy. Censure [criticism] will not drive Trade, or make the Jacke go [turn the spit to cook the dinner]. And though you be a Magistrate [Judge] of wit, and sit on the Stage at Black-Friers, or the Cock-pit, to Arraigne [assess] Plays dailie [fashionable male playgoers liked to sit on the stage to comment and be seen, as well as to get the best view], know, these Plays have had their triall already [on the stage], and stood out all Appeales [stood up to all challenges]; and do now come forth [a]quitted rather by a decree of Court [by the court of public opinion], than any purchas'd Letters of commendation [rather than by paying any individual to praise them in print].

It had been a thing, we confesse, worthy to have been wished, that the Author himself had liv'd to have set forth, and overseen his own writings; but since it hath been ordaine'd otherwise, and he by death departed from that right, we pray you do not envie his Friends, the office of their care, and paine, to have collected & publish'd them; and so to have publish'd them, as where [before] you were abus'd with diverse stolne, and surreptitious copies, [ie, the Quartos, put together by someone in the audience memorising them, or by bribing the actors, and then selling the script to a printer] maimed, and deformed by the frauds and stealths of injurious impostors, that expos'd them [incompletely and inaccurately printed, as frail babies were exposed in classical times]: even those, are now offer'd to your view cur'd, and perfect of their limbes; and all the rest, absolute in their numbers [all their lines complete and correct], as he conceived them. Who, as he was a happie imitator of Nature [human nature], was a most gentle expresser of it. His mind and hand went together: And what he thought, he uttered with that easinesse, that we have scarce received from him a blot in his papers. But it is not our province, who only gather his works, and give them you, to praise him. It is yours that read him. And there we hope, to your diverse [different] capacities, you will find enough, both to draw, and to hold you: for his wit can no more lie hid, than it could be lost. Read him, therefore; and again, and again: And if then you doe not like him, surely you are in some manifest danger, not to understand him. And so we leave you to other of his Friends [contemporary writers who praise him in the prefatory material to the First Folio], whom if you need, can be your guides; if you neede them not, you can lead yourselves, and others. And such Readers we wish him.

John Heminge
Henrie Condel

WORKS AND FILMS CITED

Alfar, Cristina León. *Women and Shakespeare's Cuckoldry Plays: Shifting Narratives of Marital Betrayal.* NY: Routledge, 2017.

Anon. *Arden of Faversham,* c. 1591. *The New Oxford Shakespeare: The Complete Works.* Eds. Gary Taylor, John Jowett, Terri Bourus, Gabriel Egan. OUP, 2016.

Barton, Anne. Introductions to the Comedies in *The Riverside Shakespeare.* Ed. Harry Levin. Boston: Houghton Mifflin, 1974.

Barton, Anne. *Essays, Mainly Shakespearean.* CUP, 1994.

Bate, Sir Jonathan. Ed. *Titus Andronicus.* The Arden Shakespeare. London: Routledge, 1995.

Belsey, Catherine. *Shakespeare and the Loss of Eden: The Construction of Family Values in Early Modern Culture.* Basingstoke: Macmillan, 1999.

Bradley, A.C. *Shakespearean Tragedy,* 1904. Often republished, for example by Penguin with an Introduction by John Bayley. London: Penguin, 1991.

Branagh, Sir Kenneth. Film: *Love's Labour's Lost,* 2000.

Bullough, Geoffrey. *Narrative and Dramatic Sources of Shakespeare.* In nine volumes. [These include extensive quotation from Raphael Holinshed, Edward Hall, Sir Thomas More, Ovid, Plutarch, French and Italian romances and many other sources worth reading for their own sakes, as well as showing what Shakespeare chose to include and what to change for dramatic purposes]. London: Routledge & Kegan Paul, 1957.

Callaghan, Dympna. Ed. *A Feminist Companion to Shakespeare.* Mass: Blackwell, 2000.

Cranmer, Thomas. The Marriage Service in *The Book of Common Prayer,* 1545.

Davies, Russell T. Film: *A Midsummer Night's Dream,* 2016.

Dolan, Frances E. *Marriage and Violence: The Early Modern Legacy.* Pennsylvania: University of Pennsylvania Press, 2008.

Doran, Greg. Film: *Richard II,* 2013.

Drayton, Michael. *Idea's Mirrour* [sonnets], 1594.

Duncan-Jones, Katherine, and H.R. Woudhuysen. Eds. *Shakespeare's Poems.* The Arden Shakespeare. London: Bloomsbury, 2007.

Dusinberre, Juliet. *Shakespeare and the Nature of Women.* Third edition with updated Introduction. Basingstoke: Palgrave/Macmillan, 2003.

Fletcher, Loraine. 'Animal Rites: a Reading of *Venus and Adonis.*' *Critical Survey,* 17 (2005): 1-14.

________________ 'Misogyny on Trial: Honour Killing in Shakespeare.' *Form and Feeling in Modern Literature: Essays in Honour of Barbara Hardy.* Eds. William Baker and Isobel Armstrong. London: Legenda, 2013, pp122-131.

Greenblatt, Stephen. The General Introduction to *The Norton Shakespeare*. Ed. Stephen Greenblatt. NY: Norton, 1997.

Greenblatt, Stephen. Introduction to *Richard III* in *The Norton Shakespeare*. NY: Norton, 1997.

Greenblatt, Stephen. *Tyrant: Shakespeare on Power*. London: The Bodley Head, 2018.

Hall, Sir Peter, and Barton, John. Film: *The Wars of the Roses,* 1963.

Hardy, Barbara. *Shakespeare's Storytellers*. London: Peter Owen, 1997.

Howard, Jean E. Introductions to the three *Henry VI* plays in *The Norton Shakespeare*. Ed. Stephen Greenblatt. NY: Norton, 1997.

Kermode, Sir Frank. Introductions to the Tragedies in *The Riverside Shakespeare*. Boston: Houghton Mifflin, 1974.

Knight, G. Wilson. *The Wheel of Fire*. OUP, 1930.

Knights, L.C. *'"How many children had Lady Macbeth?": An Essay in the Theory and Practice of Shakespeare Criticism.'* London: The Minority Press, 1933.

Kott, Jan. *Shakespeare Our Contemporary*. NY: Doubleday, 1964.

Lenz, Carolyn Ruth Swift, Gayle Greene and Carol Thomas Neely. Eds. *The Woman's Part: Feminist Criticism of Shakespeare*. Urbana: The University of Illinois Press, 1983.

MacCulloch, Diarmaid. *Thomas Cranmer: A Life*. New Haven: Yale University Press, 1996.

Maguire, Laurie E. 'Feminist Editing and the Body of the Text'. *A Feminist Companion to Shakespeare*. Ed. Dympna Callaghan. Mass: Blackwell, 2003, pp59-79.

Mandeville, Sir John. The Voyage and Travels of Sir John Mandeville, 1568.

Marlowe, Christopher. *The Jew of Malta.* First performance probably 1592.

Martino, Davide. 'Art, Religion and Diplomacy in the Life of Costantino de'Servi (1554-1622)'. Submitted as part of the Tripos Examination in the Faculty of History, Cambridge University. April 2016. (Unpublished).

Maus, Katharine Eisaman. Introduction to *Richard II* in *The Norton Shakespeare.* NY: Norton, 1997.

Moschovakis, Nicholas Rand. '"Irreligious Piety" and Christian History: Persecution as Pagan Anachronism in *Titus Andronicus.*' *The Shakespeare Quarterly,* Vol 53, Winter 4 (2002): 460-486.

Moshinsky, Elijah. Film: *A Midsummer Night's Dream,* 1981.

Neely, Carol Thomas. *Broken Nuptials in Shakespeare's Plays.* Urbana: University of Illinois Press, 1985.

Nicholl, Charles. *The Reckoning: The Murder of Christopher Marlowe.* London: Vintage, 2002.

Orgel, Stephen. *Impersonations: Gender and Performance in Shakespeare's England.* CUP, 1996.

Ovid, *Metamorphoses.* Translated by David Raeburn. London: Penguin, 2004.

Rackin, Phyllis. *Shakespeare & Women.* OUP, 2005.

.... 'Misogyny is Everywhere'. *A Feminist Companion to Shakespeare.* Ed. Dympna Callaghan. Mass: Blackwell, 2000, pp42-56.

Radford, Michael. Film: *The Merchant of Venice*, 2004.

Shakespeare, William. *The New Oxford Shakespeare: The Complete Works.* Eds. Gary Taylor, John Jowett, Terri Bourus, Gabriel Egan. OUP, 2016.

__________________ *The Riverside Shakespeare.* Boston: Houghton Mifflin, 1974.

__________________ *The Norton Shakespeare*, NY: Norton, 1997.

Shapiro, James. *Shakespeare and the Jews.* NY: University of Columbia Press, 2018.

Sidney, Sir Philip. *Astrophil and Stella* [a sonnet sequence], c. 1591.

Sinfield, Alan. Introduction to *Macbeth: A Casebook.* Basingstoke: Macmillan, 1992.

Smith, Molly. 'Mutant Scenes and "Minor" Conflicts in *Richard II.*' *A Feminist Companion to Shakespeare.* Ed. Dympna Callaghan. Mass: Blackwell, 2000, pp263-275.

Sokol, B.J. and Mary. *Shakespeare, Law and Marriage.* CUP, 2003.

Spenser, Edmund. *Poems* [Sonnets and *Epithalamion*], 1595.

Suzman, Janet. Film: *Othello*, 1988.

Taylor, Gary, and Terri Bourus. Introduction to *The New Oxford Shakespeare: The Complete Works.* Eds. Gary Taylor, *et al.* OUP, 2016.

Taylor, Gary, and Gabriel Egan. Eds. *The New Oxford Shakespeare: Authorship Companion.* OUP, 2016.

Taymor, Julie. Film: *Titus*, 1999.

Ann Thompson. Ed. *The Taming of the Shrew.* The New Cambridge Shakespeare. CUP, 2003.

Tillyard, E.M.W. *Shakespeare's History Plays.* London: Penguin, 1944. [with care].

Walter, Harriet. *An open letter to Shakespeare on behalf of women.* Internet.

Webster, John. *The Duchess of Malfi*, 1613-14.

Wilde, Oscar. *The Portrait of Mr W.H.* Ed. Vyvyan Holland. London: Methuen, 1958.

Wingfield-Stratford, Esme. *A History of English Patriotism.* London: John Lane, 1913.

Winterson, Jeanette. *The Gap of Time.* London: Vintage, 2015.

Wyatt, Sir Thomas. *Poems* [unpublished in his lifetime].

Index